MW00781940

RADIX | 2014

Martin Heidegger

The Philosophy of Another Beginning

ALEXANDER DUGIN

Edited and Translated by
Nina Kouprianova

Preface by Paul E. Gottfried

English Translation © 2014
By Radix / Washington Summit Publishers.

Radix / Washington Summit Publishers
Arlington, VA

email : Info@WashSummit.com
web: www.WashSummit.com

Cataloging-in-Publication Data is on file with the Library of Congress

ISBN: 978-1-59368-037-4
eISBN: 978-1-59368-039-8

Printed in the United States of America
10 9 8 7 6 5 4 3 2 1
First Edition

CONTENTS

PREFACE
TO THE ENGLISH EDITION

By Paul E. Gottfried

This major study of the German philosopher Martin Heidegger by Russian thinker Alexander Dugin (b. 1962) has been made available to English readers thanks to the painstaking efforts of an able translator, Nina Kouprianova. One cannot understate the difficulty of this demanding translation or the value of what the translator has given us.

Dugin is one of the world's most renowned critics of the American cult of Liberal democracy, and his work published in English in 2012, *The Fourth Philosophical Theory*[1], sets out to examine the problem of the failed (or at least vulnerable) ideologies of the 20th century, extending from Communism and Fascism to what has become the preferred American political doctrine of Liberal materialism based on universal equality. Dugin views Liberal democracy as the ideological idol of the last century that is still standing and, given the extent of American power and influence, still flourishing on this continent and among American vassal states in Western Europe. Dugin famously, or notoriously, calls for a "fourth way," just as Heidegger in the midst of the Cold War proposed a "third way" and, from the 1930s on, spoke of "another beginning" that would lead toward a new "openness to Being." In these cases, these men sought alternatives to the materialist and consumerist ethos of late modernity—and to the ideology of universal political sameness that has accompanied it.

---

[1] Alexander Dugin, *The Fourth Political Theory* (Budapest: Arktos Media, 2012).

It would be an oversimplification to reduce this ambitious and exhaustive examination of to the critique of *"techne,"* which is characteristic of Heidegger's later work. Dugin pays scrupulous attention to all the phases in the philosopher's evolution, starting with Heidegger's attempted separation of a proper analysis of *Being* from received metaphysical traditions. This study engages Heidegger's definitions of ontic and ontological and such concepts as *Sein, Dasein, Sein-zum-Tode,* and *Zeitlichkeit,* which punctuate Heidegger's early masterpiece *Sein und Zeit* (1927). Heidegger's *magnum opus* treats our growing awareness of *Being* as something that presents itself to us, to whatever extent we grasp that existence is to be understood beyond the obvious or what Heidegger calls "ready to hand." Heidegger is dealing with the self-revelation of *Being,* and not simply with the awareness of a multiplicity of *beings,* and this process unfolds in experienced time. The progressive revelation of *Being* carries us toward a future that stands before us as an unfinished project. That project (*Auftrag*) becomes apparent to us only as we exist in time, and Heidegger stresses that our particular *Being* (*Dasein*) is shaped by future-oriented labors, up until the point when our future is overshadowed by the expectation of death. This is the *Being-toward-death,* which, for Heidegger, brings the possibility of entering an undiscovered realm of existence.

Dugin is justified in linking his study to the overarching concept of *"Seynsgeschichte,"* the history of the consciousness of *Being* as it presents itself to us in human life. Like his predecessor Hegel, Heidegger stresses the historical context in which *Being* is present for us, although, unlike Hegel, he does not essay to chart the course of Progress taken by Spirit in political and cultural affairs. This would not be possible, given Heidegger's frame of reference. Like Dugin, Heidegger is starkly pessimistic about the direction in which modernity has moved. This is particularly true of Heidegger's later work, beginning in the 1930s, after his "turn" (*Kehre*) into what could be described as a mystical direction. Thenceforward, Heidegger became preoccupied with certain themes that Dugin examines at length. These include the importance of pre-Socratic Greek philosophers, like Heraclitus, in keeping open the question of the nature of *Being*, before Plato changed or limited that focus by dragging in theological answers; the enclosed rectangular space (*Das Geviert*), consisting of the divine and the mortal, and the sky and the earth, in which the quest for understanding our specific being and *Being* in general must take place; and the intrusion of *techne* as a cultural and historical diversion from serious philosophical thought. Dugin shows in detail how all these themes become interrelated in Heidegger's works, especially after 1945, and how the triumph of a purely technical culture destroyed the search for truth marked by a sense of the divine (though not necessarily by monotheistic belief) and a sense of human limits in relation to the universe.

Dugin notes that the triumph of certain modernist characteristics spelled "the End" of an age that has become increasingly closed to *Being*. It was therefore not surprising that, for Heidegger, this development gave rise to nihilism, that is, the devaluing of everything that had once been deemed holy. In a technical age, in which thinking stresses material relations that can be scientifically controlled, nothing has intrinsic value except for what can be made materially usable or manipulated according to learnable instructions. This, too, argued Heidegger, had a certain connection to traditional metaphysics, to the extent that technicians and their adepts claimed to be revealing what had been hidden as undisclosed in *Being*. *Techne* was a "manner of demystifying" ("*Weise des Entbergens*") the nature of existence, by avoiding a continuing search for *Being* and by positing superficial answers. Indeed, *techne* may be described as a *simulacrum* of the philosophical quest.

Techne imitates philosophy "by bringing forth that which was absent as something present."[2] It is, therefore, in this sense similar to the activity of pre-Socratic thinkers, says Heidegger, who saw philosophical knowledge as what had been removed from oblivion (whence the Greek word for truth, "*aletheia*"). But unlike true philosophers, technicians don't raise ontological questions. They simply fill space with a multiplicity of objects, whence Heidegger's designation of "the essence of modern *techne*" as *Gestell*, as a soulless structure that is placed in space. What the technician places before us (*stellt*), and which represents a travesty on philosophy, is summed up by Heidegger as "*Gestänge, Geschiebe, und Gerüste*"—struts, detritus, and scaffolds."[3]

Like Dugin, Heidegger regarded all modern ideologies as variations on the ascent of *techne*. Communism, National Socialism, and, finally, Western Liberal democracy all became associated, for Heidegger, with manipulation, *Seinsvergessenheit*, and the mastery of material objects. All these tendencies of the modern age pointed toward the end of an epoch and the beginning of a possible return to what Heidegger viewed as a more authentic existence. Such an existence, particularly after the *Kehre*, was to be pursued in austerity, with a sense of duty toward others and, on the philosophical level, with openness toward the mysteries of *Being*. Though one could describe the author of *Sein und Zeit* as an individualist, with a minimal sense of communal attachment, the later Heidegger is clearly a

---

[2] Martin Heidegger, *The Question Concerning Technology and Other Essays* (New York: Harper & Row, 1977).
[3] *Ibid.*

6

social traditionalist, whose emphasis on rootedness and whose love for his ancestral land of Swabia comes through in his tracts. Dugin does not shy away from explaining Heidegger's straying into the Nazi movement in 1933, when he became the enthusiastically pro-Nazi Rector at the University of Freiburg. Dugin treats this misadventure, which was followed by Heidegger's cooling toward the Nazis, as at least partly occasioned by a hope for a new, higher-minded era than the one he had lived through. Heidegger's association with a movement he later criticized as symptomatic of *techne* indicated his turning toward what he hoped would be "another beginning." He would continue to be drawn toward this ideal after World War II, albeit in a less unsavory form than had been the case following Hitler's accession to power. This envisaged epoch, to judge from Heidegger's statements, may be seen as a return as much as a point of departure (*Aufbruch*).

Dugin has been sufficiently inspired by Heidegger's work to devote this dense volume to expounding its fruits. Presumably, the Russian has been influenced by Heidegger's ontology, which is explored here with remarkable thoroughness. From this book, we discover that Heidegger is returning to a branch of philosophy that reveals a traditionalist character, in opposition to such trendy pursuits as utilitarian ethics or defenses of "social justice." But Heidegger approaches what had been a Medieval and ancient field of study without the theological emphasis of earlier generations. Of course, this must be qualified. The late Medieval philosopher Duns Scotus was the subject of Heidegger's *Habilitation* in 1915[4], and he owed a great deal to the "subtle doctor's" concept of truth and his commentaries on Aristotle. Indeed, it is impossible to read *Sein und Zeit* without noticing how deeply immersed

---

4 Martin Heidegger, *Die Kategorien und Bedeutungslehre des Duns Scotus* (Tübingen: J. C. B. Mohr, 1916).

Heidegger was in the entire history of Western philosophy. For all his complaints about the false path taken by Socrates and Plato—a notion that is recognizably Nietzschean in origin—Heidegger overwhelms his reader with quotations from Plato, Aristotle, and the Medieval schoolmen, and with his long glosses on others who came before him.

Like Dugin, one discovers in Heidegger, whom Dugin routinely calls "the greatest thinker," a combination of traditional philosophical interests with self-consciously modern concerns. But again, like Dugin, Heidegger was a reactionary modernist, someone who combatted modernity by underlining its defects and shallowness and by trying to prove that the modern enterprise was headed in a very bad direction. Heidegger tried to do this without returning to metaphysical assumptions that he believed belonged to a vanished past. This, too, as in the case of Dugin, is not as simple as it would first appear. There is something backward-looking in both thinkers, as the past is for them a source of creativity. This is totally different from the kind of "cultural conservative" this writer has often encountered: a tedious eccentric who manifests his "conservatism" by making himself the butt of gentle jokes. Such a person may frequent clubs where tea and crumpets are served or may introduce himself as a liturgical traditionalist with an ostentatious interest in Gothic architecture, but he is, above all, an expert at staying out of controversy that could threaten his career or social calendar.

This is not the kind of person we have in mind when we look at such widely hated, contentious figures as Heidegger and Dugin. These are adversaries of a deeper mettle. They approach their opposition frontally without trying to be "nice." And they are resourceful and deeply knowledgeable of the fields they set out to transform. Such thoughtful reactionaries frame a critique of late modernity with the tools of the past, while understanding that one can't go back in time. And there can be no doubt that Heidegger is operating with the tools of the past, and even distant past, as the multilingual glossary to this work amply demonstrates. He is a reactionary modernist who goes back to pre-Socratic Greek epigrams and then recapitulates the history of philosophy in order to find a way out of the implications of a wrong turn.

Heidegger is looking for the beginnings of a disaster (*sphalma*); and although his subject, as Dugin properly indicates, traces this misstep back to Plato, it is in the same philosopher that we learn the valuable lesson that there is a connection between "learning thoroughly" (*katamanthanein*) and "undertaking a correction" (*poiein to epanorthoma*)." Studying Heidegger and then reading Dugin's demanding, comprehensive explication, one comes to understand this necessary connection. For both the "greatest thinker" and his faithful Russian disciple, the improvement of our culture and spiritual life requires nothing less than a detailed examination of our traditions extending back to antiquity. There are no short cuts on the road to correcting the faults of our late modernity.

PAUL E. GOTTFRIED is Professor Emeritus of Humanities at Elizabethtown College. His books include Conservatism in America *(2007),* The Strange Death of Marxism *(2005),* After Liberalism *(1999),* Multiculturalism and the Politics of Guilt *(2002), and* Leo Strauss and the Conservative Movement in America *(2012).*

MARTIN HEIDEGGER
The Philosophy of Another Beginning

PART 1

Seyn und Sein

I. MEETING HEIDEGGER: AN INVITATION TO A JOURNEY

Thought and its Authorities

Martin Heidegger is, to the greatest extent, a foundational author. He belongs among those figures in the history of thought that are unavoidable. Much can be omitted, considered optional, and perused at leisure. But there also are other things that demand careful and thorough study. Without them, our notions and ideas about thought, philosophy, and the history of culture will be defective, incomplete, fragmentary, and, therefore, unreliable.

Heidegger is indispensable for anyone who lives in today's world and tries to at least somehow ground the fact of one's *actuality*—one's *presence*. Of course, more often than not, we do not have to speak of presence: after all, in Russian, the word "presence" etymologically means *"to be close to the essence,"* but who is *"close to the essence"* now? Perhaps, we can at least ponder over *actuality*. Even he who raises a question about his actuality cannot pass by Heidegger.

It is impossible to think, and, in particular, to think about one's actuality, about oneself, about the world, about life and death, without relying on one or another school of thought. If we ourselves do not know which philosophical system is at the base of our thinking, that does not mean that there is no such system. There certainly is one: after all, our thoughts and notions are drawn from somewhere. If we carefully treat the content of our own consciousness, take an approximate inventory of it, we may then realize that one thing in it is from Plato, another—from Aristotle, the third is accordant to René Descartes's teaching, the fourth is from G.W.F. Hegel's dialectic; some thoughts are taken from the arsenal of theology, others—from Marxism; in certain things the influence of Immanuel Kant is apparent, and somewhere else a fragment of Nietzscheism glitters. The fact that philosophy does not reach us directly, not immediately, but through hundreds of half-anonymous echoes—in school, family, society, media, education, everyday conversations, and disjointed consumer culture—changes nothing.

It seems to us that we think *independently*, but such an illusion arises only from ignorance or a poor education. It suffices to start working on ourselves, and it becomes obvious that we constantly *quote*, and, more often than not, we quote those sources the existence of which we do not even suspect. For precisely this reason, any person who wishes to think *honestly* will begin to locate the authorities and reference systems of thought in philosophy, science, and art.

A thinking person is always somewhat of a philosopher. A philosopher always belongs to some school of thought: either he follows religious philosophy, or he is a Kantian, or a Hegelian, or a liberal, or a Marxist, or a Freudian, or a positivist, or a Nietzschean, or a structuralist, or an advocate of the "philosophy of life," or a solipsist, or an existentialist, or a materialist, or a Darwinist, etc. In very rare instances, a philosopher is capable of carrying out an interesting and original synthesis of different schools; and even more rarely, with intervals measuring in centuries, those thinkers appear that blaze new trails and truly open new horizons for the rest of mankind. These are great people, who mark the milestones of thought for all humanity; and they will be remembered for centuries.

The one who understands the great thinkers and acquires one of the possible philosophical positions secures for himself the status of a philosopher, a full-fledged thinking being. And here is the most crucial truth: one must first *bow* before an authority (even if also with a "secret wish" of later overthrowing this authority) and think about oneself and the world in the inner hall of great ideas and theories. Yet those who strive for originality—immediately and at any cost—do not stay long in the field of philosophy; their place is the market.

Heidegger: the Great or the Greatest?

Among great thinkers, two places can be set aside for Heidegger, depending on how we look at him, to what degree we study him, and how much we believe him.

At the very least, Heidegger is the greatest contemporary thinker, joining the constellation of Europe's best thinkers from the pre-Socratics to our time. In this sense, some refer to him as the "philosopher king." Even those whom his philosophy leaves indifferent or those who disagree with it recognize his indisputable greatness.

Heidegger is universally recognized as a great philosopher of world history. No one seriously contests this kind of recognition, but some easily pass him by, relying on other trends in philosophy, while others keenly respond to his message, using his terms (*"Dasein," "existential," "Angst,"* etc.), allowing themselves to treat his thoughts with enthusiasm.

A different, special, exclusive place in the history of philosophy that can be set aside for Heidegger should be recognized in the case when we fully trust Heidegger, immerse ourselves in his thinking, and make him our highest authority. In other words, Heidegger examined within the space of Heideggerianism will significantly differ from Heidegger in the average and conventional history of philosophy. In the former case, we will realize that Heidegger is not only a great philosopher, on par with other greats, but, in fact, the greatest of them all. He occupies the place of the *last prophet*, concludes the development of the first stage in philosophy (from Anaximander to Nietzsche), and serves as the *transition*, the *bridge to a new philosophy*, which he only anticipates in his works. In that case, Heidegger is an *eschatological figure*, the final interpreter and clarifier of the most profound and enigmatic subjects in world philosophy, and the creator of a radically *new way of thinking*. As a result, we can view him as a figure in a religious pantheon, as an "envoy of *Being* itself," a herald and organizer of the greatest *event*. In it, the old history of the European world will end and a new one, which has yet to exist, will begin.

It seems to me that the second approach is more productive for a true understanding of Heidegger (even if, at some time in the distant future, it may be revised). It allows for full and complete immersion into Heidegger's thinking, without hasty attempts at interpreting him through appeals to other authorities (and to disparate traces they left in our consciousness) and allows Heidegger to communicate to us what he intended to communicate without hindrance. And only after accepting this message on general terms and believing in its importance and inevitability, can we, if need be, take a certain position in regard to Heidegger.

It is hardly necessary for everyone to become a Heideggerean forever, but this thinker is absolutely deserving of a certain amount of intellectual time, enough to be able to say, with slight apprehension in one's voice, "It seems that I understand a bit of his work." For some, this will take years; for others—decades. Others yet will slip when taking their very first steps. Yet the experience is worthwhile. By studying Heidegger, we study philosophy in its contemporary state. It is precisely what it is, and there is nothing to contradict to it.

Heidegger is important not only for professional philosophers— for them, he is simply indispensable. A contemporary philosopher who does not know Heidegger looks ridiculous. But he is also meaningful for those who aspire to have minimal competence in questions of culture: for scholars in humanities, politicians, artists, psychologists, and sociologists; all those who by the call of their hearts or due to professional obligations are involved in the fate of man and mankind, society and history.

Martin Heidegger in the USSR: A Distant Shelf in a Library's Special Collections and the Futile Diligence of Vladimir Bibikhin[1]

Heidegger's legacy in the Russian-speaking context is a profoundly peculiar phenomenon. First, in the Soviet period, his works, his ideas, his philosophy, as well as his intellectual standpoint and his worldview were attributed to the most dangerous and unacceptable ideological compartments, placed in the most distant and closed-off sections of libraries' Special Collections, and were essentially considered "non-existent." Any and all interest in Heidegger was looked at as a gnoseological crime or an absolutely futile pursuit. Even the criticism of Heidegger's ideas received little attention. Thus, Heidegger, like many other non-Marxist philosophers, was *closed* to late-Soviet (not to mention, early-Soviet) philosophy. He was read, translated, and discussed "underground," which affected the quality of these readings, translations, and discussions.

[1] This publication uses the Library of Congress transliteration for the Russian language, unless a different spelling had been previously accepted.

Nevertheless, a group of Soviet philosophers, led by the late Vladimir Bibikhin, the founder of the late-Soviet Heideggerean School, reclaimed the right to engage in critical readings of Heidegger. This rather small group of scholars was responsible for the majority of extant translations, many of which were made in the Soviet era and circulated in *Samizdat*.

Without doubting the sincerity on the part of these enthusiasts, we must note that their translations and the depth of grasping Heidegger proved entirely unsatisfactory. The complexity of the ideological conditions, limited access to sources, specificity of their philosophical education, limitations of philosophical knowledge, and, in general, the inadequacy of the late-Soviet social space for the scope of Heidegger's thinking were responsible for the fact that we can—without any regrets— part ways with the intellectual body of work produced by this group, so as to avoid struggling with the chimeras of a historical period so worthless, that in some ways it cannot come to an end even today.

It appears that Bibikhin and his circle of like-minded thinkers were, in fact, passionately captivated by Heidegger. But there is nothing more to the translations or explanations of Heidegger apart from this passion. It is completely impossible to read them, since these texts are very expressive in terms of the conditions, effort, and suffering on the part of Bibikhin himself, as well as his translator-colleagues. However, apart from certain accidental coincidences, these works say practically nothing about Heidegger or, worse yet, present such an image that makes one's hair stand on end. If we accept these texts as an accurate translation of Heidegger, then we would have to admit rather quickly that, regrettably, Heidegger himself did not understand what he was saying and writing. In short, we are dealing with complete nonsense.

Heidegger as the Most Western of all Western Philosophers

The second issue with Heidegger's peculiar legacy in the Russian-speaking setting is that Heidegger is a *fundamental link in the chain of Western European philosophy* and corresponds to the internal logic of its development. Therefore, generally, he is intelligible to the Western European philosopher, who can move freely in the taxonomy of ideas and theories of Western European culture. To understand Heidegger, one must be, in the very least, a European. After all, Heidegger himself constantly emphasizes that he thinks in Europe, of Europe, and for Europe, conceiving of it as a particular historical-philosophical and civilizational whole.

Dogmatic Marxism and the Russian intellectual milieu, rather complicated both in the last decade of the USSR and today, intersect with the main trajectory of Western European man largely in a fragmentary, episodic, and tangential way. We, Russians, conceive of ourselves as Europeans, and we resemble them in some ways (external appearance, phenotype, language, religion, socio-political system, etc.). However, philosophy highlights those nuances, in which it is most difficult to deceive or manipulate the state of affairs, and it is in this sphere that there is very little Western European in us all. If it exists at all, then it resembles a caricature. More likely, however, is that we are dealing with a particular kind of Russian thinking, of which we are barely cognizant ourselves, let alone of other cultures' particularities.

In a way, Heidegger represents quintessential Western thought: it is more profound, central, and, at the same time, more Western than in the case of other European thinkers, who are more accessible (although not by much).

A relaxed, even-paced, and careful reading of Heidegger, along with maintaining one's own dignity—this, perhaps, is the most serious test of a Russian-European dialogue.

Heidegger and the Metalanguage of a New Philosophy

And finally, the third point: Heidegger consciously aims to establish a *new language of philosophy*—a kind of metalanguage. This is based on his specific *philosophy of language (Sprachphilosophie)*, which he formulated along with the general development of his thought. The essence of this approach consists of the following:

1. removing the influence of Western European philosophy and metaphysics (with their logic, grammar, implicit ontology, etc.) on language and its structures; that is, rejecting the presentation of philosophical terms in the context of that metalanguage that Western European philosophy developed and sanctioned over the period of its two and a half thousand-year history;

2. returning to words (instead of terms, categories, and concepts) and their original meaning outside philosophy, their etymology, as well as their own pre-logical and pre-metaphysical content;

3. developing a new metalanguage for a new philosophy, which will be built upon the basis of words, *disseminating information about Being* and having a radically different trajectory from the kind of communication that was used in previous philosophical discourse.

The level of Heidegger's texts demands great effort even from a full-fledged European philosopher (in general, from a thinking European), which is quite difficult for German-speaking readers and even more difficult for native speakers of other European languages. The question of correctly interpreting and adequately translating Heidegger was being settled in European philosophy throughout the entire 20th century. The latter led to the creation of a kind of "Heideggerean dictionary," which philosophers use in addition to a range of translations, each nuance of which presents a subject for specialized discussions. In addition to philosophers, other academics, such as philologists, historians, scholars of antiquity, and psychologists, are also involved in comprehending and translating Heidegger. After all, the difficulty of understanding Heidegger is not a technical problem, but rather a question of choosing a *radical turn* on the path of Western philosophy urged by Heidegger. Europeans *participate in making this turn* by translating, interpreting, and commenting on Heidegger. There are no fewer complexities in the translation of his texts into French or English than into Russian. Yet the best minds of Europe have struggled with this problem for almost a century, starting with those who read and attempted to understand him in the original from the outset (Jean-Paul Sartre, for instance, owes much to early Heidegger, even including the name of his philosophy, "existentialism").

Heidegger's Silence

Getting acquainted with Heidegger, we cannot omit the historical fact that during the 1920-1940s, he belonged to the philosophical-ideological school of the "Conservative Revolution" (along with such eminent thinkers as Ernst Jünger, Friedrich Georg Jünger, Oswald Spengler, Othmar Spann, Carl Schmitt, Arthur Moeller van den Bruck, Werner Sombart,

Friedrich Hielscher, and others). Finding themselves in opposition to Hitler's National Socialism and repudiating the racism, primitivism, and brutality of his populist propaganda, these thinkers were forced to cooperate with this ideology in one way or another, not only as an attempt to survive under a totalitarian regime, but also because they shared (independently and much earlier than the Nazis) a number of ideas, including:

- the political romanticism and idealism of the new Germany;

- the notion that it is necessary for Europe to return to its roots, Tradition, and myth;

- the imperative of a simultaneous war with Liberalism (Britain and the U.S.) and Marxism (the USSR) as the two expressions of the same kind of nihilism (pragmatic, in one case, and proletarian, in the other);

- a Nietzschean diagnosis of Europe's humanitarian disease and the need to establish a "new heroism," etc.

With that in mind, in the 1930s and 1940s, Heidegger openly criticized those aspects of National Socialism that he considered erroneous from the standpoint of his philosophy. In his book *Introduction to Metaphysics* in particular, Heidegger wrote, "The works that are being peddled about nowadays as the philosophy of National Socialism, which have nothing to do with the inner truth and greatness of this movement (namely the encounter between global *techne* and modern man)—have all been written by men fishing in the troubled waters of 'values' and 'totalities.'"[2] It is important to note that the term "National

---

[2] Martin Heidegger, *Einführung in die Metaphysik* (Tübingen: Niemeyer, 1935;1953), 202; Martin Heidegger, *An Introduction to Metaphysics*, trans. Ralph Manheim (New Haven, Conn.: Yale University Press, 1959), 199.

Socialism" emerged in Germany to designate one of the schools of "Conservative Revolutionary" thought long before Hitler came to power and, more important, prior to the formulation of Nazism as an ideology. Only subsequently was it usurped by the racist theoreticians in Hitler's circle.

Evidently, Heidegger conceived of National Socialism through the filter of Ernst Jünger's manifesto, *The Worker*.[3] In it, National Socialism was presented as the answer to the challenge of Modernity[4] for contemporary European man. The answer paradoxically consisted of liberating the deeply rooted, basic, and titanic foundations of mankind through the domination of *techne*. According to Jünger, a 20th-century European was losing his rapidly evaporating cultural heritage in the mechanical grinder of modern warfare—its gas attacks and the rattle of tank treads. Yet, at the same time, and despite everything, he was heroically returning to basic human impulses, including the vivid experience of camaraderie ("frontline socialism") and an acute sense of the nation as a project directed toward the future ("nationalism"). Jünger's "national socialism" and "total mobilization" appealed to the existential roots of the European on the other side of petty xenophobia, chauvinism, and, especially, any kind of racism. This type of "national socialism" was European rather than German, humanist rather than statist, and existential rather than totalitarian and ideological. Heidegger considered Jünger's ideas to be perfectly acceptable and believed, at first, that National Socialism was capable of evolving in the direction of the "Conservative Revolution."

Initially, Jünger's national socialism left a tremendous impact on the entire "Third Way" movement in Germany in the 1920s.

---

3 Ernst Jünger, *Der Arbeiter: Herrschaft und Gestalt* (Stuttgart: Klett-Cotta, 1982).
4 The author uses the term "New Time" in reference to Modernity (*Ed.*).

However, it came gradually into harsh conflict with Nazism's official dogma and was eclipsed by the much less intellectual, but incomparably more wide-spread Hitlerism (including its criminal consequences), which triumphed in Germany in the 1930s and which appropriated the name of this school of thought, distorted it, and tainted it for a long time to come, if not forever.

The same fate befell the ideological legacy of other representatives of the European Conservative Revolutionary movement. Starting in the 1920s, Germany's "right-wing" and "left-wing" intellectuals—from Thomas Mann to Oswald Spengler, from Heinrich von Gleichen to the communists Fritz Wolffheim and Heinrich Laufenberg, from Arthur Moeller van den Bruck to Carl Schmitt, and from Ernst Niekisch to Harro Schulze-Boysen—searched for a new worldview, philosophical and political horizons beyond the limits of Liberalism, dogmatic Communism, and the old, narrow conservative tradition. They actively experimented with the riskiest combinations of tradition and revolution, historical constants and innovative technologies, religious values and progressive social theories. Far from any kind of dogmatism, they developed many original doctrines, theories, and philosophical conceptions. Yet the tragedy of their situation was the fact that when it comes to mainstream politics, this entire broad spectrum of pursuits, revelations, and intuitions has been directly linked to Hitler's totalitarian regime since the victory of NSDAP in 1933. And although all these thinkers gradually ended up in opposition to Hitler's regime—from "inner emigration" (the Jünger brothers, Heidegger, and Carl Schmitt) to direct participation in anti-fascist activities and the Resistance movement (Niekisch, Schulze-Boysen, and others)—the totality of their views was excised from political thought in the West for quite some because of its superficial and deceptive resemblance to the political declarations of the Third Reich era.

Heidegger's formal collaboration with the Nazis did not last long—as he fulfilled his duties as the rector of the University of Freiburg and was forced to follow certain orders on the part of the official leadership.[5] It is quite noteworthy that Heidegger was likely the only cultural figure of such calibre (if his calibre is at all comparable to that of anyone else) that never apologized for his past after 1945. He was simply "silent." In his philosophy, *silence* has the fundamental significance as one of the dialectics in which *Being* speaks of itself, therefore we can interpret "Heidegger's silence" in various ways (like all other aspects of his work), but certainly we can do so *philosophically*.

During the 1920-1940s period, Heidegger exerted decisive influence on many outstanding intellectuals who found themselves in 1945 in the camp of the victors (from the Freudo-Marxist Herbert Marcuse and Jean-Paul Sartre, a Communist, to Heidegger's former student and lover, Hannah Arendt, who strongly criticized all forms of totalitarianism and emigrated to the U.S., where she had a brilliant academic career). As a result, in the general philosophical context, the collaboration with Hitler's regime and even Heidegger's later "silence" were politely forgotten (despite the fact that the 1933-1945 period was one of the most fruitful for Heidegger's philosophy). No one, except for certain superficial troublemakers (like Chilean Communist Victor Farías), dealt with this subject.[6] Heidegger means too much to the West to be treated this way, even if his

---

5   He became a member of the NSDAP on May 1, 1933 and remained one until 1945, despite serious complaints about him from the official Party organs and his gradual marginalization within the regime.

6   Victor Farias, *Heidegger and Nazism* (Philadelphia: Temple University Press, 1989).

actions went beyond the accepted social mores. Geniuses can be forgiven for anything.

Obviously, both in the case of the USSR and contemporary liberal-democratic Russia, these political details of Martin Heidegger's personal life did not help in developing an adequate understanding of his work, encouraging a deliberate bias and selective treatment of his ideas and texts (those of the 1930s and 1940s, first and foremost).

Accidental Successes

In view of these circumstances, Heidegger represents an almost unknown quantity for us. If there were something coherent in what was written about him in Russian or in the way he was translated, then this is, most likely, a coincidence or a successful imitation. Russians are, in fact, very successful imitators: often, we can easily reproduce that which we do not at all understand and that which remains profoundly alien to us. Herein lies the flexibility of our culture.

But even the automatic, mechanical translation of Heidegger's texts into Russian can, in rare cases, produce a curious result. This type of success does exist among Russian body of work on Heidegger. However, without a preliminary comprehension of Heidegger either in the original or through an accurate translation into other European languages, it is impossible to distinguish successes from failures. Thus, it would be more useful to face the task of building everything up from square one. Construction engineers know that rebuilding a damaged building is considerably more expensive, time-consuming, and prone to additional problems than the complete demolition of the old and the construction of a new building from the ground up.

That is an offer for those who have taken an interest, accidentally or deliberately, in studying the person and philosophy of the greatest thinker—Martin Heidegger.

And so, inasmuch as we do not know Heidegger, I propose to carry out *a journey in his direction in order to get closer to him*, similar to the way in which Evgenii Golovin (incidentally, one of the first and most profound experts on Martin Heidegger in Russia) proposed to "move closer to the Snow Queen." [7]

Philosopher as Identity

Heidegger, as we already mentioned, thinks and presents himself exclusively within the framework of Western European philosophy. This observation is exceedingly important in order to precisely determine the location of Heidegger's thought. It might be quite tempting to consider Heidegger as the religious type (as many of his researchers do) and to draw a parallel between Heidegger and the traditionalists with their criticism of contemporary Western civilization. [8] Yet we should postpone

---

[7] Evgenii Golovin, *Priblizhenie k Snezhnoi Koroleve* (Moscow: Arktogea, 2003).

[8] Dealing with the philosophy of traditionalism for quite some time (see, in particular, *Absoliutnaia rodina* [*Absolute Motherland*], *Filosofiia traditsionalizma* [*The Philosophy of Traditionalism*], and *Radikal'nyi sub'ekt i ego dubl'* [*The Radical Subject and its Double*]), I have not emphasized Heidegger's teaching, despite the fact that it influenced my intellectual development in the most direct and immediate manner. My views are indebted to Heidegger's philosophy only slightly less so than to the ideas of René Guénon. Heidegger is a part of our worldview, our political theory, and our philosophy; he is a *sine qua non*. Heidegger is no less fundamental than Guénon. But he is different. A comparison of Heidegger and Guénon must not be carried out too hastily. We must thoroughly master Guénon and Heidegger separately. And then—only *then*!—should we determine where they overlap (and where they differ). Interpreting one by using the other is erroneous. In his *Ride the Tiger*, Julius Evola made the mistake of interpreting Heidegger hastily and superficially from the traditionalist perspective (Guénon's generalized standpoint), in which he presents

similar comparisons for as long as possible and first familiarize ourselves with Heidegger in that context to which he belonged and wanted to belong, and in which he himself comprehended his place and significance.

Heidegger is a philosopher; more specifically, a Western European philosopher, who addressed the entire legacy of Western European ontology—and metaphysics formed by it—and was familiar with its most minute nuances. Throughout his entire life, Heidegger attempted to operate within the framework of Western European philosophical axioms, even when his goal was to blow them apart, transform, or overthrow them. With German precision, he proceeds from the moment that is conventionally described as the Beginning of Western European philosophy, i.e., the pre-Socratic philosophers, to that which is conventionally (or a little less strictly so) believed to be its *End*; i.e., Friedrich Nietzsche.

Heidegger sees his place in this sequence as the summation of the entire Western philosophy. Thus, he recognizes all its stages: he separates each of them into an entire spectrum of meaningful, telling detail. Anaximander, Heraclitus, and Parmenides are a brilliant trio in pre-Socratic philosophy; Plato and Aristotle represent the highest achievement in Greek thought, and are the creators of all subsequent European philosophy and culture. Heidegger considers the Middle Ages and Catholic Scholasticism only an episode, and the metaphysics of Modernity (from René Descartes through to Immanuel Kant, Gottfried Leibniz, Friedrich Schelling, Johann Fichte, Johann Goethe, and G.W.F. Hegel and up to Friedrich Nietzsche and Henry Bergson) is the logical conclusion of that which the Greeks initiated.

Heidegger's ideas and terminology in a highly inaccurate and distorted manner and criticizes them in an even less justified, naïve way.

Keeping a certain approximation in mind, Heidegger's philosophy is like a pastor's funeral speech, "The deceased was a very good man, helped the poor, did not mistreat younger kids during his childhood, lived a worthy life, worked a lot, and then passed away; may his memory be eternal." Afterward, the pastor begins to go over all the episodes in the life of the deceased in detail ("studied, married, divorced, fell ill, changed careers, retired, fell ill again. . ."). Heidegger's philosophy is a detailed requiem for Western European philosophy, based on the assumption that "something was," "something began," then "something ended, finished, and died." Later, we will discuss what the *"beginning"* means to Heidegger, along with the meaning of "something was"—"to be" is the most important concept for him—and what it means to say "that which was, is no more."

Heidegger proposes to address Western European philosophy, first, as that which once *was*, and second, as that *which is no more*. After all, that which exists now is not Western European philosophy. According to Heidegger, the latter ended with Nietzsche. Heidegger himself is on the borderline. It is from this sepulchral abyss (*Abgrund*) that Heidegger narrates on the subject of that which has died.[9]

Adding religion, traditionalism, or mysticism to this narrative would be incorrect. For Heidegger, only philosophy is of decisive importance, only its processes and twists and turns, its stations and postulates, its highs and lows are of interest. Herein lies his peculiar asceticism: in coping with the rather profound crisis of contemporary nihilism, Heidegger does not look for support in exotic cults, initiations, or secret doctrines. He courageously chooses to be accountable for the fate of all Western European

---

9 The German word *"Abgrund,"* i.e., "abyss," a very important term in Heidegger's philosophy. It originally meant "precipice," "steep vertical slope," and "chasm," specifically.

thinking in its most Western, *logos-based* aspects, for which no analogies exist in other cultures, and which comprises the *essence* and the *fate of Western civilization, specifically.*

To Think with Words: Indo-European
Areas of Thought

In order to understand Heidegger, we must learn to perform two operations based upon the aforementioned peculiarities of his thought process. First and foremost, we must carefully listen to his language—not the concepts or categories but the *words*; not the ideas, principles, and fundamentals but the *stems of words.* His thinking is verbal and stem-based. This is what we must consider when dealing with his texts. Their reading and comprehension demand a certain, even basic, level of linguistic and philological training.[10] In addition, we, like Heidegger himself in his relation to German, must learn to think with words and stems in our native language. Therefore, when reading Heidegger, we must simultaneously:

- listen carefully (to the German words);

- comprehend (the meaning, concept, and intention of thought);

- translate (looking for verbal counterparts capable of transmitting their meaning).

The reading of Heidegger must become our chosen path to *our language, in my case, Russian, as a language of thought and a language of philosophy.* This creates a serious problem. If

---

[10] Nietzsche called one of his works *We Philologists* (Friedrich Nietzsche, *We Philologists*, tr. J. M. Kennedy [Teddington: The Echo Library, 2007]). The reading of Heidegger's philosophy is specifically for "philologists" in the Nietzschean sense.

we take a good look at Indo-European languages in terms of their distribution area, we shall see that each major linguistic group has its own philosophical system with a more or less developed apparatus. The latter is based on determining the philosophical significance of certain basic words in each language, either fully or interspersed, in part, with concepts borrowed from related languages.

This is also the case with European culture, which possesses three basic language groups: Greek (including the language of philosophy's *origins*), Romance languages (which, in addition to Latin, includes French, Spanish, Italian, Romanian, and others), and the Germanic group. All three groups have an established philosophical language with a long-standing tradition of translating certain basic meanings. Heidegger breaks this rule and proposes to introduce new meanings by paying attention to the word stems. At the same time, the work of "breaking" the philosophical metalanguage comprises the lion's share of his texts dedicated to the European philosophical tradition, which is native and intelligible for Heidegger.

This continent of European meanings—with three linguistic bases—is not self-evident to us. Learning Latin and Greek, even in an adequate manner, is becoming exceedingly rare. Our mastery of contemporary European languages (at least, German and French) is not necessarily up to par. This would not be fatal if we at least possessed the basic knowledge of the *Russian philosophical language*. By making a comparison with European meanings, we could destroy old meanings together with Heidegger, knowing *what* we are engaged in, and *what* we are destroying. We could then build something new together with Heidegger, following the wreckage trajectory and adding the treasury of Russian word stems to this new undertaking. Thus, in principle, this is how we should act. However, we have *nothing* to destroy, since our culture has not established a metalanguage of Russian philosophy along with conventional translations of European meanings. This leads to certain problems.

In order to reject European metaphysics together with Heidegger, we must understand it accurately and unequivocally. Otherwise, we would not be able to grasp either the meaning or the range of his philosophizing. This is a serious obstacle. Prior to outlining the way out, let us consider this issue in terms of other Indo-European cultures. Do they have their own philosophical metalanguage?

In the case of Indo-European Iran, there is an extensive tradition of a particular philosophical language, in which true Persian word stems are combined with the vast reservoir of Arabic terminology, which were introduced during the course of Islamization. Henry Corbin, French philosopher and historian of religion (whose work includes the first fragmentary translations of Heidegger's main book, *Sein und Zeit*, into French), in his numerous and well-supported scholarly works, demonstrated the breadth and specific character of Iranian thinking, including its own metalanguage, meanings, as well as particular linguistic and hermeneutic rules and practices.[11] Corbin offers us an insightful and detailed presentation of "*res iranica*"—the "Iranian thing." Heidegger's treatment of "*res europae*" is almost identical. [12]

---

[11] Henry Corbin, "A Shi'ite Liturgy of the Grail," "Sufism and Sophia," and "The Musical Sense of Persian Mysticism" in *The Voyage and the Messenger: Iran and Philosophy* (Berkeley: North Atlantic Books, 1998). Also by Corbin: *The Man of Light in Iranian Sufism* (New Lebanon: Omega Publications, 1994).

[12] Take into account that Henry Corbin informed Europeans about Iranian thought, while Heidegger did so with their own tradition.

Another Indo-European culture, namely that of the Hindus, also possesses an extremely developed and perfected philosophical apparatus based on the Sanskrit language. Here, Sanskrit can be considered a kind of a metalanguage of the *Vedanta* and Vedic cycle. At the same time, the Hindu Mimamsa school represents a separate domain within the framework of the Hindu religion, set aside for the systematization of Sanskrit sounds, letters and word stems, their combinations, etc.[13]

Among Indo-European cultures, only the Slavic world does not have its own established, stable, straightforward, and understandable philosophical metalanguage, which is available to those who think in Russian, despite having similar socio-political, demographic, territorial, and historic parameters to other great peoples.[14] This forces us to contemplate the meaning of this anomaly: why does the unquestionably existent *Russian thing* (*res russica*) lack its own *logos*?

In the 19th century, the Slavophiles sought to bridge the gap in search of the *Russian logos*, while the Westernizers attempted to artificially transfer the European *logos* onto the Russian cultural soil. We should appreciate their efforts, even though they were nullified in the wake of the Bolshevik Revolution. "Philosophical Russia" once again entered the area of twilight consciousness, like in many previous historic instances, when it had every possible thing, except for a full-fledged and suitable philosophical thought.

---

[13] Outside the Indo-European context, equally well developed is the philosophical terminology of the Jewish Kabbalah (in which sounds, letter forms, and basic stems have meanings) or Islamic esotericism, based on the Arabic language and the sacred book of the Muslims, the *Koran*.

[14] In terms of the fundamental and philosophical power in the general fabric of Indo-European culture, "abortive civilizations" (using Arnold Toynbee's terminology) remain in the shadows. These include the Celts, Letto-Lithuanians (including Prussians), Phrygians (including their descendants, the Romans), as well as the extinct civilizations of the Minoans, Pelasgians, Hittites, Tocharians, Scythians, and Sarmatians. Perhaps, the reconstruction of their philosophical message waits for its time to emerge.

I will make a risky suggestion that, out of all the Indo-European cultural areas, it is the Russian one that "*lies fallow.*" The latter is not an accident or the result of our deficiency and backwardness. We are quite advanced in terms of other matters (statehood, economy, technology, science, and military power). It seems that Russians simply waited for the right moment to produce a *new philosophy*. At the same time, we rejected the old European metaphysics, which the West has persistently imposed on us, not out of foolishness, but deliberately, not wishing to participate in it, guarding and saving ourselves for something more interesting and important—something more fundamental. If this suspicion is accurate, then we have awaited our hour: the old European metaphysics has collapsed, and the most profound, serious, and responsible of the European thinkers confirmed this fact and urged us to think in a radically different way. Perhaps, now is the right time to participate in the process of true philosophizing and to unseal the virgin treasure of the Slavo-Russian language in order to create new meanings and to reach new intellectual horizons, based upon the newly grasped Russian antiquity.[15] Perhaps, we "*lay fallow*" in anticipation, waiting specifically for the proper kind of turn in the world history of thought.[16]

Evening's Thinking

At the same time, we should not let the profoundly *European* essence of Heidegger's thinking out of sight even for a moment. For Heidegger, Europe and the West are synonymous, denoting

---

[15] Vladimir Kolesov published a brilliant work on the roots and meaning of ancient Russian words and their evolution. See Vladimir Kolesov, *Drevniaia Rus': Nasledie v slove* (Sankt-Peterburg: Mir Cheloveka, 2000.)

[16] The works of René Guénon and Henry Corbin possess fundamental significance. They will help us methodologically understand what exactly we strive to discover in the general legacy of the Slavic, and now—the Russian-Slavic cosmos.

a specific form of philosophizing, historical being, and cultural path, which express the idea of an "evening." Heidegger emphasizes that "Europe is an evening land" ("*Abendland*" in German). The kind of philosophy that suits it is an "evening philosophy"—an "evening metaphysics." The task of Western European philosophy is "*to put Being to sleep.*"

In Heidegger's book *Die Geschichte des Seyns*, in the third section's ("European Philosophy") footnote, we read:

> *Der seynsgeschichtliche Begriff des Abendlandes. Das Land des Abends. Abend Vollendung eines Tages der Geschichte und Übergang zur Nacht, Zeit des Übergang und Bereitung des Morgens. Nacht und Tag.*[17]

> The *Seynsgeschichtliche* understanding of the West (the land of the evening). Evening land. Evening (West) — the completion of History's day and the transition to night, the time of transition and preparation for the morning (tomorrow's day). Night and day.

Clearly recognizing his identity as a European and a European thinker, Heidegger, like all other Europeans, has no doubts that the path of the West—its "evening path"—denotes the universal trajectory of *Being*, followed by all peoples and cultures, but where the Europeans were first to go. This means that they would be the first not only to descend into the night, but also to see the dawn. Heidegger writes, "Today, the entire planet had become European (Western). . .When we say "European" (Western), we do not mean geography or the expansion of influence, but rather, history and the origins of the Historical in it."[18]

---

[17] Martin Heidegger, *Geschichte des Seyns (1938/1940)* (Frankfurt am Main: Vittorio Klostermann, 1998), 6.

[18] Martin Heidegger, *Über den Anfang* (Frankfurt am Main: Vittorio Klostermann, 2005), 107.

By "history" Heidegger means Western history, i.e., the history of Western philosophy as the quintessence of history, and he believes that its most important moment, the "*beginning*," is the emergence of philosophical thought in Greece.

Conceiving of Western European culture as a universal culture reflects "cultural racism," common for people of the West, which was completely typical for Heidegger, too.[19] However, to his credit, we must note that he himself was never mistaken. He believed that the West does not bring others "progress" and "development," but rather nihilism, "desert," "oblivion of the question about *Being*," decomposition, and downfall (i.e., all the joys of the night). The contemporary West is universal in as far as decomposition and downfall are universal. Heidegger saw the most profound form of this degeneration in "Americanism," which he viewed as "planetarism" (today we would say "globalism" and "globalization"). "Planetarism is the inversion of the beginning (of Western philosophy) within the beinglessness of its development."[20] At the onset of its evening path, the West still illuminated the world with rays of the setting sun for other cultures. In the latest period, "Americanism," "pragmatism," "*techne*" and "calculation" only bring decay to mankind. Yet Heidegger found meaning and universal significance even in the decay, perversion, and insignificance of the modern-day West.

---

[19] Just like his teacher Edmund Husserl. For Husserl, the question was whether "the European man possesses the absolute idea, whether he is an empirically measurable anthropological type, like the inhabitants of China or India are; in this case, whether the Europeanization of other peoples is evidence of the absolute meaning entering the world's meaning and is far removed from historical meaninglessness?". This question was purely rhetorical; of course, "the European man possesses the absolute idea." (Edmund Husserl, *The Crisis of European Sciences and Transcendental Phenomenology* [Evanston: Northwestern University Press, 1970].) Heidegger thought likewise. Implicitly or explicitly, practically all the people of the West are certain of this.

[20] Martin Heidegger, *Über den Anfang, op. cit.,* 107.

As a thinker of the West, Heidegger thinks in terms of the evening; even more than that, he thinks *nocturnally*. He sees his mission in summarizing the entire Western philosophical tradition. In a way, his books are the last thing that could be said using the "evening language." Heidegger's language is not the language of Heidegger as a person; it is the final chord of the Western European language. He is the last point of Western European thinking. He and his philosophy are not a specific case; they are destiny, fate (in the sense of fulfilling that, which had been *foretold*). "At the beginning of language is a poem," says Heidegger. At the end of language is the philosophy of Martin Heidegger. And it seeks to become the beginning of a new language, foreshadowing the morning's language.

Heidegger believed that in the most recent centuries, Germans, out of all Europeans, starting with Goethe, Leibniz, Kant, the Romantics, Schelling, Fichte, Hegel and up to Nietzsche, had been accountable for the fate of the world (Heidegger's "world," *die Welt*, is the totality of *beings-as-a-whole—das Seiende-im-Ganzen*). He draws a straight line from the ancient Greeks to classic German philosophy and finally—to himself.

II. BEING AND BEINGS

Differentiation ("Ontologische Differenz")

At the root of Heidegger's philosophy—at the root of all his thought—is the notion of ontological differentiation (*"ontologische Differenz"*). This concept (*"la différence"*[1] in French and *"Unterschied"* in German) becomes a fundamental philosophical act for Heidegger. We are not talking about just any differentiation, but the differentiation of all differentiations, that is to say, the differentiation between *beings (Seiende)* and *Being (Sein)*.

Beings and Being are not one and the same. This gap encompasses the astuteness of Heidegger's philosophy, in terms of the existence of sameness and non-sameness (simultaneously) —the pair (and the non-pair) of these two concepts. Having been "anointed" by Heidegger, comprehending the very nature of thought and metaphysics as well as the depths of human existence, affected by the essential dyad of *"Being and beings,"* as Heidegger understood it, from now on, we will think like Heidegger in any situation, when solving any problem, and reading any philosophical work.

It is important to determine which German words correspond to these fundamental words in Russian. In German, Heidegger calls *"Being" "das Sein,"* based on the infinitive form of the verb *"sein"* (that is, the Slavic *"бытие"* [bytie], the English "being," and the Greek *"εἶναι"* [einai] are somewhere between a verbal noun and a gerund). The German language has a particular form for constructing a verbal noun, which requires using the

---
[1] Or *"différance,"* as per Jacques Derrida.

neuter article with a verb. If we were to translate "*Sein*" literally, we would have to use the Old Church Slavonic verb "to be" (*быть* [*byt'*]) in the infinitive, that is "*быти*" (*byti*), instead of the extravagant, somewhat recent, and artificial Russian verbal noun "*Being*" (*бытие*), which is quite useful in the translation of theological texts and Western philosophy. We do not have the direct opportunity to use the infinitive form of this verb in Russian, therefore we use the noun "*Being*" (*бытие*). However, we must always keep this consideration in mind, otherwise we will fall into error, the significance of which will eventually become clear. We will not be able to understand Heidegger unless we clarify for ourselves what is at stake.

Das Sein and das Seiende

Thus, we translate "*Sein*" as "*Being*," keeping the Old Church Slavonic word "*быти*" (*byti*) in mind. In German, *Seiende*— "*beings*" (or "*сущее*" [*sushchee*] in Russian)—is formed by using an active participle from the same verb, "*sein*"—"*Seiende*."

What are "*beings*"? Old Church Slavonic had one particular form, "*сый*" (*syi*), meaning the "*one, who is.*" The difference between *beings*, on the one hand, and *Being*, on the other, the difference between *Seiende* and *Sein*, is the purpose and foundation of Heidegger's entire philosophy. And, therefore, we must return to grammar once again. Heidegger emphasizes the fact that the conjugation of a verb or the formation of different grammatical forms is always the result of its inflection[2], its linkage to something, its elastic bending. In its pure form, the infinitive, the verb "*sein*" (or the verb "*быти*" in Russian) exists by itself and does not relate to anyone or anything, does not signify anything, and does not "bow" or "bend" before anyone.

---

2 From the Latin "*inflexiō*," a bending, or the Russian "*наклонение*" (*naklonenie*) with the same literal meaning.

Let us consider a simpler verb: what does "*to do*" mean? We understand what "*he does*" signifies: we are able to recognize the "*one who does*," and we see the results of "*what had been done.*" But are we capable of conceiving or imagining what "*to do*" means in its purest form? Its infinitive does not have a clear image, and nothing pertaining to *beings* directly corresponds to it. "*To do*," ("*деяти*" [*deiati*] in Old Church Slavonic) is something that is realized by an unknown someone in relation to an unknown something. This level of abstraction is unimaginable. Nonetheless, if we attempt to deal with the infinitive of the verb "to do" in search of corresponding images, then we will immediately end up in a peculiar situation. On the one hand, this will tell us something, but on the other, we will not be able to grasp what we are dealing with no matter how hard we try. This "*deed*" (*деяние* [*deianie*]) only acquires meaning when it undergoes conjugation, i.e., when it works together with a pronoun or a noun, that is, with a subject or an object. We grasp the meaning of the verb when it is clarified by a person or number, when it is already inflected ("bent"). In its pure form, when the verb exists by itself as a ῥῆμα (*rima*), as an infinitive, we do not comprehend it; it eludes us—even as concrete a verb as "*to do.*"

In that case, what can we say about the verb "*to be*," which is much more complex and elusive in its deceptive clarity?

If we attempt to grasp this verb's meaning (in an analogous way to the verb "*to do*") in the infinitive, it will elude us even more decisively. The infinitive is the fundamental operation on the part of our consciousness concerning the disincarnation of demonstrable *beings* in action. This operation is linked to the very roots of thought, and the entire thought structure greatly depends on the way it is carried out. This structure is built

43

upon its own basic foundations, in which thought is obtained in close contact with *beings*.

Herein lie the principal difficulties and problems of Martin Heidegger's philosophy.

It is Easy to Understand Beings: The Foundation of Thought

What are *beings, Seiende?* This we understand perfectly well. We are talking about that which *is actual*, that which *is present*, and that which *is in front of us. Beings are,* and the fact that they exist as *beings*, in actuality, makes them clear and obvious. *Beings* are intelligible. The direct nature of such clarity is located at the basis of thought as such, in the sense that the confirmation of their actuality strictly corresponds to the first operation in thought. Thought may have different forms, even the most fantastic; but in all its twists and paradoxes, it always refers us to *beings* as its principal assertion. Thought asserts that *beings are.* They begin here. If there is any doubt as to whether *beings are,* and that they are *beings,* then thought strays, meaning gets lost, and madness ensues.

The experience of *beings* is the primary and initial experience of thought. The verb is in the third person is quite specific. The whole aggregate of things and each of the things, including ourselves, can grant itself the status of *beings,* of that which is, without any issues. This is not complicated: we can easily run into *beings.* All that we see, all that has been, all that we think about or remember are *beings. Beings* are, perhaps, the most intelligible and basic idea about the relationship between man and the world as well as himself. It is quite simple to understand *beings:* they represent that which gives itself to us, that which is actual, that which is *present.*[3]

---

[3] Alexander Dugin uses the Russian verb *"присутствовать"* (*prisutstvovat'*)

Of course, the field of philosophy could pose a question, which, at one point, concerned the Sophists in antiquity, Immanuel Kant, and the phenomenologists: does the knowledge that *beings* are relate to *beings* themselves or to knowledge? Is existence intrinsic to *beings*, or is it a predicate of reason, which we can grasp through basic thought process?

Kant clearly formulated this problem, having raised the question of the *"thing-in-itself"* and the *"thing-for-us"*; that is, the question of *noumena* and phenomena. Edmund Husserl, the founder of phenomenology and Heidegger's teacher, proposed to introduce the concept of *"noēma,"* in order to avoid this question—that is, *beings* which are *beings* in the area of thought, and are intellectual objects, the phenomena of thought. *Noēma* does not correspond to *beings* themselves, but to thoughts about *beings*, including the attribution of *beings'* traits. "

Despite this apparent complication, everything remains fairly simple. It is not all that important whether *beings* are *beings* by themselves, and whether it is at all legitimate to raise the question of anything "by itself" when we are dealing with philosophy. In other words, in the area of thought, there are only the laws of thought that are unconditional and fundamental, determining how thought deals with everything else. Whether *beings* exist by themselves as *noēmata*, or whether their existence is the predicate of reason, that is, "that which was declared earlier" (*"praedicare,"* "to proclaim" or "to say beforehand" in Latin or the German *"Zuspruch"*), has no decisive significance for reason. In both cases, we are dealing with *"noēma."* In

in order to emphasize its link to the Russian translation of *"Seiende,"* *"сущее"* (*sushchee*). This verb shares the stem *"сущ"* (*sushch*), also found in such words as *"existence,"* *"существование"* (*sushchestvovanie*), and uses the prefix *"при"* (*pri*), which means "near." The English word "(to be) present" has links to the Latin *"præesse,"* which refers to being in front of someone or something or to being at hand. (Present, Dictionary.com, Online Etymology Dictionary, Douglas Harper, http://dictionary.reference.com/browse/present [accessed: October 09, 2012].) (*Ed.*)

one case, it has an object that strictly corresponds to it, and is independent of it; and in the other, it has an object that does not strictly correspond to it, and is not independent of it, or has no such object at all.

As objects, or as phenomenological "*noēmata*," *beings are*, and this is obvious for thought. Thought deals with this as with something that is obvious from the outset. Accepting the opposite—that *beings are not*—we demolish the mechanism of consciousness, disable it, and thereby cease to be thinking entities. After hypothetically ceasing to be thinking entities, we can no longer be certain as to whether we exist, i.e., whether we are entities, inasmuch as we no longer possess the methods to determine the existence or non-existence either of ourselves or of that which is around us. In this case, someone else—one who retains reason— will decide for us whether we are or not.

"Man" was defined by the ancient Greeks, starting with Aristotle, as ζῷον λόγον ἔχον (*zoon logon echon*), that is, as an "*animal, endowed with word-language-thought*." Losing our *logos*, we not only lose our humanity, but also our animality, leaving the concern with our species classification to others.

Being is a Problem: The Key Question in Philosophy

Beings are intelligible and transparent, and their intelligibility and transparency comprise the foundation of thought. When it comes to *Being*, however, everything is much more complicated.

When thought takes its first step, often unnoticed by the thinker himself, it asserts (implicitly), that *beings are*. This is not a problem or a question, but the basis of thought. One who simply thinks always makes this initial move.

46

Yet if the thinker begins to think about how he thinks, i.e., thinking about thought, then the reflection about *beings* acquires a completely different character and occurs on a different, higher level of consciousness. Reflecting upon our own thinking, we apply the features of *beings* to it, too, in one way or another. Perhaps, this does not occur as clearly as with Descartes, with his "*cogito ergo sum*" ("I think, therefore I am"; I exist), but the ancient Greeks were already aware of something along these lines. This time around, this issue demands questioning *beings* in order, in the very least, to separate their properties imagined by the thinker, from those properties of *beings* that the thinker is.

This, according to Heidegger, is the "key question in philosophy" (*Leitfrage*), which is formulated as follows: "What is the *Being* of *beings* as such?" In other words, "What is common to all *beings* that makes them *beings*?" or "What is generally intrinsic to *beings*?"

What this "key question in philosophy" addresses is *Being*. It is conceived of through *beings*, but as something different from *beings*, although intrinsic to them. We can describe the genesis of this question in two ways: empirically or rationalistically. Empirically, this will look like two consecutive stages of "natural" speculation about the fact that *beings* are a given. The first stage is a simple affirmation that *beings are*. The second stage strives toward generalized observations about *beings*, toward the systematization and hierarchization of the features of *beings*. Observing *beings*, consciousness begins to notice certain regularities and, at a point in time (the appearance of philosophy in the ancient world), reaches the realization that *beings as a whole* have a common property. Thus emerges the notion of *Being* and the corresponding question, "What is this *Being*?"

47

The second way to address the same question could focus on thought regarding thought, with an underlying and growing conviction that *beings* capable of thinking about other *beings* are *beings* of a higher order. Their existence demands a different higher form; i.e., thinking *beings* are principally different from non-thinking *beings*. This highest form of *beings* is also associated with *beings as a whole*, with *what beings have in common*, and leads to the following question, "What is the *Being* of *beings*?"

Thus, *Being as Sein*, as the Greek εἶναι (*einai*), as the infinitive appears in the area of thought at that very moment when thought begins to examine something that goes beyond the consideration of *beings* as such. This is the beginning of philosophy: leaving the framework of initial assertions in the vein of *"beings are."*

And herein lies a fundamental issue. Thought focused solely on *beings* as they are in direct experience is potentially boundless. Thought can sort *beings*, rearrange, compare, differentiate, and combine them, without moving up to the next level—that of speculation about *Being*. For this reason, ancient Greeks considered thought about the essence of *beings* as an invasion of something divine. The first fragment about the unity of *beings* and *logos*, written by Heraclitus of Ephesus, refers to this point, specifically:

> οὐκ ἐμοῦ ἀλλὰ τοῦ λόγου ἀκούσαντας ὁμολογεῖν σοφὸν ἐστίν ἕν πάντα εἶναι (If you do not listen to me, but to the *logos*, it would be wise, abiding by it, to say: everything is one[4]).

---

4 Hermann Diels, *Die Fragmente der Vorsokratiker. Griechisch und Deutsch* (Berlin: Weidmannsche Buchhandlung, 1903), fragment 50; here, translated from the Russian.

In lectures about Heraclitus's *logos*, Heidegger emphasized the fact that Heraclitus associated *logos* with d*ivine lightning*.[5] Only the lightning of divine *logos*, surpassing the intellectual capabilities on the part of the philosopher himself ("do not listen to me"), can push one to conceive of *beings as a whole*: in this excerpt described as "the unity of all."

Heidegger also underscored the fact that in Aristotle's philosophy, unity is almost a synonym of *Being*—ἕν (*hen*) is a synonym of ὄν (*on*). Therefore, we can interpret this fragment specifically as one that links *logos* with *Being*, thereby elevating the entire problem of thought to the second—highest—level. The "key question in philosophy" is formulated at this level.

The place where the question of *Being* is raised is where philosophy begins. This boundary separates a mere thought from philosophical thought.

"The Key Question in Philosophy" was
Formulated Incorrectly

All that has been said above about *beings* and *Being* is yet to contain anything new and unusual, perhaps, apart from the stubborn fixation on the relationship between *Being* and *beings*. This relationship (*Bezug*) is the single most important problem for Heidegger's entire philosophy. The classical history of philosophy describes the set of ontological problems somewhat like this, assuming this to be a common issue.

---

[5] Martin Heidegger, *Heraklit 1. Der Anfang des abendländischen Denkens (Heraklit) (1943); 2. Logik. Heraklits Lehre vom Logos (1944)* (Frankfurt am Main: Vittorio Klostermann, 1987).

Heidegger's radical novelty is expressed in his obvious dissatisfaction with the very formulation of the "key question in philosophy," starting from his initial texts on phenomenology. He is wary of the original philosophical fundamentals, which substantiate the idea that *Being* is the common property of *beings*. He views this idea as something profound, foundational, and decisive for the entire process of Western European philosophy and interprets it as a fatal error, a mistake, and an omission of something that is vitally important. It is not that easy to express or describe the latter, but he grasps it intuitively as the turning point of world history.

According to Heidegger, the relationship between *beings* and *Being* was already interpreted incorrectly in antiquity. Although this mistake was infinitely small during the initial stages, it grew alongside all the consequences of philosophy's establishing foundations until ultimately transforming into the total ontological nihilism of Modernity, especially during the 20th century. According to Heidegger, we must seek the key to understanding the present state of affairs in philosophy, culture, and even politics at the dawn of Western European civilization, in the way in which the very first philosophers resolved the question of correlating *Being* (*Sein*) and *beings* (*Seiende*).

Even at that point, *something went wrong* in terms of clarifying the relationship between *Being* and *beings* in the way the "key question in philosophy" was raised. "*What* went '*wrong*'? *Why* did it go 'wrong' exactly, and *what should happen* to make it *right*?" These questions comprise the core of Martin Heidegger's philosophy.

III. FUNDAMENTAL-
ONTOLOGY[1]

The Complexity of Bezug

Working out the nature of ontological problems, Heidegger advances the following thesis, *"Sein ist das Seiende nicht"* — *"Being* is not *beings."* On the one hand, this means nothing but the fact that thoughts about the *Being* of *beings* as *beings* must take us away from *beings*, which is almost obvious. They do take us away, but not in the fashion that this should be done. Here, the structure of *Bezug* (relationship) moves to the forefront.

Bezug, relationship, clarifies the correlation between *beings* and *Being*, and is structured in a very specific way in the field of ancient philosophy. Reflection on the *Being* of *beings* leads ancient Greek philosophers to the concept of essence, as the common attribute

---

[1] In order to emphasize the specific way in which Heidegger understands the question of *Being*, I propose to utilize the German formula *"Fundamentalontologie," "fundamental-ontologische,"* which Heidegger uses himself. This strategy is not unlike using other Heideggerean terms, such as *"Dasein," "Geviert," "Ge-Stell,"* and *"Das Man,"* leaving them untranslated in order to emphasize the unique meaning that this philosopher put into carefully selected words, taking them back to the source of their philosophical-poetic and etymological significance. "Fundamental-ontology" is not "fundamental ontology," but rather the way in which Heidegger understands the most profound level of ontological analysis. However, the latter is only applicable within the framework of his unique teaching concerning nature and the structure of *Dasein* (Part 3, "Dasein," and the second part of the book are dedicated to this subject) as well as in the context of the new Beginning. In some cases, he uses the expression "onto-ontology," in order to underscore that "fundamental-ontology" is not just another level logically constructed over the ontic, but, on the contrary, the kind of thought about *Being* that preserves the continual freshness of direct contact with the ontic as a form of *Dasein's* existence.

that unites all *beings* in their greatest *shared* quality. "Essence" (*οὐσία* [*ousia*] in Greek, *сущность* [*sushchnost'*] in Russian) is a feminine noun, formed from the present participle of the verb "to be," "*εἶναι*" (*einai*), "*быть*" (*byt'*), "*sein*." This term was later translated into Latin as "*essentia*" or "*substantia*," which obscured its meaning. In Russian, the word "*сущность*" (*sushchnost'*) is the most precise translation of this term.

Here, we must once again address Heidegger's metalanguage. He insists that *οὐσία* is *Seiendheit*, i.e., a particular way to conceive of *Being*, in which it is equated with the *exact shared quality of all beings as beings*. It is this kind of understanding that determines the particular path of development in Western philosophy, where *Being* as *εἶναι* is persistently and invariably thought of specifically as *οὐσία*, expressed in the formula *Sein = Seiendheit*, "*Being is the essence of beings*."

This is the *Bezug* of Western European philosophy, which is structured upon this particular ontological picture, and is based specifically on this way of thinking. "*Being is the essence of beings*"; and, consequently, this leads to the establishment of two parallel levels: *the level of beings and the level of essence* (*οὐσία* [*substance, ousia*], *Seiendheit*). And here, Heidegger makes a highly critical assertion: ancient philosophy, and all contemporary Western European philosophy following it, which differentiate *Being* and *beings* through essence, effectively overlooked the difference between *Being* and *beings*. Thus, they created an abstraction from *beings* based upon the direct analogy with *beings* themselves. As a result, Western European philosophy conceived of *Being* (as the essence of *beings*) as distinct from unique and concrete *beings*, but coinciding with *beings* in their universality. In other words, it ultimately viewed *Being* as *beings*. This was, of course, a different kind of *beings*, one from the highest, supreme rank, but an example of *beings* nonetheless. Ultimately, *Being* acquired the attributes of *beings*, i.e., it then became possible to make statements, such as "*Being is*," as Parmenides had done. This kind of an assertion is possible only in relation to *beings*, even the most sublime, primordial, simple, and unified kind. If "*Being is*," then it belongs to the category of *beings*, even if not simply as one of *beings*, but rather as the essence of *beings*.

The Greeks, like other people of the West, loved *beings* too much and became victims of this fatal love, which predetermined the entire system of Western European philosophy. Heidegger mentions the latter not with irritation and arrogance, but rather with profound understanding and empathy. *Being*—as that which makes *beings* what they are—must somehow be combined with *beings* and connected to them. And if we follow this idea through, at some point, we would, indeed, become convinced that *Being is*, that it is *beings*, and that it is the most important and purest of *beings*. The opposite assertion—that *Being* is not *beings*—can only be accepted up to a certain extent. At that point, we would have to emphasize that *Being* as the shared feature is not the same as *beings* as particulars. However, both the particular and the shared have one attribute that unites them: they both are.

Yet, understanding the depth of ontological differentiation and *Bezug* in traditional philosophy, Heidegger tells us: this is the whole point, and the principal error is rooted here; if *Being* is not *beings*, then it is the latter that must be the object of ontological study. However, in this case, it cannot be identical to the *essence of beings*, and, consequently, it is not a shared attribute for *beings*. Here, *Being is not, it is not beings, it is none of beings* (this also includes the non-essence of *beings* and the non-shared attributes—not οὐσία or κοινόν [*koinon*]).

In other words, Heidegger asserts that *"Being is Nothingness"* (*das Sein ist das Nichts*), making Western European philosophy a great delusion, lasting two and a half thousand years, as it failed to recognize this issue.

Ontics

Analyzing the relationship (*Bezug*) between *beings* (*Seiende, ὄν [on]*) and *Being* (*Sein, εἶναι*), Heidegger introduces three levels of ontology, which would allow us to consider this problem from another perspective. Heidegger gives their definitions in his most important work, *Sein und Zeit.*[2]

First comes the "ontic" level, from the Greek *ὄν—beings: ὄντος* (*ontos*) is the genitive case, which usually helps form compound words in Greek. When we attempted to answer the question about what *beings* are in the most direct and accessible manner, we were in the domain of the ontic. The ontic dimension assumes the mind's direct grasp of the outside world with all its distinctions and variety. At this point, the mind is yet to question what the *Being of beings* or the *essence of beings* are, and restricts itself to basic affirmations that *beings* are *beings*. Thought as such in its most natural and basic form operates specifically in this dimension. To think about *beings* as *beings* means to compare one to the other, to line *beings* up, and to juxtapose them amongst themselves, always remaining at the same level in terms of thought topography (i.e., the space of thought), without going beyond its limits; i.e., not raising the questions as to *where beings originated, what the Being of beings is, where the end of beings is,* and *of what this end is.*

The ontic sphere is typical for both hard sciences and everyday thought; it ranges from the highly developed calculation

---

[2] Martin Heidegger, *Sein und Zeit (1927)* (Tübingen: Max Niemeyer Verlag, 2006).

systems and classification to the most banal mental reactions on the part of an average person in the most diverse cultures, from the most primitive to the most sophisticated.

The ancient Greeks defined the sphere of *beings* by using the collective concept "φύσις" (*physis*), and, according to Aristotle, the area of ontic thought can be called "physics." A little later, we shall see just how much is invested in this concept.

In regard to philosophy, ontic thought establishes its groundwork. This is already considered thought, but is not yet philosophical (in the fullest sense of the word). This is thought based on words, but not concepts; thoughts about the obvious, but without abstraction. These thoughts operate with things, but not essences, even if these things have a mental nature; i.e., are "*noēmata*" in Edmund Husserl's sense. For Heidegger, this thought level is extremely important, since this is where philosophy originates. And how it begins, how it deals with the stratrum of the ontic worldview and reflection about the world, in which direction it sets off, and where it moves on—all have the principal significance for the entire trajectory of philosophy's development, and, in fact, predetermines its fate and its end.

Ontology

Heidegger calls the second level ontological. Ontology begins by asking "the key question in philosophy," "What is the *Being* of *beings?*" "What are *beings* as a whole?" and "What is the essence of *beings?*" The problem of qualitative differentiation between *beings* and *Being* appears at this point. And, consequently, ontology is based on clarifying the structure and quality of the relationship between one and the other. Here, the question of *Being* is placed at the very core of thought. These are philosophy's origins, which, in contrast to thought as such, move to a principally new level. At this level, the question about the *Being* of *beings* and the fact that *Being* and *beings* are not identical, is the focal point.

According to Heidegger, pre-Socratic philosophers founded ontology, like philosophy ("philosophy" and "ontology" are identical concepts from the standpoint of *Being*). Plato and Aristotle definitively established these two subjects, which entered Christian theology and modern philosophy in their completed form. The way in which the first philosophers comprehended the question about the *Being* of *beings* turned out to be both destiny and fate for all Western European philosophy. Their choice and their solution to this set of problems laid down the fundamental groundwork for the entire subsequent philosophical process. They are the founders of Greeks' ontology, which became the ontology for the entire field of European philosophy.

Solving the question of *Being*, ontology identifies the *Being* of *beings* with the essence of *beings* (*οὐσία*) and, asserting the difference between *beings* and *Being* (as an attribute common to all *beings*), at the same time relates to *Being* as a kind of *beings*, only one of a higher rank. According to Heidegger, the most important point is that ontology strays from its predestined path during the very first stages. The birth of philosophy and the breakthrough to *logos* at lightning speed separated thought from ontics and pushed it to *leap* beyond the horizons of *beings* and to the discovery and revelation of *Being*. This would have been genuine *transcendence*; i.e., a true surpassing of limits. It and only it would have secured an irreversible and incontrovertible significance for philosophy. Grasping *beings* ontically from the outset, the Greeks' fierce thought, which had developed a taste for freedom, should have leapt into *Nothingness*, into *non-beings*, where it should have searched for *Being* as the authentic basis of *beings*. But the Greeks did otherwise and created an ontology that was not based on *Nothingness* but on the *essence of beings*, i.e., on *Being* as the general attribute of *beings*. They had thus given birth to "fictitious transcendence," which did not break through to the true source of *beings*—their hidden foundation—but doubled the topography of *beings* with an additional level. The latter remained part of *beings* (however they might have called it), but, at the same time, served as the supreme source for *beings* in the ontic arena; i.e., as *Being*.

In later works (especially of the 1936-1946 period), Heidegger introduced a very important element of his metalanguage—spelling the word "*Sein*," "*Being*," in two variants: the regular "*Sein*" and the archaic "*Seyn*." This spelling variation possesses radical significance. (In Russian, there is no possible way to convey the two spellings; in English, we occasionally see "*Beyng*" [*Seyn*].)

Ontology operates with *Being* as *Sein*, meaning *Seiendheit*, essence. *Seyn* is the kind of *Being* that, on the contrary, entirely eludes ontology and is not grasped through *beings*, but otherwise (most likely, in terms of *non-beings*; i.e., Nothingness). Seyn represents genuine transcendence and authentic philosophy, which Heidegger proposes to create. Thus, ontology, in its extant form, devises the artificial construct of "essentialism" over *beings*. This construct becomes the domain of philosophy, while philosophy itself is considered the Queen of the Sciences. In turn, philosophy determines the principles, foundations, and methodologies of physical sciences, as well as those of ethics, grammar, mathematics, geometry, philology, aesthetics, etc. All this is the result of one original and infinitely small error.

59

Instead of becoming a truly more profound, essentialist, and original form of thought, ontology, as it developed, only continued to distort the normal functioning on the part of ontic thinking, created obstructions and dead ends, distorted and warped *beings* and the understanding of *beings*. Instead of explaining φύσις, ontology violated it, imposing abstract constructions onto *beings*, rooted in the incorrectly oriented basic movement of the *logos*.

Greek philosophy configured the *logos* in ontology, differentiating it from ontics, in such a way that it operated with essence as though with *Being*, equating *Being* to *beings* (i.e., the source of Parmenidean "*Being is, Nothingness is not*"). This excess of false positivity brought the negative, destruction, and death into the ensemble of *beings*. Instead of the salvation of *beings* through *Being*, *logos* destroyed *beings* through the conjuring up of a generalized essence.

With Aristotle, the philosophical intuition of the first Greek philosophers acquired a completed and systematized form. And it is significant that one of his works bears the title *Metaphysics*: "that which follows 'physics'" ("physics"—as a phenomenon and as one of Aristotle's other treatises). Metaphysics proves to be practically identical to ontology (and Western European philosophy in general), because its task is to substantiate the domain of origins beyond physics (i.e., ontics).

Heidegger insists that all Western European philosophy is actually metaphysics (i.e., ontology), even the kind that explicitly rejects any appeals to metaphysics, for instance, the philosophy of Friedrich Nietzsche, the "philosophy of life," positivism, or pragmatism. Metaphysics as ontology became the sole and compulsory style of Western European thought long ago, which is essentialist in each and every case. It is irrelevant whether we are dealing with a system of ideas (idealism), things (realism, materialism), concepts (conceptualism), or values (axiology), a system of the practical (pragmatism), vulgar political worldviews, or even nihilism. All these are an expression of metaphysics, because the thought matrix is one and the same in all cases, and is based upon the false ascription of transcendence to one's preferred position.

Toward Fundamental-Ontology

Let us move on to the most important point—the core of Heideggerean philosophy. Criticizing ontology (and metaphysics) as false and identifying the sources of the key error in terms of the first steps taken by Greek philosophers (which predetermined the subsequent course of Western philosophy) already presupposes the existence of alternatives. If we recognize *what* was "*wrong*," then by using reverse analogy, we can attempt to determine how things *should be* or should have been in order for everything to be "*as it should.*"

Heidegger takes us up close to the following train of thought. The question of ontic thinking—natural thought prior to the question of *beings' Being*—remains the basis of subsequent philosophical development. However, as philosophy develops, and as ontology (metaphysics) becomes more structured and extensive, we move further and further away from *the ontic*, replacing it with *the ontological*. At the same time, there is an increase in technological displacement of nature and in the artificial products of human society. Ontology crushes everything, including its ontic foundations.

Since we are about to reconsider ontology at its source, it is necessary to revisit the ontic—in the exact form that it had at the beginning of philosophy's history, when it was new and fresh. (Heidegger solves this problem in the book *Sein und Zeit*[3] by focusing on *Dasein*[4]). In order to make this happen, Heidegger has to sort through the massive deposits that comprise the edifice of European philosophy from the pre-Socratics up to the 20th century. However, this crucial operation cannot yield any results and will only take us to the base level—toward clarifying ontic thought and its structure. To some degree, phenomenology, including the "*Lebenswelt*" (lifeworld) concept and its basic methodologies, proposes to tackle the same task.

Reaching the ontic and clearing away the ontological, we end up in the same position as the creators of Western philosophy, responsible for establishing the basic trajectory of its future development. This means that the same problems and the same questions now face us. It is at this point that things must happen differently. We must address the *basic questions in terms developing the logos in a different way*, but at the same time, we must ask all the *basic questions all over again*. Heidegger mentions that if the "key question in philosophy" (*Leitfrage*) targeted the essence (as a common attribute) of *beings*, then the "basic question in philosophy—one found at the base" (*Grundfrage*) must be the question about the truth of *Being* (*über Wahrheit des Seyns*: that is, "*Seyn*" with the "y").

Philosophy originates at a point when we ask the question about the *Being* of *beings*. This is a flash of the divine *logos*, illuminating a new dimension of thought and leading to new horizons. But we know that in the case of ontology, this question was formulated in an exceedingly poor manner, whereas its answer was truly catastrophic. Ontology, in an attempt to rise

---

3 *Ibid.*
4 The third part of this book is focused on this subject.

above the ontic, created false transcendence—metaphysics doubled the topography of *beings*. In it, the blueprint for the same kind of *beings* was added to *beings*, but this time—in its essential section, that of its essence. In ontology, the Greek *logos* severed its ties to *beings* and their ontic perception, thereby deforming them, but it could not break through to *Being* as such. This tragedy is responsible for the history of Western Europe and its philosophy.

Heidegger proposes to focus our attention on this point. Returning to ontics, that is, to what is readily accessible to perception, in its uncorrupted state is insufficient; we must undergo the explosion of the *logos* the second time and live through the new experience of the lightning. This time around, learning from the bitter experience of making a critical mistake, we must formulate the question of *Being* directly—not through *beings* (*Seiende*) and the dead-end road of essentialism (*Seiendheit*—*Sein* with an "i"). This time around, *ontological differentiation* must be carried out radically, focusing philosophical attention on *Being* itself—*Seyn* (which is not part of *beings* and cannot be determined by assigning the "is" attribute to it); i.e., on *Being* that is not and, consequently, is Nothingness. Starting out from the ontic (from *beings* in their most obvious, accessible characteristics), this time we must progress in another direction: we must not rise *above beings*, remaining bound to them and destroying them with this ambiguous relationship, as in the case of European metaphysics. Instead, we must glance *below*, delve into *beings' primordial source*—a place where nothing exists and where *Nothingness* is. But this *Nothingness* is not simply *non-beings* (generated from *beings*). This is Nothingness, which makes *beings* what they are, but which does not turn into *beings*. This *Nothingness* is life-giving, constituting all with its quiet power.

63

This is what *"fundamental-ontology"* is: the kind of ontology built along principally new patterns as compared to the entire preceding philosophy. *"Fundamental-ontology"* will let the new kind of *logos* shine. This time, however, it will not focus on *beings*, but on *Nothingness*.

The *logos* of classical metaphysics conceived of Nothingness as the antithesis of *beings*—or generally, as the antithesis of essence and ultimately as the antithesis of itself, which led to total nihilism. After all, operating in this manner, it destroyed —by ignoring—that very *Nothingness* (*Seyn* = *Nichts*) that gave life to *beings*. In turn, the *logos* of "fundamental-ontology" will conceive of *Nothingness* not as the antithesis of *beings*, but as their *life-giving and eternally present source*, which, removing *beings* as *beings*, confirms that they are part of *Being*.

How is *fundamental-ontology* possible? It is possible inasmuch as philosophy is an arena of absolute freedom, one in which thought can complete the most daring and most unimagined turns. But this is possible only if the thinker's *freedom* is combined—*risking everything*—with the truth of *Being*, and will allow this truth to come to fruition.

Martin Heidegger's philosophy is the transitional philosophy on the way to creating *"fundamental-ontology."*

IV. DAS
SEYNSGESCHICHTLICHE

Die Geschichte and Seyn

The noun "*Seynsgeschichte*" and the adjective "*seynsgeschichtliche*" that it forms play an enormous role in Heidegger's philosophy. They are directly connected to the project focused on developing "*fundamental-ontology*." We saw the depth and complexity of this project, which requires the construction of an ontology that serves as an alternative to the entire body of Western European thought. Therefore, the range of expressions and words employed in the realm of "fundamental-ontology" require greater attention on our part.

Before we begin to clarify the significance of the compound word "*Seynsgeschichte*," let us consider its two word stems. We already encountered "*Seyn*." In Heidegger's work, this word spelled with a "y" signifies "*Being in the fundamental-ontological* sense.*" This is not *Being* as the *shared attribute of beings*, an *essence*, or an affirmation of the *logos* built on the basis of examining *beings* through *beings* themselves, but rather— a *breakthrough into the pure element*, free from tight links to *beings*, i.e., *Nothingness* (*Nichts*).

Now let us turn to the word "*Geschichte*," which unequivocally translates as "*history*." But Heidegger himself—we must be used to this by now—not only refuses to identify "*die Geschichte*" with "history" (*die Historie* in German), but contrasts them. Therefore, if we translate "*Seynsgeschichte*" as the "*history of Being*," we would

67

misunderstand Heidegger's intention. Things are even worse with the adjective *"seynsgeschichtliche,"* which is nearly impossible to translate: *"Being-historical"* not only sounds absurd, but also distantly recalls an entirely different range of convergences and meanings contrary to those which Heidegger has in mind.

The Message and the Leap

Let us address the etymology of the German word *"Geschichte."* It comes from the verb geschehen, which means "to occur" and "to happen." Its initial meaning is close to the German *"Ereignis"*[1] (literally, the "event" or the "incident"). By using this word, Heidegger nears the meaning and form of another German word, *"Geschick"* (most commonly used today in its *"Schicksal"* form)—"fate," which, in its turn, is formed from the verb *"schicken,"* "to send," "to dispatch," etc. Therefore, Heidegger sees "fatefulness," "non-randomness," and, more profoundly, *"message"* in the word *"Geschichte,"* as a message about events deserving attention. That which occurs in history in its most essential dimension is a kind of a *message, which acts as that which happens and occurs, imparting meaning to everything.* If "history" is a narration about incidents, phenomena, deeds, and events, then *Geschichte* is the path of meanings, which travels through history as though it was sent. "History" is the envelope, *"Geschichte"*—its contents. Fate consists of all things that happen, representing an overall connected and deliberate action, in which something is passed from someone onto someone else through something and for the purpose of something.

If we delve even further into etymology, we can see that the words *"geschehen"* and *"schicken"* can actually be traced to a common Indo-European stem *"skek,"* which signified "sudden movement,"

---

[1] We will consider the subject of *Ereignis* a little later in this section.

a "jump," "burst," "impulse," "impulsive gesture," as well as "run." In Russian, the verb *"скакать"* (*"skakat'"*), meaning "to jump," comes from the same stem. This is quite noteworthy, since in Heidegger's work, we encounter the interpretation of the word *"jump"* or *"leap"* (*Sprung*) *as the basic philosophical undertaking, leading us into the domain of "fundamental-ontology."* In order to proceed from ontology to "fundamental-ontology," we must make a leap. This will not be a smooth transition, evolution, or an overflow, but a sudden, traumatic, and risky *leap over an abyss (Abgrund)*. At the same time, Heidegger emphasizes the fact that this leap could be fatal, since we stand on the edge of a cliff and have no room for a running start.

Thus, *Geschichte*, according to Heidegger, is not the gradually unfolding canvas of history and the historical process, but rather the totality of individual abrupt *leaps* over the abyss, preparing the way for the last and most crucial (the most difficult and dangerous) *final leap*. The use of the word *"Seyn"* informs us about the message content of these leaps in preparation for the last leap. Thus, we learn that the sender, much like the addressee of this message, was *Being (Seyn) itself, notifying itself about itself by the means of these leaps* (each *leap* represents a stage of philosophical thought, associated with a particular great philosopher and his discoveries). This communication occurs in order to culminate in a transition from ontology (which had revealed itself as contemporary European nihilism) to *"fundamental-ontology"* (the eschatology of *Being*). This is *Seynsgeschichte*.

Seynsgeschichte as Participation in Being (Seyn)

Seynsgeschichte is not just an area of thought or a branch of science. It is an intense effort to recognize the *message of Being (Seyn)* embedded in the historical process by deciphering

69

the profound philosophical intention of those thinkers who have raised ontological questions, spoken about it indirectly, or have been silent about it (which is no less important). In *Seynsgeschichte*, culture and all social and historical events and transformations can serve only as secondary decorations and distant consequences of questions that philosophy resolves.

Seynsgeschichte is possible as the comprehended and the affirmed, based on the framework of "fundamental-ontology." Without the latter, this would simply be *Geschichte*: in it, we would be able to see both the *message* and the *leaps*, but we would not be certain that *authentic Being (Seyn)* is part of this message, rather than the false transcendence of the old ontology. For instance, G.W.F. Hegel's philosophy of history is *Geschichte*, i.e., it is no longer simply *history*, but not *Seynsgeschichte* either. Therefore, *Seynsgeschichte* and its very existence directly depend on whether a *decision (Entscheidung)* would be made concerning the *transition* to "fundamental-ontology," and whether this *transition (leap, jump)* would be carried out successfully.

For this reason, *Seynsgeschichte* is a project rather than something actual—not a given, but a task. If we could learn the truth of *Being (Seyn)* through itself, rather than through *beings* or the their *shared attribute*, then we would discover *what* the historical process really was, and, ultimately, *what* the great thinkers communicated to us about the furthest reaches of their thought. At that point, we will enter the domain of *Seynsgeschichte*, not only having become aware of what had been, but also having won the right to be present there. We will then have the opportunity to be within the *Being of the future* (the *Being* that will be). However, if this does not happen, and we decide to remain under the "yoke" of the old metaphysics, then we will not even have *Geschichte*. Only dead history will remain, with its meaningless and endless list of details about the past, saying nothing to the spirit of the Last Men and embodying nothing but a cultural convention.

It is only possible to understand the *message of Being (Seyn)* in the state of *jumping (leaping) over the abyss*, and this awareness would be a statement on the part of *Being (Seyn)* itself. In turn, this is why *Seynsgeschichte* can serve as a starting point for all philosophizing within the framework of fundamental-ontology: after breaking through to *Seynsgeschichte* and comprehending the meaning of this word, by the very virtue of this act, we already constitute the process of developing *fundamental-ontology* and express the *message of Being (Seyn)* through our own selves.

Yet once we take part in the *leap*, we would not only radically alter the trajectory and order of our actual existence, moving toward new horizons along an entirely new path, but we would also and for the first time discover that which once was. That which once *was*—was a *message from Being*, which always remains invariably fresh and acute, new and alive. For this reason, the adjective "*seynsgeschichtliche*" signifies grasping *that which once was as if it were the present*. It means to become a contemporary of that which not only occurred and was completed in the past (but proved unimportant, became outdated, and passed), but also that which *truly* was. By using the adjective "*seynsgeschichtliche*," we become contemporaries of great ideas and people, since we ourselves reach the ultimate heights. There, other mountain peaks are clearly visible, whereas the insignificant swarms in dark valleys below are indiscernible in the present much like long ago. A true thinker knows as little about the details of society in which he lives as he does about those of the times long gone. Yet the voice of *Being* is audible to him, as it emanates from the lips of the ancients clearer and louder than the itching on the part of the senseless masses, both ancient and modern.

Seyn ist Zeit

Viewing history as *Geschichte*, and especially as *Seynsgeschichte*, may confuse those who uncritically absorbed the normative Western European ontology and metaphysics as undeniable axioms and who are accustomed to conceiving of time as something objective or, in the very least, independent and autonomous. Modern philosophy and science—and the man in the street— think of *time as that in which Being develops.*[2]

But for Heidegger, *Zeit* (time[3]) is not something separate or additional to *Being*. It is not an area where and in which *Being* is realized, or not some *a priori* condition (even if subjective or transcendental, as in Immanuel Kant). For Heidegger, *Being is time*, and, consequently, *time is Being (Seyn ist "Zeit"* [4]).

Heidegger sees *Zeit* as *Seynsgeschichte*, i.e., the development of *Being* in time (although, he does not consider *Being* as something separate, developing in time, but as time itself). However, this is not time in the natural or scientific sense (an a priori mode of object's existence) or history as the field of humanities understands it (as an aggregate of human actions, responses to challenges, and so on, the subject of which is man and all things human). The *Seynsgeschichte* version of time (*Zeit*) has no independent object (nature) or subject (man). *Being*—time— itself is the protagonist of *Seynsgeschichte*. This kind of *Being*

---

[2] The latter do not even realize that they think in this exact manner, or that they think at all.

[3] The difficulties of translating the word "Zeit" by the Russian analogue "time" are considered in detail in Part 3, "Dasein."

[4] Martin Heidegger, *Geschichte des Seyns, op. cit.,*142.

(*Seyn*) relates to itself and to *beings* (*Seiende*), developing as time. Yet we must also note that we are talking about *Being* as *Seyn*, not as *Sein*! That is, Heidegger understands time (*Zeit*) in the *fundamental-ontological* sense, rather than ontologically.

In a time like *Seynsgeschichte*, *the past*, in the sense that it *was*, still *is*. And that which *is not, never was*. And *the future* (*das Künftige*), meaning that which *will be*, already *is*, and certainly *was* earlier. The present time is the *presence* (*parousia*) of *Being* (*Seyn*); any other present with the exception of the presence of *Being* (*Seyn*) is unreal.

Since *Being* (*Seyn*) is time (*Zeit*), then, consequently, not everything in history out of all that seems to *have been*, really *was*, while much of what truly had been is not known to us, to the same extent as we ourselves are not. Here, we could recall the formula coined by the poet and philosopher Evgenii Golovin, "He, who had died, has never lived."[5] That which passed and became the past, *that which had passed* (*Vergangene*), never was. Yet that which had actually been, the truly having-been, is never *Vergangene* (*that which had passed*): it is immortal.

Three Layers of History

The introduction of the *Seynsgeschichte* dimension, and the analysis of time with its events and patterns from the standpoint of "*fundamental-ontology*," differentiate three levels in the area that is usually referred to as "history."

It is noteworthy that this word migrated into Russian from the German language in the 17th century, during the reign of Peter the Great, and it entered German from the Greek language

---

5 Alexander Dugin, "Smert' i ee aspekty," in *Radikal'nyi Sub'ekt i Ego Dubl'* (Moscow: Evraziiskoe dvizhenie, 2009).

(ἰστορία [istoria]) by the way of Latin (historia). Prior to this point, no concept of "history" existed in the Russian language: it was the chronicles (for instance, the *Primary Chronicle*) and ecclesiastic literature (the Old and New Testament, patristic literature, sermons, lives of the saints, the explanatory *palaia*, etc.) that communicated historical information. Russian "byliny" (*былины, pl.*) "byli" (*были*), and "bylichki" (*былички*), corresponding to Heidegger's *Seynsgeschichte* in terms of meaning, were either part of the heroic epic tales or the part-mythological-part-historical stories about daily life. This makes these words unsuitable in the given context. In the Orthodox tradition, *Seynsgeschichte* comes closest to the concepts of "fate" and "providence." "Fate" (*sud'ba* [*судьба*]) is the "original justice" (from the Russian word "*sud,*" "*justice*"). "Reasoning," *rassuzhdenie* (*рассуждение*), shares the stem "*sud/suzh*" with "*sud'ba*" which predetermined the development of world events, assigning the place, order, and meaning to each of them. *Providence* (*promysel* [*промысел*]) is a direct reference to divine thought, the Wisdom of God (Sophia), which intentionally (in eternity) organized *beings*, as well as the order and character of their emergence (γένεσις [genesis]) and disappearance (φθορὰ [fthora]). These parallels are important to us because Heidegger performs two operations with the concept of "history": on the one hand, he employs familiar ("academic") Western European concepts as they are typically and generally interpreted; on the other, he etymologically brings these concepts back to the original meaning of ancient words and, at the same time, overthrows the established constructions, encouraging the creation of radically new "*fundamental-ontological*" ones.

In order for the Russian consciousness to strictly follow *what* Heidegger is doing and what he encourages, it is always necessary to take into account the distance between Russian culture and its tradition of thought (for now, I refrain from speaking about Russian philosophy and, especially, Russian ontology), on the one hand, and the structure of the Western mentality and intellect, on the other. Battling the axioms of Western European historicism, Heidegger fights against what is far from evident to us and what we were late in taking from the West, fragmentarily and superficially—what had ample time to pollute our consciousness, but did not become a full-fledged system of *a priori* concepts, giving way under the necessity of clear reflection.

Here, we should once again recall what Heidegger says about Western European history, which he (by default, like all Western people) considers to be universal and the only one. We, Russians, are not at all obligated to recognize the latter as such, but we should take this into consideration in order to better understand the context of Heidegger's thought.

Thus, from the standpoint of *Seysngeschichte*, we can highlight the first layer of history, corresponding to the *ontic dimension* and narrating about *beings as such*. This kind of ontic history could represent an account that one of the *beings* collided with, diverged from, conflicted with, or reconciled with another, that *beings* were born and disappeared, then appeared anew, transformed, and grew dim once again. On a purely theoretic level, ontic history could represent a documentary account of *beings as such*. Modern historians (especially, the "Annales School") tried to reconstruct a model of history based on the painstaking study of everyday notes, household documents, and other practical texts, which recorded an average person's life routine in the previous centuries. It quickly became clear, however, that it is impossible to obtain an accurate picture of *beings* in the past. After all, the selection of examined documents, and, even more so, its multilevel interpretation (from the original author to the copyist and the historians themselves), reflects every possible thing, but not *beings* as they are by themselves.

In other words, when dealing with *history*, we always encounter *interpretation*, which is not a neutral description of *beings*. Rather, this description reflects the ontology and metaphysics of those who write, their audience, and those who will study this writing after a certain amount of time. Ontic history as an aggregate of atomic historical facts is a purely theoretical hypothesis unconfirmed by the empirical experience of researching historical documents, which directly or indirectly bear traces of metaphysics.

This is the second level—the ontological or metaphysical interpretation of *beings*—which are developing in time, from the standpoint of imagining *Being* as the *essence of beings*. This type of history is history as *Geschichte*, since it develops within a *two-level topography*: the *topography of the event* and its *meaning*, where the event's meaning not only refers us to the level oaf *beings*, but also that of the essence of *beings*. History as *Geschichte* narrates about *beings* in their connection with *essence*. Therefore, the content of this type of history would depend on the configuration that metaphysics acquires, determining the philosophical axiomatics of this or that era. Each serious change of axiomatics signifies a change of the historical paradigm and, practically, the emergence of a new version of history. This kind of history is ontological, which ultimately does not focus its attention on *beings*, but on the *metaphysical message* that is encoded in the dynamic development of *beings* and in the dialectic of multiple *beings*.

An image of *ontological history* was most fully presented in Hegel's philosophy of history.[6] He created the grand panorama focused not on the history of people, things, and events, but on

---

[6] G. W. F. Hegel, *Lectures on the Philosophy of World History*, tr. H.B. Nisbet (New York: Cambridge University Press, 1975).

concepts and ideas, and, more specifically, of the Absolute Idea, which develops its *"message"* through multifaceted dialectical stages of mankind's path throughout time.

Heidegger emphasizes the fact that after Hegel, this question was completely resolved: any history is not an account of *beings*, but, rather, the *essence of beings*, i.e., metaphysics' account about itself. In this way, Western European history is an account of Western European metaphysics, i.e., history is nothing other than the *history of philosophy*.

However, according to Heidegger, *ontological history* is the history of *Sein*, not *Seyn*. It is founded upon an incorrect understanding of the *relationship (Bezug)* between *beings* and *Being*. Consequently, this history is subject to reconsideration. This kind of reconsideration is the discovery of the *"fundamental-ontological"* dimension, which proposes not only to raise *beings* to *Being-Sein* (as is the case in ontological history), but also to meticulously investigate how the concept of *Sein* altered throughout the course (this time around) of the ontological-historical process. In other words, Heidegger is not concerned with the simple construction of history as the history of an Idea (*Sein*), but with examining the history of an Idea (*Sein*) as it correlates with *Being* as *Seyn*.

At this point, we reach the very core of *Seynsgeschichte*. *Seynsgeschichte* comprehends the variations of *Being* as *Sein* seen through the eyes of *Being* as *Seyn*.

Sein in the Ontological Section of History

At one point, Heidegger provides an extremely brief but expressive sketch featuring the basic stages of *Sein's* transformation in Western European metaphysics.[7] Essentially,

7 Martin Heidegger, *Geschichte des Seyns, op. cit.*, 26.

it represents the creation of a *"fundamental-ontological"* scale, the framework of which should be used to construct *Seynsgeschichte*.

Seyn		
φύσις (*fysis*)		
ιδὲα (*idea*)		
οὐσία (*ousia*)		
ενὲργεια (*energeia*)		
actus (actuality)		
perceptum (re-presentation) *objectum* (objectness)	}	Subjectivity a
Actuality (*Wirklichkeit*) (*energia—vis primitiva activa*, Leibniz) Will and reason (German Idealism)	}	Subjectivity b
Power (*Macht*, the Will to Power, Nietzsche)		
Machenschaft		
Seinsvergessenheit (the abandonment of *Being* as *Sein*, i.e., the rejection of ontology: pragmatism, utilitarianism, Liberalism, Marxism, technocracy—A. D.)		
The delay in the arrival (*Verweigerung*)		
Expropriation (*Ent-eignung*) Coming to fruition, enownment (*Er-eignung*)		decision (*Ent-scheidung*), "transition"? (*Übergang*)
The event (*Ereignis*)		
Outcome-conclusion-carrying out and settling (*Austrag*)		
Geschichte (either as *Geschichte* proper—ontological history—or as *Seyngeschichte*—this depends on the decision—A.D.).		

An explanation of this dry schema could occupy an entire volume. Later on, we can have a look at selected fragments that clarify its meaning. Heidegger's philosophy developed certain

78

aspects of this schema; others remained undeveloped intuitions or sketches. The basic trajectory of Heidegger's intuition may be reduced to the following.

Seynsgeschichte views history not as the history of ideas or a single idea, but as the history that tracks the transformation of the *relationship between thought and Being*: both when this relationship *(Bezug)* is described explicitly and when it ends up concealed or implicit. Furthermore, this examination does not begin with *Sein* (i.e., the source of ontology) but with *Seyn*, which is postulated by *"fundamental-ontology"* and, as a result, changes the entire philosophical topography.

Seynsgeschichte outlines the stages in terms of establishing other authorities in the place of *Seyn* (at the very peak— at the source): *nature-ideas-essence-energy-actuality-will and reason-the will to power-Machenschaft,* and others. At this point, we could stop reading the items off the list and assert that Western European history represents the degradation of thought about *Being* from the standpoint of *Seynsgeschichte*: from *nature* to the *will to power* to *mechanicity* *(Machenschaft)*. Fundamental changes occurred within this two-tiered ontological topography itself, serving as the framework of historic development. Their main trajectory was the gradual *oblivion of Being (Sein)*. In other words, that which created this topography (thought about *Being*) in the first place was gradually lost sight of, while being replaced by surrogates, increasingly more rough and removed from *Being*. Occasionally, Heidegger includes "categories," "concepts," "values," "world-views," etc. in this progression. But everything rests on the *"oblivion of Being,"* on *nihilism* and *"desertification."* At every stage of descent, the second— metaphysical level of this topography is gradually distorted, perverted, and appears more and more nihilistic and misshapen (from the point of view of *Seyn-Being*). We may encounter something similar in the ordinary understanding of history. However, instead of Heideggerean pessimism, there is every chance to find either a neutral announcement of these changes, or an optimistic assertion that man thus frees himself from the external restraints of metaphysics. Heidegger asserts that all of this is pure metaphysics, which created a false topography and now supports it, independent of the perpetual change in the nature of the ontological argument found at its base.

"*The oblivion of Being*" is the final point in *Seynsgeschichte*. From this moment on, the turn toward *fundamental-ontology* begins. *Seynsgeschichte* prepares itself for radically switching its mode—from *Geschichte*'s inauthentic development to the authentic onset of *Seynsgeschichte*.

The encounter with "delay" (*Verweigerung*) is the first phenomenon of *Seynsgeschichte* in the new standby mode waiting for the register's shift to *fundamental-ontology*. It would seem that the "midnight moment" has been reached, but, apparently, this is "not yet" the case. "*Always this 'not yet,'*" Heidegger marvels. "*Fundamental-ontology*" is hesitant.

Nevertheless, the delay comes after the "*decision*" (*Ent-scheidung*). This is the most important category of *Seynsgeschichte*. This "*decision*" is a *decision* concerning the transition (or lack thereof) to *fundamental-ontology* (therefore, in the schema, the word "transition" is written in quotations and ends with a question mark). The choice is between the *refusal* (of *Seyn-Being*) and its *coming to fruition*. The event (*Ereignis*) takes place if the latter is chosen: *Seyn* reveals its truth. Next comes the development of *beings* along the trajectory of *Seyn* rather than *Sein*. That is, *"fundamental-ontology"* is realized, asserting the primacy of *Seyn* in relation to *Seiende* and the manifestation of the kind of *beings* that will be conceived of not from their own selves or their *shared attribute (essence)*, but from the standpoint of *Being (Seyn) as Nothingness*. Heidegger calls this "carrying out and settling" (*Austrag*) or the "*Fourfold*" (*Geviert*).[8]

All together this results in history (*Geschichte*) taken as *Seynsgeschichte*.

Language and the Verb "to Be" in Seynsgeschichte

Having added the dimension of *Seynsgeschichte* to the analysis of Heidegger's topography, we can better understand the emergence of symmetry between the most vital words and their meaning pertaining to *Being*. Separating *Sein* and *Seyn*, Heidegger is forced to construct a double semantic structure associated with the formation of secondary words.

In terms of the ontic, we are dealing with *beings* (*Seiende*). "*Beings are (das Seiende ist)*"—this is an accurate ontic assertion. It is located at the basis of language and thought. Language allows *beings* to state the most important thing, which they cannot do in any other way: it provides the opportunity to express that *beings are*. The predicate "*beings*," employed or implied in speech, makes this speech (whatever it might be expressing) a unique and exceptional phenomenon. Men are *speaking beings, thinking beings*; and the uniqueness of this lies in the fact that we assign the status of *beings* to the subject of our speech. This ontic language predates metaphysics and relates to prehistory, to the era when philosophy had not yet begun, had not yet come into its own. The presence of *Seyn* is apparent in this kind of language, but *Seyn* is not comprehended; it surrounds *beings* spontaneously and naturally, regardless of human freedom or choice. This *Seyn*

---

8 The next part of this book deals with *Geviert* in detail.

does not yet join the *message*, fate, *Seynsgeschichte*, or *Geschichte* (history as an ontological phenomenon).

The ontic language is prehistory and pre-philosophy. In this kind of language, *beings are*, but the nature of what "are" means is not conceptualized. Here, all *beings* live alongside other *beings* and have not been separated from them yet.

Take, for instance, a path and its undergrowth. In the ontic prehistoric *Being*, they can freely spill over into one another. The path gets lost in the woods and disappears gradually and imperceptibly. Culture gets lost in nature. And in exactly the same way, thick undergrowth gradually thins out and opens up a free pathway. Furthermore, this does not happen when the hiker wishes it do be so, but independently, forming a pathway in a place and at a time when no one asked for it or awaited it. Thus, *beings* freely play in themselves; and the fact that they *are*, and that there is somebody speaking about them and about the fact that they *are*, in no way harms this ontic game.

Everything changes with the origins of metaphysics. Pondering about the *Being of beings* and arriving at the conclusion that *Being* is the *shared attribute* of *beings*, i.e., their essence (*Seiendheit, essentia*), man begins to create history as *Geschichte*. This leads to the emergence of a new language—one of concepts and categories. It introduces additional *beings* to *beings*—the essence of *beings*.

In terms of language, from this point forward *beings* are not conceived of and named *per se* but through their correspondence to something else, like the *essence of beings* or to *beings as a whole*. *Beings* as a whole become an intermediate authority; the essence of concrete *beings* emerges as the primary attribute *linked to Being* between *concrete beings* and *beings as a whole*

(*Being as Sein*). Thus, the path becomes a concrete expression of "pathness," while the undergrowth—that of "undergrowthness." At the same time, the path no longer has the right to be lost (what kind of a path is this, if it leads nowhere?), and the undergrowth must be thick (otherwise, it transforms into an open woodland, forest marge, or meadow). An abyss emerges between *beings*, which is covered over only through an appeal to their *essence*.

Thus, a distinctive language emerges comprising logical rules and rigid structures. Most important, it is built on reference—the correlation of *beings* and *essence*, appearing as an idea, concept, universality, and so on. *Beings* are bifurcated. Language transforms from functioning as an expression of *beings* to imposing particular representations onto them.

Tracing the establishment of metaphysics, Heidegger shows that on the way to clarifying the *Being of beings*, thought seizes *Being as a whole* and hypostasizes it as the essence of *beings* identical to the sought-after *Being*. But this *essence* is thought of as *new beings*, gradually becoming independent in relation to the initial moment, when it was confirmed to be *beings as a whole*.

According to Heidegger, this sequence contains subtle deception: *Seyn-Being is "beings* as a whole," and, consequently, the given development in thought is accurate. However, *Seyn-Being is not solely and exclusively "beings* as a whole," inasmuch as it is "the nihilation of *beings*," i.e., "Nothingness," "*non-beings*," more precisely, it is that which makes "*beings*" greater than "*non-beings*." It is the disregard for this nuance that guided the trajectory of the entire subsequent development of Western European metaphysics. Asserting *Being* as essence and operating with this essence as a result, Western European metaphysics doubles "*beings*" and thereby loses sight of *Seyn-Being* in its fundamental-ontological *essence* (*Wesen*). Constructed by this metaphysics, this essence gets transformed during the various stages of its development along the following transformation trajectory: "*Being as Sein, rather than Seyn,*" "*nature,*" "*the idea,*" "*οὐσία*" (*ousia, substance*) "*energy,*" "*reality,*" etc., right up to "*the will to power*" and "*global machinery.*"

In this process, the significance of the verb "*to be*" undergoes fundamental change. In metaphysics, which deeply affected the language and thought of Western European mankind, *beings* cease to be *by themselves: by themselves* they no longer *are*—they draw their *Being* from *essence*. They no longer are directly, but indirectly, by belonging to essence. Thus emerges the concept of *Being* (*Sein*) as *essence* (*Seiendheit*), which lends their principal marker to *beings*—the fact that they *are*. From now on, the verb "*are*" must be understood differently than before. Instead of thought, it is philosophy as well as theology and sciences based upon it that now determine whether *beings are* or *are not*. It is as if *beings* "sort of" are from this point forward. Maybe they *are*, but maybe they *are not*: it all depends on something radically different than *beings* themselves.

Western European philosophy does not immediately reach this radical conclusion. This becomes obvious after Kant and Hegel, in Schopenhauer, Kierkegaard, and Nietzsche, as well as the philosophy of the phenomenologists. Initially, *beings* were to the degree that they corresponded to an *idea* (Plato). At the end of Modernity, *beings* became *beings* because the "will to power," "reason," and "representation" required this (by using other terms, this was "useful," "valuable," "comfortable," etc.). Whatever the authority might have been asserting that *beings* are or *are not*, this was no longer direct thought, nor *beings* themselves expressing their ontically understood presence in *Being*.

Here Heidegger reconsiders anew the treatment of the word "*to be*," proposing to deal with it differently—according to the structure of *Seynsgeschichte*. *Beings* in the ontic (pre-historical and pre-philosophical) sense *are* only in the case when we ignore metaphysics and history. If the ontic and the ontological are superimposed, their meaning gets mixed up. We cannot view *beings* without accounting for Western European metaphysics and, consequently, getting distracted from *Geschichte*. For this reason, when we say that *beings are*, we most often mean the ontological sense, specifically—i.e., that they *are* by pertaining to *Being* as *beings as a whole* (*Sein*). But this "are" is no longer an ontic "are" in its unconditional pre-ontological, non-referential expression. This is the "are" in philosophy, rather than thought in its ontic simplicity and naïveté; this is no longer the "are" of language. For the purpose of differentiation, Heidegger recalls the existence of archaic (Homeric) forms of the Greek participle ὄν (*on*, *beings*), where the first sound ε was preserved: it sounded not like ὄν, ὄντα (*onta*), but like ἔον (*eon*), ἔοντα (*eonta*).[9] *ἔον* is *beings ontically*; they are in a way that does not require proof through any references; *ὄν* is *beings in the philosophical sense*—ontological and drawing their *Being* from something else.

In order to simplify the nuances containing the core of his philosophy in terms of the naming convention, when it comes to the ontic level, for certain contexts Heidegger proposes to apply the Latin verb "*existere*," "to exist" (which he tries not to translate into German)—instead of *Being*. *Beings exist*. This is undoubtedly so either from an ontic or from an ontological

---

9 Martin Heidegger, "Der Spruch des Anaximander," *Holzwege* (Frankfurt am Main: Vittorio Klostermann, 2003).

point of view. Yet whether they are—that is the question. And although in ontics *beings are,* and this is obvious (so say language and direct pre-philosophical thought), this "are" may be incorrectly understood in the space of metaphysics. Yet the *existence* of *beings* is beyond doubt. [10]

But at the same time, fearing the distortion of his thought due to an incorrect interpretation of "*are*," Heidegger is forced to take radical language-forming steps and to advance a new verb "*wesen.*" The latter is formed from the past passive participle of the verb "*sein*" (*to be*), i.e., from "*gewesen.*" The German language also contains the noun "*Wesen,*" formed from this same form and signifying the "*character of something*" (*sut'* [*суть*]) or an "*essence*" (*сущность* [*sushchnost'*]). Heidegger, however, strictly separates *essence* as *Seiendheit,* i.e., *Being,* grasped as the *shared attribute of beings* and constructed based on *beings,* from *Wesen.* The latter expresses the relationship to *Seyn* and *Being* in its *fundamental-ontological* sense. *Wesen* is an artificial verb[11], which Heidegger conjugates as *ich wese, du wesest, er / sie / es west, wir wesen, ihr weset, sie wesen.* It applies to what is an expression of *Seyn,* and truly *is Seyn-Being.*

It is here that the Russian verb "*существовать*" (*sushchestvovat'*) can come in handy. Fortunately, it is completely unendowed with any philosophical meaning and signifies the bare fact of *beings' Being*—without clear references to ontics, ontology, or fundamental-ontology. It seems to me that it would be entirely

---

[10] The verb "to exist" is formally translated into Russian as "*существовать.*" But this is entirely unacceptable for the transmission of Heidegger's thought. "*Существовать*" either means to "be a *being*" (ontic), or "to be through essence" (ontological). And in no way can we use this verb in places where Heidegger speaks of *existence* specifically in order to avoid all kinds of misunderstandings and ambiguities pertaining to the correlation between the ontic and the ontological, and, consequently, to the particular moment of *Seynsgeschichte* that we are considering.

[11] *Wesen* also means "to inhere in."

correct to reserve for it the *fundamental-ontological* significance, specifically in order to transmit the meaning of Heidegger's philosophy. *"Существовать"* can become the leitmotiv of a new *fundamental-ontological* language in Russian. There is a no-less interesting and simple opportunity in the Russian language to separate *"Seiendheit"* and *"Wesen,"* which in German signifies *"essence."* We could translate *Seiendheit* as *"сущность"* (with an additional ontological and metaphysical significance), whereas *Wesen*—as *"суть"* (*sut'*, nature, character, meaning) with particular emphasis on fundamental-ontology.

Thus, in Heidegger we encounter *beings* in three different positions relative to *Seynsgeschichte*:

- ontically (pre-philosophically and prehistorically), *beings exist* (*Das Seiende existiert*);

- ontologically (philosophically, metaphysically, as well as both ontically and fundamental-ontologically), *beings are* (*Das Seiende ist*);

- fundamental-ontologically, *beings come into their essence* (*Das Seiende west*).

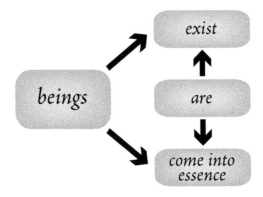

"*Is/are*" can always be understood in three ways: as "*comes into its essence,*" as "*exists,*" and strictly speaking as "*is/are*" (i.e., by *belonging to Being as the shared attribute of* all *beings*).[12]

The use of the verb *wesen* in Heidegger is the starting point of a new language—the kind of language that "fundamental-ontology" must speak. This language must express the *decision to make the leap* toward the final and principal chord in *Seynsgeschichte*. The very phenomenon of this *fundamental-ontological language* must be not only an instrument of *Seynsgeschichte* but its fundamental-ontological *essence* (*Wesen*).

---

[12] But in any case, we rid ourselves of the insufficiently thought-out and hasty Russian neologism "*бытийствовать*" (*bytiistvovat'*) in which many translations of Heidegger abound.

V. THE BEGINNING AND END OF WESTERN EUROPEAN PHILOSOPHY

Why Evening?

Having determined the general trajectory of *fundamental-ontology* and clearing up what *Seynsgeschichte* is, let us trace the basic stages of the history of Western European philosophy, as Heidegger saw it. Here, we once again turn to the subject of the "declining West," a civilization in which the sun is setting, and to *Abendländische Geschichte*, the history of the "evening," and the history of the "evening" countries.

In terms of this kind of history, Heidegger advances a fundamental thesis: from the point of view of *Seynsgeschichte*, the history of Western European philosophy is *a process of progressive oblivion of ontological inquiry* right up to pure nihilism. It is the process of gradually losing *Being*, the abandonment of *Being* and by *Being* (*Seinsverlassenheit*). In other words, the history of Western European philosophy, with all its brilliance, splendid breakthroughs, revelations, and deviations, is nothing more than *the process of parting from Being*. Consequently, this is the *history of sunset*, an extended catastrophe, wanderings, and errors. It is not by accident that Heidegger calls one of his books *Holzwege*.[1] In French, this title translates as *Les chemins qui ne mènent nulle part*—literally, "Roads that lead nowhere"; in German, the expression "*Holzwege*," literally, "arboreal paths," can also be understood as "wooded paths," and as "untrodden

---

1   Martin Heidegger, *Holzwege* (Frankfurt am Main: Vittorio Klostermann, 2003).

paths, overgrown with trees". This kind of wandering leads from clarity to darkness, which is why we are dealing with the evening. This is the process of parting with *Being*, its loss, and gradual impoverishment. Ceasing to think about *Being*, philosophy gradually ceases *to be*.

As early as the dawn of philosophy, *Being* as *Seyn* (*fundamental-ontology*) hides behind *beings-as-a-whole* (the ontological *Seiende-im-Ganzen*). Merging with it, it becomes *Being* as *Sein* and, ultimately, yet another variety of *beings*.

Then, *Being* (*Sein*), as *beings-as-a-whole*, is replaced by the notion (*Vorstellung*) of it. Next, this *notion* acquires a more and more disconnected, abstract, mechanical, and conditional character, in which all connections with *beings* collapse until, at last, the era of *nihilism* arrives. Friedrich Nietzsche recognized and described the latter—that very moment, when *Being* finally disappears beyond the horizon, revealing the ever-present *Nothingness*.

We can designate (*fundamental-historically*) the entire segment of Western European philosophy as mankind's final six hours—the time before midnight. And it is not surprising that in this sector of a cosmic day, it is the *Western* civilization that moves to the forefront, establishes laws and norms, conquers all others and forces them to unequivocally accept its forms, thoughts, and values as something universal. The West comes into its own because the night's fate is entrusted to it, because it acts in the name of the night and uses its power. *Being*'s sun is setting. And so, civilization finally goes to sleep, and the last candles go out, still illuminating people's homes with a farewell, artificial, and nostalgic light.

92

In this case, asking "Why Europe? Why the West? Why does Western European civilization present itself as something inevitable and universal?" would be equivalent to asking "Why evening?".

The Great Beginning and the Philosopher's "Daimon"

Heidegger considers pre-Socratic thought to be the start of Western European philosophy and calls it the *great Beginning*, or sometimes, the *first Beginning*.

At this stage, philosophers appear as an independent type of person occupied only and exclusively with thought. Most often, these are thoughts about the beginning, *Being*, and thought itself.

Thought is an attribute of man. It is, of course, inaccurate to assume that people did not think before the onset of philosophy and outside the area of its dissemination. They certainly *thought*, but did not *philosophize*. What is the difference?

This difference is between the *ontic* and the *ontological*. *Ontics* simply corresponds to thought, i.e., the attribute that defines man *per se*. Man speaks and thinks, and thereby he stands at a distance in relation to his surroundings. This distance emerges with man simultaneously and is expressed in the ability for thought. In turn, thought is based on differentiation of things in the world. Differentiation is the main attribute of thought, because a man is such only to the extent that he is able to differentiate himself from the rest of the world. This is the principal distinction that becomes the key feature of man. Distinguishing himself from the rest of the world, man begins to differentiate things in the world. And the more acutely he becomes aware of his distance from his surroundings, the more precise are the boundaries he establishes. Thought can occur in the sphere of myth, archaic cults, rites, and legends. It can be rudimentary or well advanced. However, regardless of how great the distance between man and the world is and regardless of his acute capacity to differentiate things in the world and their attributes, this is not yet philosophy. This kind of *ontic* thought is indicative of the *pre-beginning*. Philosophy begins at a different point.

Man takes a fundamental *leap* into a certain domain, which differs radically from the sphere that houses the one who simply thinks and the world about which he thinks. This is the moment when philosophy begins. A philosopher, by the virtue of a certain miraculous and unique ability, suddenly finds himself in the position of the one *who does not simply differentiate himself and the world, but who recognizes within himself the one who is capable of such differentiation and the one who recognizes the one who recognizes.* A philosopher is a thinking man, who is capable of thinking *how, of what, and why* he thinks.

According to Heidegger, this *leap* takes place through an attempt to understand *beings* and the emergence of *inquiry about the Being of beings.* At a certain point, man is no longer satisfied with differentiation within the framework of the ontic system of coordinates, and he discovers a new dimension as a result of a unique feat. This is the dimension of *Being.* Asking himself, "What comes prior to *beings,* what is the *Being* of *beings,* why and whither *beings?*" man realizes the greatest form of his freedom, which reveals itself as his nature at that very moment. The freedom of distance within *beings* turns out to be a half-freedom, and man lunges. It is at this specific point that philosophy begins.

Philosophy, as Plato defined it[2] (and Aristotle later reaffirmed it[3]), is "a *sense of wonder and amazement*" (θαυμάζειν [*thaumazein*] in Greek).[4] Both Russian words used to translate the Greek "θαυμάζειν" or the German "*Erstaunen*" are highly expressive: "*удивляться*" (*udivliatsia*) is formed from "*диво*" (*divo*)—marvel, i.e., "*чудо*" (*chudo*)—miracle, something "sacred," going beyond ordinary perception; "*из-ум-ление*" (*iz-um-lenie*) is formed through an analogy with the Greek word ἔκστασις (*ecstas*), literally, "going out of oneself"; "going out of the mind". Wonder—the basis of philosophy—is the realization of gestures, acts, and movements, which are in no way contemplated in ordinary human thought. The capacity to be amazed (to go beyond the bounds of the mind), to wonder, to discover a "marvel" or a "miracle" in the world stands very close to the *leap* that thought performs when it begins to think about the *Being* of *beings*. This very *leap* along with posing the question, which lies at the basis of philosophy, sends us toward the presence of something that surpasses the limits of the human. Amazement, in the original sense of the word "θαυμάζειν" triggers something divine and superhuman, which does not fit into the space of ordinary human thought, and which surpasses the limits of the ontic.

Therefore, the first pre-Socratic philosophers—Anaximander, Heraclitus, and Parmenides—perceived their own *leap from ontics to ontology as an encounter with the divine and as the discovery of the divine dimension.*

---

2 "Truly, a philosopher is he whose pathos (whose passion) is wonder (amazement—θαυμάζειν); a philosopher has no other source." (See also Plato, *Theaetetus* [London: Penguin, 1987], fragment 155 d.)

3 "It was through the feeling of wonder that men now and at first began to philosophize." (See also Aristotle, *Metaphysics* [New York: Cosimo, 2008], fragment 982b12.)

4 Martin Heidegger, *Was ist das—die Philosophie?* (Pfullingen: Gunther Neske Verlag, 1956).

Heraclitus's statement about the *logos*—"If you do not listen to me, but to the *logos*, it would be wise, abiding by it, to say: everything is one"[5]—contrasts Heraclitus himself as a man with the *logos* as the source of the divine. It is at the very moment of the leap toward the divine *logos* that, for the first time, man can think about the way in which he thinks and, consequently, philosophize. Philosophy is possible as a result of discovering the divine dimension and establishing this dimension as a new plane of consciousness. It is on the basis of the latter that man and the world reveal themselves from now on. Heidegger shows that the *logos* of Heraclitus has all the qualities of a divine source, just like the Moira of Parmenides (which holds the sphere of *Being* in shackles) and the "*chreon*" of Anaximander. [6]

This *leap*, which opens up the divine, or, from a different perspective, constitutes it, is that very *great Beginning*. The philosopher, having torn himself away from simple thought (the ontic) and going beyond the limits of the mind in ecstasy, actualizes the fullness of human freedom and establishes divine horizons for the first time ever. The distinction between this philosophical act and a religious experience lies in the fact that it is in philosophy, specifically, that consciousness turns out to be at a distance in relation to itself.

The sacred in myth and religion originate in *beings*, which strikes the imagination and forces man to tremble before its implacable power. It comes from the outside. The sacred in philosophy reveals itself from within, not as the great power of *beings*, but as a fallout thereof—a sudden acquisition of a unique inner space, which not only illuminates, with lightning speed, *beings-as-a-whole* predating man, but also man himself

---

5   Hermann Diels, *Die Fragmente der Vorsokratiker. Griechisch und Deutsch* (Berlin: Weidmannsche Buchhandlung, 1903).

6   Martin Heidegger, "Der Spruch des Anaximander," in Heidegger, *Holzwege, op. cit.*

as *a part of beings* and as *the differentiating part of beings*. The *inner sacred* on the part of the philosopher lies on the opposite part of man, just as he himself is on the opposite side of *beings*, thereby creating a truly new dimension in the topography of consciousness. From this moment on, a point appears in this topography, located on another plane as compared to the entire plane of the ontic, including the thought center and the thought periphery of the ontic.

At the time of the *great Beginning* of Western European philosophy, man encounters the sphere of divine thought. Based on the latter, he can think about *the way in which* he himself thinks from this moment on. In the Greek world during the era of the great Beginning, the belief in "*daimons*," "lesser gods" (the "*numen*" of the Latins), was quite common. Yet only with the rise of philosophy does *daimon* become not an object of worship—a powerful and invisible kind of *beings*, endowed with special energy—but as a point radiating thoughts about the thinker. Such is the meaning of Heraclitus's statement, "ἦθος ἀνθρώπῳ δαίμων" (*ethos anthropo daimon*), which can be translated as "a demon (a god of a lightning-fast moment) is order for man." Based on other fragments of Heraclitus's writing, we can infer that this δαίμων is identical to his *logos*, "The self-multiplying *logos* is inherent to the soul." [7]

Socratic δαίμων belongs to the same category: in his stories it acts as a special authority, at times illuminating the actions and thoughts of Socrates-as-a-man with a special light.

Philosophers' *daimon* is not simply a subdued god of *beings* placed on the inside. It is an element of a radically new model of consciousness, which, from now on, has a point—a fulcrum—

---

[7] Hermann Diels, *Die Fragmente der Vorsokratiker. Griechisch und Deutsch* (Berlin: Weidmannsche Buchhandlung, 1903).

from which man can look at *beings* surrounding him and at himself with an equal degree of abstraction.

The Beginning comprises the establishment of this point— the arrival of this key figure at center stage. In the Beginning, the question concerning the *Being* of *beings* crystallizes; i.e., ontology arises. This is possible only because an authority appears (philosophers' "*daimon*"), glancing from which, it is possible to embrace *beings-as-a-whole* as something complete and unified. "Everything is one," asserts the "*daimon-logos*" of Heraclitus.

ΦΥΣΙΣ Η ΛΟΓΟΣ

Heidegger provides a detailed description of the establishment of the *first Beginning* through pre-Socratic introduction of two fundamental terms: φύσις ("*physis*," "nature") and λόγος ("*logos*," "thought," "the word"). The word "φύσις" became a philosophical concept long ago, applicable to nature as something strictly distinct from man (the subject, culture, society, consciousness, etc.). In the modern period, it lost its original meaning completely, having transformed into a ready-made concept, the semantics of which nobody considers. Etymologically, this word traces back to a pre-Indo-European stem: "*bhū*," "*Being*." Based on its meaning, "φύσις" signifies "sprouts."

Heidegger sometimes replaces the Greek word "φύσις" with the German "*Aufgehen*," in order to emphasize its pre-philosophical semantics. The Greek "φυσειν" (*physein*) signified "to rise up," "to vegetate," the way that sprouts come up, bearing fruit, but also—"to beget," not in the sense of "separating from oneself," but rather "to knock out from underneath," "to lead to presence." This is how the earth acts—a primary element, producing sprouts, pushing different entities out from within itself. Earth, water, air, and fire are the primary elements in the teachings of various pre-Socratics, which realize the action of φυσεῖν, throwing out, pushing out, and emptying *beings* from within themselves.

The very thought concerning φύσις as something complete, as *beings* in their generality, is, according to Heidegger, a trace of the ontological leap: "φύσις" is the name given "by the philosophical *daimon*" (not by man!) to *beings-as-a-whole*. He thinks that *beings* ascend like grains from the soil. And *the essence of beings* comprises the very act of ascension—this formation.

According to Heidegger, the entire subsequent development of philosophy arises from the fact that it is φύσις that became the principal word of the *first Beginning*. It is here that its fate lies— its *Geschichte*. By leaping beyond its limits, human freedom was able to justify a point from which all *beings* were embraced by a general image. But it was also this point that dictated the kind of name for the *Being* of *beings* that was fatal. At this decisive moment, European history made the choice in favor of interpreting *Being* as φύσις. And this was irreversible. The fact that *beings* are is obvious. But the search for the *Being* of *beings*—the "are" of this very "are"—was the volitional decision on the part of a thinking man who leapt higher than himself. *Beings are*, but by defining *beings* as φύσις, we unnoticeably come to the conclusion that *Being* also is. Thus, *Being* itself becomes an example of *beings*, even if it is the very first one, the universal, and the highest of *beings*; nevertheless, it still belongs specifically to the sphere of *beings*.

For the first time, φύσις does not become a word but a concept, a unique phenomenon which already belongs to the sphere of ontology; i.e., to the sphere of *logos* and not the sphere of simple ontic existence or pre-Socratic differentiating thought. It is around this concept that ontology begins to form as *Physics*. [8]

The verb "*φυσειν*" ("to sprout," "to give shoots," "to foster"), which generated the first philosophical concept "*φύσις*," corresponds to another verb, no less important for the history of the *first Beginning*, "*λέγειν*" (*legein*)—the source of "*λόγος*"—"word," "thought," and "reading." Originally, "*λόγος*" signified nothing more than "harvest" and "the gathering of fruit." *Λέγειν* and *φυσειν* were closely interrelated. *Being (Sein) as the essence of beings produces "shoots"* (*φύσις*) *and reaps* (*λέγειν*) them, laying them out before the gaze of the *philosophical daimon*, which passes judgement on the quality and quantity of harvest. *λόγος* and *φύσις* are two sides of the new philosophical ontological topography, in which safe distance in regards to *beings* had been conquered.

Within that topography, *Being (Sein, Seiende-im-Ganzen* as *beings-as-a-whole, Seiendheit* as the essence of *beings*, as the pair *λόγος / φύσις*) is conceived as something that precedes *beings* and is different from them. Thus, it manifests both as the dynamics of ascension and as the regularizing static of the harvest (*Being-Sein* vivifies and kills with the same gesture). Through the *φυσειν / λέγειν* pair (two forms of essenting *beings*), a new kind of *beings* advances, *Being-Sein* as *beings*, free from *beings* in terms of the specifics of their dynamic circular rotation. Parmenides's philosophy already clearly describes *Being-Sein*, in which the question of *εἶναι* arises, i.e., that of *Being in its disembodied form*, torn from *concrete beings*. *But this Being-Sein is conceived precisely as an exemplar of beings of the highest order.* Herein lies the problem in a nutshell, according to Heidegger.

After making the *leap* toward the divine *logos-daimon* and toward the clarification of the *Being* of *beings* in amazement and wonder,

---

[8] Aristotle, *Physics* (Cambridge: Harvard University Press, 1970).

i.e., leaving the sphere of the ordinary and the boundaries of (pre-philosophical) thought, the creators of the *first Beginning* slightly *under-jumped* (or over-jumped). With safe distance separating them from the the soil of *beings*, they were not able to give into flight and built a new level, i.e., that same soil, only artificial, cultural-social, in no way resembling nature, but repeating its structure unbeknownst to them. A walk along an elevated platform replaced the flight in heavenly abyss. And after some time, at the next stage of the first *Beginning*—with Plato and Aristotle—the instantaneous divine *"daimonic" logos* transformed into "Logic," and the infinitely powerful, all-generating element *physis* turned into a carefully worked-out *Physics*.

Pre-Socratic gnoseology, established by the new authority of the *daimon*, still hesitates to finally recognize *Being-Sein* as the highest instance of *beings*. As one of the founders of philosophical topography, Heraclitus's entire order of thought resists betraying flight and replacing it with a platform. By introducing λόγος and φύσις, Heraclitus clearly avoids describing *Being-Sein* as a hierarchical, structured gnoseological system. This is the source of his paradoxes and his serious attacks against Pythagoras. Heraclitus, more than any other philosopher of the *first Beginning*, bears the possibility that this Beginning, having begun, will become different. He does not move too far ahead or lose it from sight and, more important, resists having it replaced with another kind of *beings*. Establishing his view on *beings* from somewhere else (*Being-Sein*), he treats this "somewhere else" exceedingly cautiously and gently. He reveres the *logos* and allows the gods to fly.

ΑΛΗΘΕΙΑ *in the First Beginning*

Among pre-Socratics, truth is conceptualized as ἀλήθεια (*aletheia*), literally, "*the unconcealed.*" In order to emphasize the significance of pre-Socratic Greek understanding of truth,

Heidegger sometimes uses the German word "*Unverborgenheit*" —"*unconcealment*."[9] During the first Beginning, there are two meanings in ἀλήθεια: in the first case, we are speaking about the *unconcealment of Being* (*Sein*), showing through "*shoots*" and "*harvest*." And had this only remained so, then the self-organizing ontology would have already been able to become *fundamental-ontology* in the *first Beginning*. Furthermore, λόγος and φύσις would not have overshadowed *Being* (gently replacing it with themselves), but would have been revealing its truth; whereas *Sein* itself would have gravitated toward *Seyn*. True, wonder (amazement) itself, too, as the principal mood in philosophy, should have gently transitioned into a more abrupt and traumatic, but also completely sacred and ecstatic, quality—*the sacred terror* (*Ensetzen*).[10]

But the fate of Western European philosophy as the philosophy of the evening was different: gently and unnoticeably, "*unconcealment*" (ἀλήθεια) slid down to the unconcealment of "*shoots*" (φύσις) and "*harvest*" (λόγος) as a new kind of *beings*— although at this moment, this is still *beings-as-a-whole* (*das Seiende-im-Ganzen*)—or even *beings* in their dynamic vivifying origins (*das Sein im Seiende*).

It is in shifting the notion of "truth" as "unconcealment" that Heidegger recognizes basic Greek philosophical thought:

---

9   Old Slavonic and Church Slavonic contained the word "*проснота*," which meant "verity," "clarity," and which was closest in meaning to the Greek ἀλήθεια, ἀληθής.

10   "*Im ersten Anfang, da die φύσις in die ἀλήθεια und als diese aufleuchtete, war das Er-staunen die Grundstimmung. Der andere Anfang, der des seynsgeschichtlichen Denkens, wird angestimmt und vor-bestimmt durch das Entzetzen.*" (Martin Heidegger, *Beiträge zur Philosophie (vom Ereignis)* [Frankfurt am Main: Vittorio Klostermann, 1989], 483–484.) The literal translation is as follows, "In the first Beginning, when nature shone in truth and as the truth, wonder was the principal stimulus. Another Beginning, the Beginning of *seynsgeschichtliche* thought, will be designed and prepared by terror."

Being-Sein is given as the *unconcealed*. He views thoughts about the truth of *Being* as the *unconcealment* of *Being*—given in the act of *sprouting* (*"φύσις"*)—as the gnoseological code of the *first Beginning*.

Even Parmenides—who equates thought and *Being* (*νοεῖν* and *εἶναι*), the unity of *Being*, and the sphere of *Being*—believes truth to be unconcealment, although here, in terms of *Being-Sein*. Heidegger actively objects to contrasting Heraclitus's dialectic with the static ontology of Parmenides.[11] We view Parmenides through the eyes of Platonism and the metaphysics of Modernity. In reality, we must read him in the spirit of the philosophical context to which he belonged.

Parmenides's thesis, *"Being is, non-Being is not"*—despite its ontological nature and the impression of trying to absolutize *Being* as the "second kind of *beings*"—is not devoid of gravitating toward the vision of *Sein-Being through beings and only through beings* that was common for the pre-Socratics. However, Parmenides stipulates two paths of learning: the true and the false. The first path recognizes the unified *Sein-Being* more deeply than all natural forms, things, and phenomena—this is ontology. The second is the path of opinion, "impression," *δόξα* (*doxa*), which only perceives *beings* in terms of their appearance, trusting phenomena's superficial side and failing to see their complexity—this is ontics.

Pre-Socratic *first Beginning* considers *Being* through the act of *self-exposure, placement, establishment, super-formation*, moving toward *visibility* and certainty of *beings*. Here, everything still breaths *Sein-Being*, i.e., that which is disclosed in *beings*:

---

[11] Martin Heidegger, *Parmenides* (Frankfurt am Main: Vittorio Klostermann, 1982).

its freshness, depth, and elusive grandiose majesty permeate everything. But this loving and passionate treatment of *beings* and their truth (ἀλήθεια) already contains the source of the subsequent catastrophe.

Yet at the same time, the ἀλήθεια of this cycle *can* still *be* interpreted as a prelude to *fundamental-ontology*. Had it not been for the entire subsequent history of Western European philosophy, Thales, Heraclitus, Anaximander, and even Parmenides could have been viewed, in their *"dash toward,"* as those who initiated the kind of ontology that was capable of being revealed as fundamental-ontology at a certain point. Herein lies the colossal significance of the *first-Beginning* thinkers for Heidegger himself and for his *fundamental-ontological* project. In preparing the space for the discovery (truth, ἀλήθεια) of *Sein-Being*, we can guess the most subtle movement of thought, which could have led to being illuminated with the truth of *Seyn-Being*.

The Catastrophe of Platonism
(Idea and Representation)

Heidegger treats those that come after the pre-Socratics, i.e., Socrates, Plato, and Aristotle, with even greater caution. He calls this second period of Greek philosophy *"the beginning of the end within the framework of the first Beginning."*[12] The Beginning persists, the evening glow continues to redden, traditional Greece lives on, but the end is in the air. The end is near.

This is a good time to bring up the analogy of the Biblical story about the serpent's appearance in the Garden of Eden. It would seem that Adam, Eve, and the earthly paradise itself exist in bliss and abundance. Yet even in this new beautiful world, the forces

---

[12] Heidegger, *Geschichte des Seyns* and *Beiträge zur Philosophie*, op. cit.

of impending doom already make themselves known. And even before that point, at the dawn of Creation itself, when universal order is only being established and all creatures are close to God, the first of Angels—entities of light and servant spirits—rebels and is cast into the abyss with his supporters. It is from this abyss that he later trespasses into the earthly paradise. And in the End Times, his power will extend over the world and the cosmos. But the devil, evil, and the harbinger of the end already make an appearance *on the first* pages of the World's sacred history. In the sunlight, joyful paradise, his flexible body twists around the forbidden Tree of Knowledge of good and evil and tempts Eve to taste its fruit.

Likewise, the end is drawing near within the first Beginning—at a time of the greatest tension of spiritual forces, original philosophizing as if in "paradise" and the great pre-Socratic *leap*—when philosophy, becoming ontology, still hesitates in indecision over the way in which it should interpret the *Being* of *beings*. This "first end" is an end *within the first Beginning*.

Heidegger never regarded this end disdainfully, lightly, arrogantly, or contemptuously. He valued and admired it, because it was, indeed, something great. Even error and delusion sometimes occur on the grand scale worthy of veneration. And for Heidegger, true *Being* (*Seyn*) speaks through the catastrophe of Socratic and Platonic thought. However, this takes place in an extremely indirect way, through the abandonment of *itself* (*Seinsverlassheit*) and through its concealment.

One principal name determines *the end* within the *first Beginning*: Plato. According to Heidegger, Plato, as well as Socrates before him, and Aristotle after him, is the actual name and historical legalization of the greatest catastrophe.

Here, the *theory about ideas* plays a fundamental role. Heidegger takes apart the main etymological-philosophical aspects of Plato's thought trajectory, which led him to the doctrine of ideas. Plato's illumination by ideas and the introduction of ideas within the framework of his philosophy simultaneously represent both *greatness* and a *fundamental* substitution for Heidegger.

Greatness lies in the fact that Plato's thought, like that of all Greek philosophy in the era of the Beginning, is motivated by the question of the *Being* of *beings*. In other words, we are dealing with that unique and unexpected leap that Greek thought carries out *from the truth of beings* toward the *truth of Being*. And it is impossible not to see this trajectory of thought in Plato—in all its triumph, risk, and tension, in all its fatality and destiny—in the very mood of his philosophy.

The substitution comprises the following. Before Plato, the philosophical thought of the Greeks still wavered between considering φύσις / λόγος ("*physis / logos*") the true name of *Being*, thereby treating *Being* as a kind of *beings*, and moving further, higher, and deeper in order to "seize" *Being* as a unique *event* (*Ereignis*), which does not contain anything in itself that belongs to *beings*; i.e., as *Seyn* (*fundamental-ontology*). We can still interpret pre-Socratic philosophy in two ways. In this question, Plato dots all the "i"s, interpreting the preceding philosophical tradition as ontological and taking one more very important step in the *ontological* direction (at this point, this is unequivocally the non-fundamental-ontological).

Plato's doctrine replaces the wavering of pre-Socratic ontology (the manifestation of *Being—Sein? Seyn?*—through *beings*) by conceiving *Being* as an *idea*. With Plato, *Being* becomes that which is placed *before* man, initiating such phenomena as "*pre-*

sentation," *Vor-stellung*. Man stands before *ideas*, while ideas stand before things of the world.

The etymology of the word ἰδέα (*idea*) is connected to visualization and originates in the power of *vision* (based on the verb ὁρῆν [*horēn*]).[13] Plato's dialogue *The Republic*, in which he offers an expanded theory about ideas for the first time—at all levels of the "cave" account—discusses "vision" specifically, at first, that of shadows, then of objects themselves, and finally, of ideas.[14] While introducing the concept of ideas into the very core of philosophical thought, Plato reduces the basic operations of cognition to clear vision and recognition of ideas, which are the heavenly models of things and phenomena. But any contact with ideas presupposes being *across from* them— they can only be "seen" in this manner.

The latter initiates an era of a very specific *direction* in the development of reason—an era of a very specific rationality, which becomes the *fate of Western European philosophy* with Plato and Aristotle. The latter completely predetermines all its stages, including Modernity, the Middle Ages, and even Late Antiquity.

For Heidegger, the pre-Socratics were located in the world, *inside* of it. They were *beings* among *beings*, thinking *beings* and *thinking of beings* among *beings*. Such were the ancient Greeks as a whole. In addition, philosophers, remaining in *beings* and thinking about *beings*, took the chance of the *divine dash* (the

---

[13] The same Indo-European stem was preserved in the Russian verb "to see" (*видеть*), as in the Greek. That is, "ideas" (*идеи*) can be thought of as "appearances" (*виды*) or "visions" (*видения*), in references to the appearance of original blueprints or images. It is rather significant that the word "to know" (*ведать*) is formed from the same Indo-European stem, which was the source of other words, such as "knowledge" (*ведение*), "information" (*сведение*), "news" (*весть*), "renown" (*известность*), "message" (*известие*), etc. In German, the word "*Wissen*," "knowledge," goes back to the same root.

[14] Plato, *The Republic*, tr. Desmond Lee (New York: Penguin, 2007).

δαίμον of philosophers) toward *Being* (*Sein? Seyn?*), without destroying the connection with mankind or "naturality" completely. And philosophizing in wonder and amazement, in a state of wonderful ecstasy at the moment of the"*daimon*," they allowed *logos* to think *through them*, giving *Being* (*Sein? Seyn?*) the opportunity to occur and *show itself by coming to fruition through them*.

And so, with the arrival of Plato and his theory of ideas, man stands before *beings*: he is no longer *in the world*, he is *before the world*—*vor-gestellt* and *pre-sented* to the world—he *stands before it*. He is no longer capable of communicating with *beings* and things of the world directly. He cannot participate in the world's "unconcealment" (i.e., in its pre-Socratic "verity"). From now on, he is doomed to constantly postulate *the idea*—an additional authority of a visualized model—between everything, before everything, and over everything.

We transition to *Sein als Idea* (*Being* as idea) from the dynamics of *concealment* and the continuous burst of *Being* in *beings*) and, consequently, to an additional authority: the idea, which replaces *Being* with itself. Plato's most terrible accomplishment comprised the fact that he equated *the idea* with Sein. The *idea* was put in the place of *Sein*.

With his "decision," Plato made two ontological gestures of critical importance for Western European philosophy: he settled (implicitly) the uncertainty in the question on the status of φύσις in favour of *beings*; i.e., he unequivocally concluded that φύσις as the *Being* of *beings* is essence (*Seiendheit*, οὐσία [*ousia*]), and then he equated *essence* with the *idea* (Plato unequivocally speaks of the *idea as essence*, οὐσία). As a result of this two-fold move, the passageway to *Seyn-Being* was irreversibly closed.

And although Plato himself and the philosophers who joined him (Aristotle, in particular) constantly raise the question about the *essence of beings,* i.e., they do not lose sight of *Being*—from now on, the discussion is only about *Sein-Being* as a "species," "image," "representation" of *Seyn-Being.* He passes the ontological visual copy off as the fundamental-ontological original.

From this point forward, everything changes in comparison to pre-Socratic philosophy. From now on, truth appears not as the *unconcealment* of φύσις (and, perhaps, as the unconcealement of the hidden *Seyn-Being*—through φύσις and through λόγος), but rather as a correspondence (reference). Moreover, from this point on, that to which *beings* correspond is the *idea,* i.e., another kind of *beings,* which *is* as *Sein* and which the mind contemplates. At this moment, the discovered ontological topography (with the possibility *to be* fundamental-ontological) of philosophy's *first leap* finally closes up in the upper limits, where the *idea* is located, including the first idea, *that of the good* (τό ἀγαθόν [*to agathon*]).

At this very moment, in which thoughts about the *Being of beings* still shine, the process of *Being's* gradually increasing abandonment (*Seinsverlassenheit*) commences along with the arrival of European nihilism. The passageway to *Seyn-Being* has collapsed irreversibly. In its place stands *Sein-Being* as *essence, Idea,* and, consequently, as *beings* themselves. From this point forward and until philosophy's ultimate ending in the 20th century, the truth is exclusively considered through reference, i.e., as the correspondence of one type of *beings* to another (at first, philosophy suggests that it corresponds to the *highest of beings,* and then merely to *another* kind of *beings*).

Subsequent post-Socratic philosophers put various ontological constructs in place of the idea as *Sein*. Thus, Plato's student Aristotle selects ενέργεια (energy [*energeia*]). Later, other philosophers will prefer different contenders for the replacement in the "office" of the highest kind of *beings*. But there will be no principal change overall. After Plato, the ontological topography is established once and for all and remains in effect from the *end within the framework of the first Beginning* to the very last and final *End*.

Heidegger and Christianity (Platonism for the Masses)

Here it is worthwhile to recall Heidegger's view of Christianity. He often repeated Nietzsche's words that "Christianity is Platonism for the masses." What did he mean? Why does Heidegger have such a condescending attitude toward Christian culture, with its intellectual elements and its complex constructions of thought?

It is rooted in Heidegger's *linguistic-philosophical* understanding of theology.[15] The Semitic origin of the *Bible* puts it outside the limits of the strictly defined Indo-European context. For Heidegger, this is an alien kind of thinking, which does not interest or impress him at all. In order to think Biblically, one must be a Semite. Of course, Christian philosophy was, starting as early as the Apostolic age, a fundamental revision of Semitic, Jewish religiosity and theology, adapted for the Greek, Indo-European way of thinking. However, Heidegger prefers not to proceed along the path of recognizing all the non-Semitic influences on Christianity, but, on the contrary, he removes the problem as such by attributing it to pure Semitic influence. This might seem like a trivialization. However, our task is not

[15] We must also take into account that when Heidegger used the term "theology," he referred to Western-Christian (Catholic-Protestant) branch of theology exclusively; his love of Greece did not encompass Orthodox Christianity.

110

to criticize Heidegger, but to understand him. In the structure of his philosophy, Semitic thought is simply left out.

Illustrating the gnoseological "naiveté" of Biblical philosophy, Heidegger literally reproduces the phrase spoken by God to Moses on Mount Sinai: "I am that I am," "I am *beings*." Let us say that this statement refers to the *highest kind of beings*, but *beings* nonetheless, Heidegger argues. By doing so, Heidegger wants to prove that Christian theology remains within the framework of *beings*, i.e., in the space of ontology, and dogmatically closes off the possibility of a breakthrough to fundamental-ontology. [16]

Heidegger views the case of theology approximately as follows. God as a kind of *beings* is not of interest for a true philosopher, adds nothing, but rather takes away from the ontological set of problems. The latter is true because the notion of God only "mystifies" the same Platonic topography and referential theory of truth under the guise of resolving it by referring to the highest and original entity. Scholasticism and theology as a whole only confuse the problem of the relationship between *Being* and *beings*. In place of this relationship, Christianity proposes to simply arrange *beings* along the hierarchy of their merit in terms of Creation; i.e., to build a ladder of *ens creatum*, deliberately responding to the question not yet raised about the *Being* of *beings* with an appeal to creationism (divine creation of entities).

Heidegger is convinced that Christian philosophy is completely enslaved by the Platonic doctrine of ideas and Aristotelian

---

[16] I realize that this might sound somewhat facile for those who understand the entire significance of Tradition (for instance, according to René Guénon's interpretation). At this point, every traditionalist (including beginners) is capable of an objection. However, let us deliberately omit such disputes. Prior to comparing great intellectual constructions, we must first understand each one exactly as it is. Let us not rush in exclaiming, "Stop, I disagree with this point!"

logic, which only serve the need to justify a Semitic religion—without addressing their Greek roots—and which participate in the philosophical process indirectly and indistinctly. Whence the Nietzschean phrase: "Christianity is Platonism for the masses." For Heidegger, this is a reason to circumvent this sphere of philosophy and to treat it with condescension. The reason is two-fold: because of the aforementioned "for the masses" and the Platonic character.

Let us recall what is said about the *"philosophical daimon."* In comparison with pre-philosophical (Homeric-Hesiodic) Greeks, who lived and thought in terms of *beings* and *myth*, philosophers discovered the domain of a different kind of miracle. We called this domain the *philosophical daimon*; i.e., the space where the *Being of beings* is questioned or the point of observing man (as the thinkable is observed by the thinker) from within. This is the sphere of *logos*, where it illumines all *beings as one* (ἕν), as φύσις. Ὄν (*beings*) and ἕν (the one) converge on one another and almost become identical to one another, according to Parmenides and Aristotle.

In the pre-Socratic period, wavering between *Sein* and *Seyn*, *Being* occupies this dimension—the place of the *philosophical daimon* ("god," *numen*). After Plato, philosophers make the unequivocal choice in favor of *Sein*. In fact, *Sein* is almost openly identified as *essence* (οὐσία), the idea, and, consequently, *beings*. Thus ontology ends up in the risky place of a leap into the abyss of questioning, established by the *daimon* of wonder, a special type of inner, philosophical sacredness (different from the pre-philosophical sacrality of sacred *beings*). This topography, in which the way out to *Seyn* flickered, which was blocked after Socrates and Plato by the theory of ideas and universal "representation" (*Vorstellung*), is preserved right up to the *End* of philosophy.

According to Heidegger, Christian theology is nothing other than an episode in the consolidation of this post-Platonic topography, where the figure of the Semitic God-Creator replaces the *philosophical daimon* and later the Platonic *idea*. Thus, the cycle of Christian philosophy fits between two philosophical periods: Late Antiquity and Modernity. The *place* constituted by the *philosophical daimon* for the leap into *Seyn-Being* remains in approximately the same state (although the passageway remains substantially collapsed and continues to collapse further and further). And when the influence of Christianity disappears ("God is dead," according to Nietzsche), the lack of change in the ontological topography becomes clear at once: it turns out that in the philosophical sense, Christianity provided absolutely nothing new and only delayed the process of truthful and consistent thought for 1,500 years.

The Scholastic God-Creator temporarily remained in the place of the philosophical *daimon*, later abandoning this philosophical *topos* once again, giving room to the "idols" of Modernity: subject, object, the soul, matter, *techne*, values, worldviews, etc. That is what the expression "Platonism for the masses" means.

Descartes: The Science and Metaphysics of Modernity

Heidegger conceives of Modernity in two ways. On the one hand, this is a very significant *turn* (*Wendung*), which, in his eyes, represents renewed contact with pre-Christian philosophizing. At this time, the ontological set of problems begins to be comprehended more clearly, rigorously, and consistently, without the apparent tranquillity of the Scholastic "Platonism for the masses." As thought thaws, it finds itself within the schematic topography of Platonic-Aristotelian metaphysics once again, without reference to Creation and its degrees.

On the other hand, the Modernity of René Descartes, Gottfried Leibniz, Immanuel Kant, and others inherits the Platonic intellectual field in its entirety. Thus, their philosophies contain nothing that is drastically "*new.*" Furthermore, the Scholastic pause that lasted for fifteen hundred years only aggravated the *abandonment of Being (Seinsverlassenheit)*. New versions of ontology in terms of Modernist thinking replicate Platonic schemata. Although instead of the idea, they rely on new "representations": the subject, apperception, energy, reality, the monad, etc. Each new essence, category, or concept only aggravates the abandonment of *Being*, responding to the question of *Being* all the more formally and indifferently, sinking deeper into the sphere of (re)pre-sentations and solidifying an exclusively referential theory of truth.

Descartes bases the metaphysics of Modernity on the subject, which he also introduces into the main trajectory of Western European philosophizing. In a way, he deals with the "*philosopher's daimon*" once again. But Descartes no longer operates in the open optics of the *first Beginning* (maintaining the possibility of a *leap* into fundamental-ontology) or even in Platonist topography, barricaded from *Seyn-Being*, though two-dimensional nonetheless, where ideas still bear a trace of the initial flight ("Ideas," said Plato, "either soar or perish"[17]). Instead, he operates in the space of strictly human thought (of the "rational mind"), where a place called the "subject" is put on the same tier under the *topos* of philosophizing and, consequently, as the point for observing man's thought. Thus, the *philosopher's daimon* ends up locked up inside man, in his "inner" dimension, which only takes on this particular form with Descartes. This is the subject, "*res cogens,*" which passes judgement on what is, and what is not. Ultimately, metaphysics

---

[17] Cited in Gilles Deleuze, *Logika smysla* (Moscow: Rariet, 1998), 251.

becomes the metaphysics of the *"ego cogens"* (the thinking "I"), which makes assertions about *what beings*, the truth, etc., are.

In the Cartesian system of coordinates, Platonism decays to its smallest components, where *Sein-Being* is lowered from the Platonist idea toward Descartes's subject (*"cogito ergo sum"* signifies that *Being* becomes a function [*"ergo"*] of the subject's act of thinking, of his gnoseology). That which set off pre-Socratic philosophical thought, rising up into the *daimonic world of the logos*, i.e., human thought, becomes the place to which the initial breakthrough returns in the final stages of Western European philosophy and its *Geschichte*.

Descartes, according to Heidegger, is good in terms of his sincerity, the candid insignificance of his primitive ontology, and his shrivelling lack of intellect. Here, Heidegger finds the very *fate of Being*, which, not having managed to concentrate on *Seyn-Being* in the *first Beginning*, at a certain point could not help but descend to the topography of the subject. The Cartesian turn and the metaphysics of Modernity, however, is the same metaphysics as in Plato's era and during the triumph of Scholasticism. But this time it enters into a phase of active decay, in which its inner skeleton is exposed.

For Heidegger, it is very important to cleanse this skeleton from pseudo-ontological super-impositions and empty not-quite-philosophical and pseudo-philosophical quirks. With Descartes, Western European philosophy takes a decisive step toward its End.

Solidifying the subject at the core of his ontology, Descartes places everything else before it in the sphere of the *(re)pre-sented*. Only now he conceives these *beings* (earlier φύσις, later *ens creatum*) as objects.

An introduction of the *subject* inevitably entails the *object*, as that which stands before it. With Plato, ideas and things are positioned vertically; with the Scholastics, God was *above* the world; with Descartes, the subject and the object end up being on the very same plane. Although it is the subject that is the source of ontological assessment, whichever member of the *subject-object* pair we take, we automatically get the second one immediately. By establishing the subject, we also establish the sphere of the objective, where everything else falls. If we begin to think from the object's perspective (as Medieval nominalists suggested, as did the empiricists, like Newton followed by philosophers such as Locke, Hume, etc., up until the materialists), then we shall also inevitability arrive at the subject as a mirror placed before the object.

In Russian, the object is *"пред-мет"* (*pred-met*). Slavs (initially, the Poles with their*"przedmiot"*) copied this word for themselves from Latin, in order to convey*"ob"* ("before," *"пред"* [*pred*]) and *"jectum"* ("that which was cast"; "that which was thrown," from *"jacere"* — "to cast," "to throw"). An object is that which is before us. The one before whom something was cast is the subject. But this subject has an important distinction from merely a man or human thought: this subject is constituted scientifically; i.e., during the course of a philosophical observation about the way in which thought develops. This is reflective thought, which lies at the basis of the modern understanding of science. The subject is the centre of science and simultaneously that which creates science. That is why in Modernity, it is science that occupies the place of religion. From this point forward, it is science that becomes the depository of assessments that are recognized as true. Furthermore, it is science that takes it upon itself the function of issuing directives concerning *what beings are* and *what* they *are not.*

116

In the same way and by using the same gesture, science constructs the object as well. That which the subject examines and recognizes as existent becomes the object. *To be* a part of *beings* and *to be an object* fuse into one another. This is the origin of the synonymous use of concepts "to exist" and "to be objective" in colloquial language. Everything that exists is objective, and everything that is objective exists. The non-objective does not exist, or exists as a blunder, an error, or a delusion. The referential theory of truth is elevated to the level of gnoseological absolute, but, within the boundaries of Modernity's science, it is the subject and object that become the poles of reference.

Heidegger sees a clear sign of nihilism in this line of reasoning. Scientific thinking is one of the most extreme forms of nihilist thought; i.e., the kind of thought in which the question about the *Being* of *beings* not only fails to be raised but *cannot* be raised.

At this point, we must note the following. In the science of Modernity, despite the apparent detachment from the transcendent dimension (whether Platonism or Scholasticism) and the lowering of attention to concrete *beings*, the basic laws of metaphysics continue to be fully operative. Let us recall that this metaphysics erected an additional superstructure over *beings* as early as ancient Greece. Science represents thought within the framework of *two kinds of beings*—exactly the same kinds as in previous forms of idealistic or religious transcendentalism. These *two kinds of beings* are the sphere of the ontic and the sphere of the ontological, in which the place of the ontological is occupied by the science of Modernity itself. The topography of scientific thinking is the topography of classical metaphysics, although it is formulated in a radically new manner.

Vorsetzende Durchsetzung

Heidegger meticulously traces the artificial formation of scientific and philosophical ontology in the period of Modernity—from Descartes to Kant, classic German philosophy, and, finally, to Arthur Schopenhauer, Søren Kierkegaard, and Nietzsche. Each step brings us closer to the *End of philosophy*.

The subjective character of the ontological argument leads to the conscious primacy of the will as the principal mechanism for the construction of *beings*. This occurred especially after Kant's fundamental studies focused on the structure of pure reason and the discovery that reason is unable to make an accurate decision concerning the *Being* of the "thing-in-itself." This is explicitly present in Schopenhauer; and, finally, Nietzsche elevates the will—as "the will to power"—as the highest form of identity.

As early as Kant's practical reason, the will—now in the form of the categorical imperative—acts as the principal moral foundation, responsible for affirming the *Being* of an object, subject, and "God." Further on, classical German philosophy—from Johann Fichte and Friedrich Schelling to Nietzsche—develops this Kantian thought.

In order to describe the last segment of Western European philosophy, understood within the optics of *Seynsgeschichte*, Heidegger uses a specific expression—"*vorsetzende Durchsetzung*," which can be translated rather approximately as "premeditated enforcement." What this means is that the one who followed the path of *(re)pre-sentation* (*Vor-stellung* or *Vor-setzung*, which literally signifies "placement before oneself," "deliberate fixation," and "that which was added in advance"), moving further and further away from *Being (Sein)* and having gradually—then completely—lost vital contact with *beings (Seiende)*, ultimately finds oneself in ontic emptiness. In a neurotic dialogue with this emptiness, he started to fill it up—"litter" it with certain representations, established within the space of ontological topography. He turned toward the domain of the "idea" (which became the concept, the subject, the object, the category, the value, etc.) and further imposed these ontologically, metaphysically, and later scientifically constructed *beings* directly onto the surrounding *beings*, not particularly concerned with them and their existence. In order to deal with *beings* that had become objects, man, at some point, was forced to "deliberately impose" something constructed onto *beings*, to pave the emptiness with the content of his own *(re)pre-senting* mind, and to forcefully impose these *(re)pre-sentations* with the help of the will, in order to later examine them, repeating a similar operation *ad infinitum*.

For Heidegger, the essence of the fundamental advancement on the part of philosophical thought during the course of its development lies in understanding the machinery of "premeditated self-imposition." Western European philosophy is a progressive *vorsetzende Durchsetzung*, moving from the pre-Socratic pole toward the nihilism of the Nietzschean "will to power" through alienating phases of Platonism, Scholasticism, and Cartesianism.

The Objectification of Things

The objectification of things (*Vergegenständlichung der Dinge*) occurs during the process of "premeditated self-imposition" (*vorsetzende Durchsetzung*).

Here, it is very important that we understand what a "thing" is. The German word "thing" ("*Ding*"[18]) bears a sacred meaning similar to the Russian counterpart. In Russian, a *thing* (вещь, [*veshch'*]) is *news* (весть [*vest'*]), something *prophetic* (вещее, [*veshchee*]), that which prophesizes ("broadcasts," вещает [*veshchaet*]) in the world, where *beings* are revered as sacred. Prophetic things prophesize or make themselves known in *beings*. But it is through representation that they become objectified— these prophetic things cease prophesizing, lose their sacred content, deform, slip away, or, in the very least, violently thrust into the human (more specifically, the ontological, philosophical) conception thereof. But people are not satisfied simply with the objectification of already existent things; they are more and more possessed by *representation (anticipation)*, *Vorstellung*, and the will. So they begin to duplicate natural things through artificial ones, "things-Doppelgangers," "things-shadows," creating such *man-made beings* that are closer and closer to representation thereof. Thus they begin to replace *Aufstellung*, i.e., *that natural and innate something that is being born*, with *Herstellung*—an artificial product.

Man plunges into *techne* as if this were predetermined and continues to move in the opposite direction of *Being* (in the direction of *Sein* as *Seiendheit*). *Beings* lose their delicate connection with *Being* (as *Sein*, or perhaps spilling over into *Seyn*) as early as Plato, and then being transforms into something manufactured. Ultimately, inasmuch as *Being* is forgotten (*Seinsverlassenheit*), *beings* become enslaved, and are replaced by that which is produced artificially. There are more and more objects, fewer and fewer things. This is the dictatorship of production (*Herstellung*).[19]

[18] We will review the significance of the German word "*Ding*" in more detail in Part 2, "*Das Geviert.*"

[19] The Russian language is an ontic language to a significant extent. Saying

Hegel: An Outburst of the "Greater Logic"

Heidegger pays considerable attention to Hegel's philosophy. From his point of view, Hegel tries to escape from the clutches of a doomed set of problems in the realm of *disontologizing*. For the first time during the entire Western European philosophical tradition, he tries to resist Aristotelian logic. Kant described the latter by saying that over the course of two thousand years no one had introduced anything new into it and failed to alter, improve, or suggest anything new for it. In a burst of genius, Hegel tries to create his own *alternative logic*, in which the third law of formal logic, the *law of excluded middle (tertium non datur)*, would be negated.

For Heidegger, this is a brilliant experiment, representing the peak of Western European philosophy. However, Hegel remains within the categories of the *concept*, where *beings* are

---

"we produce" (*производим* [*proizvodim*]) means that "we help nature," "we take things out of it." (*выводим из нее* [*vyvodim iz nee*], *изводим* [*izvodim*]). "To produce something" signifies "to push something out of somewhere" (for instance, from *Being-Sein*). There is only a single word in the Russian language for the concepts of "*Aufstellung*" and "*Herstellung*," "*proizvedenie*" ("production," "creation"). The German word "Herstellung" signifies "to set outside" or "to place in front of," specifically, in an artificial, forceful manner. We, Russians, even think of industrial production as an almost magical, mystical feat. For instance, Russian author Andrei Platonov describes proletarians digging a trench, thereby collectively accomplishing a great national archetypal gesture. It is unclear what the trench is for: a building will not be built anyway, and no one is planning on doing so; but everyone continues digging, convinced that this process is necessary on a fundamental level. Platonov's other protagonists have deep conversations with steam locomotives, engines, and machines tools, perceiving industrial manufacturing as one gigantic *living* organism (to be fair, it also exhibits certain infernal attributes). Among Russians, even technical production is understood (more specifically, was understood until recently) with a certain level of sacredness. That is why it is difficult for us to imagine an objectified thing or an object in pure form: for us things still *prophesize* (although more and more quietly). (See "Magicheskii Bolshevizm Andreiia Platonova" chapter in Alexander Dugin, *Russkaia veshch'* [Moscow, 2000].)

121

enslaved by reason and are not able to free themselves from "premeditated self-imposition" (*vorsetzende Durchsetzung*). Hegel accomplishes as much as can possibly be accomplished within the framework of *Vorstellung*. Nothing else can be done. It is not until night reaches the point of midnight that morning could arrive. Therefore, poor Hegel appears to be a certain kind of a *morning thinker*, who wakes up in the middle of the night and begins to act as though he were just in time for breakfast.

Heidegger is amazed by Hegel, but at the same time, he thinks that this is not a *breakthrough* toward fundamental-ontology but rather a *dash* toward it, since conceptual thought envelops the movement of Hegel's spirit like a fishing net, taking it away from the most acute and potentially explosive moments every time.

To Hegel's enormous credit, he transitions from history to the history of philosophy, convincingly demonstrating that the historical process is nothing other than the deployment of concepts, the work of the "global mind." The latter—either openly or covertly—predetermines the logic of events, remaining the sole content of mankind's world history, which must be considered the *subject* only at the eschatological moment when "history comes to an end." Hegel essentially reestablishes Platonism in its own right, which was subjected to numerous distortions over the course of more than two thousand years. He speaks of history not only as the history of philosophical ideas but as the history of an Idea, the Absolute Idea, the transformations of which comprise the fabric of Western European historical *Being* (referring to his own philosophical period, from the pre-Socratics until Modernity). Hegel raises the question of *Being*, *Nothingness*, negation, and dialectics, substantially reestablishing the ontological set of problems of the Greeks, but only in the ultimate, post-Platonic, strictly metaphysical context.

122

Hegel summarizes Western metaphysics in its most complete form. But this entire process of restating the question of *Being* (*Sein*) anew not only fails to lead us to reconsider ontology, but also negates the possibility of thinking about *beings* and *Being* (*Sein*) outside the intellectual context of Western European metaphysics once and for all.

Striving to respond to the difficult questions of Kant's critique of pure reason, Hegel merely exhausts the standard spectrum of answers to the ontological challenges of nihilism through formal repetition of pre-Socratic theses (Parmenides and Heraclitus) within the topography of post-Platonic philosophy. He examines the *first Beginning*, but repeats its set of problems within the framework of the *End*.

Only a step separates Hegel from Nietzsche.

Nietzsche and the End of Philosophy

Western European philosophy ends with Friedrich Nietzsche, who calls things what they are. Heidegger devoted a number of scholarly volumes to Nietzsche's philosophy.[20] For Heidegger, the latter is the most significant and principal thinker of

---

[20] Martin Heidegger, *Nietzsche I (1936–39), Nietzsche II (1939–46)* (Frankfurt am Main: Vittorio Klostermann, 1996); Martin Heidegger, *Nietzsche: Der Wille zur Macht als Kunst (1936)* (Frankfurt am Main: Vittorio Klostermann, 1985); Martin Heidegger, *Nietzsches Metaphysische Grundstellung im abendländischen Denken: Die ewige Wiederkehr des Gleichen (1937)* (Frankfurt am Main: Vittorio Klostermann, 1986); Martin Heidegger, *Nietzsches II. Unzeitgemässe Betrachtung (1938)* (Frankfurt am Main: Vittorio Klostermann, 1989); Martin Heidegger, *Nietzsches Lehre vom Willen zur Macht als Erkenntnis (1939)* (Frankfurt am Main: Vittorio Klostermann, 1989); Martin Heidegger, *Nietzsche: Der europäische Nihilismus (1940)* (Frankfurt am Main: Vittorio Klostermann, 1986); Martin Heidegger, *Nietzsches Metaphysik (1941–42), Einleitung in die Philosopie—Denken und Dichten (1944–45)* (Frankfurt am Main: Vittorio Klostermann, 1990).

Modernity and even of Western European philosophy. This is completely understandable: according to Heidegger, Nietzsche is the final philosopher, and so it is difficult to overestimate his significance in this capacity. That which began at the time of the pre-Socratics ends with Nietzsche. In terms of his authority and significance, he is a key figure, since the End of philosophy explains or substantially clarifies its Beginning. This helps us understand what exactly began at the time of this Beginning; how it came to be that; now having commenced, this certain something came to an End—and to what kind of an End?

Nietzsche asserts that nothing apart from subjectivity remains, and that the meaning of subjectivity is in the will and self-imposition. *Being* is no longer an idea—it is simply a *value*, development, life, and the will to power. In other words, it is an arbitrary decision on the part of the subject. Because *Being* became the function of values, we find ourselves in the space of total nihilism, having lost absolutely everything that at one point connected us to *beings* and ourselves.

According to Heidegger, Nietzsche does not overcome Western European metaphysics in his philosophy—he extends it in an attempt to save it. The Nietzschean critique of Plato, his appeal to the pre-Socratics, his battle with static ontology, which has been blocking access to the flow from the vivifying source—none of this takes him toward a new turn. It does not bring him closer to truly overcoming Western European philosophy, but both sums it up and brings it to the burial ground. Striving to overcome Western European metaphysics, in reality, Nietzsche tried to save it. "The transvaluation of all values," "the will to power," "life," "the Superman," "the eternal recurrence"—all these Nietzschean propositions, according to Heidegger, represent the agony of philosophical thought, thrashing about in snares of a once falsely established topography, where the breakthrough to *Being* was irreversibly closed off by its entire structure. But in contrast to his direct predecessors—Kant, Hegel, and Schopenhauer—Nietzsche truly yearns to overcome all of this; he thirsts to break through to new horizons, but fatally remains within the limits of the old. This is the End comparable to the Beginning in terms of its scope, tragedy, and relevance. In terms of risk, it is comparable to the entire process of Western European sunset, evening-time philosophizing. Nietzsche is a worthy End.

Nietzsche is the guard heralding the coming of midnight. "Watchman? What is left of the night? "Morning is coming, but also the night."[21]

The *"destitute time"* has come, according to Nietzsche, "God is dead," and the midnight of the world arrives. Speaking of the fact that "midnight has arrived," Heidegger added, "What are poets for?" to the text, "It is already midnight, but maybe *'not quite yet,'* always this *'not quite yet.'"*

We can return to this *"not quite yet"* a little later. In the meantime, let us consider why the oblivion of *Being* occurs.

---

21 "Someone calls to me from Seir, "Watchman, what is left of the night? Watchman, what is left of the night?" The watchman replies, "Morning is coming, but also the night. If you would ask, then ask; and come back yet again." (Isaiah 21:11-12.)

VI. HEIDEGGER'S ANTHROPOLOGY OF SEYNSGESCHICHTE

Man's Guilt

The question as to why the *oblivion of Being* occurs, i.e., the question about the source of *Seinsvergessenheit* as the principal content of the historical-philosophical process, leads us to a quite profound level of analysis, and we confront the problem of man and anthropology in the same vein as that of Heidegger.

In one of his works of 1935, *Introduction to Metaphysics*[1], Heidegger poses the following questions directly: Why does the *fate* of Being turn *away from Being?* Why does the *oblivion of Being* take place? Why did Platonic ideas emerge, and what pushes philosophy in the direction of its End? What lies at the basis of the End? And consequently, *why midnight?*

When meaning is obscure, philosophers turn to poets. Poets are not limited by anything providing philosophers with what they essentially lack. And in this case, Heidegger turns to Sophocles—in particular, an excerpt from his tragedy *Antigone*[2] where the choruses, symbolizing *beings* (*Seiende*), sing the following (in Heidegger's literal translation):

---

1 Martin Heidegger, *Einführung in die Metaphysik* (Tübingen: Max Niemeyer, 1953); Martin Heidegger, *An Introduction to Metaphysics,* tr. Ralph Manheim (New Haven: Yale University Press, 1959).

2 "The Ode on Man in Sophocles' Antigone," Martin Heidegger, in *An Introduction to Metaphysics,* tr. Ralph Manheim (New Haven: Yale University Press, 1959), 86-87.

Chorus

Strophe I

There is much that is strange (πολλὰ τὰ δεινὰ), but nothing
that surpasses man in strangeness (δεινότατον).
He sets sail on the frothing waters
amid the south winds of winter
tackling through the mountains
and furious chasms of the waves.
He wearies even the noblest
of the gods, the Earth,
indestructible and untiring,
overturning her from year to year,
driving the plows this way and that
with horses.

Antistrophe I

And man, pondering and plotting,
snares the light-gliding birds
and hunts the beasts of the wilderness
and the native creatures of the sea.
With guile he overpowers the beast
that roams the mountains by night as by day,
he yokes the hirsute neck of the stallion
and the undaunted bull.

Strophe II

And he has found his way
to the resonance of the word,
and to wind-swift all-understanding,
and to the courage of rule over cities.
He has considered also how to flee
from exposure to the arrows
of upropitious weather and frost.
Everywhere journeying, inexperienced and without issue,
he comes to nothingness.
Through no flight can he resist
the one assault of death,
even if he has succeeded in cleverly evading
painful sickness.

Antistrophe II

Clever indeed, mastering
the ways of skill (τέχνη) beyond all hope,
he sometimes accomplishes evil,
sometimes achieves brave deeds.
He wends his way between the laws of the earth
and the adjured justice of the gods.
Rising high above his place,
he who for the sake of adventure takes

the nonessent for essent loses

his place in the end.

May such a man never frequent my hearth;

May my mind never share the presumption

of him who does this.

Heidegger finds a concise description of the entire historical-philosophical process (i.e., the formula of Western metaphysics) in these choruses about *beings*. It is because man, at least Greek man, *Western European* man is the kind of man that Sophocles depicts—this leads to everything else.

Man, as one of *beings*, gets removed from the general system of *beings*, is accentuated, falls away, and embodies something unique and special, housing catastrophe within. On the one hand, he is as "terrible" (strange) as all *beings*. His "terrible" nature must be understood in its original Greek sense, Heidegger insists. This is the way in which the Greek term "δεινόν" (*deinon*, suffering) translates. Heidegger interprets this term as "coercive," "aggressive," "subordinating," and imposing." Certain aspects of *beings* are also terrible: among them are storms, hail, deadly diseases, savagery, unruliness, aggression, risk, and threat. But man, partaking of "terribleness" with all *beings*, surpasses everything else with it. Many things are terrible, but man is the most terrible of all. Herein lies his uniqueness: he is the most terrible of all that is terrible; he is the most aggressive of all that is aggressive; and he is the most subjugating among all that subjugates.

Moreover, he turns aggressiveness into his fate. According to Heidegger, man's specific δεινόν is fully captured in "τέχνη," "techne," the ability to create special *beings*, which can serve

130

him more completely than those *beings* that he conquered, subjugated, and placed under his control.

The ability to create *per se* is neutral with respect to good and evil, but in every case this ability is based on aggression, imposition, and terror. After all, it is the qualitative concentration thereof.

At the same time, "*δεινόν*" is, in a certain sense, "*δίκη*" (*dikē*, justice), i.e., the "higher law" or the "higher order" which subjugates all *beings*. Heidegger interprets "*δίκη*" as "*φύσις*" (*physis*) and "*λόγος*" (*logos*), i.e., as *Being* of *beings*. Δίκη imposes itself onto everything on the scale of *beings*, whereas man imposes himself onto *beings* through τέχνη. This leads to the fundamental confrontation between man and *Being*. Man places himself in opposition to δεινόν as the expression of Δίκη through τέχνη as the expression of δεινόν. It is for this reason that man becomes "more terrible" than all *beings*. There no longer is a point within *beings* where the two terrors could collide: the terror of *beings'* Being and the terror of man, who copies them. This is the point of a schism in *beings*. Man as the kind of *beings that are being split* represents the point where an incursion of the terrifying power of *Being* (*Sein* or *Seyn*—this is yet to be clarified) occurs. Yet manifesting itself in this way, it pushes man away from the rest of *beings*.

As the greatest and most important of *beings*, while towering over *beings* at the same time, he is excluded from *beings* and is banished from them. He is not welcome at the source of *beings*. In fact, he is cast out from that which comprises *beings'* knowledge about himself.

131

Techne as Western European Fate

Therefore, we should search for the source of Western European philosophy's fate in the roots of European—Greek—anthropology. At his core, man is doomed to conflict with *beings* and, indirectly, *Being*, which is the order of *beings* as well as their *logos*. Yet man is also doomed to conflict with himself, since he, too, is part of *beings* and an expression of this order. However, this order of *beings* (its *Being*) is exhibited in man in an essentially different way than in the rest of *beings*. Heidegger reaches the assertion that there is "excessive *Being*" in man, and it is this factor that is manifested in his having too much power and terror directed toward the overcoming of *beings* and toward exiting their boundaries. This departure is an attempt to break through to the *Being* of *beings* that comprises the *essence* of man's *Being*.

Thought is a characteristic of man. It is the latter that distinguishes him from other *beings*. Man is capable of acutely differentiating one thing from another when it comes to *beings*, i.e., thinking ontically. After all, he himself is distinct from *beings*, because he occupies a special place in relation to them. "Man, ruling over places (*beings*), placed outside of places" (as Heidegger translates Sophocles). Thus, the very act of thinking already contains the possibility of turning into a *breach in beings*.

However, man does not attempt to draw the necessary conclusions from this. He is satisfied with differentiating that which is around him and with consolidating his position, although he is periodically thrown from side to side in his attempts to reach the edge of *beings* and to battle with them as *beings-as-a-whole*.

During the course of mastering the limits of his own freedom and distancing himself from *beings*, at a certain point man discovers τέχνη, the ability to create *beings* for himself. This allows him to acquire an even greater power over them and to measure distinctions between *beings* even more precisely and accurately. Through τέχνη man approaches the final barrier, the other side of which reveals the horizon of the *leap*; beyond the limits of all that is human, the place which we described as "*daimonic topos*" earlier. With this leap, man considers himself to be among *beings*, i.e., distances himself from himself. He, thereby, realizes the greatest possible violence and undermines the last foundation for remaining in *beings*. When he thinks of himself as a kind of *beings* in the same way as he considered other *beings* (in opposition to himself) earlier, he constitutes a new place, which in a certain sense is no longer located in *beings*. This place can only be *Being*. Furthermore, this is *Being* as *non-beings* (*Seyn als Nichts*).

This gesture initiates philosophy. Yet at the same time, τέχνη does not become one of the manifestations of human distance, but is instead comprehended as man's fate, as the principal thing in him, as *Seynsgeschichte*. By undertaking the *leap into non-Being*, man himself becomes a "product," a "means," and something technical. And the potential of *an-nihil-lation* (*Seyn = Nichts*) contained in *Being* begins its lengthy work against *beings* and, for that matter, against man as one of *beings*. It is for this reason that Heidegger identifies τέχνη with fate and sees in this the manifestation of man's ontological depth as a phenomenon of *Seynsgeschichte*.

But not every man moves in the direction of complete and final acceptance of responsibility for *double distancing*: both from *beings* and from *man* as part of *beings*. Only the Greek man in the earliest days of philosophy makes this choice. And from this initial point onward, the leap, *double topography*, *daimonic place*, and τέχνη become his evening fate. Ultimately, the first gesture of self-awareness as a breach within *beings* already opens up a path toward the gradual formation of Western European nihilism and the *"desert's" advance*.

Freedom and Will

At the heart of the catastrophe of Western European fate lies the most profound truth of human freedom. *Being* reveals itself in man in a completely different way from its revelation in other *beings*. Man lives in *Being*, and his home is *Being*, not *beings*. As one of *beings*, he, however, is not at home among *beings*; this is not his home. His authentic home is *Being*; that is why he acts so repugnantly when he is only immered in *beings*.

Being, having brought man *into presence* and supporting him *in presence* until the moment of death and simultaneously leaving him to his own devices, remains in him in a special way. It expresses itself through his special position—the *will*. Man places himself before *beings* and imposes himself onto *beings* through his will. In this way, he moves toward the replacement of *beings* by the created and the *technical*. Herein lies his will. Man is a wilful entity. This relationship between man and *Being* as well as that of *Being* and man comprises the source of *vorsetzende Durchsetzung* (*"premeditated enforcement"*).

The impulse to move away from *beings* and toward *Being* as the source of philosophizing is an echo of *Being's* boundless freedom in the depths of man. Sensing the very possibility of this impulse, man enters the riskiest zone of his essence: he throws himself into *Being*. In the first Beginning, the boundless nature of freedom signals the greatest risk in terms of the possibility of flying over the abyss. Becoming alien to *beings* and interpreting this as his fate contrary to the fate of *beings*, man begins to philosophize.

At the same time, this impulse is the realization of the greatest violence over *beings* and over oneself: from now on, man is irreversibly alien within *beings*. But whether he would find his home in *Being*—this is the big question. At this moment, he becomes man for the first time because there now is a *place*, from which one could say, "*Ecce homo!*"—"Behold the man!"—pointing at himself from somewhere within (the *daimonic topos*). But at the same time—exactly at that same moment—man ceases to simply be man and begins to be the one who *philosophizes*, a man with a fate correlated with *Seynsgeschichte*. From now on, he is no longer free of his freedom, and is condemned to philosophical thinking, despite all attempts or desires to slip back into "simple thinking," i.e., the ontic. Having identified himself as man, as *beings* in what is human, man makes the lightning-bolt of the *logos* a reality. In a certain sense, the Superman appears for the first time at this very moment as *logos* is discovered. It is not a coincidence that Heraclitus tells us about this as already mentioned, "If you do not listen to me, but to the *logos*, it would be wise, abiding by it, to say: everything is one". "*Not to me but to the logos.*" Philosophy is not about Heraclitus as a man, but about the *logos*, and we must only listen to it; it philosophizes, and it truly risks.

And here the exact moment of making the *greatest decision* reveals itself: to what limit will man follow the path of the *logos*? How will he deal with his boundless freedom? After all, he reclaimed it by taking the terror of *Being* in its ultimate concentration upon himself as its first-priority recipient (through death), bearer, and inspiration for all others (through will and power).

Today we know the answer. Establishing philosophy, the ancient Greeks did not know it. Terrified and amazed, advancing toward that which they themselves did not know, they created a work of art unique in its tragedy: Western European history—the history of the *world's evening*.

As we have already noted on a number of occasions, the fluctuation between *Sein* and *Seyn* in the works of Aristotle and Plato unequivocally resolves itself in favor of *Sein* as *Seiende-im-Ganzen* and *Seiendheit*. This means that the process of soaring in a leap was interrupted, and the very element of the *leap into the abyss* was replaced by an artificially created campsite, a temporary stop, established somewhere halfway between the abandoned home of *beings* (ontic thought) and the true home of yet-to-be-acquired *Being* (*Seyn*, fundamental-ontology). But will as the tragic banishment from *beings* and as violence and destruction nevertheless became man's *fate* to drift along every possible road in a deliberately wrong direction. Always prone to turbulent destructiveness, man created a planned schedule for it. Stopping in his tracks at an intermediate station, he intensified the technical destruction of *beings* along with their artificial counterfeiting and, at the same time, extended his war with δίκη as the *Being* of *beings*, with the *dash toward Being* (*Seyn*) no longer on the agenda.

Τέχνη became the two-fold fate of man: he began to transform *beings* into products through his will, and, consequently, he himself (like *beings*) became more and more reminiscent of a machine (this is the source of Julien Offray de La Mettrie's "machine man"). At the same time, *Being* became the question about the *"techne"* of thought for him, which he used to consolidate the barricades in the face of dangerous questions about death, *Nothingness*, the *abyss*, and *Seyn*.

This process reaches its peak in the metaphysics of Modernity and with René Descartes's introduction of the subject and object. From this point forward, there is only the reasoning, representing, and willing subject and before him—the object, "*res extensa*," the ob-ject, *Gegenstand*. It is at this point that the *final ob-jectification of things occurs.*

Heidegger designates this process by using a special term, "*Machenschaft*." It is formed from the German stem "*Machen*," "to make" or "to do," which is also the source for the concept "*Macht*," "power," "might," and "dominion." The Russian language conceives of "power" and "dominion" as something from the domain of the "po-ssible", the potential (not unlike the Latin "*potentia*"), that which might be, but might not be. The German words "*machen*," "*Macht*" and "*Machenschaft*" are linked, on the contrary, with actuality, action, act, and with that which not only might show or impose itself, but which already shows and imposes itself at the given time. This is an active and operating volition, operation, deed, action, and activity. It is possible that the assonance of the German stem with the Greek stems μάχομαι (machomai) and μηχανική (mechanike) influenced Heidegger in his selection of this group of words; the first signifies "fight," "battle," "aggression," and "attack," and in the figurative sense, "machination"; and the second, "mechanical invention" and the "machine." *Machenschaft* is absolutized τέχνη. It is taken as a positive program for man and mankind no longer implicitly, but rather explicitly.

In this inferior, pragmatic, and objectified madness of production, which swept over the West in the era of Modernity, Heidegger sees the same original anthropological gesture on the part of the ancient Greeks realizating the greatest, unlimited freedom. Man lowered himself to a production frenzy, utilitarianism, pragmatism, and materialism, precisely because at one point he faced the sources of his humanity (superhumanity) as something *distinct* from *beings*. He discovered his fate in *logos* and will, constructed a metaphysical topography of the relationship to the world and a referential theory of truth. That is why the ultimate nihilism of disastrous present-day circumstances and man's complete and hopeless abandonment of *Being* (*Seinsverlassenheit*) contains the profound mystery of the relationship between man and *Being*, the fateful history of his rebellion against the limits of *beings*, and his descent into nihilism. Yet all of this is not simply an accident on the part of someone who participates in the independent course of something that is distinct from him. It is man that creates himself and determines himself before the face of *Being* (*Seyn*), which never lets itself be known directly through *beings* or through death, but which can happen to man or not happen at all.

Herein lies the fundamental character of the relationship between *Being* and man: for man, *Being* is something accidental —specifically, that which may or may not collide with him. And at the same time, *Being* needs man in order to immediately, accidentally, and whimsically reveal itself in his brokenness, separation, and tragic mortality.

Thus, man's will is his fate and *Being* itself. This is expressed at all stages of Western European philosophy through φύσις *(physis)*, ιδέα *(idea)*, ψυχή *(psyche)*, subject, object, concept, value, and, finally, *Machenschaft*.

Why is this the case? Because *Being* is not a kind of *beings*; consequently, it is Nothingness. And since it revealed itself in the great Beginning as the *Being* of *beings*, then in the End it reveals itself as *Nothingness* out of *beings*. Thus, man at the foundation of his will actually wills *Nothingness*.

The sun moves towards night not because it or someone else made a mistake. The light simply expresses itself through light and shadow, and day transitions into night, in order to meet the new day. As early as the *first Beginning* of Western European philosophy, *Being* manifests itself as will, moving *Seynsgeschichte* toward the point of mindnight.

VII. ANOTHER BEGINNING (DER ANDERE ANFANG)

Background for Another Beginning

Gradually, we arrived at the main subject of Heidegger's philosophy, which he called "*another Beginning*" (or the "*second Beginning*").

There are three works that were not published in Heidegger's lifetime, consisting of the outline for courses, lectures, and other works. They are dedicated specifically to the subject of *another Beginning: Contributions to Philosophy (of the Event)*[1], *Geschichte des Seyns*[2], and *On the Beginning*[3]. They were all written between 1936 and 1956, i.e., at the time Heidegger theorized about the subject of *Ereignis*, which had direct correlation to the subject of the *second Beginning*. Heidegger's thought appears much more clearly and precisely in these loosely designed fragments than in stylistically perfected texts. They also demonstrate the questioning and fluctuations on the part of Heidegger himself, revealing his process of searching for appropriate words and expressions.

In all three books, the idea of the *second Beginning* serves as the author's focal point. It is this question that makes other subjects that Heidegger considered earlier (until the mid-1930s) truly piercing. These include *Sein und Zeit* as well as ideas primarily

---

[1] Martin Heidegger, *Beiträge zur Philosophie (vom Ereignis)* (Frankfurt am Main: Vittorio Klostermann, 1989).

[2] Martin Heidegger, *Geschichte des Seyns (1938/1940)* (Frankfurt am Main: Vittorio Klostermann, 1998).

[3] Martin Heidegger, *Über den Anfang. Gesamtausgabe* (Frankfurt am Main: Vittorio Klostermann, 2005).

concerned with language and ancient Greek thought (which he made a priority after the end of World War II and the collapse of the Third Reich).

With the *second Beginning*, Heidegger equated his own philosophy, thought, and ultimately himself. It is that with which he completely identified his own philosophical and personal fate.

According to Heidegger, the *first Beginning* comprises pre-Socratic philosophy (especially Anaximander, Heraclitus, and Parmenides); it lays the foundation for philosophy as such and determines the fate of two-thousand-year-long Western European history. This Beginning is a unique transition from the *ontic* to the *ontological*; from simply human thought to the type of thought that considers man a special kind of *beings*. It involves fully accepting the responsibility for the fate of this transition, man, *beings*, and *Being*, conceived in a completely different way from this point forward.

Within the framework of the first Beginning, thinkers prior to Anaximander, Socrates, Plato, and Aristotle determined whether Western European *Seynsgeschichte* would be ontological or fundamental-ontological, whether the daring leap of ontological thought would result in a flight toward boundless *Seyn-Being*, or whether it would stop halfway, replacing *Seyn* with the greatest manifestation of *beings* (ὄντως ὄν [*ontos on*]).

We know what decision was made and whence it led. The fundamental-ontological prospect was not realized. And the kind of ontology that prevailed is the one which Western European philosophy has been demonstrating to us until its latest nihilistic manifestations. Recording theoretical moves by the process of *Seynsgeschichte*, we can ask ourselves the following question about a certain daring endeavor together with Heidegger. Should we discard two and a half thousand years of Western man's fate and thought thereby transitioning to a *new Beginning*? Should we raise the question about the *Being* of *beings* anew and in a completely different way than was done in the *first Beginning*—taking into account the entire available Western European philosophical experience? What does this "different way" mean? It means posing this question not by using *beings* as the starting point or equating *Being* with *beings*, but surging directly into the pure element of *Being* through terror and abyss.

We saw that the first Beginning opened up the possibility of a *leap* and *flight* toward *Seyn*. We also saw that it was not realized and was completely taken off the agenda by Platonism. But we also saw how this was done, how the *logos*—the place of the philosophical *daimon*—revealed itself in the highest dash on the part of man's thought, which established philosophy in place of simple thought, and ontology instead of the ontic. Indeed, thinkers transitioned from the ontic to the ontological in the *first Beginning*. But in the *second Beginning*, we must transition into fundamental-ontology, realizing that very possibility which was lost, discarded, and failed.

This comrpises the new Beginning—a different Beginning. We are not simply raising the question about *Seyn-Being* with all of its rigid and radical qualities, by asking ourselves, "Why are there *beings* rather than Nothingness?"[4] This is a transitional question according to Heidegger. Let us recall that the "key question of philosophy" (*Leitfrage*) since the introduction of the Greek concept of φύσις was about determining the essence of *beings*, i.e., what is *Being* as *beings-as-a-whole*? This is the question asked at the end of the first Beginning. "Why

---

[4] Martin Heidegger, *Einführung in die Metaphysik* (Tübingen: Max Niemeyer, 1953).

are there *beings* rather than Nothingness?" is a transitional question (*Übergangsfrage*). "What is the truth of *Seyn-Being*?" is a fundamental question (*Grundfrage*).

We know that the "key question" was formulated incorrectly, whereas its responses led to a catastrophe. We also know that "Nothingness" of the transitional question is not an empty concept, but rather a sophisticated expression of the incongruence between *Being* and *beings*. In addition, the latter emphasizes the profound significance of *Seyn-Being*, which is *Nichts*, but also *Seyn* of beings (*Seiende*), i.e., *Sein*. And, finally, we know that not only the referential theory of truth, but also the understanding of truth— *ἀλήθεια*—as the unconcealment of *beings* inherent to the pre-Socratics, is a fundamentally wrong way to raise the question. Unconcealment must refer to *Seyn-Being* and be drawn directly out of it, bypassing *beings*, including man as a kind of *beings*.

The *new Beginning* is also possible based on the following criteria:

1. The historic-philosophical process of the European man has exhausted itself, and the era of total nihilism has arrived.

2. Recognizing the will to power, *Machenschaft*, values, worldviews, *techne*, and all other versions of Plato's idea as the expression of *Seyn-Being* itself, indirectly proving the latter's non-equivalence with *beings* through a schism in *beings* embodied in the philosopher-man.

3. Tenacious will toward thinking philosophically and the greatest risk in any situation that pertains to man's *seynsgeschichtliche* dignity and his dignity as a species—as the bearer of greatest freedom.

4. Martin Heidegger's philosophy focused on the fundamental-ontological trajectory in the history of philosophy. It spurred the reading of Western European history in terms of its most significant aspects.

The new Beginning will open up if we are to believe Heidegger and follow him, thereby taking on the new version of thinking and philosophizing. But if we are to consider carefully the scale of this philosophical act that we are to undertake, then we will feel uncomfortable because of the fundamental nature of the task that we are supposed to solve. The transition to the new Beginning translates into ceasing to live by the rules of Western history and the history of the evening. It means to not only topple metaphysics but also the original source—the first nerve of Greek thought about *beings*, ἀλήθεια—truth and φύσις at the deepest level under the strata of Latin, Scholastic, and contemporary philosophical concepts, which continue to predetermine the fundamentals of Western thought, Western logic, and Western consciousness, not to mention culture, science, education, social relations, politics, and economics.

Heidegger offers the total overcoming of the West and the beginning of a new history, new *Being*, and new humanism. At the same time, he does not point the way back or look for the alternatives in other cultures and other eras. His invitation is as follows: it is necessary to accept Western *Seynsgeschichte* as one's fate, recognize the inevitability and justification of each of its phases, decipher them grasping the message sent by *Seyn-Being*, which is implicitly contained in the approaching coming of the night and the kingdom of total nihilism. It is especially important to focus on the initial roots of Western philosophy during the era of the first Beginning and take one more step— toward the abyss—in order to immediately and radically pass on the truth's initiative onto *Seyn-Being* itself in its pure form.

Transition (Übergang)

Here is what Heidegger writes about the transition into a different Beginning,

> In preparation for the transition from the End of the first Beginning into another Beginning, man not only enters a never-before-experienced "period" but into a completely new area of history (Geschichte). This transition and even the different Beginning itself, will both include a long phase of overcoming the End of the first Beginning.[5]

Further:

> This transition is the running start for the leap, with the help of which the Beginning can commence—and another Beginning to an even greater extent. Here, in this transition, the most initial and, therefore, the "most historic" (geschichtlichste) decision is being prepared. This is an either-or decision from which one cannot take refuge in a burrow or a secret hiding place: one will either remain imprisoned by the End and its final consequences, i.e., the renewed modifications of "metaphysics," which become more and more crude, more and more meaningless (the new "Biologism," etc.), or one will initiate the new Beginning, i.e., undertake its lengthy preparation.

> And since the Beginning only occurs in a leap, then this preparation, too, has to be a leap and should originate from the confrontation with the first Beginning and its history (Geschichte). (. . .)

---

[5] Martin Heidegger, Beiträge zur Philosophie (vom Ereignis), op. cit., 227; here, translated from the Russian (Ed.).

In another Beginning, all *beings* will be sacrificed to *Seyn-Being*, and only because of this will *beings*, as such, acquire their own truth for the first time.[6]

Ereignis

Heidegger points directly to the main barrier to this transition—*human reason (ratio)*. Reason in its *re-pre-senting* role is the obstacle for fundamental-ontological thought.

Seyn-Being in another Beginning is not physics (and is not perceived as a meta-physics). It is thought of in a radically different way: through simultaneously grasping and holding on to it as the *Being of beings and Nothingness simultaneously*. At the same time, it is incorrect to consider it as something that should *always* be (it is incorrect to think of *Seyn-Being* through the prism of permanence). According to Heidegger, *Seyn-Being is not*—it exists (*Seyn west*), i.e., *remains in essence*. This means that it is not permanent and unchangeable, but rather extremely rare. It occurs, comes true, and is unique.

Herein lies the fundamental-ontological core of another Beginning: it grasps *Seyn-Being* as *Ereignis* (literally, the "event").[7]

In order to clarify the term "*Ereignis*,"[8] Heidegger uses artificial syncretism. Etymologically, "*Er-eignis*" comes from "*Er-augen*," in which the meaning of its stem is "*Auge*"—the "eye," more broadly, "vision" and "observation" in the old German. Yet Heidegger interprets the term as the similarly sounding "*eigene*," i.e., "one's own,"

---

6 *Ibid.*, 228–229; here, translated from the Russian (*Ed.*).
7 Unlike a simple "event," *Ereignis* "befalls," "attacks," and "falls with lightning speed." It is the midnight storm in which the lightning illuminates the black landscape with a sudden, piercing, and unnaturally bright light.
8 We will discuss this subject in more detail in the upcoming sections of the book.

"genuine," and "authentic"—"*Er-eigene*."[9] Heidegger conceptualizes *Er-eignis* in two ways: as a unique one-off (*seynsgeschichtliche*) event in which *Seyn-Being* instantly manifests itself in its truth, and as the immediate transition from the inauthentic mode of existence to the authentic kind and, accordingly, to *Being* (*Sein*) and existence according to the fundamental-ontological essence (*Wesen*).

The *Seynsgeschichtliche* horizon of Heidegger's philosophy is oriented toward *Ereignis*. *Ereignis* is the culmination of *Being's* history, because at this point the whole process of *Seynsgeschichte* manifests itself in its true dimension: as *Being's* narration about itself in a reversed (inverted) form— in the form of *Being's* oblivion (*Seinsvergessenheit*) and the triumph of nihilism. *Ereignis* is directly linked to the fact that at a certain point the entire cycle of Western European philosophy is being grasped in its true proportions and in terms of fundamental-ontological significance. And this process of grasping and comprehension forms the premise for *Seyn-Being's* advancement as it truly is—this time not through continuance in which it conceals itself, but rather through the single moment in which it reveals itself.

Heidegger uses the metaphor of *maturity* and ripeness to describe *Ereignis*. In the context of *Ereignis*, *Seyn-Being* becomes a fruit and a gift. At the same time, *Ereignis*, looking ahead and having an instant place in the future, is also present in the past—in so far as the past was, i.e., correlated with *Being* (*Seyn*). Thus, *Ereignis* becomes a moment orienting the development of the historical (*geschichtliche*) process that generates the eschatology of *Being*. Heidegger wrote about this subject in a text dedicated to Anaximander:

9 The terms "*eigene*" and "*uneigene*" ("authentic" and "inauthentic") are applicable to the fundamental concept of "*Dasein*," which we will discuss in the third section.

Beings' Being gathers (λέγεσθαι, λόγος) in the final moments of its fate (*Geschick*). *Being's* previous existence collapses in its still-concealed truth. *Being's* history gathers in this parting. The gathering in this farewell comprises the eschatology of *Being* and is akin to harvesting (λόγος) the ultimate (ἔσχατον [*eschaton*]) expression of its former existence. *Being* as *seynsgeschichtliche* (that which was sent) is eschatological.[10]

Er-eignis is, therefore, an eschatological event. In it, the evening fruit of fatally articulated questions in the first Beginning falls into the hands of the one who is ready to undertake the transition over the point of great midnight and come out on the other side—the morning side. At the same time, Heidegger believes that the salvation of the West— which was the first to follow the trajectory of ontological philosophy and metaphysics and was also the first among all others to have reached the critical end point of cultures (the End of philosophy)—must occur in the West itself— realized by the latter itself. Taking on the fatality of making the initial choice, a new philosophy of the second Beginning must make the new choice and, pushing off from its tragic history, focus on the problem of *Seyn-Being* anticipating or preparing for *Er-eignis* as *Being's* ultimate coming to fruition.

Er-eignis is the keyword of the New Beginning. This is another Beginning in its fundamental-ontological essence. "*Seyn-Being* exists as an event" ("*Das Seyn west als das Ereignis*"), writes Heidegger.[11]

---

10 Martin Heidegger, *Holzwege* (Frankfurt am Main: Vittorio Klostermann, 2003), 327; here, translated from the Russian (*Ed.*).

11 Martin Heidegger, *Beiträge zur Philosophie (vom Ereignis)*, op. cit., 256.

The Last God

The eschatology of *Being* takes Heidegger to the introduction of a certain figure, to which, as far as I know, very few people have paid serious attention. He outlines his assumptions about the *Last God* (*der letzte Gott*).

Heidegger speaks of him as follows:

> The Last God
>
> The most coming in coming and which, constituting itself, occurs as an event.
>
> The arrival as the essence of *Being*.
>
> Ask *Seyn-Being* itself! And in its silence, God will answer as the Beginning of the word.
>
> You will be able to encounter all *beings*, but you will never find the trace of God.

In German it sounds like this:

> *Der letzte Gott*
>
> *Das Kommendste in Kommen, das austragend sich als Er-eignis ereignet.*
>
> *Das Kommen als Wesen des Seyns.*
>
> *Frage das Seyn! Und in dessen Stille als der Anfang des Wortes antwortet Gott.*

Alles Seiende mögt ihr durchstreifen, nirgends zeigt sich die Spur des Gottes.[12]

"Frage das Seyn!"—"Address *Being,* ask *Being (Seyn)!"*

The very structure of this text makes it clear that this is a kind of prophecy about the fundamental-ontological vision, which is conceived, established, and postulated as part of an entirely new cycle in the history of philosophy. This is a prophecy about a unique event that must occur strictly at the point of the Great Midnight.

The Last God is a unique figure in Heidegger's philosophy. He appears through *Ereignis,* passes people by, leaving them only with a *nod* and a hint (*Wink*). He is neither part of *beings,* nor the Creator of *beings,* but he manifests himself at the moment when *Being* as *Seyn* comes to fruition during the one-time event.

Heidegger writes,

> In the hint's (*Wink*) *Being, Seyn-Being* itself reaches maturity. Maturity is the willingness to become fruit and to be given as a gift. There is the last End, which in its essence (*wesentliche*) is anticipated from the Beginning and does not happen by chance. The latter reveals the profound finality of *Seyn-Being*: in the Last God's nod."[13] And further, "The Last God is not the end but another Beginning of immeasurable possibilities for our fate (*Geschichte*).[14]

The Last God is a mysterious figure. Heidegger carefully differentiates between him and the protagonists of all known

[12] Martin Heidegger, *Geschichte des Seyns* (1938/1940), op. cit., 105.
[13] Martin Heidegger, *Beiträge zur Philosophie (vom Ereignis),* op. cit., 410.
[14] *Ibid.,* 411; here, translated from the Russian (*Ed.*)

religions. However, this is not an empty individual image or a metaphor. In Heidegger—who rejected both religion and atheism on the basis of their total dependence on the philosophical topography of the first Beginning, i.e., ontology and metaphysics—one can find hints at a very peculiar theory of the divine. He does not discuss this subject directly, but we can attempt to reconstruct the course of his thought leading to the introduction of the Last God into his eschatology of *Being*.

Heidegger thinks primarily about the other Beginning, which must proceed according to a different scenario (as compared to the first Beginning) and lead to *Ereignis*. The first Beginning, on the other hand, comprised the transition from the ontic to philosophical and ontological thought. But the ancient Greeks, who established the first Beginning, believed in gods. Heidegger is not interested in the structure of the ancient Greek religion. He is interested in the way in which the philosophical consciousness of the Greeks, making a leap into the abyss, conceived of gods and divinity. The most important aspect thereof is that the gods are not *Being*, but they are not *beings* either. In addition, gods are not people; they are completely not human. According to Heidegger, these gods, however, need *Seyn-Being* to record their divinity. They are *not essence* or *non-essence*. Their main feature is lightness. Furthermore, gods are indifferent to people: they neither save nor punish them. Gods walk past people, but this happens only when people turn to their humanity's *Being* and sufficiently honor *Being* as *Seyn* by doing so. In that case, people orient themselves toward the *sacred*. And the *sacred* offers space to the *divine*, while the divine allows gods to gather around the hearth of *Seyn-Being*. The people responsible for *Being* must, in contrast to other *beings*, correctly structure this responsibility and serve *Being* as a result. This will enable gods to appear. If, however, man substitutes *Seyn-*

Being with *Sein-Being*, metaphysics, ontology, the will to power and, ultimately, *Machenschaft*, these lightweight gods will easily fly off, leaving no trace behind, distancing themselves. After all, nothing connects them to that which is human. Gods get away from Platonism, theism, deism, atheism, i.e., from all that "intentionally imposes" preconceived *re-pre-sentation* onto *beings* and does not allow *Seyn-Being* to shine through and illuminate *beings* so that the gods would gather around this glow.

In the *first Beginning*, the Greeks conceived of gods through *Being*. Heraclitus wrote that "*ethos* is the god of man," explaining to the curious newcomers that he is getting warm by the fire because "the gods live there, too." In *struggle*, he saw the source that makes gods godly, and humans—human. Parmenides was dedicated to the goddess of justice, Dikē. Gods and goddesses settled, hid, and manifested themselves around *Being*, revered by the first philosophers. They were incredibly important for thought and for man, comprising a sophisticated and paradoxical pair at the opposite ends of *beings*. Gods and men were the two poles of the most complex, silent, poetic, and thinking dialogue about *Seyn-Being*.

Thought about *Being* as *beings-as-a-whole*, about *essence*, and about the *idea* scared the gods away. They had nothing left there anymore, because everything was already clear to the people. The gods are obtained only as part of prayer questions or ceremonial singing.

Heidegger's Last God is the kind of God that returns as part of the development of *another Beginning*. He does not arrive as a savior. He passes by. But he leaves a sign, slightly nodding, which is almost an invisible gesture that was also made by judges in Antiquity or the Basileis, working on some important matter. The more serious the decision—the shorter, less noticeable, and more significant the gesture. For this reason, the Last God does not arrive, he walks by. He gives nothing to the people and changes nothing. He simply ensures the fact that this time the Beginning is truly the Beginning, or, more specifically, *possibly*, the Beginning. Thus, the ripening *Ereignis* receives a small, hardly noticeable, and not even a necessary "certification." The event had come to pass. A place for the Last God to walk by is being conquered through silence, a new sacredness, and men's reverence.

When it comes to the Last God, Heidegger uses poetic language. He deliberately relies on vague and paradoxical expressions, expecting that in the realm of ultimate penetration into the possibility of another Beginning, consciousness is geared toward grasping the subtlest hints.

The Last God is the Beginning of the longest fate (*Geschichte*) along the shortest path. Lengthy training is essential for the great moment of his passing by. For the purpose of this training, peoples and countries are too insignificant; they are inaccessible for authentic growth, and are dedicated to *Machenschaft*.

Only the great and concealed individuals will prepare silence for this God to walk by, and create the silent atmosphere among themselves."[15]

The Role of Man in Another Beginning
(New Humanism)

Heidegger refers to these "great concealed individuals" as "the future ones" (*Künftige*), after Friedrich Nietzsche. In his famous

[15] *Ibid.,* 414.

letter to philosopher Jean Beaufret on the subject of humanism, Heidegger describes in detail the fundamental-ontological understanding of man.[16]

The content of this oft-cited text will become clearer to us if we localize man's place within the structure of Heidegger's philosophy. Heidegger rejects humanism, much like other versions of Western European philosophy, due to its direct dependence on metaphysical topography. He has zero interest in this kind of humanism. In contrast, he is concerned with man and the human within the structure of the Beginning (both the first and the *other*).

Man is the breach in *beings* through which *Being* bursts in, blowing up *beings* and man himself. He is what he is in terms of his relationship with *Being*. Only this relationship between man and *Being* is his essence. All the rest—animality, reason, spirituality, soulfulness, psychological qualities, sociality, and ethnicity—is secondary. Man is man only in his essence, in the fact that he *is*, which means that he is man through the relationship (*Bezug*) to *Being*.

The one who does not think about *Being* or does not think about it in the right way, who clogs questions about *Being* with self-explanatory babble, who is unable to feel wonder and terror, who does not experience problems having been "cast" into *Being*, who does not create the greatest freedom in noble thinking or quiet sacred labor, he renounces his humanity and loses it. For this reason, Heidegger's new humanism is exceptional, in which human dignity is measured by the level of participation in the fundamental-ontological act, in questioning *Seyn-Being*, in the preparation of *Ereignis*, and in an anticipation of the Last God to pass by.

---

16 Martin Heidegger, *Brief über den Humanismus (1946)* (Frankfurt am Main: Vittorio Klostermann, 1949).

Heidegger refers to this kind of man—the man of the future— as the "watchman of Being" (*Wächter des Seins*) or the "shepherd of Being" (*Hirt des Seins*). Man is intimately connected to *Being*, but at the same time, he is independent from it. *Being* needs man not in order to be (*beings* can be non-human, and through them *Being* is), but in order to prepare a place for it to glow amidst *beings*—for the light of its truth. Man is that very place. If the place is proper and sacred, then it is suitable for sacred acts, blessings, and for the unconcealment (truth) of *Being*. If it is not, then man and mankind turn into the garbage dump of the world (as is the case at the end of Modernity, that is, today).

Man worthy of being one is the kind of man that is the alternative to what we understand by using this term today—the one who remains under the yoke of ontology and its nihilistic deritivates. Nietzsche's "Last Man" (comprising the majority) and his Superman (expressing the greatest will to power and domination) remain within the framework of the *old humanism*. Heidegger crosses them out with fatigue and sadness. These have no entry into the "future." Man is only the bearer of questioning about *Being*, its truth, its remoteness, and the possibility of its return through the *event* and the Last God. The one who does not bear all this is not man. In the very least, he crosses the boundaries of Heidegger's humanism—the *humanism of another Beginning*.

Man is defined by his relationship with *Being*. The notion that man possesses *Being* as something permanent and guaranteed, and correlates to *Being* in general through his *Being* as that of a man, is a delusion on the part of metaphysics, which should be completely rejected in the other Beginning. Heidegger writes, "*Seyn-Being* for man is based on chance (*Zu-Fall*); the fact that man comes to fruition in *Seyn-Being* does not depend on him, nor does it mean that *Seyn-Being* has any responsibilities with respect to man, as if it needed

156

him."[17] And a bit earlier on, "*Seyn-Being* does not exist for man, but man exists for *Seyn-Being*, at best; for *Seyn-Being* in the sense that man would have earned for himself his own essence in this way." [18]

The fact that man is not merely a kind of *beings*, but the *place where Being's encroachment occurs*, is incorporated in his capacity for speech. Speech is not merely one of man's attributes. It is not by accident that the latter is called "ζῷον λόγον ἔχον" (*zoon logon echon*), i.e., an "animal endowed with speech." Speech *per se* is not man's attribute, but rather an attribute of *Being*. *Being* exists through speech. Speech is that through which *Being* is in the capacity of *Being*. Therefore, in the context of new humanism man must speak differently. He must address words and realize what they tell him. And then, he must begin to think and talk with the help of that which he realized. We must preemptively undertake the "destruction" of the old language based on the rules of grammar and logic, i.e., the rules of metaphysical thought of the first Beginning, so that this new kind of speech could be born. The latter is the speech of another Beginning, the speech of *the future (Künftige)*.

The *new humanism* presupposes new speech, because the fate of *Being* and the greatest moment of *Seynsgeschichte* lie in speech and language.

The new man of another Beginning will speak in new ways, in a new language, stating new thoughts and things. Everything he says will be be linked directly with the nature of *Being*, i.e., with the way in which *Being* exists in its spotlight. This will be fundamental-ontological speech about the anthropology of *Ereignis*. Only this kind of speech could express the sacred silence, in which it becomes possible for the Last God to walk by.

[17] Martin Heidegger, *Über den Anfang, op. cit.,* 127.
[18] *Ibid.,* 127.

VIII. SEYNSGESCHICHTE AND POLITICAL IDEOLOGIES OF THE 20TH CENTURY

The Fundamental-Ontological Method and Its Application Area

Following our general excursion into the structure of Heidegger's thought, it is not difficult to grasp that in terms of Western metaphysics, he is interested only in its most principal aspects. These aspects focused on the relationship of this metaphysics to *Being (Sein)* as *beings-as-a-whole* or *beings* of the second order, and, consequently, the progressive distancing from *Seyn-Being*, which presupposed—at a certain stage—the oblivion of the ontological set of problems as such (*Seinsvergessenheit*). For this reason, the technical questions of this metaphysics—theology, gnoseology, humanism, axiology, epistemology, philosophy of science, philology, ethics, and especially political philosophy—did not have any independent significance for Heidegger, being individual cases of using the basic principles of this metaphysics.

However, at all those times when Heidegger had to make a judgment on these particular issues, he was forced to take them back to their metaphysical roots. In some cases, he had to sketch out the potential direction in which respective schools of thought and culture should be interpreted in the fundamental-ontological way. This means that Heidegger, together with criticism of specific aspects of Western European metaphysics, also sketched out ways of a radically new interpretation of these subjects in *another Beginning*.

This dual operation—tracing a particular subject under consideration to the general context of Western European ontology and the attempt at its alternative interpretation from the perspective of fundamental-ontology—comprises the main course of action in the transition to another Beginning; consequently, it is the principal methodological tool in Heidegger's philosophy. In its initial gesture, this methodology is a "phenomenological destruction,"[1] which Heidegger did not conceive in the negative sense of the term "destruction." Instead, he understood the term as "de-structuring" and "de-con-struction" in the opposite direction of that which was "con-structed" artificially, as a way of returning the term to its original context within the structure of metaphysics. Later, in French structuralism, Heidegger's operation of "destruction" was renamed "deconstruction" by Jacques Derrida.

The second gesture of Heidegger's "phenomenological destruction" is more complex, since it is focused on correlating the question of *Seyn-Being* traced back to its metaphysical context, i.e., placing it back into the Beginning (either the first Beginning or the new one). This means removing the given question from the context of Western European philosophy and including it in a radically new fundamental-ontological context. It does not appear as something readily available, but as that which is being created, composed in the process of correlating the given thing, question, object, or phenomenon directly with *Seyn-Being*. If the new fundamental-ontological context were already known and given, then this operation would only constitute a technical problem. But it is not given. It is only

---

[1] Martin Heidegger, *Sein und Zeit (1927)* (Tübingen: Max Niemeyer Verlag, 2006), 19–27.

asked as the horizon of the possible, but not an assured new Beginning. This Beginning may commence and, having begun, it will implement a total revision of concepts, words, topics, areas of science, disciplines, things, and thoughts. However, if we capture the essence of Heidegger's method[2], we will be able to carry out this operation on our own and, in particular, correctly decipher and even extend Heidegger's own indirect hints regarding certain issues that he touched upon only briefly.

Thus, we can sketch an image of Heidegger's relationship to contemporary political ideologies, in which he was never interested *per se*. However, the *seynsgeschichtliche* approach to this subject area will clarify many things in the history of the Modern world and will provide us with the most important clues to deciphering the real history of the 20th century.

Americanism and the Planetary Idiocy of Liberals

The 20th century experienced three major political ideologies: Liberalism, Communism, and Fascism. In one way or another, Heidegger spoke about each one of them. These assessments were segmented and unsystematic (Heidegger was never interested in the sphere of ideology as a subject matter of any significance), but are still worthwhile on their own.

According to Heidegger, all ideologies (and it follows naturally from the preceding discussion), contain the essence of contemporary nihilism. They express one thing only: the triumph of τέχνη ("*techne*"), the "oblivion of *Being*," "premeditated self-imposition," the "will to power," and *Machenschaft*. All three

---

2 The word "method" comes from the Greek "μέθοδος" (*methodos*), where "μετα" means "through," "on," and "after," whereas "ὁδός" translates as a "path" and "road", and originally meant the "placement of road signs", "*Wegmarken*" in German.

political ideologies are the greatest expression of total nihilism; these are the ideologies of the night, in which Western thought has reached its lowest point. They are not simply the essence of "false consciousness" according to Marx's definition of ideology. They express the falsity of consciousness as an ontological and metaphysical kind of consciousness. Moreover, these ideologies operate with metaphysics in its Modern edition, and, consequently, they place the most primitive and poor idols of the "subject-object" pairs in the place of the essence of *beings*, *Being* as a whole, the ideas, or God.

Liberalism equates the Cartesian subject with the individual and pragmatic calculations in the area of countable tangible and intangible objects (mainly products) generated by its ratio. Heidegger calls this "Americanism," which represents the ultimate expression of capitalism. There exists nothing more vile and treacherous than this degeneration of philosophy, because here nihilism reaches such a level of intensity that it no longer recognizes itself as nihilism. At some point, the night becomes so familiar that it no longer identifies itself as night.

Calculating reason at the basis of Liberalism and its values are the last stage of degeneration of Western European ontology. It is impossible to go any lower. We must look for the roots of Liberalism as a fatal and deadly pandemic in Europe, but it is in the U.S. that this political phenomenon has acquired its ultimate form. *Being* completely insignificant from a philosophical standpoint, it continues to expand on a global scale, creating the phenomenon of the "giant," becoming more and more "vast," while its meaning and significance shrink to a microscopic size. The global rise of Liberalism is equivalent to the spread of total imbecility.

Heidegger refers to this phenomenon as "planetarism" (today we talk about "globalism" and "mondialism"); he equates it with global "idiocy." In essence, this is none other than "desertification," which Friedrich Nietzsche described: "The desert grows, and woe to him who conceals the desert within."[3]

Heidegger writes, "The greatest development in the essence of power (power in the Nietzschean sense, *Macht*) does not appear via the previously known form of desertification and the loss of roots but in the norm of direct opposition to this kind of desertification and uprooting. Historically recorded signs of fully realizing the very essence of power are embodied in two specific phenomena—"planetarism" ("globalism") and "idiocy." "Planetarism" ("globalism") marks the spread of the essence of power (*Machtwesen*) throughout the entire world, though not as a result of a conquest, but rather as the beginning of a special kind of planetary domination. "Idiocy" (ἴδιος)[4] translates into the triumph of egotism over everything, thereby expressing the most extreme form of subjectivity."[5]

Reading these lines, one might think that they were written today, not in 1938.

Man of the global world, a Liberal, accepting and recognizing the normativity of the "American way of life," is the kind of person who is a patented idiot from the philosophical and

---

3 See Friedrich Nietzsche, *Thus Spake Zarathustra*, tr. Alexander Tille (New York: Macmillan, 1896), 447.
4 "Ἴδιος" (*idios*) in Greek means "private (individual)," "applies only to this individual and no one else." In ancient Greece, "idiots" were the kind of people who did not represent anyone but themselves, neither the *polis*, nor the procession, neither class, nor clan.
5 Martin Heidegger, *Geschichte des Seyns (1938/1940), op. cit.*, 74.

etymological point of view, a documented idiot, an idiot parading his foolishness above his head like a banner.

Liberalism embodies the metaphysics of Modernity in its driest and most primitive but, at the same time, purest form. One could treat Modernity and its philosophy in various ways even being closely and consciously tied to it. One could try to construct a critical theory in an attempt to overcome this inherent alienation (as per Marxism). One could endeavor to go deep into the roots of the problem, courageously accepting the real status quo in the face of nihilism (i.e., German philosophy at its peak—from G. W. F. Hegel and his "negativity" to Nietzsche). Or it is possible to express the core of this metaphysics with the least amount of mental strain, surrendering to the element of alienation, expressing naïve solidarity with it, telling it a deliberate and submissive "yes," and not even caring much as to what this "yes" represents. It is the latter option that is Anglo-Saxon Liberalism and Americanism. It is this factor that is the most terrible and fatal. It represents the ultimate choice in favor of abandoning the *other Beginning*—and such a degree of *Being*'s oblivion—that the very fact of oblivion is forgotten. This is nihilism in its greatest expression, when the very awareness of nihilism as such becomes impossible.

The global power of idiots does not simply embody the abuse and exploitation of one people by another. This is pure nihilistic violence, the victims of which are everyone: both those who carry it out, and those who submit to it. Narcissistic planetary idiots stand closer to *Nothingness* not when they lose something or are subjected to violence but rather when they exist in comfort, security, and under the illusion of complete subjective freedom. In this case, the power of *Machenschaft* over them is absolute, and their dehumanization reaches its limits.

An idiot of the global market society is no longer man, having fallen into a *Nothingness* that he does not even notice.

The Metaphysics of Communism: Machenschaft

According to Heidegger, things are more complex with Marxism. Unlike Liberalism, Marxism possesses serious philosophical energy drawn from classical German philosophy (Hegelianism) and focused on the problem of alienation. It was this particular aspect of Marxism, according to Heidegger, that made it so attractive and successful.

Uncovering the problem of alienation contains the core of the entire process of Western European history (*Geschichte*). It is this history that is the history of alienation. Acknowledging and focusing on this is the appeal to the *truth of Seynsgeschichte*. In this respect, Marxism is the philosophical challenge that must be taken seriously. Interpreting history as the accumulation of alienation's qualitative properties, Marx hits the target and touches upon the essence of truth. If we are to think from this point onward, then any consideration on the part of the thinker gains significance. *Seynsgeschichte* of the *first Beginning* until the *End* is the process of alienating thought from *Seyn-Being* and the *oblivion of Being (Seinsvergessenheit)*. This is what determines the logic and structure of all cultural, social, political, ideological, and economic processes. Marxism puts this at the center of its attention and, consequently, conquers its rightful place in the history of thought.

But here limitations from Hegel's own philosophy become relevant. Hegel rightly views history as the history of philosophy and, more important, as the history of ideas. But he remains completely within the framework of the *first Beginning* and classical ontology and cannot arrive at the the correct formulation of the question about *Seyn-Being* (*Grundfrage*) precisely because of these reasons. Hegel thinks within the element of τέχνη via philosophical concepts relying on Plato's understanding of ideas as the *essence of beings*. He remains within the framework of Western European metaphysics—although nearing its end—in scope, penetration, and totality of his thought, summing up its main points in his teaching.

Marx inherits this feature from Hegel and stays loyal to the metaphysical topography of Modernity: he thinks in terms of the subject (society, class) and object (matter, product, thing), time (as an objective phenomenon), etc. Marxism suggests to overcome the problem of alienation—*Machenschaft*—by the means of *Machenschaft* itself. He contrasts bourgeois ideology (the false consciousness of one class) with proletarian ideology (the false consciousness of another class). The struggle is taken into the realm of manufacturing and production. Thought in terms of the subject (this time, the subject is collective, represented by society) is fully preserved. This path starts with acknowledging alienation, but can only lead to further alienation.

Heidegger fully records this in the case of Soviet Russia, in which the structure of Marxist philosophy is implemented in socio-economic and political practice. Industrialization, technological development, totalitarian mobilization of the Soviet communist society, the struggle for political power and geopolitical domination—all these are clear signs that Communism does not overcome Western European metaphysics but is the final (and brightest) expression of its fate (*Geschichte*). At the same time, Communism is more loyal to the essence of *Machenschaft* as compared to all other

166

political ideologies. Communism is *Machenschaft* in its pure form and is thus the fate of Western European philosophy and a highly eschatological phenomenon. Communism is the ultimate expression of metaphysics which establishes total dominion of the *essence* of *beings* over *beings*. And if it is the idea that expresses this in the Beginning, then in the End it is power, might, and *Machenschaft* in its greatest and most obvious form. *Machenschaft* is the total dominion over *beings* by that which is conceived as their essence, which in terms of Modern metaphysics can be described as the "objectness of the objective" or the "materiality of the material." Communism is not the power of some over others regardless of which class they belong to. Rather, it is the power of power over everything. This is the highest form of disembodied power on the part of pure objectness. This is why Heidegger writes that "nothing human remains in Communism."[6] "The essence of Communism is pure legitimation (*Ermächtigung*) of power (*Macht*) within absolute *Machenchaft* and through this absoluteness."[7]

Communism is pure metaphysics of Modernity in the form of its End. But it can only be recognized in the form of metaphysics within the optics of fundamental-ontology, which captures the *seynsgeschichtliche* significance of this phenomenon, correctly decodes it, comprehends its nonrandomness, predetermination, fatefulness, and fatality. And, only having recognized *Being's* own voice under this utter oblivion of *Being*, it announces its true attitude toward the incompleteness of thought about *Being*, pushing off *beings*, through ruthless and total dominion of *Machenschaft* over *beings*. According to Heidegger, it is only possible to overcome and defeat Communism upon understanding it.

---

[6] *Ibid.* ,195.
[7] *Ibid.*, 191.

"Americanism" (Liberalism, "planetary idiocy") and Communism (Soviet Bolshevism) are the opponents of *fundamental-ontological* transition into another Beginning, both being the two extreme expressions of Western European metaphysics and two versions of *Machenschaft,* embodying the final stages of nihilism and the spirit of the End itself, i.e., being expected, justified, and fateful forms. They embody a different decision— the decision to remain loyal to Western European metaphysics not only until the End, but also afterward, when the End as such had been fixed, recognized, and correctly interpreted by the German (Old European, not American or Soviet) philosophy of Modernity in its last version. Therefore, only the return of the End's phenomena to their end, i.e., the final destruction of Liberalism and Communism, will be the manifestation of mankind authentically taking the *leap* into another Beginning and the dawn of *Being's* return.

At the same time, Heidegger is convinced that the victory over Liberalism and Bolshevism by using purely technical means is impossible, since we are dealing with metaphysical and ontological phenomena that have to be conquered in the space of metaphysics and ontology. Therefore, when it comes to their destruction, the main objective is to bring them back to their hidden nature, to their ontological roots, thereby releasing their true nihilistic meaning. In this respect, Heidegger utters a phrase about the political fate of the 20th century that has become truly prophetic, "The danger is not in 'Bolshevism,' but *in ourselves.*"[8]

The Political Ideology of the Third Way

Now we arrive at Heidegger's political position. He conceptualized his place in the history of thought, as well

---

[8] *Ibid.,*120.

as in *Seynsgeschichte*, as something directly associated with Germany. He conceived of his ethnic and cultural roots metaphysically in the context of belonging to the German philosophical and poetic tradition. The very *fact of thinking in German* was highly significant to him. After all, in his opinion, *language is the house of Being*. Thus, the nature of this house—German, Greek, Latin, English, French, Russian, Semitic, and so on—largely depends on the nature of man's relationship to *Being*. German philosophy is the German path to *Seyn-Being*, which Heidegger often emphasized in respect to both German philosophy (repeating Hegel's words that "a great people should have a great philosophy"), German culture, and poetry (he considered Hölderlin's poetry its greatest expression).

German philosophy is linked to the *fate of Seyn-Being* no less than was that of the Greeks. It all began with the Greeks and ends with the Germans. Therefore, according to Heidegger, Hegel and Nietzsche are the last philosophers, who recognized the End of philosophy earlier, better, and clearer than others. Those who have recognized the End have also opened the path to another Beginning. This is the reason why the last ones—the Germans—are so in tune with the first ones (the ancient Greeks and especially the pre-Socratics). The mission to start philosophy anew belongs to the Germans—Heidegger and other "future ones." For this reason, Heidegger reduces the fate of the West and Europe as a whole to the fate of Germany. This is the source of Heidegger's fundamental-ontological patriotism; the kind of patriotism that rejects nationalism, collective egotism, and other forms of superiority based on the metaphysical understanding of subjectness. In Germany and Germans, Heidegger sees *Seyn-Being*, the language of thought and poetry, a people comprised of those "singular" and rare ones who are capable of inquiring about the *truth of Seyn-Being*. Heidegger's patriotism is the patriotism of the "basic question of philosophy," the patriotism of *Grundfrage*. Being German, it is equally European, Western. This is also the patriotism of all mankind having set upon the evening path and reached the point of midnight.

In terms of specific political geography during Heidegger's lifetime, Germany (Europe) was the center of philosophical thought, clinched by proverbial pincers on two sides by the derivative forms of Western European metaphysics: from the West came "Americanism" and, broadly speaking, Anglo-Saxon Liberalism ("planetary idiocy"), whereas Soviet Bolshevism, Marxism, *Machenschaft* in the most blunt and totalitarian form came from the East. Metaphysically, they both corresponded to the kind of thought that ignored (Liberalism) or misinterpreted (Communism) the End, which German philosophy had discovered and had chosen to extend that which had already concluded after this End. Europe ended up under the double blow of the final incarnation of the first Beginning in its ultimate form—that of totalitarian and planetary domination of τέχνη.

For Heidegger, Europe (and Germany as its philosophical eschatological equivalent) embodied the possibility of transition to *another Beginning*. Europe was the place of writing, publishing, and reading *Sein und Zeit*. Thus, Heidegger consciously ended up in the camp of those forces in Europe that considered its identity at a profound level in an attempt to penetrate its *Seynsgeschichte*, desired follow its philosophical fate until the End, and at the End and on the other side of the End—into *another Beginning*. Furthermore, these forces, by definition, had to be immersed in the spirit of German culture and philosophy, or, in the very least, had to recognize the significance and content of this spirit. And finally, these forces ended up in the position of a radical confrontation with American (Anglo-Saxon) Liberalism and Soviet Bolshevism, not for political but for metaphysical reasons. Prior to transitioning to the possibility of preparing *another Beginning*, it was necessary to do away with that which persisted in ignoring the fact that the End has come to fruition even after this has come to be. Heidegger not only logically ended up among these forces, but in a certain sense, was their philosophical pole, center, and core in the fundamental-ontological and philosophical sense. Heidegger's thought is what constituted them.

Judging by its formal qualities, the political ideology of the Third Way was consistent with this metaphysical position to a certain extent. They were oriented toward patriotism, were pro-European, anti-liberal, and anti-communist. They addressed the roots and sources that went deeper than Modernity and laid claims to the revival of European heritage. They raised the philosophy of Hegel and Nietzsche into the category of the greatest achievements in thought. The lack of strict dogmatism or a system allowed them to offer a variety of epistemological and philosophical models and hypotheses within the framework of these movements. The eschatological sense of a critical turning point in world history—from the lived experience of the First World War, brutal realization of an offensive by *techne* on a global scale, acutely suspecting the proximity of the *Decline of the West* (Oswald Spengler)—completed the picture.

Most fully, these trends have been presented in the ideological movement of the "Conservative Revolution,"[9] which included such thinkers as Oswald Spengler, Carl Schmitt, Othmar Spann, Thomas Mann, Friedrich and Ernst Jünger, Arthur Moeller van

---

9 Armin Mohler, *Die konservative Revolution in Deutschland, 1918–1932* (Stuttgart: Friedrich Vorwerk Verlag, 1950).

den Bruck, Heinrich von Gleichen, Ernst Salomon, Friedrich Hielscher, Ernst Niekisch, Ludwig Klages, and hundreds of other prominent German intellectuals, thinkers, poets, and artists. Heidegger was, by all accounts, systemic connections and contacts, thought power lines and political sympathies, an integral part of this movement. He was a "conservative revolutionary" in the sense that, as he understood it, man was called upon to be the "guardian of *Being*" (in this sense, the "one who conserves" *Seyn-Being*), and at the same time—to take a risky *leap into another Beginning* (the "Revolutionary" moment, the orientation toward the future).

In a certain sense, the Conservative Revolution in Germany and its counterparts in other European countries, notably in Italy, Spain, etc., were that very ideological environment in which Fascism and National Socialism—Third-Way ideologies— sprung up. At the same time, we can argue that the main object of criticism from the leaders of the Conservative Revolution was the spirit of Modernity and its most striking manifestations: individualism and rationalism, utilitarianism, dogmatism, materialism, subjectivism—in other words, *nihilism* and *Machenschaft*. The political ideology of National Socialism and Fascism, partly based on the ideas of the Conservative Revolution (anti-Liberalism, anti-Communism, anti-utilitarianism, etc.) to a great extent also contained the features of that same Modernity that the Conservative Revolution criticized. Whence came its political pragmatism (all the way through to opportunism), absorption by practice and *techne*, the industrialization and militarization of economics, subjectivism (of nation and race), intellectual stagnation, primitive racial dogmatics, and many other traits that are typical of the metaphysics of Modernity. The bearers of the spirit of the Conservative Revolution saw their greatest enemies in Liberalism and Communism (the U.S.

and USSR). Thus, no form of any, even relative, solidarity with them was possible. Yet the ideologies of the Third Way—in the form that they embodied in German and Italian political regimes in 1930-1940s—were not acceptable to them either. After all, they possessed the principles and theses with which the essence of the Conservative Revolution was at war.

The most astute representatives of the Conservative Revolution, such as Ernst Niekisch, as early as the early 1930s, saw that the rise to power of Adolf Hitler's Party would result in a fatal disaster for Germany—not from the standpoint of Liberals and Communists (this was of secondary importance) but from the perspective of those ideas and principles that National Socialism allegedly sought to defend. That is exactly why Niekisch's book was called *Hitler–Germany's Doom* (*Hitler Ein deutsches Verhängnis*).[10] Following Niekisch, and sharing his fears, many went into the anti-Hitler underground. The rest ended up in "internal emigration". Ernst Jünger found himself in a similar situation—as one of those thinkers who formulated the main ideas of the "Conservative Revolution" more fully and vividly, while remaining overboard from the Nazi Party, refusing to compromise with vulgarity, populism, and unprincipled pragmatism of Hitler's Party.

We can fully consider Heidegger one of the Conservative Revolutionaries who remained in "internal emigration," in which he ended up soon after agreeing to become the rector of the Freiburg University and joining the National Socialist Workers Party for pragmatic reasons. His rectorship lasted only nine months, and soon his ideas were being aggressively attacked by the officials of Hitler's regime. But despite public

---

10 Ernst Niekisch, *Hitler—Ein deutsches Verhängnis* (Berlin: Widerstandsverlag, 1932).

criticism of many fundamental points in Nazi ideology in his speeches from the 1930s up to 1945, Heidegger did not absolve himself of the responsibility for the decision he made, continued to wear the Party badge, and shared the fate of his people and the political regime that this people had chosen.

All the drama and the depth of the paradox in the relationship of the Conservative Revolution with National Socialism is expressed in Heidegger's words uttered at the beginning of the Second World War, when the collision with Bolshevism became inevitable: "The danger is not in "Bolshevism," but in ourselves."[11] This meant that, in the eyes of Heidegger, the impending war with the Soviet Union was not merely a military conflict between two powers over vital interests or access to natural resources, not merely a grandiose turn in the battle for global power, but a clash between two beginnings, in which the "silent force of possibility"—the possibility of another Beginning—had to counter Marxist metaphysics (*Machenschaft*). But while Germany and National Socialism had not recognized the fundamental-ontological significance of their own historic (*seynsgeschichtliche*) mission, while they themselves were not free from the mass character, rationalism, τέχνη, old European metaphysics, from the same *Machenschaft* as the Communists, this battle could not be won, as it was not the kind of battle that it should have been.

The discrepancy between the Conservative Revolution and the political movements of the Third Way embodied the core in the political history of the 20th century if we were to view it from the Heideggerian perspective. Offering hope to raise the kinds of questions considered by the thinkers of the Conservative Revolution (of *Being*, the meaning of authentic

---

[11] Martin Heidegger, *Geschichte des Seyns (1938/1940), op. cit.,* 120.

174

history, the spiritual place of Europe and the West in the global cycle of metaphysics, etc.), National Socialism was profoundly and fundamentally inadequate. In it, it seemed to Heidegger, emerged the possibility of transformation, the ability to raise the question about *Seyn-Being*, the possibility of another Beginning, but this *possibility* not only remained unrealized, but was not even established as a *possibility*, proving to be illusory and deceptive.

Following the war, philosophers and intellectuals wondered how Heidegger could have been so wrong in terms of his political choices. They, however, did not account for the fact that the political ideologies that triumphed in the war (Liberalism and Communism) had always been repulsive and alien to him, because they embodied what Heidegger wanted to bury, overcome, and close as the final stage of history (*Geschichte*). In turn, the history and the unsurprising end of National Socialism only confirmed that this political regime was about substitution and parody (about premature and distorted simulation of another Beginning, the imitation of *Ereignis*, etc.). Profound questions about *Being* had been replaced with technical questions of power, control, domination, subjugation, enslavement, and conquest, i.e., things and values that directly embodied Western nihilism. Heidegger always considered it his task to oppose the latter.

IX. "NOT YET"

The Metaphysics of Delay

Clarifying the relationship between Heidegger's philosophy and the political ideologies of the Third Way brings us to a very delicate issue, which could be called the *"problem of delay."*

German philosophy recognized the End of Western European metaphysics. Friedrich Nietzsche formally established it, and Heidegger interpreted it. The *seynsgeschichtliche* localization of the "Great Midnight" was theoretically carried out. But does this really mean that it had been reached? This question, which already contains uncertainty and fluctuation, largely explains the paradoxes of the links between the Conservative Revolution and the history of the Third Reich. If the End had come and was interpreted as such, then the transition to *another Beginning* and, in fact, *Ereignis* could and should have come to fruition within the framework of the *seynsgeschichtliche* history of Germany as the center of European thought. Friedrich Hölderlin's prophetic visions and Hegel's philosophical predictions about a "philosopher-people" should have reached their culmination resulting in something great and unprecedented.

At one point it seemed that it was "about to happen," and what was happening was, indeed, that very *other Beginning*. However, in reality, it turned out that the possibility was ephemeral, which means that the point of Midnight had not been reached yet again. "Always this 'not yet," as Heidegger states in the most crucial text, "What Are Poets For?"[1]

---

[1] Martin Heidegger, "What Are Poets For?" in *Poetry, Language, Thought* (New York, Harper Perennial, 2003), 87-140.

The fate of Nazi Germany and Heidegger's witness to it, as well as his personal fate and the fate of his philosophy unequivocally demonstrate that this time around it was still the "not yet," and that the occasional flashes of light were mistaken for the first distant rays of dawn. And because of them, darkness got all the more dark. For this reason, Heidegger's postwar texts are full of courageous despair. That which should have happened in the only place where it could have happened— did not happen. Once again, "has not happened yet." The two ideologies with blunt ontological nihilism at their core— Liberalism and Communism—triumphed not only militarily but also philosophically. The latter's significance is all the more powerful since it was achieved not only from without but also from within, because the political ideologies of the Third Way failed to follow the path of *another Beginning*. Consequently, they lost even prior to the decisive military battle. And so did Germany—split into two parts. So had Europe, being half-USSR and half-U.S., as the two forms of a single evil, infinite in its worthlessness.

At some point, one could detect the sound of despair in Heidegger's voice: *techne* as the fate of the West has entered into the totality of its rights; nuclear weapons are ready to destroy the entire earth—already steeped in nihilism—and turn it into *Nothingness*. No one remembers that the Night approaches because the memory of the light (even that of the twilight and the evening) has been completely erased. Man, in his "inauthenticity," has forgotten about *Being* to such an extent that he no longer understands what that means.

In an interview with *Der Spiegel*, published after his death, Heidegger states, "Only a God can save us."[2] This phrase is quite

---

[2] "Spiegel-Gesprach mit Martin Heidegger am 23. September 1966," *Der Spiegel*, 30. Jg. N 23. 31 (Mai 1976).

telling for a thinker who has always insisted that the purpose of the Last God is not to save anyone: the latter simply arrives and passes by, nodding to those whose vocation it is to "guard Being." Now, the arrival of the Last God is no longer an option. The very possibility of "the future ones" (*Künftige*) to become such has been shut down by the totalitarian planetary power of the past—not the one that *was*, but the one that *passed, is passing*, and *will pass* at the very moment when it comes. This means that there is no one to sing paeans to the arriving God. Ultimately, there is no one left to save.

So where does this "not yet" come from? The answer to this question is tantamount to unravelling the secret *seynsgeschichtliche* rationale for the external and internal defeat of the Third Way as well as the logic of Martin Heidegger's fate.

This "not yet" coupled with expecting *Ereignis* to arrive soon, sensing the breath of *another Beginning* nearby, announcing one's course toward fundamental-ontology—what are these? An imprecisely determined moment in time and place? A mistake in calculations, anticipation, localization, or is it something else altogether?

Man of the Beginning

The way Heidegger poses the question about this "not yet" leaves the impression that *something else is at play*. But what?

We can only guess. It may be that man in his classic status, that is, as a *Westerner*, constructed along the lines of Western European metaphysics, because of his identity, will never be able to approach the point of the Great Midnight face to face. Perhaps, in the sense that man is man (in terms of this metaphysics), he

179

will endlessly circle the labyrinth of this "not yet." Maybe this "not yet" is one of the constituent parts of a human being. In that case, the Great Midnight will never arrive. It will never arrive for *man*, that is. Therefore, it is man that is the reason for this "not yet." And it is not just a matter of his not being ready. Perhaps, his essence is to delay *another Beginning* whenever he feels its breath, closeness, and coming to fruition. But in this case, the problem of this "not yet" is resolved through the final decisive battle between the *man of the End* (which includes subhumans, the Last Men, and even the Superman himself, in the Heideggerian sense, as the greatest embodiment of τεχνη [techne] and the will to power), and an alternate man, a *man of the Beginning*.

Man of the End seeks to be endless. And when, it seems, all that remains for him is to go out as the lights of all *beings* are turned off, in his electronic *Nothingness* of a "provoked life" (as per Gottfried Benn), he manages to multiply the meaningless turns of his absurd return—again and again—with an increasing degree of "planetary idiocy" (Liberalism), which (as we know after the experience of the 1990s in Russia) turned out to be a more advanced stage of nihilism even as compared to the totalitarian mass-metaphysics of Bolshevism.

Man of the End is going to "not be" for eternity, thereby exacerbating his "*non-Being*." We cannot exclude the fact that this "not yet" comprises the final identity of man himself as the one "postponing," "pausing," "delaying." In that case, who is the *man of the Beginning?* Who is he who can turn this almost-midnight into a full-fledged Midnight, pushing the last moment that is frozen, shot up, woven deeply into time, and unwilling to be cut off?

It would be tempting to identify him with Nietzsche's Superman, if it were not for Heidegger's interpretation of this figure.

According to Heidegger, Nietzsche is the fundamental thinker of the End. He even sees the "future ones" as the maximization of the will to power which drives the world. Thus, the Superman, despite all his metaphysical charm, is not suitable for the role of the man of the Beginning. The new man must relate to the old one like a vertical line perpendicular to the horizontal one: for him, all that is human in its trajectory is always that "not yet..."—both in the heroic splendor of this "delay" and in the chafed banality of shallow subhuman cowardice. But this perpendicularity contrasts with the definition of man. If man is that "not yet," then no matter how much he transforms inside his identity, he would continue thrashing about only within the framework of this "still not yet . . ." And if we were to recall the First Beginning and the acuteness of Heraclitean thought, then we will see in it a clearly delineated horizon of that which lies beyond man. This is the *logos* (whose voice is radically different from the voice of the thinker); this is the *daemon*, which is the ἦθος (*ethos*) of man. Heidegger interprets Heraclitus's statement "ἦθος ἀνθρώπῳ δαίμων" (*ethos anthropo daimon*, "ethos is a demon for man") as one referring to the "place" (ἦθος) inhabited by a deity (δαίμον) as man's true center. If anthropos is that "still not yet," then the δαίμων is the "already yes"! We cannot exclude the possibility that the final desperate hope for salvation in Heidegger's later works referred to salvation from "man" as such—toward salvation by "God" (δαίμων) and his "place" (ἦθος) of *beings* in the rays of *Seyn-Being* from the metaphysical infection of the human. For this reason, it is the *man of the Beginning* who is capable of abolishing the lingering *man of the End*, the meaning and essence of which comprise this delay, that will be the "Last God." And in this case, the Last God's passing by will be endowed with dramatic significance: saving *beings* and illuminating the truth of *Seyn-Being*, the "Last God"—in his "most-arrived arrival"—will bypass the raging people of the End, which will indefinitely continue thrashing about in the suffocating nets of this endlessness. Thus, the *man of the new Beginning* could already be here, be already arrived, already passing by, even if the *man of the End* is ignorant of his existence. The most terrifying end for the *man of the End* would be to make this end infinite.

But in that case, fundamental-ontology must be constituted in a certain special, unique direction, without any correlation with anthropology in general, since any kind of anthropology immediately immerses us in the "*not yet.*"

But somebody has already overcome the "*still not yet.*" And Midnight took place in him.

.

X. HEIDEGGER AS A GREAT MILESTONE

Returning to the beginning of this section, we can now understand this thinker's trajectory in a new way, in light of discussing his philosophy, its structure, and eschatological orientation. Heidegger considered himself to be somewhat analogous to a prophet or seer, who, at the most dramatic moment in the history of the West, not only discovers the upcoming resolution, but also foresees the meaning and cause of its source and the significance of the present moment in time. By accepting or not accepting his "prophecy," interpreting it in one way or another, we must always remember that this is a "prophecy" within the framework of Western European philosophy, and only there does it have content, value, and meaning. If we look at it from the outside rather than the standpoint of Western European philosophy, religion, or some other particular school of this philosophy, we would not only miss the acuteness of his message but also its direct and clear meaning. Therefore, understanding Heidegger requires a cardinal and fundamental rethinking of Western European philosophy. If the former understanding thereof was quite approximate (which occurs in Russian philosophy), then we must speak not of rethinking but rather about the responsible and correct understanding for the *first time*. Morever, this kind of rethinking must not occur *prior* to getting acquainted with Heidegger, but rather *simultaneously*, and even *through* this acquaintance.

Today we cannot say what the Russian religious philosophy of the 19th and 20th centuries really was since the *seynsgeschichtliche* succession has been lost. Even less clear to us is the Soviet Marxist philosophy, which for such a long time was everything only to suddenly become nothing (having experienced—in the reverse direction—the fate of a messianic phenomenon on the historical stage of the proletariat). It seems that we could acquire foothold in religion, but a substantial part of religion comprises the kind of thought that is associated with the *logos*, that is, theology. Whether our theology survives in its current complicated and discordant state in the face of philosophical generalizatios and "phenomenological destruction" of Heidegger's thought we can only state after getting acquainted with the latter. Not any time earlier.

For this reason, Heidegger, with his amazing radicalism and dizzying acuteness of his statements and assessments, may become the greatest stimulus for our rethinking the West and ourselves faced *vis-a-vis* the West.

But at the same time, we must avoid the danger of absolutizing Heidegger and accepting each of his statements as the ultimate axiom. Sad is the fate of a seer if he turns into an idol or a graven image. A clairvoyant tells the story of *Being*, life, gods, and the fate of the world, about the present moment and that which was and will be. His words live on and are animated by the life of those who understand them and who ponder through them. And thus through this living understanding, these words and he who expressed them continue to live and, in some cases, only begin truly living. If we manage to understand Heidegger, then we will be able to move in any direction pushing off from this realization. Furthermore, it is absolutely irrelevant which direction this will be—whether we confirm certain key points of his philosophy or discover something else, for instance, something that his philosophy does not contain or even something that contradicts it. He who lives in thought animates those who once thought. We must interpret Heidegger as a *Wegmarke,* a *road sign,* which in Greek sounds like "μέθοδος," a "method." We have the pathway and a sign. What remains is to read it correctly. And then we will be free to do as we please.

PART 2

Das Geviert

I. AN INTRODUCTION TO GEVIERT

The Meaning of the Term "Geviert"

In German, *Geviert* means "quaternion," "four," "quaternity." The image and structure of *Geviert* represent a fundamental moment for Heidegger's thought. By introducing *Geviert*, we will be better equipped to understand the primary structural lines of his philosophy: the distinction between *Seyn* and *Sein*, the *second Beginning, Ereignis,* the chasm between ontology and fundamental-ontology, and so on.

Geviert can be represented symbolically as two intersecting lines resembling St. Andrew's cross.

In some cases, Heidegger himself uses two vertical lines crossed at a 90-degree angle.

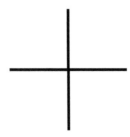

Let us record both possibilities. In the first case, the emphasis is on the relative opposition of the top ends of the cross to the bottom ones; in the second—the placement of vertical opposition onto a horiziontal one.

We must keep in mind that this schematic diagram does not represent a spatial image, but rather the structure of a philosophical and fundamental-ontological topography. This is an image pertaining to *Seyn-Being* and thoughts about its truth. This is not *beings* or a depiction thereof; but, at the same time, this is not a symbol pointing toward something other than itself. Heidegger conceives of *Geviert*, both as a word and a sign, as an expression of a method (in Greek, this literally means "pointing the way") of the fundamental-ontological look at *Seyn-Being* itself through the light of its presence. Therefore, it makes sense to refrain from any hasty comparisons of *Geviert* to everything that is known about the meaning of the cross, the number four, and so on. Any and all analogies will turn out to be misleading and inapplicable, especially at the first stage, when the intensity of Heidegger's thought is not yet clear to us. Any attempt to compare *Geviert* with something already known to us or with what we ourselves think will be fatal. *Geviert* is most likely something that we do not know, have not heard, and have never encountered. Only in this case, the freshness of this phenomenon—of something that never appeared previously—will truly open up to us.

The word *Geviert* and its schematic depiction appear in Heidegger's work in the late 1930s in lecture and book notes for a cycle related to the subjects of *Seynsgeschichte* and *Ereignis*.[1] Later, in the 1950s, he develops them further in the context of interpreting Hölderlin's poetry[2] and studies on the subject of

---

[1] Martin Heidegger, *Beiträge zur Philosophie (vom Ereignis)* (Frankfurt am Main: Vittorio Klostermann, 1989); Idem., *Geschichte des Seyns (1938/1940)* (Frankfurt am Main: Vittorio Klostermann, 1998).
[2] Martin Heidegger, *Erlauterung zur Hölderlin Dichtung. Holderlin und das Wesen der Dichtung* (Frankfurt am Main: Vittorio Klostermann, 1981).

language problems[3]. Heidegger investigates this subject most fully in his highly poetic texts, such as the *The Thing, Building Dwelling Thinking*, and so on, which were included in an anthology called *Lectures and Essays* (1936-1953).[4] It has become customary to consider the problem of *Geviert* as part of Heidegger's late period, being a *leitmotif* of the final part of his later works.

From the point of view of subject periodization in Heidegger's philosophy, one could say that the issue of *Geviert* comprises the culmination of his thoughts of the middle period (1930-1940s) about *Ereignis* and *another Beginning*. At its core, *Geviert* is a flash illuminating the entire structure (*Gefüge*) of Heidegger's philosophy with its final light. This is *Lichtung* (lighting, flooding with light, highlighting) of *Seyn-Being*, which opened up at the peak of thought, focused on *another Beginning*. The introduction of *Geviert* in itself is *Ereignis*.

The Fourfold (Geviert) and Seyn-Being

Heidegger approaches the subject of *Geviert* through deciphering his favorite poet, Hölderlin. The philosophical interpretation of the latter's hymns brings Heidegger to the construction of a special kind of envisioning *beings* through *Seyn-Being*.

Geviert opens opens up for Heidegger as a *structure* (*Gefüge*) of *Seyn-Being* in its pure form. *Being is fourfold*. This Fourfold always exists as such and only as such. In other words, nothing can be removed from it or added to it.

Heidegger introduces *Geviert* in order to replace Hegel's trinitarian dialectic. If Hegel spoke of thesis-antithesis-synthesis,

---

3 Martin Heidegger, *Unterwegs zur Sprache (1950–59)* (Frankfurt am Main: Vittorio Klostermann, 1985).
4 Martin Heidegger, *Vorträge und Aufsätze (1936–53)* (Frankfurt am Main: Vittorio Klostermann, 2000).

then Heidegger stated, *"not three, but four."*[5] Morever, he speaks of *all four simultaneously.* In a certain sense, addressing the four was a critical step in terms of the Christian triplicity. But let us note immediately that Heidegger viewed Christianity as a model of Western Christian theology and was exclusively interested in the philosophical significance of triplicity: the way in which this principle was included in the explanation of *beings' structure* and the organization of *ontology.* For this reason, Hegel's triad was more important to him than the Christian dogma.

Triplicity expresses the topography of the old metaphysics and Platonic ontology, where *Sein-Being* takes the place of

---

[5] Here we can use the example from a completely different field. However, we must also keep in mind that there are no direct parallels between Heidegger's philosophy and the subject that we are about to address. The following example skips over the most complex work that was not really carried out—of comparing the philosophies of two major 20th-century figures—Heidegger and Jung. Carl Gustav Jung paid great attention to the symbolic meaning of the numbers 3 and 4. He relied on the hermetic text of Maria Prophetissa who alchemically interpreted the structure of the Pythagorean tetractys $1 + 2 + 3 + 4 = 10$ (i.e., 1 again since the Pythagorean $10 = 1$). In this formula, Jung singled out the first three numbers, which, in his interpretation, are linked with rationality, the "ego," and transcendence, and which constitute the triad; he correlated the fourth number—4—with nature and the collective unconscious. Jung believed that 3 (the triad and the trinitarian principle) refers to Christianity (as a rational transcendentalist kind of theology), and 4—to paganism. The greatest distinction, according to Jung, was the fact that the pagan quaternity included the principle of evil (the devil, shadows), which is completely excluded from the light of triplicity. This is how Jung interpreted the disputes among the students of Paracelsus (in particular, Adam von Bodenstein and Gerhard Dorn) with respect to certain aspects of his teachings, especially in the debate with critics from the Church. Despite the fact that Jung's psychoanalytic reconstructions and hermetic reasoning belong to a completely different level of philosophizing than that of Heidegger, there are certain similarities since, evidently, Heidegger implicitly contrasted the quaternity with triplicity in the spirit of his "Greek," "Hellenic," and, in a certain way, "pagan" approach. See: Carl Jung, "Paracelsus as a Spiritual Phenomenon" in *Memories, Dreams, Reflections* (New York: Vintage, 1989); Carl Jung, *The Spirit Mercury* (New York: Analytical Psychology Club of New York, 1942); Carl Jung, *Arkhetip i simvol* (Moscow: Renessans, 1991).

Seyn-Being as the *essence of beings*, as *beings-as-a-whole*. This trinitary topography contains the referential theory of truth always seeking to trace the relationship of the knower to a third party, which comprises the basis of metaphysics. *Fundamental-ontology* must treat the *ontic field of beings* and the thinking man standing amidst it (the first level of distancing) in another way, avoiding the trap of the trinitary principle, the meaning of which is the domination of τεχνη (*techne*). The latter is ultimately expressed in contemporary Western European nihilism—the final embodiment of triplicity. *Geviert* is both the instrument of "phenomenological destruction" (deconstruction) of the old metaphysics and the triumphant result of its realization.

Seyn-Being, having found itself, illuminating itself (*Lichtung*), letting itself be known, *opens itself up through Geviert*, through the Fourfold. *Being* is never *alone*; it is not monistic (but neither is it threefold or twofold). It expresses itself as the totality of *four*, but at the same time *no one element of this Fourfold ever acts alone*. *Seyn-Being* and *Geviert* are almost the same thing, because where *Being* does not generate (pro-duce [*duco*, Latin, "to lead"]—φύειν [*phyein*], Ed.) *beings*—we cannot speak of *Being*; where it produces *beings*, it is necessarily *pre-sent*, but never fully and is always simultaneously *absent* in its presence. At the same time, always and under any circumstances, *Seyn-Being* lets itself be known (without letting itself be known, hiding itself) in the *Fourfold*.

We cannot conceive of *Seyn-Being* in some other way, coming at it "from the other end." One of the most erroneous positions in regard to *Being* was thinking about it from the standpoint of *beings*. When it comes to this approach, no matter how far we move away from *beings*, sooner or later, we are bound to project them toward the abyss, the terror of which will only increase as the distance from *beings* grows. Instead of flying, we will create a shore, a stop, solid ground, hardness. We will not acquire the experience of the sky and will certainly start thinking of an "earth of the sky" or a "sky of the earth." Therefore, it is *not a gaze at Being* from the standpoint of *beings*, but rather—at *beings* from the standpoint of *Being* that will be a *fundamental-ontological* act. This gaze in its concreteness and radical overturning of all proportions is *Geviert*.

In the moment when we envision *Seyn-Being* correctly—through the light of its own truth, through its existence in the terror of absolute loneliness, at the outmost distance from all *beings*, in the experience of the abyss—it is then that we will encounter the entire *Fourfold* simultaneously, it is then that it reveals itself to us.

It is extremely important to understand in advance that *Geviert* does not amount to an ontic perception of the world, and that it would be erroneous to conclude the latter by contrasting the *Fourfold* with the trinitarian ontological topography, although there is some truth to this observation. But ontic thought, direct analogies of which we can actually see in the *Fourfold*, does not know anything about *Being*, nor does it entertain this question in the first place. It is dissolved in the *Fourfold*, but does not know about it. It flows out from the *Fourfold*, but fails to grasp it in the living moment of this fundamental event. It does not suspect that *Geviert* is *Geviert*; it does not call it by name or express its *Being*. Therefore, it, being located in *Geviert*, is lost in it, dissolved in it, is not in it, does not exist (in essence— *west da nicht*). Therefore, the discussion of *Geviert* pertains to *fundamental-ontology*, not ontics or the old ontology. This discussion occurs in the register of *another Beginning*, and it can only be carried out in the case if we, in one way or another, follow

196

Heidegger and the main stages of his review of *Seynsgeschichte*, another Beginning, and focus on *Ereignis*.

Geviert is given to us like an open window to the abyss, i.e., as the greatest gift, and it is assumed that we will value it accordingly.

The Contents of the Fourfold (Geviert)

The *Fourfold* is the *Sky* (Himmel), *gods* or *God* (the divine in general), (mortal) *man*, and the *Earth*. These *four* figures, four realms of the World, comprising *Geviert*, remained unchanged for Heidegger. However, until the 1950s, instead of talking about the *Sky* (*Himmel*), Heidegger discussed the *World* (*Welt*), equating the "world" with the "sky." Later, he began to speak about the sky, specifically. Nonetheless, let us keep in mind the interchangeability of the *Sky* and the *World* in the *Fourfold*. The Sky and the World express an open order.

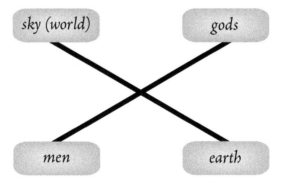

Pre-Socratics used the word "cosmos" to define the world, which did not mean the "world" in our current usage but rather "order," "harmony," "organization." Cosmos is an order or a beautiful order, that is, something organized into a perfect formation. The ancients also used a synonymous concept *ουράνιος* (*ouranious*, celestial), *ούρανός* (*ouranos*, sky), because they considered the sky to be the source of order, the essence of order, and the world as such. They equated the world and the sky. It is for this reason that Plato placed his ideas into the sky. This inner identification of the sky with the world is crucial for understanding *Geviert*. Later on, Heidegger states that *die Welt* (world) is *Geviert*, but at the same time, he represents the sky on its own as an independent element of *Geviert*.

War in the Fourfold (Geviert)

Heidegger sees the source of *Geviert* in Heraclitus's formula about *war as the father of all things*. Heraclitus stated, "War is both father and king of all, some he has shown forth as gods and others as men, some he has made slaves and others free."[6] He also wrote, "We must know that war (*πόλεμος* [*polemos*]) is common to all, and strife is justice, and that all things come into *Being* through strife necessarily."[7]

For Heidegger, *Being* as war, Heraclitean *πόλεμος* (*polemos*) as the "father of things," is the form of *Being* in the genetic sense (*Being* from the standpoint of origin). Thus, the fundamentally *fourfold beings* outstretched in front of us, above us, and around us are created through the *pressure of war*, present in every point, in every segment of *Geviert*. We are none other than a *product of war*, because war *separated* us from gods and made us into men; on the other hand, it is war that *connected* us to gods, put us on earth, and covered us with the sky.

---

[6] *Fragmenty rannikh grecheskikh filosofov* (Moscow: Nauka, 1989), 202; see also Daniel W. Graham (ed., tr.), *The Texts of Early Greek Philosophy: The Complete Fragments and Selected Testimonies of the Major Presocratics* (Cambridge: Cambridge University Press, 2010).

[7] *Ibid.*, 201.

War—πόλεμος—is the name of *Being* as *Seyn*. According to Heidegger, herein lies the actual depth of fundamental-ontology as such. The roots of understanding *Being* as *war* trace back to the problem of *Nothingness*. Heidegger defines *Nothingness* in the structure of fundamental-ontology as the "*nihilation in Seyn-Being*" (*das Nichten im Seyn*). It is deeply erroneous to assume that *Seyn-Being is*, and always is something immutable and eternal. *Seyn-Being comes to fruition* (*sich er-eignet*), it is always fresh, always at risk, and never a given. Furthermore, in order to break the illusion of guaranteeing its unchanging existence, it turns to *beings* and man with its "*nihilating*" side. Thus, it proves the mortality of the mortal, the finitude of the finite, and the uniqueness of itself as an event (*Ereignis*). *Being* makes itself felt not in peace but in war, precisely because it simultaneously introduces a "yes" and a "no." Here, we can recall Heraclitus once again, who claimed, "Homer, praying that 'Discord be damned from gods and men,' forgot that he called down curses on the origin of all things."[8] Separating "*Nothingness*" as "nihilation" from *Seyn-Being*, we lose it in itself, because we deprive it of the opportunity to occur and, therefore, *beings* to be born in battle and for battle. Having turned *Being* into *beings-as-a-whole*, we lose its creative power to transform *beings* into *non-beings* in order to bring *non-beings* to *beings* and, consequently, we substitute it with something else. *Geviert* is specifically *Seyn-Being*, which, occurring in *Ereignis*, brings war into everything, establishing tension of the great axes of the world. The world is war.[9]

---

8 *Ibid.*, 202.

9 The Russian word "*мир*" (*mir*) as a "universe" can be traced back to the ancient Slavic conception about three phenomena, which developed from the same roots but later received distinct interpretations. "*Mir*" as a community, "*mir*" as non-war and peaceful existence, and "*mir*" as a universe. Prior to the 20th-century reforms of the Russian language, the word "*миръ*" (*mir*, non-war) and "*мiръ*" (*mir*, the universe) were distinct, but in the old Slavonic language, they were written in the same way as in the contemporary Russian language (even though in contemporary Russian, these are interpreted as homonyms, i.e., words that sound, and are written in the same way, but that designate different things). The German word *Welt* most likely comprises two stems, "*wer*" and "*alt*," which, according to one of the etymologies,

The Sky

The Sky is that which establishes order, that which makes any and every thing what it is. It highlights, determines, organizes, supplies the world and parts of the world, as well as *beings* with that which Heidegger calls "*dignity*" (*Würde*), ἄξιος (*axios*). It makes a thing valuable precisely because it is that *very thing*, and it determines its inner worth secretly and mysteriously. These are ordered *beings, beings-as-a-whole*.

The Sky opens itself up and unfolds, thereby opening and unfolding things. It divides and endows. The Sky is the world in its openness. This is the face of the world facing itself and those who look at the world. A gaze toward the world is a gaze toward the Sky and the Sky's gaze toward itself. The Sky is the domain of light that highlights, enlightens, opens up.

The Sky is fundamentally open. It has no limits or boundaries in itself. So the Sky is not an essence, an object, a phenomenon, but rather the orientation, an area, the boundless edge of the sacred geography of *Being*.

The Sky and the World

We stated above that, for Heidegger, the Sky serves as a fundamental-ontological synonym for the world (*die Welt*).[10]

---

pertains to the idea of antiquity, eternity, strength, and seniority. In terms of meaning, this could be close to the old Slavonic "*род*" (*rod*) and the Sanskrit word "*rita*"—"eternal immutable order." For this reason, the Russian word "*мир*" carries an entire chain of meanings different from the German "*Welt*" and the Greek "*κοσμοσ*" (*kosmos*).

[10] The old Russian language contained two words that designated the world—"*свет*" (*svet*, light) and "*мир*" (*mir*, world). It is interesting to note that the term "*world*" pertained to the glance from the standpoint of the earth, whereas "*svet*"—to that of the sky, κοσμος (*kosmos*), ουρανος (*ouranos*, heaven). It is the old Russian word "*свет—белый свет*" (*belyi svet*, white world) that corresponds to the German "*Welt*" and Latin "*mundus*."

The World and the Sky express something close and almost identical, hence their interchangeability in *Geviert*.

The *World* (as the light and the Sky), according to Heidegger, is an expression of openness (*Offene*)—herein lies its main attribute. The *World* opens up and illuminates, making things clear and uncovered. At the same time, *beings*, becoming the World, establish themselves in the World, receive the stamp of orderliness; each thing gains its own attributes and places.

Heidegger writes,

> At the same time, as the World opens itself up, all things obtain their delay and acceleration, their distance and nearness, their vastness and its narrowness.[11]

The World is that which opens up the pathways. It is extremely important to note that Heidegger understands the World (and, consequently, the Sky) as something that is profoundly connected with a people (*Volk*). The World is comprised of peoples, and so is the Sky. Outside of a people and its language and art, the World loses itself, scatters about, and ceases to be the World. Conversely, the openness of the World is directly conencted to opening the pathways for the people.

"The world is an opening openness of vast pathways, simple and meaningful (*wesentliche*) decisions in destiny (*Geschick*) for a historic (*geschichtliche*) people."[12] The people at their core are the ones who make the decision, where a decision is made, and how it is made. The people are a place for decision-making. The people's ways in history express their

---

11 Martin Heidegger, "Der Ursprung der Kunstwerkes" in *Holzwege* (Frankfurt am Main: Vittorio Klostermann, 1994), 31; here, translated from the Russian.

12 *Ibid.*, 35.

attitude toward the World and the Sky manifested through fateful decisions.

It is important to note that we are talking about a people (*Volk*), specifically, not man (on an individual basis). This is due to the role that Heidegger assigns to speech. Speech is the existence of *Seyn-Being* manifesting through man. But speech is always based on language. And it is language that differentiates non-man from man and one people from another. The differences between peoples and languages comprise the wealth of *Seyn-Being*. For this reason, the people, along with language receive a certain angle of viewing the World and the Sky. It is this gaze that is language. Therefore, the World opens up to the people in language, and through language the people make the decision that will be their destiny. It is not man that makes this decision, but the people. And this decision is always connected to language. The World, as *openness*, acts as the possibility and necessity for this decision. The World's openness is reflected in the decision of the people.

"The world is the illumination of roads that point to meaning (*wesentliche Weisung*), in which all decisions are structured."[13] The decision (through speech) welcomes a people, but the world dictates (points to) the structure of this decision.

The Earth

The Earth in Heidegger is that which leads everything to presence (*Anwesen*). Thanks to the Earth, many things, objects, sensations become present, actual. The Earth is that on which one *stands*, and is, therefore, real. The Earth makes *beings* real. Thanks to the Sky, things are what they are, but because of the earth, they are real, they lie before the world, they are stretched, they are present.

---

13 *Ibid.*, 42.

The most important attribute of the Earth, according to Heidegger, is its being closed and sealed. The Sky and the World open up; they exist as the open and the opening. The Earth conceals, covers, locks, hides. But at the same time, it preserves. In the initial fundamental-ontological act of *Seyn-Being*, openness is adjacent and alternates with non-openness, closedness.

Earlier we stated that Heidegger correlated the World with the people (*Volk*). Less explicitly, he linked the people and the Earth. The latter can only be derived based on his indirect observations. At one point, discussing the fundamental-ontological significance of the war between the Germans and Russians[14], Heidegger wrote,

> Every World opens itself and remains paired up with the Earth. Every World and every Earth—the significance, as a whole, lies in their mutual belonging to each other—this is a historical (*geschichtliche*) phenomenon. (. . .) The Earth of the future lies fallow in a not-yet-freed-for-itself Russianness. History (*Geschichte*) of the World (*Welt*) has been layered upon the self-awareness (*Besinnung*) of the Germans.[15]

It is important to note that Heidegger connects the *World* (*Welt*) and the *Earth* with a people and peoples. In a way, this is somewhat reminiscent of the theory by the ancient Greek pre-Socratic philosopher Xenophanes of Colophon, who believed that in different regions of the universe there are distinct skies and earths, similar to each other but different nonetheless. Heidegger explains this hypothesis through language as the core

---

14 This is a reference to World War II, which Heidegger conceptualized as the German nature in opposition not so much to the Russian counterpart, but rather to the Bolshevik, Communist kind—as an extreme expression of Western European metaphysics in the form of *Machenschaft*.

15 Martin Heidegger, *Geschichte des Seyns (1938/1940)* (Frankfurt am Main: Vittorio Klostermann, 1998),108; here, translated from the Russian.

MARTIN HEIDEGGER: The Philosophy of Another Beginning

of what is human. Heidegger himself considers the difference in languages and dialects a consequence of the diverse geographical landscapes reflected in speech. But since language is a way for *Seyn-Being* to exist, then the people (*Volk*) with their Earth and their Sky (world) always represent a unique attitude to *Seyn-Being*. It is the people, not a single individual (the subject), that is relevant, since language is entrusted to the people as a whole.

In Germans, Heidegger sees the beginning of the open pathways, self-awareness, the World, the Sky. In Russians, he foresees the essence of the Earth, as one of preserving closedness, the keeper of the future. The battle between Russians and Germans becomes one of cosmogonic dimensions, which establishes a new Sky and a new Earth—the German Sky and the Russian Earth.

Uranogeomachy

Between the Sky and the Earth there is tension, an axis of war. The Universe is constructed along this axis.

The Sky and the Earth are opposite in everything. The Earth, unlike the Sky, is always closed; it turns its back toward the world, and its face is hidden. No one knows what the latter looks like, and whether it has a face at all. The Sky has no end inward and upward, the Earth is infinite in its breadth. But at the same time, the battle of the Sky (World) and the Earth is not a clash between two rigidly and strictly separated entities.

The World (Sky) and the Earth are essentially different from each other, but are never separated from each other. The World is based upon the Earth, and the Earth rises up through the World. But the relationship between the World and the Earth does not fade in the empty unity of contentless opposition.

The world in its quietus on the Earth seeks to raise, elevate it. The World, being self-opening, cannot handle being closed. The Earth, as the keeper of all, is inclined toward absorbing the World and keeping it in itself.

The confrontation between the World and the Earth is a real war, a battle.[16]

This war—uranogeomachy (or cosmogeomachy)—opens its "is" for each side, its relationship with *Seyn-Being*, which is the same for both, but treats each of the two differently. In the Sky (World), *Seyn-Being* expresses itself as lighting, openness, unconcealment. This is ἀλήθεια (*aletheia*), the truth of *Being*'s unconcealment in *beings* and through *beings*, through a designated spot in the middle, where *Being* makes itself known through *openness* The Earth opens up another side of *Seyn-Being*—the "nihilating," concealing, but at the same time keeping, preserving, closing, and harboring side. In its relation to *Seyn-Being*, the Earth is bottomless, it is the *Abgrund*. Xenophanes of Colophon, according to certain ancient authors, taught that the Earth is the principal source of all and that its roots go all the way to the abyss, eternally falling into their bottomlessness.

Uranogeomachy is a natural and the only expression of *Seyn-Being* through *beings*, in *beings*, through *beings*, and against *beings*. In this war between the Sky and the Earth, where everyone, fighting, returns to his nature and begins to authentically be, an even more profound process occcurs—the *war between Seyn-Being against beings, which makes Seyn-Being and beings them themselves.*

---

16 Martin Heidegger, "*Der Ursprung der Kunstwerkes*" in *Holzwege* (Frankfurt am Main: Vittorio Klostermann, 1994),35.

Gods of the Beginning

The *Divine* (*gods*) and men are the poles of the second axis. Heidegger uses the words "god", "God" very carefully, although in later works he increasingly speaks of the "divine", "divinity," and the "divine ones." These essences are fundamentally necessary for *Geviert*, but Heidegger avoids giving them a clear and precise definition.

If man as a thinking entity is always present in *Geviert*, and his presence is unquestionable, then it is customary for gods to escape.[17] In fact, the *divine ones hide even when they show themselves.*

The "divine ones" are a special kind of *beings* (and, at the same time, *Being*), which is extremely *light* and *subtle*, and whose function is exceedingly non-utilitarian. It is as if the "divine ones" "tickle" the world, without adding any heavy fundamental elements to it, teach people nothing (stealing fire and establishing crafts are up to the titans and tricksters). Instead, the "divine ones" give *Geviert*, the entire Fourfold, a certain kind of *transparent intoxication.*[18] Divine presence, even traces of deities, introduce the Fourfold of unfolded things, objects, states, and thoughts, giving them a discreet internal current.

It is the relationship to *Seyn-Being* that, first and foremost, separates gods and men. Perhaps, this is one of the most difficult aspects of Heidegger's philosophy. He asserts, "The gods need *Seyn-Being*."

---

[17] Fleeing gods are a consistent subject in Heidegger's metaphysics. In some of his statements, he makes it clear that the willingness and ability to escape from the human presence is a basic property of divinity. Man with his familiar metaphysical attributes—in particular by continually emitting the *Gestell*—always scares the divine away, drives it away, and does not allow the divine light to quietly shine at the center of the Quaternion.

[18] *Lucida ebbrezza.* This was discussed, in particular, by Julius Evola, see *Ride the Tiger* (Rochester: Inner Traditions, 2003).

Further, he writes,

> *Being* does not stand "above" the gods, but neither do they stand "above" *Being*. Yet gods use *Being*, and *Seyn-Being* is conceptualized in this statement. Gods need *Seyn-Being* in order to belong to themselves through it, even though it does not belong to them. *Seyn-Being* is that which the gods require; it is their necessity, their need; they lack it.[19]

Then Heidegger specifies the relationship between gods and philosophy,

> Since *Seyn-Being* is gods' need and, at the same time, it is found only in thinking over one's own truth, and this pondering, in turn, is none other than philosophy (of another Beginning), then gods require *seynsgeschichtliche* thought, i.e., philosophy. Gods do not need philosophy as if they planned to philosophize on the subject of their deification, but philosophy must occur (be, become, *sein*), if (*wenn*) gods must, once again, enter the element of the *decision* and obtain—for *Geschichte* (history as fate)—the basis for its meaning. *Seynsgeschichtliche* thought as the thought of *Seyn-Being* will be predetermined by gods.[20]

It is important to note that Heidegger conceptualizes "*gods*" outside of any particular religion. A god of religion, he argues, is nothing but a name inside metaphysical topography, where *beings* are placed in the place of *Being* as the greatest *beings*, highest *beings*, the original *beings*. So the gods of religion are powerless and die when metaphysics collapses into contemporary nihilism. These are gods in the name only and in the structures of false thought. The only kind of divinity that is worthy of itself and

---

[19] Martin Heidegger, *Beiträge zur Philosophie (vom Ereignis)* (Frankfurt am Main: Vittorio Klostermann, 1989), 438; here, translated from the Russian.
[20] *Ibid.*, 439; here, translated from the Russian.

of gods themselves—and within the limits of one God (if gods themselves decide that among them there is only one that is truly God)—is the the kind of *divinity that is linked to Seyn-Being*, not various versions of "Platonism for the masses." If this kind of divinity is possible, then only at the ecstatic horizon of fundamental-ontology, balancing on the verge of the truth of *Seyn-Being* as the core of *Seyn-Being*.

We can say that Heidegger's gods are the gods of fundamental-ontology and are intimately connected to it, with its possibility, with another Beginning. This is why Heidegger conceives of the Last God as the "god of the Beginning."

Heidegger's gods have another important attribute. These are the gods who *are not* (*sind nicht*), in the sense that they are not *beings* (*Seiende*). They are removed from *beings* by the greatest distance. These gods *are not*. But the fact that they are not makes them truly alive and sacred. With their "not," they constitute the sacred (*Heilige*) dimension. In contrast to the old ontology, which conceived of *Being* as the *greatest kind of beings* out of all *beings*, and in contrast to apophatic philosophy, which conceived *Being* as Nothingness, *non-beings*, and even more *non-beings* than gods, fundamental-ontology places *Seyn-Being* and its "*in between*" truth *between* gods and *beings*.[21]

From a certain angle, *Seyn-Being* itself can be conceived from the standpoint of the gods. In this case, "*Seyn-Being* is the trembling of gods (the echo of gods' decision regarding their God)."[22]

But at the same time, gods are neither an abstraction, nor a metaphor, nor an artificial construct of an atheistic consciousness. Atheism for Heidegger is as metaphysical as is theism or deism.

---

[21] *Ibid.*, 244.
[22] *Ibid.*, 239.

Gods of the Beginning are the direction of philosophical geography of that world, which manifests itself in the *event* (*Ereignis*), in an instant flash of light (*Lichtung*) of *Being*'s truth. Gods and men belong to the same axis, establishing opposite directions. Gods are those who need *Seyn-Being*, for whom it is home and hearth. Men are those whom *Seyn-Being* needs, in order for them to guard the truth. This dual need of *Seyn-Being* and in *Seyn-Being* constitutes, in relation to itself, the "gods-men" pair. Indifferent gods, subtle and light, and sorrowful, poor men, ripped out of all *beings* by the flash of *Seyn-Being* and thrown into the abyss of the Sky.

The Men of Geviert

We can imagine *Geviert* as the geography of another Beginning, the schematic diagram of the fundamental-ontological topography. Therefore, even men whom Heidegger prefers to call "Mortals" in *Geviert* are men of another Beginning, men as "guardians of *Seyn-Being*'s truth" (*Wächter der Wahrheit des Seyns*) based on their main attribute, "Being-towards-death". These are the men of a new fundamental-ontological humanism.

It is very important to note that they do not stand at the center of *Geviert*, but at one of its ends. Man, even one facing his truth like the truth of *Seyn-Being*, is only one of the dimensions of *Seyn-Being*'s spark along with others. Yet even man's neighbors in *Geviert* are fundamental—gods, the Sky, and the Earth. Man, as the guardian of *Seyn-Being*'s truth, is comparable to them, but in no way is something unique among them. He is different from them like they are different from each other, but, at the same time, he is unthinkable without them, unimaginable; he is not without the other three.

Man of *Geviert*, explains Heidegger, is in no way a "subject" or an "object" of history; he is not a "rational animal." Furthermore,

209

he is not defined through belonging to a human essence, since he, out of all *beings*, lacks this essence. In place of this essence, which would have served as the basis for anthropology, founded on the principles of the old metaphysics, there is a chasm, a hole, a window into the abyss. This abyss, which distantly lets itself be known through death, terror, extreme forms of risk, the feeling of abandonment (like falling) is the form of *Seyn-Being*'s own expression, which announces itself as something that does not correspond to *beings* and even the greatest kind of *beings*. "Man is cast in a free throw into unfamiliarity and never again returns from the abyss remaining in the unfamiliar next to *Seyn-Being*."[23]

Man does not have an essence, and his core (*Wesen*) does not belong to him, but to *Being*'s need to possess a guardian. *Seyn-Being* constitutes a fundamental-ontological place for a guardian next to itself, and he who occupies that place becomes man. Taking this place, man as a guardian of *Seyn-Being* remains in the structure of *Geviert*. *Beings* open up to him, as something unfamiliar, as part of an event-opportunity from the standpoint of *Seyn-Being*'s proximity, even though as one of *beings*, man was at home among them. Settling next to *Being*, he becomes a guest among *beings*, in exile, he finds himself "thrown" into *beings*. Only this kind of man is truly "mortal," since his *Being* is "Being-toward-death."

Wars between Gods and Men

The divine and the mortal, men and gods, reside, according to Heidegger, within the framework of *Geviert* in a continuous *encounter* (*Entgegnung*), that is to say, in an encounter in every sense of the word: they *collide* as opponents and *encounter* each other as creatures located on the same axis. It is possible to

---

[23] *Ibid.*, 492.

collide as two enemies, or meet each other as two neighbors in a grove or near a creek. And in this encounter, it is gods that *escape* more frequently, and only the most subtle of all mortals—poets and sages—escape from them, sensing the presence of a deity, thereby honoring its subtle nature and allowing gods to go where they want, so that the earth and the world could be filled with this subtle light of the *sacred* (*Heilige*).

These and many other meanings are part of the term *Entgegnung*— the *collision* between men and gods. War, as the father of things, according to Heraclitus, separates men from gods, puts them on opposide sides and makes them non-identical. On the opposite sides of what? On the opposite sides of *Seyn-Being*, which remains *"in between."*

This *non-equivalence,* this constant and principal distinction *constitutes them both.* This is the most accurate and precise understanding of what divinity and humanity are. Men become men and gods—gods through the expression of their nature in comparison (*Bezug*) to *Seyn-Being*. War (*Streit,* πόλεμος) is the name of *Seyn-Being* when it constitutes *Geviert* as the intersection of the fundamental-ontological power lines. Through the *event's* explosion (*Ereignis*), *Seyn-Being* casts men and gods, the Sky and the Earth, into different points of the philosophical geography, thereby creating four regions, each of which contains a vibrating impulse which has brought them into presence and takes it to the source (*Seyn-Being* as war).

As a rule, men treat divinity in an *excessively rational, utilitarian,* and "technical" way even in their greatest theologies and theosophies. The gods of religion turn into mechanisms of punishment and forgiveness, salvation and damnation. They become "human, all too human," revealing the fact that they had been replaced. These gods do not struggle against men—nor men against gods—for one reason: they are not, they are constructed through being torn away from *Seyn-Being*. Therefore, skillfull techniques of clever men are capable of forcing them to do everything that men desire. These gods are tamed gods, *dei ex machina*.

True gods stand apart from men on the other side of *Seyn-Being* and observe men through the light of war. This does not mean that they are aggressive. It means that they are gods.

The ancient Greeks intuitively grasped the nature of deities better than people in conventional organized religions: in gods, they saw a *game*. But games and wars share their source: war is a game, and a game is always a war.[24] A presence was similar to a subtle dawning, intuition. The *divine* almost imperceptibly comes over and steps on man, attacks, falls on him, softly extracting him from the roughness of the everyday. This divine attack exposes the place for a *daimon* (Heraclitean *logos*) in man. Man's counterattack may drive a god away from his chosen place or hold him captive (the appropriation of the divine spark as the soul, consciousness, the humanization of the divine *logos* as one's own rational mind). Man wins the war (note "beating" one at war, for instance, that is, he "plays") only when gods are victorious, conquer man, and hold him captive. Then and only then does the following truth come into its own right, "ἦθος ἀνθρώπῳ δαίμων (*ethos anthropo daimon*)," that is δαίμων (*daimon*) becomes ἦθος ἀνθρώ (*ethos anthropo*).

The *Bible* consecutively mentions—in the story of the prophet Elijah, when the Lord appeared to him—that the Lord was not in the fire, the wind, the earthquake, the rocks, but very subtly,

---

[24] Johan Huizinga, *Homo Ludens* (London: Routledge & Kegan Paul, 1949); Eugen Fink, *Spiel als Weltsymbol* (Stuttgart: Kohlhammer, 1960).

in the "gentle blowing," almost silent and imperceptible.[25] This Biblical description of a "gentle blowing" contains a very perceptive understanding of a deity. This is the element of the divine. The essence of divinity is that it almost is not, and that it stands at the opposite pole from *beings in all its clarity*, concreteness, tangibility, and grandeur. *Beings*, despite all their scale, do not contain God. And Heidegger constantly emphasizes, "You can go through all *beings*, but you won't find a trace of God."[26]

"We Think of the Other Three"

In his fundamental, albeit brief, 1951 article, *Building Dwelling Thinking*[27], Heidegger defines *Geviert*[28] as follows, "The *Earth* is the serving bearer, blossoming and fruiting, spreading out in rock and water, rising up into plant and animal. When we say *"earth,"* we are already thinking of the other *three* along with it, but we give no thought to the simple oneness of the four."[29]

Using the same poetic rhythm, Heidegger describes the Sky, "The sky is the vaulting path of the sun, the course of the changing, moon, the wandering glitter of the stars, the year's seasons and their changes, the light and dusk of day, the gloom and glow of night, the clemency and inclemency of the weather, the drifting clouds and blue depth of the ether. When we say sky, we are

---

[25] *The Bible*, Old Testament, 3 Kings 19:12.

[26] Martin Heidegger, *Geschichte des Seyns (1938/1940)* (Frankfurt am Main: Vittorio Klostermann, 1998), 211.

[27] Martin Heidegger, *Vortrage und Aufsatze* (Stuttgart: Klett-Cotta, 2004).

[28] Dugin's translation here and further on (*Ed.*).

[29] Martin Heidegger, *Vortrage und Aufsatze* (Stuttgart: Klett-Cotta, 2004), 143; also see Martin Heidegger, "Building Dwelling Thinking," from *Poetry, Language, Thought*, tr. Albert Hofstadter (New York: Harper Colophon Books, 1971), 141-160.

already thinking of the other three along with it, but we give no thought to the simple oneness of the four."[30]

Now let us have a look at the way in which Heidegger defines the divine ones: "The divine ones are the beckoning messengers of the godhead. Out of the holy sway of the Deity, the God appears in his presence or withdraws into his concealment. When we speak of the Divine ones, we are already thinking of the other three along with them, but we give no thought to the simple oneness of the four."[31]   Note, in particular, "Out of the holy sway of the Deity, the God *appears* in his presence or *withdraws* into his concealment," and "out of the holy sway withdraws and appears." From the standpoint of *Seynsgeschichte*, this is always the *same* movement, difference and unity, opening and concealing, appearance and withdrawal, presence and absence. In *Seynsgeschichte*, these things are not opposed to each other. Herein lies the core of *Seyn-Being*: opening is not an antithesis of concealing and vice versa—otherwise, we are trapped by the old metaphysics, where *Being* is equated to *beings* (which are certain and always are), whereas *non-Being* strictly is not. Divinity is not exclusive: we cannot say that it is (obvious), or that it is not (concealed); it is both simultaneously.

When we say "*Geviert*," we must also mention all others, regardless of where we began this incancation. And finally we reach ourselves, the Mortals, *die Sterblichen*, "The Mortals are the human *beings*. They are called Mortals because they can die. To die means to be capable of death *as* death."[32] Everyone dies (others, not men), but in dying they (others, not men) cannot die, because they will never be able to master death as death. Death is given to men for their personal use; death is what makes men

---

[30] *Ibid.*,144; see also Martin Heidegger, "Building Dwelling Thinking," in *Poetry, Language, Thought*, tr. Albert Hofstadter (New York: Harper Colophon Books, 1971), 141-160.
[31] *Ibid.*
[32] *Ibid.*

214

men, death is *Being-in-death* and *Being-toward-death*—the fact of a presence or annihilation does not add anything to death; it has nothing to do with death. Death, conceived ontologically, fundamental-ontologically, is the same thing as life. "Only man dies, and indeed gradually, as long as he remains on Earth, under the Sky, before the Divine ones. When we speak of Mortals, we are already thinking of the other three along with them, but we give no thought to the simple oneness of the four."[33]

Further, "The Mortals live saving the Earth. Leaving it for itself."[34]

Mortals live perceiving the Sky as the Sky. They allow the celestial bodies to take their course; they do not try to make bad weather good and vice versa; they do not turn day into night and night into day.

Mortals live to the extent that they wait for the Divine ones as such. Hopeful, Mortals offer to them that which was unfulfilled. They expect a hint about their imminent arrival and do not confuse the signs of their absence with anything. They do not make gods unto themselves or replace them with idols. In suffering and misery they foresee Salvation."[35]

If the Fourfold (*Geviert*) cannot be conceived in a one-sided way, if only one part of the Fourfold (*Geviert*) cannot be imagined separately, then any mention of the Earth, Sky, Gods, and Men automatically calls for the presence (specifically, "*prae-esse*," "tearing away from the essence," and "submerging into essence") of all others.

Heidegger also states,

---

[33] *Ibid.*
[34] *Ibid.*
[35] *Ibid.*

215

Mortals dwell in that they initiate their own nature—their being capable of death as death—into the use and practice of this capacity, so that there may be a good death. To initiate Mortals into the nature of death in no way means to make death, as empty Nothing, the goal. Nor does it mean to darken dwelling by blindly staring toward the end. In saving the Earth, in perceiving the Sky, in awaiting the Divine ones, in initiating Mortals, dwelling occurs as the fourfold preservation of the Fourfold (*Geviert*).[36]

Crossing out Sein

Heidegger's manuscripts from the second half of the 1930s contain an interesting image.

or

This means that there is no *Being* without the Fourfold (*Geviert*), and the crossed-out *Being* is *Geviert*. At the same time, when *Being* appears, it makes *Geviert* appear, which means that it cannot be written in some other way. It is never given to us on its own, that is, without the Fourfold (*Geviert*) or outside of the Fourfold (*Geviert*). As soon as we focus on *Seyn-Being* as such, *Geviert* manifests itself. As soon as we come to fruition in the event (*Er-eignis*), *Geviert* simultaneously splashes in four directions of *Geviert* and covers *Seyn-Being* with itself. *As soon as Being expresses itself, it crosses itself out. But as soon*

---

[36] *Ibid.,*145; here, translated from the Russian.

as *Geviert* in its pure form moves away from *Seyn-Being*, when it conceals *Seyn-Being* fully, it also breaks, disappears, and *Seyn-Being* once again begins to show through it (only with another side—through "nihilation," "*nichten*").

Geviert and *Seyn-Being* are always together, always one and the same, although their relationship is not dominated by constant statis, but rather a complex, unpredictable, and eventful dynamic of revelations and concealments.

This fundamental dynamics of *Seyn-Being* as *Ereignis* animates the relationship of all four *Geviert* regions with one another. Waves of revelations and concealments, arrivals and departures, ebbs and flows, advances and retreats, the tense element of war and game permeates *Geviert*, separating and uniting the orientations of philosophical geography.

Perhaps, there is nothing more fundamental than the "St. Andrew's cross" of *Seyn-Being*. Something similar must be printed on our philosophical gonfalons. Observing *Geviert*, we observe the crossed-out *Seyn-Being* (as well as *Nichts* together with it: after all, *Seyn* is crossed out here in every sense!), we simultaneously observe the Sky, Earth, Divine and Mortal ones.

Note the subtlety with which Heidegger depicted the original *Geviert*. When one has a fundamental metaphysical prophecy in mind, everything matters.

This writing, name, image, and graphic illustration represent the synthesis of the most profound fundamental-ontological knowledge. Correct thinking is equal to something that we could call "illumination" (*Lichtung* in German, ἔλλαμψις [*ellampsis*] in

Greek). *Geviert* is the fruit of that illumation and, at the same time, an invitation to this illumination directed at those who will focus their entire life's thought-oriented attention on it.

Men and Gods as Neighbors

In certain manuscripts, Heidegger depicts *Geviert* vertically as a regular cross.[37]

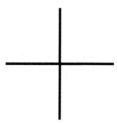

In this case, the Sky (World) is located above, the Earth—below, which is obvious even in the metaphysical sense (order is above, chaos is below; light is above, darkness is below; transparency is above, opacity and concreteness are below).

But with this turn of events, we will see a remarkable thing: men and gods are positioned next to each other on the same line between the Sky and Earth. And this is fundamental. From the standpoint of the Earth and the Sky, men and gods are located on the same plane, in the same circle, as part of the same roundelay and, strictly speaking, it is impossible to differentiate between "right" and "left." Gods and men are gathered *around* the light of *Seyn-Being* and are engaged in a roundelay. Gods gathered at a meeting, an assembly (Scandinavian *thing*) around *Seyn-Being*, and ended up next to men, since they are neighbors in *Geviert*. It is this kind of neighborship that makes the games between gods and men possible. Indifferent to men's problems, gods occasionally

---

[37] Martin Heidegger, *Beiträge zur Philosophie (vom Ereignis)* (Frankfurt am Main: Vittorio Klostermann, 1989), 310.

encroach on the sphere of men (and this intrusion is blessed), visit them at home, find themselves in the oven, in the icon corner, at the home's hearth, in bread, wine, the wind's blow, in the sacred tree. All of this becomes possible if we organize *Geviert* in this manner.

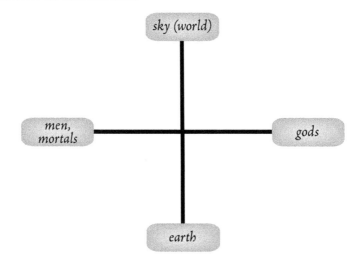

Gods end up being men's *neighbors*; they live in the nearby grove, in the spring, in the stream, in spring air, in the fear of the night, in midday heat, in ripe wheat; they visit men and vice versa, compete for owning the spring, young beauty, or a skillfully executed vessel in the same way that men act toward each other and in relation to those whom they are not. The *Bible* contains a troubling story about close contacts between men and "God's sons," which describes how "God's sons" were once mesmerized by the beauty of men's daughters and came down to the earth. Their descendents were an ancient race of giants later gone extinct from the face of the earth.

This coexistence of men and gods on the *shared* plane is one aspect of the fundamental rethinking of the fundamental-ontological schematic diagram of *Geviert*.

219

And, at the same time, the position of the Sky and the Earth on the vertical axis underscores the kind of war that they carry out against each other. The Sky attacks the Earth, the Earth hides from these attacks, defends itself, gathers into itself in the face of a self-scattering open Sky. This is Uranogeomachy—the war between the Earth and the Sky (World). In this war, *Seyn-Being* is the constant dynamic of life. The order of *Geviert* has not been set once and for all. The Sky as the expression of the ordering region of fundamental-ontology cannot impose its order onto the Earth once and for all. The Earth is too large and primordial for this, too vast, too heavy. It never stops its life's work for a second, which is expressed in the stirring of a great weight. No matter how decisively the Sky acts, the Earth does not allow peace to occur as simply peace, hiding from the Sky's rays; the Earth makes everything earthly, envelops the Sky's volition with a thick presence and thereby saves things from immobility and perfection. The Earth gives things that are established by the Sky the opportunity to decay and return to the Earth. This is the Earth's revenge, its counterattack. No matter what the Sky gives birth to with its creative power, the Earth will, sooner or later, dissolve it in its sacred primordiality. The Sky strikes the Earth for this; the Earth suffers, suffers through this, and, once again, contracts in pristine freshness after the splitting strikes of the Sky's thunder.

The Sky and the Earth are not separated from one another— they are the waves of *Seyn-Being*, its means to existence. These are regions and directions of *Being*.

Uranogeomachy can be dramatic and turbulent. At times, however, the passion subsides. The battle between the Sky and the Earth brings *beings* so that they become. A truce puts out the trembling of *beings*. The Sky tends to always fight, whereas the Earth is always ready for a truce. Peace is the Earth's revenge, since peace is a period of dissolution. Peace does not give birth to anything. Everything that is born is born in war.

The Axis of Anthropotheomachy

We could try turning the cross of *Geviert* in some other way. Then we will end up with another vertical axis and a different structure of fundamental-ontological tension. I have not located this kind of a schematic diagram in Heidegger's work. It is theoretically possible, however, if we start at the primacy of its position as St. Andrew's cross, in which one of the vertical poles can be taken as the absolute vertical line. With the Sky's leadership, this kind of a possibility is supported by Heidegger's own manuscripts. But we can also put the Divine at the top of the vertically positioned cross.

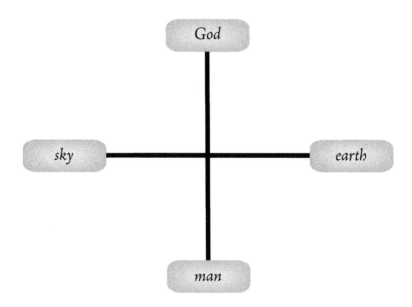

The very symmetry of depicting *Geviert* pushes us toward placing God, in the singular, at the very top. Perhaps, the absence of this version is explained by Heidegger's stubborn lack of desire to somehow address the question about the "multiplicity of gods or the presence of a single God." But at the same time, he clearly holds onto the possibility of a single God within the fundamental-ontological system of coordinates, as evidenced by his usage of the term "God" in the singular and, more specifically, the "Last God" ("God" in particular, not "gods"). But Heidegger carefully avoids forcing any discussion about a God based on a justified fear of slipping back into the old metaphysics and ontological theology, which would be the equivalent to refusing to philosophize within the space of *another Beginning*. The question of the one God should be resolved at the assembly of gods, in their trembling, in the sacred inaccessibility of their secret meeting at the hearth of *Seyn-Being*. We can—approximately—judge only the divine horizon as one that opens up inside the sacred, sacral (*Heilige*). But it is the sacred that is the other (poetic) name for *Seyn-Being*. "The sacred and *Seyn-Being* both name one and the same and not one and the same (...). The sacred and *Seyn-Being* are the names of another Beginning tested through experience and thought through."[38] Each of these names belongs to a different sphere: one to poetry (the sacred, *Heilige*), and the other to philososhy (*Seyn-Being*). The divine in relation to the human is located on the other side of *Seyn-Being*, on the other side of the sacred zone (*Heilige*). This is why man in his essence, as the guardian of *Seyn-Being*, always sees the divine only as the farthest horizon and cannot judge the number of gods, their multiplicity, or singularity. This is not men's business, but that of gods—to count themselves, if numbering for gods has any kind of meaning.

---

[38] Martin Heidegger, *Über den Anfang* (Frankfurt am Main: Vittorio Klostermann, 2005), 157.

Therefore, it would be more accurate to represent this schematic diagram as follows:

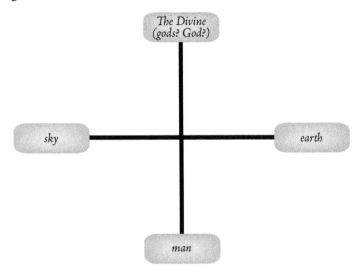

In this positioning of *Geviert*, there develops the greatest kind of opposition between gods and men, which were more like neighbors in the previous version. Here, their relationship becomes more hostile. Gods fight men, attack them, send them sores and suffering, mock them, despise them. Gods can kill men, laugh at them, turn their lives into hell. At times, men begin to storm the light, airy citadels of the gods and, on occasion, they manage to kill them ("God is dead," writes Nietzsche, "And we have killed him."). In comparison to men, gods are immortal, but in comparison to *Seyn-Being*, they are mortal, since *Seyn-Being* is the *event* that carries *Nothingness* in itself as the possibility to "nihilate," "annihilate." Sometimes, gods die (as the great Pan once died).[39] Let us also recall the Biblical subject about Jacob wrestling with the angel (God) until dawn.

---

[39] The novel *Malpertuis* by the Belgian author Jean Ray ([London: Atlas, 1998]) tells a different story of certain great Greek gods: they degenerated and turned into a sinister family of humanoid dolls. Unable to die, they dried up and transformed into pathetic dummies. (See also Jean Ray, *Tochnaia formula koshmara* [Moscow: Yazyki russkoi kul'tury, 2000].)

As we have already mentioned, anthropotheomachy, the struggle between gods and men (men's defeat), not only means that gods win but that men also do. Gods, having taken men hostage, captive, enslaved, liberate men from their dependence on *beings*, making them truly free for the first time. This is related to the term "rapture," which literally means being taken into the sky, an abduction on the part of something greater.[40] Thus, Saint Paul the Apostle was "caught up" to the third heaven. The poetic epithet of admiration and rapture at one point meant the brute act of man being kidnapped by muses or spirits and taken into heavenly captivity.

And vice versa, men's victory over gods, the storming of Olympus, leads to men's defeat, since by destroying and burning down the farthest horizon of the divine, men lose their connection to *Seyn-Being*, drop it, lose the thread of *Geviert*, are thrown into the abyss of *Nothingness*. This is not the revenge of the gods, but rather a self-inflicted punishment, their conscience, their *"ethos"* (as the place of gods in men) that pushes them into the desert of nihilism and *techne* as the price for a victory they should not have achieved under any circumstances.

There is another conclusion that could be drawn from observing *Geviert* in this particular orientation: when gods are above and people—below, then *the Earth and the Sky are located in equal positions* by moving onto the same plane. This means that this time around, they lost their vertical opposition, stopped fighting, reached a truce; this means that they are now *together*, which, in turn, means that it is their turn to engage in the roundelay. We can call this moment the marriage of the Sky and Earth, their engagement.

---

[40] The author uses the term "*voskhishchenie*" (*восхищение*), which contains the word "abduction" after the prefix, to emphasize the etymology. In Latin, "*raptus*" is "seizure," "abduction." (*Ed.*)

When the mortal man begins to realize himself on the same vertical axis as the gods, when anthropotheomachy is set aflame, then the Sky and the Earth are made equal, interlock with each other in a chaotic connection, and their sacred marriage takes place.

When man feels the weight of a deity not *next* to himself (then it's not its weight but, rather, lightness), but *above himself, against* himself, then he is located on the line of *"polemos"* with gods, and the Earth and the Sky become equals, then the world falls into chaos (sacred or otherwise).

Seyn-Being as the "In Between"

Here we should ask the following question: *what* stands in the middle of *Geviert?* In different texts and manuscripts, Heidegger put different things at the intersection of *Geviert.* We saw that in Heidegger's depiction of a crossed-out *Seyn-Being,* the center can only be taken up by *Seyn.*

Seyn-Being lives between gods and men, between the Earth and Sky; *between (Zwischen), in between (Inzwischen)* is where *Seyn-Being* is located. If it had specific localization then we would be dealing with *Sein-Being* of the old metaphysics. But in fundamental-ontology, *Seyn-Being* does not have a specific place; its place is alwys between places. Furthermore, this *"between"* is the name of *Seyn-Being.* But since *Seyn-Being* is what is most fundamental, then everything that has anything to do with it— first and foremost, *Geviert* and its regions—also become that "in between," defining their position through their relationship with the other. The meaning of the abyss is that it has no bottom. It is not that it is simply too deep: there is no bottom at all. Similarly, the "in between" is not "between one and the other." On the contrary, "one" and the "other" are hypothetical directions taken from the starting point of this "in between," where the ends' own *Being* is taken from their relationship with the "in between." The intersection of the *Geviert* axes is the most important "in between," which means that it is where *Seyn-Being* hides and opens up through everything that radiates from it in all directions. Heidegger warns that the poles of *Geviert* and their struggle against each other cannot be understood as self-sufficient entities. "The Earth is not a section of *beings-as-a-whole*. The World is not a section of *beings-as-a-whole*. *Beings* are not separated into two sections. The Earth is existence (*Being* as essensing, *Wesung*) of *beings-as-a-whole*. The World is the existence of *beings-as-a-whole*. The Earth and the World belong to *Sein-Being* of *beings-as-a-whole*. This is why we can never understand the war between them if we imagine it as a competition or battles between different things."[41] The Earth fights to become the World (Sky). The World fights in order to instill order on the quiet and rebellious Earth. But both the Earth and the Sky (World) must be conceived from what is between them which is *Seyn-Being*.

Geviert and Ereignis

In other cases, Heidegger places *Ereignis* at the center of *Geviert*. This is not different than the same picture from before, only *Seyn-Being* is described in it as the event, as something exceptional, unique, final. Conceiving of *Seyn-Being* as *Ereignis*, we end up in

---

[41] Martin Heidegger, *Geschichte des Seyns (1938/1940)* (Frankfurt am Main: Vittorio Klostermann, 1998), 21.

the very moment of another Beginning, initiate the Beginning with this thought. *Geviert* is not and does not become, it happens, comes to fruition as an event in the dynamic explosion of *Seyn-Being*. This explosion is something *seynsgeschichtliche*, and which occurs only once. *Geviert* is invalid until the event comes true, and another Beginning activates, and, thus, now we are dealing only with guesses about it. *Geviert is*, and to such an extent that *Ereignis is*.

For this reason, Heidegger's work contains the following diagram.[42]

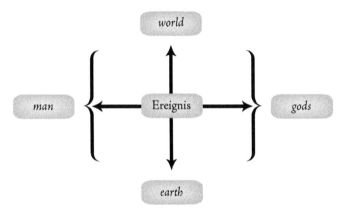

Placing *Ereignis* at the center of *Geviert* shows its *seynsgeschichtliche* character. *Geviert* is not simply *beings* (*Seiende*) or *beings-as-a-whole*. These are *beings* and *beings-as-a-whole* when the event (*Ereignis*) occurs, when *Seyn-Being* explodes, and when the Last God arrives. This means that it is accurate to conceive of *Geveirt* from the standpoint of *Being's* eschatology. *Geviert* is an attempt, a fundamental-ontological impulse, in which *Seyn-Being* is recognized as the "in between" and not in any other way. Without this impulse, there is no *Geviert*. This is incredibly important to remember in order to understand Heidegger's thought process correctly.

---

42 Martin Heidegger, *Beiträge zur Philosophie (vom Ereignis)* (Frankfurt am Mein: Vittorio Klostermann, 1989), 310.

The Thing (das Ding)

The third candidate for being placed at the center of intersecting fundamental-ontological orientations of *Geviert* is the *thing, das Ding*.[43] Heidegger warns that we must refrain from conceiving of the thing at the center of *Geviert* as the fifth element. The intersection of two axes in *Geviert* does not represent something new. This point does not possess independence. Outside of *Geviert*—as a functional, dynamic fundamental-ontological model of relationships inside a living rhythm along both of these axes—there *is no* thing.

Any thing—for instance, a tree which we observe—*is*, is present. And being in presence, it, as a result of this fact of being present, represents the necessary *crosshairs* of *Geviert*. This is why any thing should be correctly interpreted within the framework of fundamental-ontology as the *crosshairs* that indicate the axes piercing it. Only in this case, being placed into the light of *Geviert*, does the thing become the thing.

Let us recall that *Geviert* is the intersection of two axes along which anthropotheomachy and Uranogeomachy develop, the war between men and gods, the war between the Sky and Earth. *Seyn-Being* itself is Heraclitean πόλεμος (*polemos*), the "father of things." We refer to the thing because this is the *crosshairs of two wars*, more specifically, of a single war, which occurs in two perpendicular directions. Herein lies the dynamic life of the thing, which is never itself—it is picked up by the regions of *Seyn-Being*, making it overflow with life and saturating it with the breath of death. For this reason, the thing in its fundamental-ontological dimension is not simply a kind of *beings*. It comes to fruition, occurs, expressing *Seyn-Being* with itself, including its

---

[43] See, first and foremost, Martin Heidegger, *Das Ding, Vorträge und Aufsätze (1936–53)* (Frankfurt am Main: Vittorio Klostermann, 2000).

"nihilating" power. The thing is therefore dangerous and risky, it is thrown into the abyss of the great war. There are no non-living things in *Geviert*. All things live here, in the field of a continuous and unpredictable battle.

It is important to mention the Indo-European etymology of the word "thing." The roots of the Latin word *"res,"* German *"Ding,"* and Russian *"вещь"* (*veshch'*) originally contain a reference to political-judicial procedures. Heidegger asks the following question: what is *Ding?* And answers himself: *Ding* is something that was presented for debate at a thing, a folk assembly, at "agora" (*Ἀγορά*) for the prupose of deciding the rightfulness or lack thereof, usefulness or lack thereof, of what was presented. *Ding*, a thing, *is that which is brought forth to be judged.* But at what kind of a trial? The kind of trial that represents the circle of people walking atop the Earth, under the Sky, and in the presence of Deities' signs, since all sacred meetings amongst the ancient peoples occurred precisely in this manner. Men gathered at a *thing* in front of the Divine; this meeting occurred on Earth under an open Sky. What was presented and placed at the center of discussion was *Ding*. *Ding* is not a symbol, a sign, or an instrument. *Ding* is the intersection of all four dimensions of *Geviert* at a single moment, when these dimensions gather for the purpose of carrying out a fundamental decision. It is important to address Russian etymology. What is the basic meaning of the Russian word *"veshch'"?* *"Veshch'"* is what is presented at a *veche*, a Slavic folk assembly, and what is decided there. Similarly, the German *Ding* is what was presented at the *thing*. It is interesting to note that even the Latin *res* initially meant "the matter" specifically because it was presented to the public, to a gathering. This is where *res publica* (republic) comes from. Therefore, we find the idea of a gathering among the Latins as well, the practice of reaching a fundamental decision with the help of the Earth, the Sky, and Gods. And this is not simply a metaphor given to us by Heidegger but an insight into the core of the way things are in thought, language, and history.

The Thing and the Gifts of Geviert

Every direction of *Geviert* brings "the thing" something of its own.

The *Sky* brings the thing what makes it precisely what it is. The *Sky* illuminates it with its light, which makes it visible as *that very* thing, *this kind* of thing. The Sky shows its place in the world, since the Sky and the World are synonymous in Heideggerian fundamental-ontology. A pine, for instance, is a pine because the Sky makes it so; the Sky illuminates it as a pine and endows it with orderly worth.

The *Earth* makes the thing present, it makes it real, while the Sky makes the thing "precisely this one," a concrete thing and a thing that is included in the general order of all things. In the same way, the Earth unites all things because they all consist of a foundation, and, at the same time, it separates them, casting them throughout its endless vastness. The Earth and the Sky unite and separate things, but do so differently.

The *Divine ones* introduce the *sacred* into the thing. When gods get closer to the thing, this thing becomes embued with their most subtle, invisible, and imperceptible vibrations. The thing becomes sacred. A sacred thing is the thing of the gods. Gods are those for whom everyone is meant. Everyone is a sacrificial offering handed to them. By accepting things, gods make them light for themselves and heavy for others. Sacred things are the most light and heavy things simultaneously.

230

Man brings exaltation to the thing, offers it a name. But this is not a name in the sense of "property" since man in *Geviert* does not yet possess the thing. In *Geviert*, man poetically *sings the thing* and often drinks (from the sacred sacrificial vessel) in order to sing on this path. Herein lies the most important aspect: *man treats the thing through language. Man extols the thing, places the thing into language, and places language into the thing.* Man pronounces the thing. Man *creates* the thing in a hymn, in poetry.[44] He creates, which means he places it where it is located, between the Sky and Earth, before Gods praised by them themselves. Therefore, according to Heidegger, the essence of the human in relation to things is the exaltation of things, it is a hymn, it is poetry.

Language is not an attribute of man, but rather man is a form of language's presence. Language is the core of *Seyn-Being's* truth. Therefore, speech and statements reach man's greatest horizon, as the "guardian of *Seyn-Being*." He introduces the most important aspect into the thing, something that exceeds himself, and that is a statement, naming as a call to presence.

---

[44] ποίησις (Greek), "poetry" means "creation," "work."

II. GEVIERT AS THE MAP OF THE BEGINNING AND THE RETREAT FROM IT

The Desert Grows

Geviert is the world as it is from the standpoint of *Seyn-Being*. This is a world understood within fundamental-ontology. For this reason, this is the world that pertains to the Beginning, to that moment in the Beginning that is, in a certain sense, shared by both the first Beginning and another Beginning. The First Beginning remained quite primal until the moment when the philosophical revelations and insights on the part of Anaximander, Heraclitus, Parmenides, Plato, and Aristotle made definitive statements in the spirit of metaphysics and ontology (in which the essence of *beings* became equated with *Sein-Being*). The deviation from fundamental-ontology could only be documented *a posteriori*. This explains Heidegger's immense interest in the pre-Socratics—he, a thinker of another Beginning, peers into the first Beginning striving to see what makes a Beginning the Beginning, i.e., what is initial. This is why his favorite poet, Hölderlin, a poet of another Beginning, is so close to the Greeks and the Greek poets of the first Beginning in his worldview.

In this sense, *Geviert* is a fundamental-ontological perspective of the world's revelation in the event (*Ereignis*), i.e., the horizon of *Being*'s eschatology and the phenomenon of the Last God's walking by and, at the same time, the immediate still frame of the kind of cosmos that opened up before the first Greek thinkers in the original movement toward philosophy and poetry. But outside of this original moment, *Geviert* can also be conceptualized, but not as an initial phenomenon and event, rather as a platform for the fundamental-ontological criticism of non-initial metaphysics and cosmology based on this metaphysics. *Geviert is* only from the standpoint of *Seyn-Being*, when *Seyn-Being* comes to fruition in a unique and singular moment. But when *Geviert is not*, in other periods, characterized by the "abandonment of *Being*" (*Seinsverlassenheit*), it still *is* in a certain sense, but only through its turn in the opposite direction, not unlike Heidegger reading the messages (*Geschichte*) of *Seyn-Being* itself in "*Being*'s abandonment" and "*Being*'s oblivion," which led to nihilism.

With the help of *Geviert*, we can also examine non-*Geviert*. In other words, we can examine Geviert as a fundamental-ontological map where through the application of other—non-initial—representations of cosmology, astrology, physics, and theology, we can measure the volume and qualitative characteristics of what Nietzsche called "desertification" (*Verwüstung*). In this case, it is the desertification of *Geviert* that is in question, the distortion of proportions between different "regions of the world," the change in their status and position, their separation from *Seyn-Being*, the violation of the fragile initial connection between them.

The entire history of philosophy, culture, and civilization can be described as the process of progressive desertification of *Geviert*. It is this that will be the *seynsgeschichtliche* procedure of correct historic analysis.

234

The Idea Covers the Sky

In the first section of our investigation (*Seyn und Sein*), we described in general terms the way Heidegger conceptualized *Seynsgeschichte* and its stages. Let us now project these stages onto the map of *Geviert* in order to better understand their content.

Heidegger defined the place of Platonism as the End in the first Beginning. Here, Greek thought carries out a radical transition from the very possibility of thinking about *Being* (*Sein*) as something different from *beings* (*Seiende*) and records the ontological set of problems with the essence of *beings* as the "second kind of *beings*," placed above all others.

Ontology is being constructed over ontics in such a way that it does not reveal the *Being* of *beings* but rather ultimately makes them inaccessible. The principal instrument of this process is the theory of ideas. If we were to project this set of problems onto *Geviert*, then the most serious transformation occurs in the region of the Sky (World).

The Sky as the world region of the fundamental-ontological map in the initial *Geviert* is conceived as being open. *Seyn-Being* reveals itself in this openness of the Sky, in its bottomlessness and depth. Plato puts the idea in the Sky and not only that, but in the middle of the Sky, indirectly, in the place of the Sky. As the greatest kind of *beings* among all *beings*, the idea overshadows the Sky, replaces it.

The Sky itself is at the foundations of seeing, since the Sky is the region of light and lighting. But the natural and open light of the Sky, tracing back to *Seyn-Being*, turns into an artificial and "closed" light of the idea in Plato.

The idea as the expression of the greatest kind of *beings* closes up the fundamental-ontological dimension of the Sky and transforms the Sky as a region of the world into a metaphysical sphere. From now on, this is the Sky of metaphysics both in the philosophical and religious senses. According to Heidegger, Plato's metaphysics enteres Hellenized Judaism through Philo of Alexandria, and then, through the Greek translation of the *Septuagint*, it enters Christianity. The Sky obtains its identity as a logical position equal only to itself and non- equal to anything else (the Earth, first and foremost).

The introduction of logic and its laws decisively enslaves the Sky within ontological statics, and all the versions of later metaphysics, including Modernity and open nihilism do not fundamentally change anything in this question.

The Sky is no longer the existence of *Seyn-Being* which battles the other existence of *Seyn-Being*, the Earth, in a creative and dramatic war-game of mirrors.

The Sky is the substance, essence, *Seiendheit*, the greatest kind of *beings* (ὄντως ὄν [*ontos on*]). The war against the Earth continues, but it is no longer a game. The goal of this war is radical annihilation.

Techne (τέχνη), *Machenschaft*, and "deliberate self-imposition" take root here.

The Earth Turned into Matter

The Earth's transformation occurs symmetrically to this. The Earth in the initial version of *Geviert* is not simply what is below, at the base of the world. It is lower and broader than that.

The Earth is also open in terms of fundamental-ontology, even though it is closed in the face of the open Sky. This mysterious openness of the Earth is the abyss (*Abgrund*). The Earth as *Grund* (foundation, ground, soil) is *Abgrund*, the abyss, in its fundamental-ontological essence (*Wesen*) because it is none other than the essensing (*Wesung*) of *Seyn-Being*. The Earth is always lower than one could imagine. Herein lies its life-giving power and dark terror. When the Sky is replaced with the "idea" (in Aristotle, this is "energy" or "*eidos*"), the Earth becomes "matter," "substance," "ὕλη" (*yli*), "wood," the foundation for embodying the idea in its concreteness. This is still that sacred Earth, sacred element, but it is already closed from below, it is the bottom, not the abys, the limit, not the dark power of birth and destruction. But in this Earth, one could already foresee the Scholastic conception of "*signata quantitate*," the amount of quantitative matter and the object of Modern metaphysics up until the "matter" of the materialists.

Ultimately, the Earth's life-giving darkness transforms into entropy, exacting revenge through the indiscriminate spread of decay to all that is being disseminated stubbornly and aggressively by the technical will to power, which was once the Sky.

Human Man

But the most important desertification, according to Heidegger, is expressed in the kind of man who begins to think differently, becomes aware of himself differently, losing his fundamental-ontological horizon. Man becomes closed, appropriates what was the horizon of *Seyn-Being*, the domain of the gods, the speech of the Sacred (*Heilige*). As a "guardian of *Seyn-Being*," the horizons of speech and thought were open to man, as the forms of existence of fragile, far-removed, and carefree gods, as flashes of *Seyn-Being* illuminating the Men part of *Geviert* through man. At the end of the first Beginning, man began considering this his property, what constituted him as a species, even though man, as a species, with his closed-off and self-identical essence, does not exist. Man is the place for language, possible zones of invasion for light gods, a chasm in *beings* through which *Seyn-Being* expresses itself as a thought. As in *Geviert*.

The man of Platonism and all following Western European metaphysics is a closed (off) man: groundlessly, he asserts his foundations and self-identity, defiantly appropriates for himself that which was handed to him for the purpose of praise, exaltation, and safe-keeping. *Logos* was a god, *daimon*, the source of ethnics and the horizon of true thought, the beginning of philosophy. In *Geviert*, *logos* owns man, not vice versa. In Greek anthropology man turns into "ζῷον λόγον ἔχον" (*zoon logon echon*), an "animal that owns the *logos*" (note "ἔχον" —"having," "owning").

In post-Socratic philosophy, this anthropology, initially discerned only by sophists (for instance, Protagoras and his "man is the measure of all things"), becomes accepted across the board. Translating into Latin, we get "*animalis rationalis*," which does not correspond to anything, since "*ratio*" is not "*logos*," but "mind," present in ordinary men rather than those who philosophize and who were illuminated by the *logos*. The same fate reaches *daimon*, which was man's "*ethos*" in Heraclitus. Man took away "*ethos*" from *daimon*, appropriated it for himself (inhabiting it with idols), and, ultimately, played with it for two millennia, only to cast "*ethos*" aside as something empty together with the Nietzschean analysis of the "genealogy of morals" and the prospect of going "beyond good and evil." That same Nietzsche recorded the "death of God."

238

The same thing occurred with language. Instead of understanding its meaning and deciphering the message of *Seyn-Being* included in it, man decided that language is his own attribute, and, through the distortion imposed by logic and grammar, turned language into an instrument of the "will to power" instead of one that highlights *Seyn-Being*. From this point forward, he became sure that thought, language, and the divine are objects fully found within his completence and dependent on his self-identifying nature. This notion was ultimately fixed with the Cartesian concept of the subject and the following metaphysics of Modernity.

Man, establishing himself as a special kind of *beings*, lost access to his own essence, which is constructed around his openness to *Seyn—Being* as something radically different and alternative to possessing an original essence. Desertification commenced when man *began to represent and create things instead of exalting them.*

In the Beginning, man praises the *thing*, names it. In Greek, this is "ποίησις" (*poiesis*), which means "creation."

When we enter the phase of Platonic thought, this sacralizing creation through exaltation of the thing turns into direct production. *Ποεσις* does not become poetry but rather the feverish creation of new *beings*, artificial *beings*, which now expresses only man's uncontrollable will to power.

Man begins to do something that is completely uncharacteristic for him. He no longer safe-guards the mystery of *Seyn-Being* or maintains the harmony inside *Geviert*. Instead, he roughly *interfers* in *beings*, mangles them, knocks out of them what he needs, and seeks to subjugate them. It is here, in Heidegger's view, that fundamental decadence sets in.

239

Here, we come to an extremely important boundary. According to Heidegger, it is to man, out of all four directions of *Geviert*, that the decision (*Entscheidung*) is given. Man is a deciding creature, capable of making a choice. *Seynsgeschichte* depends on this choice. Man's freedom, his openness, his groundlessness, disunity, and bottomlessness, his mortality comprise the fact that he is capable of disposing of his vocation to guard *Seyn-Being* according to his own will. He can guard it, or he can evade doing so and leave his guard. This decision is fundamental and cannot be corrected by anyone or anything in the moment when it is taken. Here the Sky falls silent, as do the Earth and the Gods. And even *Seyn-Being* itself leaves man in a free fall, since the freedom entrusted to him is that very illumination of *Seyn-Being* in that place of *beings* that is called "man." Man can choose to be or not to be, to exist as a guardian of *Seyn-Being's* truth, or to be in some other way, accordingly, someone else. Man damaged *Geviert*. He paved over the Sky with ideas and flattened the Earth down into matter. He dispersed, enslaved, and killed the Gods. He armed himself against *Being* and chose to forget about his own mortality. And he was free to do this since it was this freedom, this decision (*Entscheidung*) that comprised his region of *Geviert*.

However, being fully and solely responsible for this decision, which was formulated during the course of the first Beginning and soon gained clear attributes of Platonic metaphysics, being completely free in this decision, man was not free in organizing its consequences. He created ontology within the emptiness of his great turbulent will, but he had no power over predetermining the End that resulted from the decision he had made. It is this that is *Seynsgeschichte*, fate's message as the power of *Seyn-Being*, even more powerful than the power of the one whom *Seyn-Being* vested with the power of his freedom. This is the eschatology of *Being*, which, having fully accepted man's decision in the first Beginning, demonstrated the true content of this *decision* as *techne* and placed man in front of the mirror of his nihilistic End. Deciding everything himself in the emptiness of the great Beginning, man could not be free of only one thing—the End itself, which was contained in that very Beginning, and which became inevitable and predetermined at that precise moment when the content of the decision that was made (even within the framework of the Beginning) became clear.

Man ruined *Geviert* himself. And he paid for this with himself.

Displaced Gods

The fall of the original *Geviert* and its damage inevitably touched upon the fourth region of the divine. Heidegger speaks about this in a figurative way by describing the *"flight of gods"* (*Flucht der Göttern*). One could describe this as the definitive and irreversible victory of men in the course of anthropotheomachy.

The subject of deicide or the death of gods has ancient roots. Many archaic cults are based on the symbolic murder of gods—such was the fate of Dionysus, Adonis, Purusha of the Hindus, and so on. The idea of deicide is also at the center of the Christian religion. Men can kill god. God can die.

But it would be even simpler to scare a god away rather than kill him. One does not need to carry out lengthy military operations that require great costs, employ cunning, divide up the resources and form squads, or think through defense and attack strategies. It is sufficient to close off at least one of *Geviert's* directions, to extract one fragment from the overall fundamental-ontological map of the world, even if an insignificant one. This will result in the flight of the gods. They cannot stand roughness, stupidity, bad language, lack of kindness, discourtesy, and, most important, they cannot tolerate enclosed spaces, slammed doors, finalized forms, ideas, thoughts, and things. Gods are openness and union. Such was the Heraclitean god-*logos*: if his whisper remains unheard, and the unity of *beings* that he opens up remains unresponded to, then he hides immediately, because those parts that are cut off from unity fall away at an infinite distance. Herein lies the secret: most of all, gods are afraid of stupidity or "conventional wisdom" (which is the same thing), the "rational mind," "practical reason," and the Aristotelian "φρόνησις" (*phronesis*). Common sense, a sober and calculated attitude, experience, and rationality are the most tried and tested weapons against gods. Gods exist where there are sages and madmen. Rational and pratical people are worse than poison for the gods.

Men triumphed in anthropotheomachy as soon as as they became simply men, "human, all too human." Thus began the word's disenchantment, its desacralization.

The Fate of the Intersection

Now let us observe what occurs with the intersection point as *Geviert* moves away from its initial (*anfangliche*) state. We already discussed the transformation of *Seyn-Being* in Platonic and post-Platonic philosophy. *Seyn-Being* begins to be conceptualized as *Sein-Being* and as "the greatest kind of *beings*" (ὄντως ὄν). Ultimately, it is *beings* (*Seiende*), no matter how great, that end up at the center. At the same time, the autonomization of *Geviert's* center occurs. It is conceived of, not as an intersection of two dynamic axes, but as an independent and fixed point, independent from these axes. This autonomization creates a new map of philosophy that stops being fundamental-ontological and becomes ontological. After recording this point of the "greatest kind of *beings*," "essence," "substance," we can step away from *Geviert* and its world regions and construct different geometric maps of thought pushing off from this point.

To an even greater extent, these transformations with *Geviert* affect *Ereignis*, the event, which we also placed at the intersection of the axes. This point is no longer conceived as *Ereignis*, the event. The singularity, uniqueness, rarity of *Ereignis*—as an explosion of *Seyn-Being* in its most direct and original expression—has been lost. *Seyn-Being* stops being the event and no longer comes to fruition. It is now conceptualized as something permanent, "eternal," "always present," "guaranteed," "in presence," as a provided, universal, and empty ontological *a priori*. *Being* outside of the Beginning is never *Ereignis*. Herein lies the most profound attribute of non-initial (old) ontology. In the place of the event, there now stands its negation, something opposed to the event—what does not come to fruition, does not happen, but always *is*. Instead of freshness, suddenness, a lightning flash, and newness, we have the case of *a priori*, familiarity, constancy, and banality.

Also changing is that third item, which we previously placed inside *Geviert*, i.e., the thing, *Ding*. The thing ceased to be a simple and oversaturated expression of *Seyn-Being* as war (πόλεμος) or as the question that was brought out to a *veche* for discussion among the Sky, Earth, gods, and men, demanding a life decision. It became something artificial, a sign, symbol, composite *beings* decomposable into an idea, form, essence, and matter, substance embued with secondary attributes and qualities—accidents.

243

We can summarize all of these transformations of *Geviert* at the End of the great Beginning in the following schematic diagram.

The Sky becomes a place where ideas flutter and cloak Seyn-Being; The Sky is covered with ideas

Living gods withdraw and retreat

-*Essence replaces* Seyn-Being (Sein als Seiendheit) -*The thing becomes a symbol, splits into form and matter* -*Ereignis does not occur* Seyn-Being *does not happen*

Man imposes himself and turns beings into re-pre-sentation

The Earth is conceptualized as matter (ΰλη) and loses the dimension of an abyss

Geviert and Scholasticism

During the era of Socrates, Plato, and Aristotle, *Geviert* stops being *Geviert per se*. Its structure falls apart, the Fourfold stops being fourfold, and we place the map of Geviert over a new structure of post-Platonic ontology only to follow the correlations between fundamental-ontological proportions and relationships that were indicative of the Beginning as well as their later distortions.

Geviert deviates from its initial structure even further when it is dominated by Christian theology and Scholastic philosophy. According to Heidegger, this period does not bring anything principally new to Platonic ontology, where the idea stands above everything else as the "greatest kind of *beings*," complementing this ontology with a theological concept of a single God, as the greatest kind of *beings*, the supreme kind of *beings*, simultaneously acting as the Creator of every other (lower) kind of *beings*. Heidegger believes that we are dealing with the next level of absolutizing the principle of *techne*, when all *beings* begin to be thought of as a certain analogy to technical production, and the demiurge is considered the supreme *being*—the master who creates things and objects.

Between the world and its Creator, there appears an impassable chasm, as if between the potter and the pot he had made. Those fundamental-ontological approaches that animated *Geviert*, the subtlest of distinctions, dramatic wars and, simultaneously, the unity of worldly regions in *Geviert*—all this ended up incompatible with the Creationist metaphysics of theology and Scholastic philosophy. It is not an accident that the Christian period of Western history occurs under the sign of Three, not Four.

Thus, the ontological structure changes appearance even further. The comparison between the new theological ontology and cosmology with *Geviert* becomes more and more difficult. Nonetheless, certain parallels remain. The most important aspect of theology is the qualitative change in the status of the divine. Instead of gods and an open question about the possibility of a single God, strict monotheism is postulated as the absolute axiom. God is the absolute subject and absolute object. He is the greatest of *beings* and, at the same time, the creator of *Being* (like the world's *Being*). There is a relationship of strict transcendence between God and the world. God cannot be evaluated like the world, he is beyond limits. He created the world out of *Nothing* and has no prospects of qualitatively changing His own "nihilating" attributes. The relationship between men and God acquire a strictly judicial and moral character. God "signs" a Testament with men (a kind of a contract) and sternly watches over the adherence thereof, penalizing the violators and rewarding those who strictly follow its points.

The monotheistic God does not have anything in common with the gods inside *Geviert*. These gods were a part of the world; it was impossible to calculate their number; they were mobile, volatile, and fragile; it would be more accurate to say that they are *not*, but, at the same time, they *are not not*. The God of theology is not part of the world, but its Creator; He is strictly unique; He is immobile and eternal, always equal to Himself; He is and, furthermore, He is the One who is.

From the philosophical standpoint, it is easy to recognize Plato's highest idea here, supplied with additional features and attributes. From the standpoint of philosophy, religion adds to its structure only a little—individual details. The entire thought topography remains the same—metaphysical and ontological.

This conception of God breaks *Geviert* apart, turns it into an asymmetric schematic diagram with God heading it at an absolute and immesearable distance from the rest.

On the other side, across from the transcendent God, there lies the Earth. But, of course, this is no longer the same Earth that we had seen in the Beginning or even the same ὕλη (*yli*), substance, or matter discussed by Greek philosophers. From now on, the Earth is only dust, expressing Nothing, that same Nothing from which the world was created—transient, temporary, and subject to decay. In Scholasticism, matter was divided into two types: *materia prima* and *materia secunda*. The former represented something analogous to that from which the world was created, whereas the latter was a plastic substance responsible for physical and specific perception of tangible and created things. Everything that was not God became the Earth. It is quite telling that even the Sky was known as the "firmament" from this point forward, i.e., soil, earth, even though it was unique and heavenly. Let us recall that inside *Geviert*, the Earth acts as the beginning of closedness and closing but, at the same time, a place of safe-keeping and hiding. The Earth as *materia* in creationism (*prima* and *secunda*) is reduced to closedness, but loses its quality of safe-keeping and hiding. Matter as an expression of *Nothingness* neither guards, nor conceals. On the contrary, it brings decay and mortality into things. According to Psalm 102:14, "For thy servants take pleasure in her stones, And have pity upon her dust."

From now on, the Sky (World) and man are creatures, created entities, *ens creatum*. In a certain sense, as a given, the Earth itself is also *ens creatum*. All that is created is earthly in some way. The Sky and its inhabitants (angels) have a certain kind of superiority within the framework of the general hierarchy of creatures, although the Sky no longer possesses ontological uniqueness. In Heidegger, the *seynsgeschichtliche* function of the Sky (World) is replaced with Divine Providence, organizing the world order in accordance with the creating, sotereological, and eschatological script.

Negatively equating the rights of the three *Geviert* members in the face of a transcendent God also has a "positive" side focused on soteriology—the teachings about salvation of the soul. Man, despite being created out of nothing, out of dust, is able to address God directly: neither the breadth of the Earth nor the height of the Skies is an obstacle. In Christianity, there is an additional and highly important doctrinal position: Incarnation. God the Creator, in one of his embodiments, assumes a human nature, thereby revealing man's path of deification.

Thus, man, while remaining a creature, earthly, made of dust, becomes higher than the other creatures and, in some ways, higher than the Sky. Christ revealed the pathway to the Sky for him.

But for Heidegger, theological statements represent only the movement in the space of Platonic metaphysics, in which the fundamental-ontological set of problems is impossible. Therefore, Heidegger does not dedicate much attention to analyzing theology, considering the Christian era in the history of Western European philosophy as an extended interlude between Plato and Aristotle, on the one hand, and Modernity, on the other. In terms of the intersecting axes in *Geviert*, where we placed *Seyn-Being*, *Ereignis*, and the thing, this point also transforms in theology. *Being* is no longer *Seyn* or *Sein*, splitting into two parts—God's *Being* (as the highest of *beings*) and the *Being* of the world as that of the creatures. In this scenario, the question of *Being* as such cannot be posed correctly. Here, too, Heidegger sees the movement away from *Being*, the abandonment of *Being* (*Seinsverlassenheit*), and the oblivion of *Being*. *Ereignis*, having disappeared from the horizon of philosophy immediately after the Beginning[1], does

---

[1] Furthermore, Heidegger is inclined to think that *Ereignis* is not an attribute of any Beginning, but rather, that of *another Beginning*; therefore, placing it at the center of *Geviert* must be done in light of this correction.

not appear in the theological depiction of the world, even though in Christianity, unlike in Plato, we encounter the event that has an absolute significance for all Christian faith. This event is the arrival of Christ, the divine *logos*. It would be completely inaccurate to examine Christian cosmology as a special version of *Geviert* with the event (*Ereignis*) and the coming of Christ at the center. Heidegger understands *Ereignis* in a completely different way, and does not connect it with redemption, but rather with fundmanental-ontology. However, at the same time, we cannot avoid noting this parallel, even though its accurate interpretation would require an in-depth course in theology.

Finally, when it comes to the thing, here it turns into a creature, *ens creatum*, and its ontological significance fully coincides with its place in the hierarchy of creation; herein lies its identity. Overall, Scholasticism takes on the Aristotelian theory of the thing (form and matter), but the general Creationist perspective unequivocally interprets the thing as a *created* thing. If in Aristotle, $\tau \acute{e} \chi \nu \eta$ still is, in a certain sense, man's imitating the creative power of $\varphi \acute{v} \sigma \iota \varsigma$ (*physis*), then in St. Thomas Aquinas, nature (*Natura*) itself imitiates God's craft. The relationship between nature and culture changes substantially in favor of culture, and man's production, elevated to the level of Divinity, becomes the model and paradigm for understanding the natural processes, which, in their turn, are now conceived as an enormous mechanism or apparatus made by the Creator. Thus, the overall understanding of the thing as *ens creatum, res creata*, brings us significantly closer to the final triumph of what Heidegger calls *Machenschaft*. We can summarize the changes in *Geviert* inside Scholastic theology in the following diagram.

249

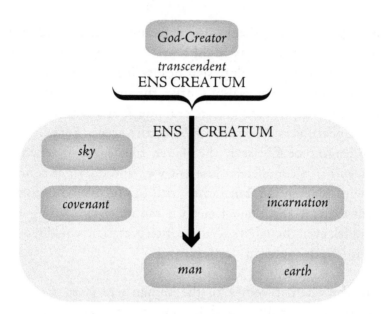

In this diagram, we must pay attention to the fact that the structure of Christian theology itself opposes being depicted inside a fourfold figure, despite the fact that the figure of the Cross is the principal symbol of Christianity. And even though the significance and symbolism of the Cross had been described in a multitude of excegetic and myical texts, and the connection of this symbol with various teachings about the fourfold structure of the world (four seasons, four elements, four directions, four evangelists, etc.) is obvious, it has no relationship with the essence of Christian ontology.

Geviert in the Metaphysics of Modernity

It is customary to periodize philosophers as Modern starting from Galileo, Francis Bacon, Isaac Newton, Baruch Spinoza, and, especially René Descartes. Following a lengthy period of domination by theology and the Scholastic (selective) Aristotelianism taken in the Latin translation (which missed many highly important aspects of Greek thought), Western Europe turned toward a new style of philosophizing, which aimed to liberate itself from Medieval dogmatism, Scholastic Aristotelianism, and the pressure of theological axioms. The Protestant Reformation offered favorable conditions for reaching this goal by challenging Catholic dogmatism and the hitherto unquestioned authority of the Church.

Heidegger, however, underscores the fact that in addition to the truly "new" (at least in comparison to the Middle Ages) elements in this philosophy, we also see in it the continuation, development, and establishment of the same Platonic-Aristotelian metaphysics, the same kind of thinking based on categories with reference to ontology, the essence of *beings*, the idea, etc. Modernity did not overcome the old metaphysics, but simply took it to its logical conclusion, extracted, and revealed all the consequences embedded in it. Therefore, in the philosophy of Modernity, we encounter the traces of several centuries of the development of the Scholastic mindset and the emergence of deeper, specifically Western European paradigms, which could be expressed with greater clarity, candor, and specificity.

From its first manifestos and programs, Modernity revealed itself to be the time of τέχνη. Furthemore, from now on, the most important pole of *techne* was moved from the Medieval God-Creator to man himself, having become, since the Renaissance, the most principal "creator" of culture, society, economic systems, politics, etc.

We have demonstrated that, according to Heidegger, it is man that was entrusted with the decision (*Entscheidung*), predetermining the course of establishing Modernity, the fate of Western European thought, and, consequently, the course of Western European history (*Geschichte*). It is man that was responsible for "destroying" *Geviert*. During the Modern period, this issue, veiled during the era of Scholasticism, is fully revealed. It reaches culmination in the philosophy of René Descartes. Descartes names the human ego, the thinking ego (*res cogens*), which is expressed in his formula *cogito ergo sum*, as the main authority in the ontological judgement of *Being*. This is how the philosophical topography of the subject is established, which ontologically constitutes the object with his thought (and God in deism). Being a radically new thought process from the formal standpoint, this change in direction, in reality, only revealed the main message of the early Greek philosophy. Behind its generalizations, gods, elements, ideas, and cosmogonic construction, the anticipated shadow of the future subject already flickered, which was called differently at that point ψυχη, νους (*psychi, nous*), etc. Therefore, the Renaissance, with newly found pathos, began to discover Greek authors for itself, in most cases incorrectly interpreting their thought and simplifying it. Renaissance philosophers intuitively guessed that the new era in Europe was profoundly linked to the period of the first Beginning, representing, in a certain sense, its mirror reflection. This explains the influence of Democritus on Galileo Galilei and Pierre Gassendi, Plato on Nicholas of Cusa; this is the source of the Neoplatonic Academy in Florence (Gemistus Pletho, Marsilio Ficino, Giovanni Pico della Mirandola, etc.), the surge of interest in the Milesian school, Parmenides, Epicurus, Lucretius, etc. Modernity was the *beginning of the End*, much like Plato and Aristotle representented the era of *the end of the first Beginning*. The Beginning was reflected in the End. To an even greater extent, this is obvious in those Western European philosophers who summed up the metaphysics

252

of Modernity, i.e., Hegel and Nietzsche: both diligently and continually addressed the Greeks (first and foremost, the pre-Socratics and especially Heraclitus).

What do we get if we superimpose the topography of *Geviert* over the philosophical schematic diagram of Modernity?

In place of man, there now stands the subject. The subject is the kind of figure that is placed at the center of an ontological construction. The subject is the essence (*essentia, οὐσία* [*ousia*]) of man and equal to his ability to reason and his rational activities. From any standpoint, the subject is a direct construction of the old metaphysical topography. First, we are dealing with *essences*, which immediately send us back to the Platonic *idea*, replacing *Seyn-Being*. Essentialist thought and essentialist interpretation of man as a *generalizing essence* (species—*εἶδος* [*eidos*]) was further strengthened in Christian theology. Therefore, the subject is based on this metaphysical foundation. Second, at the basis of a subject there lies the definitionof man as *animalis rationalis*, a "thinking animal." When it comes to "*animalis*," Charles Darwin and other evolutionists will deal with this issue later all the way through to ethology (Konrad Lorenz), whereas it is Descartes who will already make "*rationalis*" into the main attribute of a subject, thereby equating the rational mind with man's essence.

At the same time, the novelty of this philosophy includes the fact that putting the subject at the forefront liberates him (as the final philosophical version of man) from his dependence on any above-standing ontological authorities, *Being*, first and foremost, which from now on derives from the subject's judgement. The subject's thought process is deemed to be the *proof* of his *Being*, therefore, *Being* is the function of thought and subjectness. Later on, this topic will be developed further by Kant, who will cleanse

253

the philosophical topography of Modernity even further by formulating the construction of "pure reason," i.e., an autonomous structure of that same old *rationalis*.

Man as a subject transforms everything else into what he is not—an object. The concept of a subject is inseparable from that of an object. An object is that which is *in front* of the subject, that which is pre-sented to him (hence the German *Gegen-stand*, "standing across" or the Russian "*пред-мет*" (*predmet*)—that which has been "thrown in front of something.") Therefore, in this system of coordinates, all other members of *Geviert* become objects—the Earth, Sky, God (note that we are dealing with God that has been rethought out of the theological context, in the singular, even though during the Renaissance, timid attempts were made at addressing a certain version of polytheism, including Bernardino Telesio's hylozoism, Giordano Bruno's pantheism, alchemical traditions, all the way through to Spinoza and, later, the German Romantics). Their objectness differs: God as an object of the highest order, as the First Principle—the existence of which is postulated by the rational mind thinking about one's own origins; the Earth and the Sky together comprise an object of the lowest order, something spatial (according to Descartes), *res extensa*, an "extended thing." Equating the Earth and the Sky on the basis of substance, that is, the earthly (material, corporeal) nature of the Sky, is justified, as a priority, in English empirical philosophy by Isaac Newton, first and foremost.

Thus, in philosophy of the Modern period, we encounter further disfigurement of *Geviert*.

We see that in the given case, the structure of *Geviert* has been distorted even further. The Sky merged with the Earth:

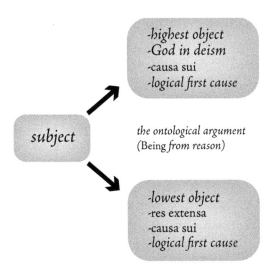

the nature of the heavenly bodies was recognized as strictly analogous to the nature of the earthly bodies (which was rejected by pervious philosophical interpretations of the world's structure). The assessment of an object's *Being* (both highest and lowest) was assigned to the subject. The God of deism gradually lost the attributes of a subject and became a mental abstraction (it is not surprising that at the next stage of philosophy of the Modern period, it was completely discarded).

This philosophical topography of the Modern era is highly significant, because its main parameters represent the map of the End, the last stage of *Geviert*, which, prior to this point, maintained a certain correlation to its initial appearance.

Gestell as Fate

Here we approach a key concept in Heidegger's philosophy from his late period—that of *Gestell* (literally: a frame, a stand).[2]

---

2 In English, *Gestell* is often translated as "*Enframing*." (*Ed.*)

Gestell may be viewed as a fundamental *seynsgeschichtliche*work in destroying (distorting, decaying) *Geviert*. Without accounting for the stages of deforming and collapsing *Geviert*, *Gestell* cannot be understood. *Gestell* is *Verwüstung*, "desertification," an inexorably approaching catastrophe, but, at the same time, a process, with the help of which the man of the West realizes his history (fate, *Geschichte*). Man replaces the thing first with a symbol, then with a created thing, then with an object. This is how the objectification of the world gradually occurs. An object is no longer a thing, but rather, a far-removed derivative thereof. When man is no longer capable of constituting and praising the *thing* (*Ding*) in its sacredness, in its presence, its poetic qualities, he reproduces the *object* (*Gegenstand*).

The object is not simply another name for the thing. An *object* is the end of the *thing*, when instead of the intersection of two live-giving axes of war in *Geviert*, we are dealing with an artificial, death-giving constructions of man's rational mind.

Gestell is the fundamental work of man's essence in destroying *Geviert*. From a poet, man turns into a "proletarian," "producer," and, at a certain stage, he wants to know nothing outside of economics. And everything started with poetry... Man tears himself away from the *world* and its regions, from free and proud *essensing* (*Wesung*) of the *thing* to such an extent that he only begins dealing with artificial objects that are fully within his will because he produces them himself. In this kind of production, there is no place for either the *Sky*, *Earth*, *gods*, or *God*. Here, man reigns supreme—only man as a *subject* (economic subject, judicial subject, political subject, etc.). Gradually, man becomes irritated not only with natural things (these he tries to exterminate as a class) but also various things he created himself. They end up being too "spontaneous," "distinct," therefore "free," and "autonomous," i.e., independent of his will. This is why man gradually transitions to mass serial production, the "eternal production of one and the same," "*ewige Herstellung der Gleichen.*" This is the industrial-economic version of Nietzsche's Eternal Return. *Gestell* is a fundamental phenomenon for Heidegger. *Gestell* is the fate of man. *Gestell* is the essence of *man* on the path to the developing consequences of the *decision* he made in the *first Beginning*. *Gestell* is the direct opposite of *Geviert*, its alternative and the process of its deformation, destruction, and overthrow.[3] But at the same time, Heidegger hears the voice of *Seyn-Being* even through this destruction. This voice is silence, abandonment of *Being* (*Seinsverlassenheit*), concealment (*Verberen*), but it, too, can be heard and deciphered. *Gestell* is the profound essence of *techne* and *Machenschaft*. And as such, it is linked to *Seyn-Being*. *Seyn-Being* exists (*west*) through this *Wesen*.

Heidegger talks about the "war of *Seyn-Being* with *beings*."[4] This war is based on the fact that the correlation between *Seyn-Being* and *beings* is problematic and not obvious. It is this factor that, more so than anything else, deserves *questioning*. If questioning is not constituted in the proper way, or if it becomes one of the questions alongside all others, if the answer given to it is too hasty or incorrect (and the decision in all cases is taken by man—the carrier of speech—as a form of *Seyn-Being's* existence), then *Seyn-Being* initiates war with *beings*. The name of this war is *Gestell*.

---

[3] "*Gestell* is what destroys *Geviert.*" (Martin Heidegger, *Zur Frage nach der Bestimmung der Sache des Denkens* [St. Gallen: Erker-Verlag, 1984], 12.)
[4] Martin Heidegger, *Beiträge zur Philosophie (vom Ereignis). op. cit.*, 310. In full, this statement reads, "*Der Streit des Seyns gegen das Seiende aber ist dies Sichverbergen der Verhaltenheit einer ursprünglichen Zugehörigkeit.*" "The war of *Seyn-Being* against *beings* is the *self-concealing* relationship of original belonging."

Here, we approach the most important issue: *how should we conceptualize nihilism and the catastrophe of philosophy's End in a non-dual way?*

In a dual shematic diagram, *Geviert* is conceived as something authentic, whereas *Gestell*—as inauthentic. *Geviert* opens up the Beginning, whereas *Gestell* is work toward bringing the End. However, Heidegger uses every possible way to make us realize that dual thinking is fundamentally inaccurate. It can never resolve a philosophical problem or even formulate it correctly. *One must think non-dually* and, if one so desires, non-logically. Opposites must not simply be overcome through synthesis (as a third given), but also must be thought of simultaneously as opposites and non-opposites.

Geviert is a world in which *Seyn-Being* is revered, a world seen in a fundamental-ontological way as it actually *exists* (*west*) in the fundamental-ontological *essence* (*Wesen*). *Gestell* is an unyielding, centuries-long, and deliberate process of destruction, distortion, and annihilation of this kind of a world, a presumptious oblivion of *Seyn-Being*, a series of foolishly formulated questions and even more foolish answers. *Gestell* is man's ultimate failure, his catastrophe, his misfortune, his self-denial, his unfulfillable goal; it is his neverending end, his unrecognized dying *per se*, and the murder of everything around him. How can all this be combined? How can one see the quiet voice of *Seyn-Being* in either one? How can one recognize *destiny* (*Geschick—Geschichte*) in this?

Gestell is the essence of the world's inauthentic contents. It appears as the world's skeleton, when *Seyn-Being* is incorrenctly conceptualized as *Sein-Being*. *Seyn-Being* opens up as *Ereignis* in *Geviert*. *Sein-Being* is the routine in *Gestell*. But even

258

though there is a fundamental (the most fundamental of all) opposition of *Seyn* and *Sein*, they are not different and, at the furthest-removed horizon—one and the same. This is not a simple thought. Perhaps, this is the least simple of all thoughts. But in understanding this thought lies the key to the entire philosophy of Martin Heidegger.

The Industrial Transformation of the Fourfold

From the philosophical standpoint, *Gestell* fully reveals itself in the metaphysical topography of Modernity together with Descartes. Here one could theoretically finalize the analysis of *Geviert*'s deformation in Western European thought. But for the purpose of a graphic demonstration, we could trace more specific transformations found at the point when Modernity turns from being a philosophical program into a political, social, ideological, and economic practice. This analysis offers certain case-in-point moments that simplify our understanding of speculative philosophical problems.

Modernity reaches its peak with industrialization, which, in practice, embodies the main tendencies present in the candor of Modern-era philosophy. In this period, the world regions in *Geviert* undergo visible changes, the main content of which one could easily find as early as Descartes. Yet there is a certain distance between the *beginning of the End* and the *End* itself. The most significant change concerns God. At the End of philosophy, "God dies." Therefore, an entire region of the world collapses, which, starting from *Geviert* and until Descartes, was part of the philosophical topography in one way or another. Nietzsche's phrase "God is dead" refers to a radical extraction from the ontological picture, not just the specific figure of God, but the entire dimension that previously was necessarily present in the philosophical topography, also having been the basis of the entire ontological construction in theology. "God is dead" does not simply mean crossing out the greatest of *beings*, the God Person, but also the annulment of an entire dimension, an independent world region, which was part of *Geviert* and all other ontological maps. This is the real end of *Geviert* (the Fourfold), since one of its dimensions disappears in the most radical way. This is called "atheism," the rejection of acknowledging God. Heidegger demonstrates that atheism, radically changing the ontological topography, still remains within the framework of Western European metaphysics. After all, another dimension is now in the place of the annulled one—either matter (for materialists and Marxists), "Nothingness" (for agnostics) or utilitarianism, value, life (for utilitarians, Liberals, and the philosophers of life). An empty space, left in the place where the Divine used to dwell, has the same role in the metaphysics of the industrial world as the one previously carried out by a deity. It remains the source of the greatest kind of legitimation, the highest soft nod that indicates "divine" approval, acceptance, and agreement. Only from now on, the insignificance of this legitimation allows us to speak about the "legitimation from the side of Nothingness." *Nothingness* approves or disapproves of man's fate. Those who can look the truth in the eye formulate this literally: "Nothingness approves or disapproves." Those whom the tragedy of the given situation escapes, prefer to say the following, "Nothingness neither approves, nor disapproves." The former are conscious nihilists (Conservative Revolution, Fascism), the latter—unconscious nihilists (Communism, Liberalism).

Starting with Plato, the Sky was the receptacle of ideas, and later, in Christianity, the Sky became God's throne, even though it was created. Newton's cosmology, principally based on the quality of the general substance, compares the Sky to the Earth in terms of shared substance. But ultimately, the Sky disappears as such during the era of industrialization, the triumph of science and *techne* through flights into space and penetration deep into substances, quantum mechanics, the theory of relativity, field theory, etc. There is no more Sky as the Sky. Man encounters only earthly substance, matter everywhere.[5] Satellites paved the Sky over with blinking apparatuses, iron bodies, and all-pervasive radio waves, finishing off desacralization, which began with Platonic ideas. Satellites are the *ideas* of the industrial era.

The Earth also stopped being *Earth*. Now it produces harvests forcefully. It is poisoned with chemicals in order to achieve the impossible. They make deep holes in it to reach its black petroleum blood. They cut out its insides to deprive it of breath—gas. The Earth is becoming a "resource," that which must be scooped out and destroyed, reduced to nothing, given into entropy. If earlier the very principle of the Earth functioned as a gentle feminine sabotage of the Sky's order, then now mankind is turning the Earth itself into dust; man mercilessly rapes, destroys, devastates, poisons, sprays with acids and civilizational waste, scorches, and tortures it.

Man of the industrial era is further removed from man of *Geviert* than one could imagine. He inflated his subjectness to such an extent that he made himself microscopic, infinitely small, nearly gone. Nietzsche wrote about this speaking of the

---

[5] German poet Gottfried Benn wrote about this in his poem "Chants" ("*Gesänge*"): "Everything is the shore, forever calls the sea." ("*Alles ist Ufer, ewig ruft das Meer.*")

"Last Men." The Last Men are men of the End. By producing mountains of garbage, they become garbage themselves.

At the same time, the *thing* turns into an industrial product, goods for sale; that is, it no longer exists at a communal *ting* or *veche*—a sacred gathering but is exclusively in the *marketplace*. Some manufacture things, others resell them, others yet consume them, and all together they create a singular stream of late-human, late-historic mechanisms—production, consumption, thirst, suffering, desires. Proletarians and the bourgeoisie once and for all crash what was destroyed before them by the titans of Antiquity, Middle Ages, Renaissance, and the heroic beginning of Modernity. It was the giants that destroyed *Geviert*, and the "Last Men" simply swarm amidst its ruins, stealing everything they can.

Man becomes the man of production, man of trade, man of consumption—*homo economicus*. And it is no longer man *per se* as a subject that becomes the master of the world's game, but *Gestell* itself, replacing *Being* with itself along with the event, thing, man, and everything else. Industrial production becomes the fate of *homo economicus* and predetermines the most sigifnicant aspects of the industrial era—the hysterical accumulation of capital and the attempts to redistribute what is produced by the revolutionary proletariat in its own favor.

Industrial topography can be illustrated according to the following schematic diagram.

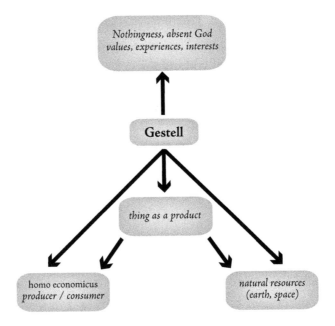

From the standpoint of a formal approach, this looks completely "new" in comparison to Cartesian metaphysics. But from the philosophical point of view, the industrial era does not add anything principal. Gernally, all of this was already obvious in Descartes and Newton, who predefined Modernity within its qualitative framework.

Simulacrum

Then follows another phase of Western European history, though Heidegger did not live long enough to see it. We are dealing with Postmodernity, in which the entire topography undergoes substantial changes once again. In the postindustrial landscape of civilizations, certain thinkers (such as Francis Fukuyama) announced the "End of History" (*Geschichte*), at the same time acknowledging that the comprehension of this end as an ontological phenomenon will not occur and that is why this

End will be "infinite." Having happened, it will never happen, will never occur, will never come to fruition, since there are no longer men capable of making the decision that the end is the End and taking on the responsibility for the profound limit of the End. Nietzsche himself spoke of the "Last Men": "His race is as ineradicable as the flea; the Last Man lives longest." "'We have invented happiness,' say the Last Men, and they blink."[6] It is indicative that Fukuyama who announced the "end of history," mentioned the "Last Man" in the title of his book as well.[7]

The primary world regions (*Weltgegenden*) of *Geviert* may be found in Postmodernity, but this is not the sight for the weak.

Instead of the Sky, there gapes a giant advertising billboard, a computerized, transparent, and alluring window display. The subject's dark desires are projected onto it, previously squeezed out beneath the perception threshold by the stoic work of our consciousness. This is *animalis*, liberated from *rationalis*, letting itself be known. But does such *animalis* exist among *beings*? Are animals, "the living," "ζῷον" (zoon), capable of doing and desiring such vile things as the Last Men? This is not *animalis* but a mechanically perverted fantasy of an eviscerated man creating images on the screen. He overthrows the rational mind and wants to be an animal, but cannot be one, because he is not an animal. Then who is he? After all, we cannot call "this" a "man" from any one of the topographies known to us. He is not an "animal" because he is no one, and his goal is not to become someone, but, becoming no one, to break through to *Seyn-Being* in order to give speech to its illumination. By failing to do so, by establishing

[6] Friedrich Nietzsche, "Thus Spake Zarathustra," *The Portrable Nietzsche*, tr. Walter Kaufmann (New York: Vintage Books, 1954), 130.
[7] Francis Fukuyama, *The End of History and the Last Man* (New York: The Free Press, 1992).

himself as man, man commits an irreversible error. Instead of the question mark of his identity, he offers a hasty and preemptively incorrect answer. This is how humanity, which is *not*, is created. Therefore, it is not surprising that this kind of humanity does not last for long and collapses into a new chimera—a chimera of a man-beast—at a certain moment (the moment of Postmodernity). No longer capable of being man (this is the kind of *Being* as a strict formula is in itself misleading), the Last Man rushes in despair to the participants of the Christian Apocalypse—those places where the Revelation mentions the "beast" and his number. Since the Last Man is incapable of doing anything other than counting, he attempts to "count the number of the beast," suspecting that he will find the beast within by doing so. Animality and demonic incarnation are the final illusions of the Last Man, since he is neither beast, nor demon. Man becomes posthuman. On the one hand, this is an *Übermensch*-technician, deftly reasoning, dealing with the mobile Web, capable of loading information streams with data. On the other hand, he is an *Untermensch* which is also a version of posthumanity. He is a consumer, a user, clicking and staring at the "user-friendly interface," going through countless links. No longer capable of comprehending text, he is simply searching in the data bases for what corresponds to his perception of the "here and now." This is constant internautic wandering through simulated, winking objects; staring at the screen, it is impossible to discern where online ends and the real world begins, as he also continues to communicate with someone via Skype.

But let us leave this terrifying issue of precisely describing our contemporaries. Thank God Heidegger did not live long enough to see this.

The Earth disappears with the ease of communications, all places become the same, and utopia is realized. *Utopia* is where there is no *place*. According to Heidegger, the Earth opens itself up through places. The Earth is that very *place*, a natural place. And nowadays, there are no places, no distances, nothing is separate; all places, cities, points, and McDonald's drive-throughs around the globe are completely identical. There are identical people with tattoos and piercings, chatting, drinking beer, using the Internet, and doing drugs.

There is no more Earth either. It has turned into a virtual space, where what is the most *far removed* is banal, whereas what is the *closest* does not exist. All that the Earth had done during its participation in *Geviert* as well as later on, in other philosophical topographies, is no longer needed. The Earth is no longer a resource, but rather a garbage dump. People fight for it as a garbage dump, including human garbage— those very Nietzschean "people of the End" who "obtained happiness." From this point forward, the Earth is a place where people bury garbage, whether radioactive, manufacturing-based, or bodies of those who died or were cremated. God becomes a joke. He returns from Modernity's Nothingness in the form of a silly caricature. No one is scaring him off anymore or killing him. His death lost all meaning, and that is why it is now forgotten. It is not that He was resurrected, but that He simply appeared again, as if nothing happened, as an independent corpse.

Today, one can speak about God, or be silent. No one is interested in Him, and if anyone is, then to no greater degree than the intrigues of a popular actor or a supermodel. No, tabloid gossip is much more interesting than God. Yet still, he returns, but this time around as a parody, as a mockery of death, which had been forgotten, and which lost all meaning. "*Who* died exactly?"

Bin Laden appears on television, saying to the cameras, "*Allah Akbar!*" "Allah is Great!" They attempt to capture him immediately but fail to do so. He is nowhere, untraceable, he is outside of places in the utopia of the television. Chasing him turns into a popular detective series. Bin Laden and Allah switch places, but the public's suspense is just as high. "When will they capture him?"

Whom? Allah? Bin Laden? Saddam Hussein? Mullah Omar?

In response to the question why he made the decision to attack Iraq, George W. Bush, the former U.S. President, allegedly proclaimed, "God told me to strike at al-Qaida, and I struck them, and then He instructed me to strike at Saddam, which I did..."[8] We are neither horrified, nor amazed by this. We accept this as a given. He is the President of the United States after all, the head of the most powerful and successful democracy in the world. It is quite possible that God himself allowed him to do so.

If someone were to say, "God is not dead," at the previous stage of *desertification* (Modernity), then he would have been put into a psychiatric ward. But now, in the era of Postmodernity, whatever one says about "god" or not about "god"—everything goes. Due to ultimate indifference. Things are turning into *simulacra* (as per Jean Baudrillard). They become derivative of fashions, which, as in its ultimate embodiment, *Gestell* captures and covers us fully.

---

8 James Gannon, *Military Occupations in the Age of Self-Determination* (Westport: Greenwood Publishing, 2008), 125.

The thing ends its journey. From now on, it is a *simulacrum*, and no longer an idea, sign, object, and not even a product, but rather a pure embodied deceipt. A product, in which the thing dies, still maintains a connection with manufacturing, usefulness, and a certain kind of rationality. But even this comes to an end. *Simulacrum*, according to Baudrillard, is a "copy without an original," akin to a poor-quality photocopy in which one's imagination allows one to see whatever it wants— a portrait of a President, a woman's body, landscapes, or fictional text. Instead of a thing, Postmodernity establishes the Rorschach test, meaningless and unnecessary ink stain, useless and empty, but as a result of limitless will to power and the power of fashion, taken to be the absolute categorical imperative. The laws of fashion as the highest level of *Gestell* proclaim:

- things live only for a moment;

- things must be meaningless, herein lies their meaning;

- things must be exchanged;

- after a thing comes another thing;

- identical things differ;

- the thing is everything; the rest is nothing;

- the thing does not die; it must be discarded;

- the thing is greater than life.

The shorter is the life of a thing-*simulacrum*, the more intense it is. The right shoes of Postmodernity are those that only get worn once. This is the logic of fashion (*Gestell*), it becomes more and more rapid. In the past, some people wore things for several years, now—for a season or half a season, but this is not the limit. The change in things at breakneck speed is their death factory, their planned and systematized genocide. Behind the entropy of things, behind the transition to the regime of total *simulacrum*, stands a culture's readiness to completely annihilate *Geviert*.

Instead of *Being*, we are now dealing with "virtual reality." The very concept of "reality" in the metaphysics of Modernity is "virtual" to the greatest extent in the sense that it is fictional and ontologically unjustifiable. When a subject postulates what he has in front of him as an object, he carries out a rather questionable operation based on justifying the ontological reality of this object. The object is objective (it is "in reality") because it is an object, i.e., because it is etymologically "in front of me" (the subject). In Descartes, Newton, Hume, and Kant, this looks serious and solemn, featuring that special pompous kind of pathos with which limited minds normally proclaim yet another meaningless absurdity. But even more limited creatures fall, even easier, for these scientific fairy tales about the nature of reality and wander through the labyrinths of these categories for centuries. The transition from reality to virtual reality is the transition from a joke, taken seriously, to a joke that should be (may be) a source of laughter. Virtual reality takes the idea of an object *ad absurdum*, thereby taking the idea of a subject *ad absurdum* as well. This is grinning Nothingness.

It is difficult to depict the topography of Postmodernity. But, as a hypothesis, the following (debatable) version may be proposed. This topography is so terrifying that it could be called "post-eschatological."

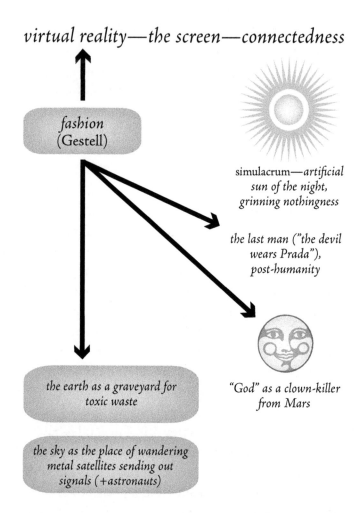

virtual reality—the screen—connectedness

fashion
(Gestell)

simulacrum—*artificial
sun of the night,
grinning nothingness*

*the last man ("the devil
wears Prada"),
post-humanity*

*the earth as a graveyard for
toxic waste*

"God" as a clown-killer
from Mars

*the sky as the place of wandering
metal satellites sending out
signals (+astronauts)*

270

III. GEVIERT IN ANOTHER BEGINNING

Geviert and Future Horizons

We examined *Geviert* as a possibility in the first Beginning and as a fundamental-ontological map allowing us to better understand those processes pushing Western European philosophy toward its End. But according to Heidegger's own thought, *Geviert* belongs to the realm of the "future," which must come into fruition in another Beginning—at the moment of *Ereignis*. And despite the fact that certain parallels exist with the first Beginning—at least prior to its reaching the point of establishing Platonic topography, *Geviert per se* was never in the form in which it must come to fruition in the future.

For Heidegger, fundamental-ontology is a project (*Entwurf*) being constructed on grasping the hidden message from *Seyn-Being* throughout the entire history (*Geschichte*) of Western thought—the kind of message that comprises the worsening concealment of *Being*. Therefore, *Geviert* should be conceived as a horizon and, in a certain sense, a goal.

Heidegger thought that our time is the time of the decision (*Entscheidung*). This is also the time of death, the grave hour. The essence of the decision comprises the following: either Western mankind recognizes that its history has been the result of the decision taken in the first Beginning and accepts the consequences of "*Being*'s oblivion," recognizes the nihilism embedded in τέχνη (*techne*) and *Gestell*, or mankind can

273

continue pretending that "everything is fine," that there is no nihilism, and that there is no catastrophe hanging over the world. In the first case, the very fact of grasping Modernity as nihilism, as the "desolate times," and the fixation of one's attention on *Gestell* as an already realized fate mean the transition to another Beginning, the transfer of attention exclusively toward *Seyn-Being*, and preparing for *Ereignis*. Then *Geviert* becomes the direct and natural extension of *Ereignis*. The event, having come to fruition, will establish man as the guardian of *Seyn-Being*, will open up the order of the Sky and the world, will save the Earth, returning to it its dignity and allowing gods (the Last God) to arrive. At the center of the four axes of *Geviert*, the sacred (*вещая* [*veshchaia*], knowing) thing will reign again. In the second case scenario, if the decision about making no decisions is made (this will be a decision in itself), the power of the unperceived *Gestell*, the force of the arrived, but unacknowledged and unidentified (to an adequate extent) End, will lead to an ultimate catastrophe. And then *Geviert* will not occur, come to fruition, and τέχνη will plunge mankind and the Earth toward imminent death. In his final years, Heidegger leaned toward the view that mankind had already made its decision—the second fatal choice, and that the situation cannot be rectified. "'Only a God can save us.'"[1]

In any case, in order to accurately understand Heidegger's philosophy, it is important to relate *Geviert* specifically to the future that is open and that depends on man's realization of his profound freedom.

---

[1] "Nur noch ein Gott kann uns retten," "Spiegel-Gesprach mit Martin Heidegger am 23. September 1966," *Der Spiegel*, 30. Jg. N 23. 31 (Mai 1976).

Geviert as a Goal (a Will Toward Making the Decision)

In terms of the decision that has already been made, there can be certain uncertainties. It is quite obvious that choosing another Beginning in the 20th century and the incipient 21st century was not made. Nonetheless, from the philosophical standpoint, events developed with outmost consistency and internal logic. At the end of the 19th century, Nietzsche, in essence, formulated the end of Western European philosophy. This is a fundamental historic (*seynsgeschichtliche*) fact. In Nietzsche, philosophy reached its "eschaton."

In the 20th century, Martin Heidegger, more so than anyone else, recognizes the meaning of the entire philosophical process from the Beginning to the End in a crystal-clear way. Heidegger philosophizes over a grave, dots all the "i's," once again gazes upon the entire history of philosophy, and marks the unquestionable periods, meanings, and transformations. Nietzsche theorized the 20th century, but it was Heidegger who did so in a more profound way. Heidegger recorded the End of the West, opened up the horizon of *another Beginning*, the trajectory of *leaping* into *Ereignis*, and outlined *Geviert* as an assignment. Furthermore, Heidegger conjugated the history of Western European philosophy and *Gestell* with a fundamental-ontological outlook in a grandiose manner, which made the catastrophic position of contemporary man not an argument against *Geviert* but rather the proof of its fateful proximity.

In the 20th century itself, *Ereignis* did not occur. The decision about transitioning to another Beginning was not made. It was impossible to make this decision within the framework of the ideologies that openly took an oath for *Machenschaft*

(Communism and Liberalism); and in the place where it could have been made, and where certain moments made one hopeful that it would be (the ideology of the Third Way), the decision was passed over (this was expressed in the chasm between the Conservative Revolution and historic National Socialism). Heidegger himself impartially interprets the fact that the decision was not made in the Germany of the 1930s-1940s as proof that National Socialism was, too, infected with *Machenschaft*, along with its inability to leave the framework of Western European metaphysics (with *Gestell*, subject, *techne*, will to power, etc.). Heidegger himself saw his philosophy as a transition to another Beginning and, consequently, as the justification of *Ereignis* and as a moving closer toward *Geviert*. Western European history (*Geschichte*) of the 20th century did not follow Heidegger, did not end up at his level, did not accept or grasp his message. Similarly, contemporaries did not understand Hölderlin, Kierkegaard, or Nietzsche in the 19th century.

Heidegger, who had done more in the 20th century—and, possibly, in the entire history of philosophy than almost anyone else—had every reason for despair. The political, cultural, and social history of the 20th century fully confirmed his assessment. During a turning point, he himself ended up where he should have been heard, in Germany. He was a German, and it was Germans, it seemed then, who were ready to take upon themselves the responsibility of changing the course of history (*Geschichte*). All elements of fate were gathered into a single whole. There was only a single moment left before reaching *Ereignis* and the universal midnight.

When everything fell apart, this became the greatest challenge for Heidegger. It is difficult to imagine the kind of trauma that he experienced observing the events of 1930s-1940s, trying to participate in them. He had every reason to think, by the end of his life, that mankind is dead-set on trying to kill itself, the Earth, and the world in no less a radical manner than it dealt with God.

Judged by the logic and significance of the events and transformations, which mankind lived through after Heidegger's death, nothing tells us that his fateful prognosis was inaccurate. On the contrary, in the last few decades, degeneration has gone so far that there are very few left of those who are capable of recognizing the depth and irreversibility of this tragedy.

But we can also look at this situation in another way. The 20th century, having recognized Heidegger as a great thinker, essentially failed to understand his thought, and even if it did understand them, then it did not accept them. Heidegger's philosophy, pulled apart into fragments, inspired hundreds of philosophers, psychologists, artists, scientists, cultural critics and to a great extent affected the establishment of the Postmodern paradigm. But practically no one fully and wholly grasped Hediegger's thought or followed the path leading to *another Beginning*. However, if mankind does not want to acknowledge the fact that the End has already occurred and persists in "planetary idiocy," dying without dying, and "stretches the rubber," tries to leave the dead end, making it eternal, then, contrary to its will, it leaves open the possibility to make a different decision in its stead.

The 21st century, in essence, has not yet begun: that which is around us today in terms of meaning is still the 20th century, which simply cannot come to an end. The 21st century will start when we truly begin to grasp Heidegger's philosophy. And then we will gain the opportunity to make another decision, a choice in favor of transitioning to *another Beginning,* in favor of *Ereignis,* in favor of Geviert.

Heidegger faced Western European philosophy focused on classic German philosophy and its Nietzschean peak. On its basis, pushing off it, Heidegger took a leap into the abyss of a new kind of freedom. We are now faced with Heidegger's philosophy. In it, there implicitly lies the entire history of philosophy comprehended by him, Hegel, Schopenhaur, Kierkegaard, and Nietzsche. However, it contains many other things, too, which Heidegger carried out anticipating the future and preparing for it. Heidegger's own appearance can be interpreted as the dawn of *Ereignis,* and this interpretation can and must become the imperative for the 21st century. *Ereignis* did not arrive in the 20th century. This is a fact. But we would not be free, would not be men, would not be thinking *beings,* would not be the carriers of great Indo-European languages, if we were to give up in the face of the mad, globalist crowds and self-entertaining, scattered masses of Postmodernity, the slaves of tolerant, alienating, nihilating, and poisonous fashions.

Therefore, the decision about *Geviert*'s arrival remains open. And this openness is established thanks to the very presence of Heidegger's philosophy. If this philosophy finds at least one adequate reader, then we cannot bury *Ereignis* preemptively. Or conversely, the living breath of *Ereignis* will cross out today's world with a life-giving cross, giving the region of Nothingness its hypertrophied and unthinkably bloated creation.

In this case, the image of *Geviert* can become a fundamental philosophical program, goal, and banner that will gather those "exceptions" around whom, according to Nietzsche, turns the

278

wheel of the Universe—those exceptions, whom Heidegger calls the "future ones" (*Künftige*). Whether there *will be* a future, whether the *Beginning* commences, whether the *Event* comes to fruition depends on them.

In this case, the structure of *Geviert* in *another Beginning* will be as follows.

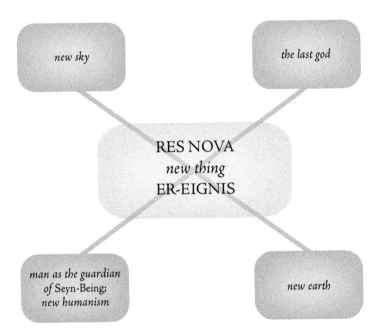

PART 3

Dasein

I. THREE STAGES OF DEVELOPMENT IN MARTIN HEIDEGGER'S PHILOSOPHY

There are tree principal stages in Heidegger's philosophical work.

The first stage: formulating the principal set of problems and introducing the concept of *Dasein*. The culmination of this period came with writing his main work, *Sein und Zeit* (1927).[1] The phenomenological approach to Husserl[2] preceeds this book, while the period of pondering the grand prospects marked in it—one that is fundamental for the entire history of philosophy—follows it.

---

[1] Martin Heidegger, *Sein und Zeit* (1927) (Tübingen: Max Niemeyer Verlag, 2006); Martin Heidegger, *Being and Time*, tr. John Macquarrie & Edward Robinson (New York: Harper & Row, 1962); Martin Heidegger, *Être et temps*, tr. d'Emmanuel Martineau (Paris: Authentica, 1985).

[2] Early phenomenological works appear in the following volumes: Martin Heidegger, Gesamtausgabe. Frankfurt am Main: Vittorio Klostermann. *Frühe Schriften (1912–16); Zur Bestimmung der Philosophie; Grundprobleme der Phänomenologie (1919); Phänomenologie der Anschauung und des Ausdrucks. Theorie der philosophischen Begriffsbildung (1920); Phänomenologie des religiösen Lebens; Phänomenologische Interpretationen zu Aristoteles: Einführung in die phänomenologische Forschung (1921); Phänomenologische Interpretationen ausgewählter Abhandlungen des Aristoteles zur Ontologie und Logik (1922); Ontologie: Hermeneutik der Faktizität (1923); Einführung in die phänomenologische Forschung; AKA Der Beginn der neuzeitlichen Philosophie (1923).*

The following texts were written immediate prior to *Sein und Zeit* developing individual topics from Heidegger's most important book of the future: *Der Begriff der Zeit (1924); Grundbegriffe der aristotelischen Philosophie (1924); Platon: Sophistes (1924); Prolegomena zur Geschite des Zeitbegriffs (1925); Logik: Die frage nach der Wahrheit (1925); Grundbegriffe der antiken Philosophie (1926); Geschichte der Philosophie von Thomas v. Aquin bis Kant (1926); Die Grundprobleme der Phänomenologie (1927).*

283

The second stage: the years 1936-1946 are the least known of all. This is the case for a number of reasons, political, first and foremost. In this period, Heidegger was involved with National Socialism. Even his gradual marginalization within that regime did not affect his careful attention to this phenomenon, comprehended in a unique, profound dimension, which coincided, overall, with the general approach by the Conservative Revolution. This period was the peak of Heidegger's creative philosophical pursuits, marked by conceptualizing *Seynsgeschichte*, *Seyn*, and especially *Ereignis*. Heidegger himself wrote in a note to "Letter on Humanism," "Starting from 1936, the main subject of my thought was *Ereignis*."[3]

At this time, Heidegger lives through the hope of transforming National Socialism into a profoundly philosophical phenomenon, which has been called upon to undertake the turning point in Western European civilization and world history in favor of *another Beginning* (*der andere Anfang*), comparable and even superior to the first Beginning (*der erste Anfang*) when Greek philosophy arose. In order for the historic prerequisites of *Ereignis* to occur, Germany (representing Europe) must overcome two forms of ultimate nihilism (*Machenschaft*)—the U.S. ("*Americanismus*" which Heidegger despised) and the USSR (in which Heidegger found the triumph of *techne* through its version of Marxism). Heidegger linked the victory of Nazi Germany with carrying out a *philosophical operation*—comprehending the essence of *Machenschaft* and its interpretation in the context of Western metaphysics and its history. Without this, he warned, the war would be lost.[4]

---

[3] Martin Heidegger, *Brief über den Humanismus (1946)* (Frankfurt am Main: Vittorio Klostermann, 1949); here, translated from the Russian.

[4] Martin Heidegger, *Geschichte des Seyns (1938/1940)* (Frankfurt am Main: Vittorio Klostermann, 1998).

284

This kind of comprehension did not occur, and the war was, indeed, lost.

Heidegger of the so-called middle period was left outside the philosophical discussion after 1945 for obvious reasons and is, therefore, virtually unknown. At the same time, it is in this period that the philosopher expresses his profound ideas in the most complete and candid manner.[5] What we know from this period is Heidegger's works on Nietzsche[6], which are undoubtedly fundamental, but not fully covering the central set of problems in those years. If we miss out on the contents of this period, we will not be able to adequately understand the ideas of the early period formulated in *Sein und Zeit*, nor those of the later period.

The third stage comprises works from the postwar period until the philosopher's death. They are the continuation of Heidegger's main philosophizing trajectory. However, they are

---

[5] We relied on the following works in the first and second parts of this book: Martin Heidegger, *Einführung in die Metaphysik* (Tübingen: Max Niemeyer, 1953); Idem., *Geschichte des Seyns (1938/1940)* (Frankfurt am Main: Vittorio Klostermann, 1998); Idem., *Über den Anfang* (Frankfurt am Main: Vittorio Klostermann, 2005), and, perhaps, the most important work of that period: Martin Heidegger, *Beiträge zur Philosophie (vom Ereignis)*. (Frankfurt am Main: Vittorio Klostermann, 1989), published, however, quite recently, after the author's death as a result of his will.

[6] Martin Heidegger, *Nietzsche I (1936–39), Nietzsche II (1939–46)* (Frankfurt am Main: Vittorio Klostermann, 1996); Idem., *Nietzsche: Der Wille zur Macht als Kunst (1936)* (Frankfurt am Main: Vittorio Klostermann, 1985); Idem., *Nietzsches Metaphysische Grundstellung im abendländischen Denken: Die ewige Wiederkehr des Gleichen (1937)* (Frankfurt am Main: Vittorio Klostermann, 1986); Idem., *Nietzsches II. Unzeitgemässe Betrachtung (1938)* (Frankfurt am Main: Vittorio Klostermann, 1989); Idem., *Nietzsches Lehre vom Willen zur Macht als Erkenntnis (1939)* (Frankfurt am Main: Vittorio Klostermann, 1989); Idem., *Nietzsche: Der europäische Nihilismus (1940)* (Frankfurt am Main: Vittorio Klostermann, 1986); Idem. *Nietzsches Metaphysik (1941–42), Einleitung in die Philosopie—Denken und Dichten (1944–45)* (Frankfurt am Main: Vittorio Klostermann, 1990).

placed into the context of humanities, in which the subjects of the second period were censored or self-censored under the influence of external factors. The collapse of National Socialism demanded the revision of certain metaphysical expectations of this thinker, which could not be done openly and transparently or, perhaps, could not be done at all. [7]

At the same time, these three periods comprise a single whole of Heidegger's philosophy, which cannot be dismembered without causing damage to each of its elements. The most accurate approach, in our view, would be to begin the historical-philosophical investigation with Heidegger's second period (the subject of *Ereignis*) as the most direct and concise presentation of the *acme* of his philosophy. Only then should we discuss his third period and only after that return to the subjects considered in *Sein und Zeit* and *Dasein* of the first period, the latter being the chosen start for most researchers.

It is this second period of Heidegger's work that contains the keys to his thought in its entirety. If we were to artificially ignore this period, then we would not be able to understand the intentions of *Sein und Zeit*, or the general trajectory of the last writing period. In this case, the first period will only appear to be as a certain kind of development in the phenomenological approach (in the spirit of uniquely interpreting Husserl), whereas the third period will be seen as a harmless version of European humanism, a certain kind of hermeneutics of European culture

---

[7] Heidegger's main texts in the late period from his collected works: Martin Heidegger, *Gesamtausgabe* (Frankfurt am Main: Vittorio Klostermann) including *Was heisst Denken?* (1951–52); *Der Satz vom Grund* (1955–56); *Identität und Differenz* (1955–57); *Unterwegs zur Sprache* (1950–59); *Zur Sache des Denkens* (1962–64); *Seminare* (1951–73). *Holzwege*, in particular, stands out (Martin Heidegger, *Holzwege* [Frankfurt am Main: Vittorio Klostermann, 2003]), containing key texts about philosophy and poetry.

and pessimistic intuitions about a technological and ecological catastrophe. But this is not Heidegger at all.

It is quite understandable why it is this kind of Heidegger that is familiar to everyone. Philosophers enslaved by his thought tried to introduce him in the context of world philosophy *despite* his political positions. Perhaps, this was justified, because preserving the grand ideas of this thinker in Western European culture was such an important undertaking that this concession was worth it. At the same time, reduced preservation of Heidegger's heritage led to the fact that most often we are dealing with *simulacra* of his thought rather than his thought itself. Referring to Heidegger without accounting for *Ereignis*, we end up making quite a rough approximation, if not a caricature.

Therefore, we chose to begin our analysis with Heidegger's middle period, followed by the section on *Geviert* in which we described the main trajectories of late Heidegger. Only then, here and now, we have arrived at the point that has become a customary start, the set of problems focused on *Dasein* and his most important work in which they are formulated, *Sein und Zeit*.

This book must only be read in German. And, in order to get acquainted with it, it is quite possible to learn this language.[8]

The first attempt to work with Heideger in the USSR took place in the 1970s and was a failure. We cannot blame amateur

---

[8] There are no Russian translations that are up-to-par. Therefore, the first generation of Russian philosophers interested in Heidegger must learn the language in which his works are written. Only in the future, after the emergence of accurate translations accompanied by an editor's commentary, will it be possible to discuss the next steps.

Soviet philosophers: it was impossible to understand anything in terms of philosophy in that intellectual atmosphere, let alone make sense of Heidegger's outmost difficult work. Starting from the middle of the 1960s until today, Russia has been experiencing an "empty" time period from the philosophical standpoint. A lot of things occur, but nothing takes place.

Despite everything, we must prepare a new turn in Russian philosophy starting from an accurate understanding of Western thought. And Western thought in its greatest embodiment is the philosophy of Martin Heidegger.

II. DASEIN AND THE HISTORY OF PHILOSOPHY (FROM THE FIRST BEGINNING TO THE END OF PHILOSOPHY)

Dasein as an Illumination and Conclusion to the Historical-Philosophical Analysis

The existential analysis of *Dasein*, according to Heidegger, is formulated as follows: "*Wie ist Dasein?*"—"How is *Dasein?*" Note that it is not "*What* is *Dasein*" but rather "*how.*"

Therefore, we must *describe Dasein* rather than define it; we must invite others to think about it rather than unequivocally postulate its meaning.

The expression "*Dasein*" is fundamental for the entire history of philosophy. Formally, it means "*Being,*" "existence," and "presence in the world." Prior to Heidegger, this expression was not philosophical, nor was it comprehended as something unique and central. Of course, speaking about the world's *Being* and space, the notion of "*Dasein*" was attached to an object, whereas discussing the presence of things—to a subject. However, this notion was not key or fundamental before Heidegger.

It is unlikely that *Dasein* could be taken out of the philosophical context. It seems that Heidegger was illuminated by *Dasein*. *Dasein* revealed itself to him as an empirical reality of language and thought.

The source of thoughts about *Dasein* lies in a certain fundamental intellectual explosion, more specifically, an *implosion*, i.e., an explosing facing inward. This is why we specifically mention the "*Dasein experience.*"

Dasein is not a category (later on, we will examine the difference between a category and an existential). *Dasein* is a certain kind of fundamental start and in another sense, perhaps, it is even the end of all philosophy. Heidegger's *magnum opus, Sein und Zeit,* addresses the question of what *Dasein* is.

If we get closer to the experience of *Dasein,* even if remotely, if we succeed in meeting *Dasein,* and if we are destined to live through *Dasein,* then absolutely everything will change. *Dasein* is what turns everything upside down. *Dasein* makes our *Being-in-the-world* prior to this experience akin to that of a man with serious vision defects: he sees everything indefinably and vaguely, undifferentiated, and can only guess what objects are. Only *Dasein* returns everything into focus, and, for the first time ever, we begin to clearly differentiate what is around us, what we are, and what seemed like mere spots to us earlier, prior to this experiment. However, the comparison to vision is limited to a single sensory organ. In order to imagine *Dasein,* we must project this scenario onto the other senses: hearing, touch, taste, etc. Furthermore, analogous changes take place in terms of consciousness and the psychological state. Encountering *Dasein,* we leave a mental coma and a psychological cloudiness. We *awaken.*

Heidegger could reveal himself to us only in the experience of our being illuminated by *Dasein.* This experience, this word descended upon him like grace or inspiration. *Dasein appeared* to Heidegger. Of course, we could say that the latter

292

was preceeded by an enormous amount of philosophical labor, etymological studies, learning about culture and history, but all this is customary to other European intellectuals. Heidegger would not have been Heidegger had he not located the very nerve of *Dasein*. Therefore, we will attempt to understand and *live through* (which is vastly more important) *Dasein*. If we succeed, then we will make it *inside* philosophy. If not, then we will be doomed to wander around its periphery.

Conceptual Background for the Emergence of Dasein

If we approach *Dasein* externally, deductively, and descriptively, then we could say that it represents what remains *unconditional* following the colossal work of Western European philosophy during the course of its entire history. This is the *remnant* and, at the same time, the *résumé* of what remained during the development of Western European philosophy, comprehended as a systematic destruction of one's own *ontological* foundations. Heidegger himself described this process as *de-ontologification* or the *oblivion of the question about Being*. All that remained from this colossal *nihilation*—which Nietzsche called "European nihilism," from the total reduction toward *Nothingness*, from doubt and questioning, and then from clearing the remaining ontological elements—is *Dasein*.

If we approach *Dasein* internally, then this is illumination, shock, direct confrontation with the *presence* even before it becomes obvious *what* this *presence* is, *who* encounters it, and *where* this occurs.

Both approaches can be used simultaneously. On the one hand, realizing the fundamental process of Western European philosophy as the absolutization of nihilism (Nietzsche: "The desert grows, and woe to him who conceals the desert within him.") brings us to a confrontation with *Nothingness* (this is how we delineate the outer boundaries of *Dasein* as a phenomenon). On the other hand, shaking off banal clichés, thoughts, and feelings, we break through to pure experience, which preceded any kind of interpretation; this experience reveals itself to us, for instance, as part of a strong feeling— intense love, deadly *ennui*, dark terror, and so on; and we end up *inside Dasein*. Philosophy gives us the opportunity to *think* about *Dasein*, the experience of terror—*to dwell inside Dasein*.

Heidegger asserts that we cannot understand *Dasein* through something else. *Dasein* must only be understood through *Dasein*. In his book *Sein und Zeit*, he shows *how* this occurs.

Historical-Philosophical Prolegomena to Heidegger's Philosophy. The Pre-Socratics

In order to trace the way in which the concept and phenomenology of *Dasein* form, we must take a brief excursion into the history of philosophy. As we already noted, Heidegger sees the source of ontological nihilism in Western European philosophy of the Modern period in the source of that philosophy, in the "first Beginning" (*der erste Anfang*): it was there that an *error*, infinitely small in the beginning, later grows to gigantic proportions and becomes the main content of philosophy.

This error involves:

- the understanding of the outside world as "nature" (φύσις [*physis*]), i.e., etymologically, "sprouts" (*das Aufgehen*);

- further conceptualizing it as "*beings*" (ὄν [*on*], *das Seiende*);

294

- forming the notion of *Being* (εἶναι [*einai*]) as a generalizing attribute of all *beings* (*Seiendheit des Seienden*), i.e., the kind of *"Being"* that Heidegger writes with an "i" (*Sein*) in contrast to the fundamental-ontological *Being* (*Seyn*).

Since *Being* is conceptualized as *generalized beings*, and is explained in relation to φύσις (*physis*), then we gradually end up at the duality of Parmenides: *"Being is, non-Being is not."* Everything about this formula is completely accurate, but something is missing nonetheless. Fundamental-ontological *Being* is broader than the generalizing attribute of *beings* (that is, *Sein als Seiendheit des Seinden*) and requires the kind of gaze that is projected somewhat differently than directly at φύσις.

Of course, *Being* is that general attribute that is inherent to all *beings*. But that is not *everything*. Forgetting about the latter, first we remain within the correct philosophical process. But with time, this oblivion will make itself be known. The error in the very design of pre-Socratic philosophy is still minimal, but already contains something fatal.

Plato

This is fully expressed in Plato.[1] Here, an ontology that was constructed earlier over φύσις and the understanding of *Being* as something common for all *beings*, reaches its crystallization in the teaching about ideas. An idea is the kind of *beings* that is thought as a model for all other *beings*. According to Heidegger, this is the "end of the First Beginning." *Beings* as an idea of the greatest kind of *beings* ultimately eclipsed *Being* with themselves. That which was a small error early on ("not everything") has been

---

1 Martin Heidegger, *Vom Wesen der Wahrheit. Zu Platons Höhlengleichnis und Theätet (1931)* (Frankfurt am Main: Vittorio Klostermann, 1988).

taken outside the framework in Platonism. The ontological set of problems is being fixed in studies about the hierarchy of *beings* (from the thing to the idea), and there is no more place for *Being* in its pure state.

Beings replace *Being* (*Seyn*). And, that very "not everything" (an initially tiny chasm between "*Being*" and the "*common attribute of beings*") ends up out of sight, since it finds itself outside of ontology's attention, begins to make itself known, constituting Nothingness and the moving force behind the rejection of *beings' Being*.

Scholasticism

Heidegger, following Nietzsche, thinks that Christianity is Platonism for the masses from the philosophical point of view. This means that the structure of Christian (Catholic) theology fully reproduces Plato's ontology, in which *Being* is measured through the correspondence between the thing and its archetype—an idea as the greatest kind of *beings*. At the same time, the given ontological position is fixed even further around the theological concept of creation. The thing's status as *ens creatum* is determined by its place in the hierarchy of creatures. Here, God replaces Plato's idea as the *supreme kind of beings*.

According to Heidegger, Scholasticism does not bring anything new to philosophy, simply making Platonism banal and transforming the hierarchy of ideas into one of created things.[2] Scholasticism forms an ontological triangle, which Modernity then inherits.

---

2 Martin Heidegger, *Geschichte der Philosophie von Thomas v. Aquin bis Kant (1926)* (Frankfurt am Main: Vittorio Klostermann, 1993).

Ontological Triangle

Let us imagine that there is a triangle in front of us, the top vertex of which represents God or transcendence. According to Augustine and the Scholastics, God's *Being* is absolute. In other words, the top vertex of the triangle resolves the question about *Being* as follows: God is absolute *Being*.

There are two more vertices at the base of the triangle: one of them contains the subject, the other—the object. Both are ontologically conceptualized in Christian Scholasticism as *created beings, ens creatum*. Consequently, absolute *Being* creates *non-absolute Being*.

Non-absolute *Being* was created, made, thereby revealing its *Being*. It contains the human soul which in terms of substance belongs to *beings* (this is a very important point), along with things from the outside world, which are also part of *beings* in terms of substance. The difference is only that the former is *beings* as a subject (our "I," the human soul), whereas the latter—as an object. But they all draw their *Being* from the absolute *Being* of God.

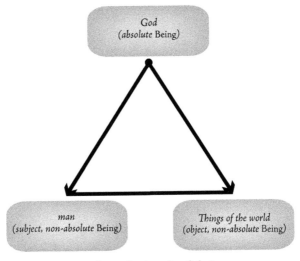

ontological triangle of theism

There is a God, and He is absolute; there is a subject, and it is non-absolute; there is an object, and it also is non-absolute. All it takes is replacing "God" in this schematic diagram with an "idea," and we end up with Plato's philosophical model. It was this that allowed Platonism to enter Christian theology (first and foremost, in the works of the Eastern Church fathers).

Ontological Transformations in the Philosophy of Modernity. Rational Ontology of the Subject in Descartes

The new time in the philosophy of deism (Descartes, Newton) substantially reorganizes the ontological proportions in this triangle. For Scholasticism (theism), God's *Being* does not require proof (Tertullian's "I believe, because it is absurd" [*Credo quia absurdum*]), and is based on faith. After this kind of an ontological assertion, it is easy to transition to *Being* in terms of the two poles of creation—subject and object. In this case, their *Being* will be justified with God's *Being* that brings creatures into *Being*.

But it is at faith that the rationalism of philosophy strikes during Modernity, encouraging everyone to "doubt everything," along with Descartes. The only thing that Descartes does not doubt is *cogito*, from which he derives the subject. The subject, in turn, based on conclusions about perceptions, records an object's *Being* (*res extensa*) and arrives at the proof of God's *Being* on the basis of conclusions about the cause of one's own *Being*.

God's *Being* is derived from the subject's *Being*, which is justified through the empirical fact of the thought process. As a result, the entire image of the ontological triangle changes. *Being's dispositif* is found in the thinking human subject, which, as the two secondary

298

operations, explains the *Being* of the two other vertices in the triangle, God and the object, on the basis of rational operations.

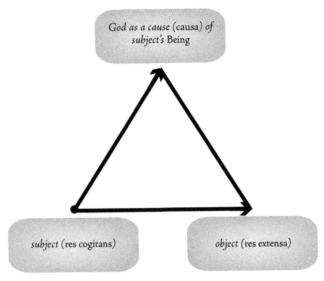

God as a cause (causa) of subject's Being

subject (res cogitans)

object (res extensa)

ontological triangle of rationalist deism

This ontology of deism, in which the *Being* of the three vertices is proven on the basis of *cogito*, ends up at the foundation of Modernity's philosophy.

According to Heidegger, this is one of the most important aspects in the history of philosophy. From Plato's transcendent idea and Scholastic theology with God at the head of the ontological triad, we transition to the dualist "subject-object" image, in which *Being* begins to act as a result of the subject's rational activity. As a result, *das Seiende, beings*, is reduced to the simplified "subject-object" pair, and ontology acquires a strictly rational character.

Empirical Ontology

In the 17th century, Newton's and Francis Bacon's English school forms a different gnoseological model. If Descartes's ontological argument was the thought process, and its principal ontological element was the subject, then in the English branch of Modern philosophy, this is the outside world, an *object*, following the same line of questioning of the ontological picture of the Middle Ages. This is a classical empirical school based on induction, experiment, and experience.

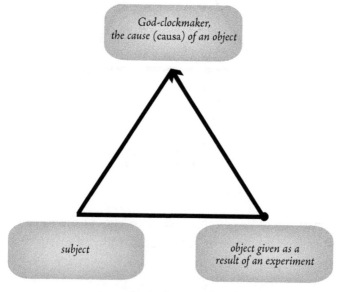

ontological triangle of empirical deism

That which is recorded by the sensory organs is considered unconditional *Being*. An object *is*, and this is the principal empirical assertion without which one cannot construct any science or philosophy. But the object (world) must have a cause. And this cause is, evidently, God. In empirical versions of deism, God is also postulated as the necessary cause of *Being's* presence, but this time around this occurs not from the standpoint of the subject but that of the object.

When we pronounce the words "really," "reality," we mean "thing-nessly," "thing-ness." In Latin, "*res*" is a "thing." In empirical philosophy, the thing is an object, and the thing is *as* an object. Whence "objectivity" as a synonym for reality. Initially, "reality" was a predicate for the empirical version of deism, and in its context, it had the meaning of an ontological argument.

Leibniz's Monad

At the dawn of Modernity, Leibniz offers an original interpretation of the ontological set of problems. His task is to substantiate theodicy, to carry out the proof of God's *Being* under radically new post-Medieval conditions. He does so on the basis of reason like the other philosophers of Modernity, but his ontology is constructed using a different schema.

Leibniz represents the world as a hierarchy of monads which hieararchically distribute *Being* into different subordinate groups. In a monad, the subject corresponds to an object.

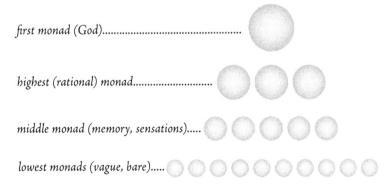

first monad (God)...

highest (rational) monad...........................

middle monad (memory, sensations).....

lowest monads (vague, bare).....

*monad schematic diagram
according to Leibniz*

The phenomena of space and matter, according to Leibniz, appear because of optical illusions that are symptomatic of the lowest monads. The latter, being vague and unclear, produce the appearance of spatial distinctions and temporal sequences. The division into a subject and object also occurs as a result of illusions. It is not the subject or object that possesses *Being*, but only the monad, keeping in mind that the quality of *Being* improves as one moves toward the highest monads and decreases as one moves down.

We may consider Leibniz' construction a certain kind of attempt to return to the Platonic and neo-Platonic pictures of the world after several centuries of Creationist Scholasticism and under the conditions of developing a new ontological paradigm in the philosophy of Modernity.

Criticizing Leibniz' work on monads is one of the most important aspects in Heidegger's philosophy.[3] Describing *Dasein*, Heidegger warns that any parallels with Leibniz's monadology are erroneous, since his philosophy places *Being* into the first monad, i.e., the highest *beings*, but *beings* nonetheless.

Kant's Ontological Doubt

Broad ontological distribution of Modernity's philosophical schools demonstrates the growing uncertainty regarding what should be chosen as the unconditional point of *Being*. Dissatisfaction with Scholastic Creationist recipes in theism forces philosophers to offer new versions of ontology— subjective (Cartesian), objective (empirical), and monad-based. The multitude of ontological hypotheses leads to generalizing the accumulated difficulties in the ontological set of problems

---

[3] Martin Heidegger, *Metaphysische Anfangsgründe der Logik im Ausgang von Leibniz (1928)* (Frankfurt am Main: Vittorio Klostermann, 1978).

through Kant's philosophy.[4] This is one of the most significant aspects in the development of Western European philosophy.

Kant was under the influence of ideas proposed by Descartes, Leibniz, and Newton, but focused his attention on developing his theory of knowledge—*The Critique of Pure Reason*. In this completely revolutionary (in an ontological sense) work, Kant definitely shows that all the proposed versions of ontology (that of the subject, object, or God, including the monad) cannot be strictly proven based on pure reason. Thus, the idea of a *noumenon* arises, a certain authority, whose *Being* cannot be proven or disproven through the rational mind. Kant does not negate the *Being* of a subject, object, or God. He simply demonstrates that *Being* belongs to the sphere of the *noumenon*, about which the rational mind cannot make any solid conclusions.

In Kant's philosophy, the ontological triangle looks as follows.

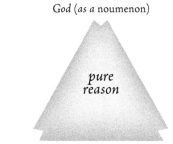

God (*as a* noumenon)

pure reason

subject (*as a* noumenon)   object (*as a* noumenon)

ontological triangle from the standpoint of Kant's pure reason

Kant has the ontology of *cogito*, which, however, does not lead to the Cartesian *ergo sum*. Of course, we can conclude, "I think,

---

4 Martin Heidegger, *Kant und das Problem der Metaphysik* (1929) (Frankfurt am Main: Vittorio Klostermann, 1991); *Idem., Phänomenologie Interpretation von Kants Kritik der reinen Vernunft* (Frankfurt am Main: Vittorio Klostermann, 1990).

therefore I think." However, "think" does not translate into "is." Pure reason has its own structure, organizes apperception, and regularizes thought processes, thereby acting *as if* the subject ("I"), object (outside world), and God existed. Yet at the same time, pure reason lacks ontological argumentation that could remove this *as if* and translate it into a strict conviction.

Faced with this purely nihilistic picture, Kant is forced to take a step back and attempt to substantiate his ontology after all. But the latter is not focused on the fundamental conclusions regarding pure reason, but rather—on moral wishes on the part of practical reason, whence comes the subject of the categorical imperative. Pure reason cannot prove the *Being* of a subject, object, or God. But practical reason, in making a *moral* choice, states that they *must* exist nonetheless, and that it would be good for them to exist. On the one hand, it seems that ontology makes a comeback, but on the other, ontological nihilism increases. At this stage, *Being* is proven not through an experience or reason, not through Revelation, but through moral considerations: "It would be good for *Being* to be."

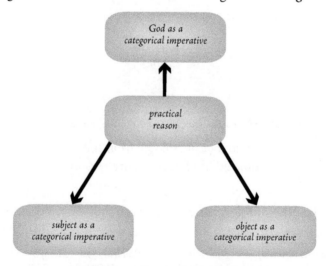

ontological triangle from the standpoint of Kant's practical reason

The idea of *The Critique of Pure Reason*, however, does not heal the trauma sustained through philosophical ontology thanks to the "critique of pure reason," but only exacerbates it. Morally supported ontology is even less thorough than the kind of ontology that is justified rationally or empirically.

Nothingness grows.

Fichte and Hegel: Overcoming Kantian Pessimism

Of course, Kant's followers attempted to deal with this challenge. Fichte, Kant's student, in response to the fact that Kant left the world without a subject, decided that there is a subject after all and, developing this idea, he added that the subject is the only thing that there is.[5]

Hegel also sensed that things are not well. He invested a colossal amount of effort in order to demonstrate that *Being* and thought correspond to each other. For this purpose, he had to construct a new logical system significantly correcting Aristotle's traditional logic, which Kant used for *The Critique of Pure Reason*. Thus arose the *Science of Logic*, in which Hegel developed a philosophical dialectic, rejecting the law of the excluded third in logic, which got Heidegger's attention. Heidegger considers Hegel's formulation about the problem of Nothingness, rejection, negation to be correct, but at the same time, he demonstrates that Hegel remains within classical philosophy[6], continuing to operate with concepts and acknowledging the referential theory of truth.

---

[5] Martin Heidegger, *Der Deutsche Idealismus (Fichte, Hegel, Schelling) und die philosophische Problemlage der Gegenwart (1929)* (Frankfurt am Main: Vittorio Klostermann, 1997).

[6] Martin Heidegger, *Hegels Phänomenologie des Geistes (1930)* (Frankfurt am Main: Vittorio Klostermann, 1980).

He attempts to answer the challenge of disontologization revealed by Kant and moves further in this direction than any other thinker. But the objective limit here is the very structure of Western European philosophy in which the ontological problem is formulated incorrectly at its very foundation, in the first Beginning, while the metaphysics of Modernity, specifically, Kant, only discovers its ultimate consequences.

Nietzsche: the End of Philosophy

For Heidegger, Nietzsche was Modernity's most important philosopher. He had the greatest and most decisive impact on Heidegger. The latter dedicated a multitude of texts to Nietzsche[7], a part of which appears in the two-volume *Nietzsche* book.

In order to approach the subject of *Dasein*, Nietzsche has the following central philosophical points:

- asserting that Western European philosophy during Modernity is nihilistic;

- stating that the cultural and metaphysical guidelines are artificial as a product of life's alienation;

- criticizing Plato and the referential theory of truth;

- addressing the pre-Socratics' search for the sources of Western European thought process in its pure form, yet to be "distorted" by the teaching about ideas;

- emphasizing the "will to power" as the principal motive in life;

---

[7] See footnote 6, previous chapter.

- overthrowing the idols and values of the West;

- calling for radically new ways of thinking.

For Heidegger, Nietzsche is the kind of figure that places the last period in the process of establishing Western European philosophy. If Plato were the "end within the framework of the first Beginning," then Nietzsche is simply the end of philosophy as such. He is the last philosopher.

Nietzsche no longer believes either in the object or the subject. He proclaims the "death of God" openly and with greatest conviction. Finding himself at the center of European nihilism, Nietzsche addresses the element of life. Heidegger interprets the latter as *Being*. That, which in the period of nihilism's greatest flourishing collides with this element, is approximately what Heidegger calls *Dasein*.

Husserl

On the other hand, such phenomenon as the phenomenology of Edmund Husserl was born, parallel to Nietzsche, out of consistent and fundamentally comprehended Kantianism. Husserl was a truly consistent Kantian, drawing the kind of conclusions that should be drawn. Even though more than a hundred years separates Husserl and Kant, it is he who brought the themes directly linked to *The Critique of Pure Reason* to their logical conclusion.

Husserl's phenomenology is based on the following operations:

- the object's, subject's, and God's existence is taken outside of the framework (the principle of phenomenological reduction);

- concentrating philosophical attention on the structure of human consciousness in the form in which it constitutes objects of its functioning (*noēmata*) through intellectual operations (*noesis*).

- introducing the concept of intentionality as the basic model of the relationship between consciousness and the observed object (which, in a certain sense, constitutes this object);

- researching the phenomenological stream of consciousness, while observing man's behavior in the realm of the "lifeworld" (*Lebenswelt*).

Husserl's phenomenology has a multitude of different interpretations. For Heidegger, Husserl's former student, the most important aspect of this phenomenology was the pursuit of identifying the purest authority that remains in place of the thinking man after consistently carrying out the *epoché* operation in relation to the basic philosophical concepts ("subject," "object," "I," "essence," "time," and so on). In essence, Husserl proceeds along the path of nihilism described by Nietzsche and, being on this path, attempts to substantiate and accurately describe that authority that remains after all the metaphysical layers have been removed. These layers include positivism, materialism, and empiricism, which, according to Heidegger, are nothing more than specific cases of the same Western metaphysics.

Phenomenology, from its perspective, gradually prepared Heidegger's approach to *Dasein*. In a certain sense, Heidegger can be called a "phenomenologist," whereas *Dasein* itself—a *phenomenological* phenomenon.

At the same time, the concept of a "phenomenon" has special significance for Heidegger. He links it to the Greek meaning of the stem in φαίνεσθαι (*fainesthai*), which means to "make oneself appear," "manifest oneself," "reveal oneself," as well as with another Greek term, ἀλήθεια (*aletheia*), "truth," which was highly important for Heidegger. He interprets "truth"— "*aletheia*" as "unconcealment" and transmits this Greek (pre-Socratic) term everywhere by using the German word "*die Unverborgenheit*"—literally, "unconcealment."

Heidegger contrasts the truth as "uncancelment" (of *Being*) with the truth as the correspondence between one kind of *beings* with another. Therefore, Heidegger's phenomenology is inextricably united with the ontological set of problems. Husserl, in contrast, seeks to isolate phenomenology from any kind of link with ontology, attempting to substantiate the new philosophical school that he created by using an innovative conceptual arsenal, completely constructed *ad hoc* at the greatest proximity to the phenomena themselves. By following this path, Husserl arrives at such points as "transcendence" or "*noesis*." This means that Heidegger connects the phenomenon and its sphere with *Being*, whereas Husserl—with the thought process, which predetermines the difference between their respective philosophical approaches.

Therefore, Heidegger formally repeats a series of classic operations in phenomenology, but, at the same time, carries out something completely different, since his philosophy and his history of philosophy are firmly fixed around the axis of the question about *Being*. Heidegger differentiates between the "key question in philosophy" (*Leitfrage*) and the "fundamental question in philosophy" (*Grundfrage*). The former pertains to *beings* (*Sein der Seiendheit*), whereas the latter—to *Being* (*Seyn*). From

309

the very beginning, Heidegger's phenomenology is placed into the context of solving the "basic question in philosophy." This is phenomenological ontology, whereas Husserl's general thought remains within the framework of gnoseology and the theory of knowledge.

III. DASEIN AND ITS EXISTENTIALS

Introduction to Dasein

If we approach *Dasein* from the standpoint of the history of philosophy, then we could say that this is the last point that can be recorded in the period of completing disontologization at the midnight of universal nihilism. Pre-Socratics equated *Being* (*Seyn*) with nature, *beings*, the universal—missing something that was initially barely noticeable but significant. Plato equated *Being* with one of *beings* (idea). Scholastics moved even further away from *Being*, establishing the theological hierarchy of created things. Deists doubted the dogmas of faith and began to explain *Being* on the basis of artificial concepts, whether Cartesian rationalism, Locke's and Hume's empiricism, or Leibniz's monad. Kant honestly admitted that the ontological argument has no rational justification.

Fichte's and Hegel's attempts to remove this problem only send us to a partial conceptual correction of the situation without affecting the essence of this nihilistic catastrophe. Nietzsche calls things what they are and demands that from now we must think harshly and in a sober way in terms of the Godforsaken world. Under the conditions of collapsing European metaphysics, Husserl introduces the phenomenological method of thought. What remains of *Being* in this case, getting futher and further removed from the main process of philosophizing, is reduced to *Dasein*.

Dasein is the ultimate fact of *Being* preceeding any kind of justification, without an adequate interpretation, placed in the desert of nihilism.

At the same time, *Dasein* is, undoubtedly, a phenomenological presence. That is to say, it is a *phenomenological point of Being*, the combination of the historical-philosophical optics of disontologization, focused on the "key question in philosophy," with the direct phenomenology of presence. This phenomenology of presence has its own features. Determining these features, i.e., the analytical description of *Dasein*, is the primary focus of Heidegger's *Sein und Zeit*.

Da and Sein

Occasionally, *Dasein* is translated as "*Being-there*." Indeed, the German word *Dasein* comprises two parts. *Da* is "(t)here" and *Sein* is "*Being*."

That kind of *Being* that is mentioned in *Dasein* is an *unconditional presence, manifest presence*, that is, a certain kind of an unconditional phenomenological fact. Heidegger does not insist upon introducing metaphysical correspondences between *Dasein* and *Sein* (and, even more so, *Seyn*). This correspondence must conclude the entire body of Heidegger's philosophy; this is the end of the road. Nonetheless, it is incredibly important to note from the onset that in *Dasein* we are dealing with *Being*, even if not metaphysically substantiated quite yet. Heidegger uses the term "ontic," from the Greek "ὄν" (*on*), "beings." *Dasein* pertains to *beings*: it is *beings*, but at the same time, it is not *simply beings*, like the rest of *beings*, but a certain kind of *special beings*. At the initial stage of Heidegger's philosophy, the phenomenology of *Dasein* may be taken as ontic (but not yet ontological, since this assertion does not yet contain the *logos*).

The second stem in the word "*Dasein*" is "*da*," "(t)here." This "*da*" shows that *Being* is located "(t)here" (as opposed to somewhere else), that we are dealing with something factual and available, present definitively and tangibly. Therefore, *Dasein* may be perceived as a specific coagulation of *Being*, *Being* in the ontic, almost empirical sense. One may live through *Dasein* if one gets accustomed to the factuality of *Being* of that which is "(t)here"— with the greatest possible separation from *what* is (t)here, *who* is (t)here, *where* is (t)here, *why* is (t)here, and so on. At the same time, the translation of German "*da*" as simply "here" (into the Russian "*здесь*," "*zdes'*") or "there" is fairly incorrect. In *Sein und Zeit*, Heidegger himself mentions the hypothesis of Wilhelm von Humboldt[1] in regard to the origins of personal pronouns based on locative adverbs. Humboldt proposed the following version: "*ich*" ("I") is derived from "*hier*" ("here"), "*er*" ("he") is derived from from "*dort*" ("there"), and "*du*" is derived from "*da*" ("here," "somewhere here," "not too far," between "here" and "there"). The adverb system in the German language has a triple, rather than dual, structure as compared to the modern Russian language. "*Hier*" is specifically "here," "*dort*" is specifically "there," whereas "*da*" is somewhere in between the two.

This-Being

We could use the Russian demonstrative pronoun "*вот*" (*vot*), which roughly translates as "this" (as in "this one," "this one here"). "*Vot*" means neither "here" nor "there," but somewhere specifically nearby where one could point. "*Da*" could be translated as "(t)here," but also as "this" ("*vot*"). In order to

---

1   Martin Heidegger, *Sein und Zeit*, op. cit., 119.

explain the significance of this fundamental term, it seems that "*this-Being* is more accurate. Humboldt's corespondence is important: "*Being,*" which is located "somewhere nearby," is a man that is nearby (not far away, not "out there"), but at the same time, this is neither "I" nor "non-I." In a certain sense, this is "you," since the experience of *Dasein* includes disidentification with the "I." In *Dasein*," "I" is perceived as "you," but this is the kind of "you" that has no subject but rather a simple presence.

"Here" and "there" clearly demarcate distance, whereas "this" does not yet have a distance—it preceeds it. "This" is something to which we pointed, which we noted through our attention. "Here" and "there" appear only after we marked "this."

La Realité Humaine

Henry Corbin[2] translates *Dasein* into French by using the expression "human reality," "*realité humaine.*" Strictly speaking, neither term is useful at all. Incidentally, throughout the entire book, Heidegger mentions that he is dealing neither with the "human" nor the "real," neither with the "subject" nor the "object," and most certainly not "God." "Neither subject, nor object, nor the human, nor reality, nor the divine" would be a much more accurate description of *Dasein*, rather than Corbin's "*realité humaine.*"

---

2 Henry Corbin is one of the most important French philosophers, a historian of religion, and a specialist in Iranian and Islamic philosophy, mysticism, and poetry. See Henry Corbin, *Le paradoxe du monothéisme* (Paris: l'Herne, 1981); Idem., *Temps cyclique et gnose ismaélienne* (Paris: Berg International, 1982); Idem., *Face de Dieu, face de l'homme* (Paris: Flammarion, 1983); Idem. *Philosophie iranienne et philosophie comparée* (Paris: Buchet/Chastel, 1979); Idem., *Corps spirituel et Terre céleste: de L'Iran mazdéen á l'Iran shî'ite* (*Paris:* Buchet/Chastel, 1979); Idem., *Histoire de la philosophie islamique* (Paris: Gallimard, 1964); Idem., *L'homme de lumière dans le soufisme iranien* (Paris: Éditions "Présence," 1971).

However, this translation does elucidate the meaning of *Dasein* to an extent. In a certain unique optics (Henry Corbin was one of the greatest specialists in the area of esoteric Islam, sacred anthropology, and mystical philosophy), *Dasein* could be understood as a "human reality" in its purest form—before man and before reality—as a structured qualitative authority developing its autonomous attributes, during the course of which "man" (subject) and "reality" (object, world) emerge. In this sense, we should consider Corbin's own theory about "*mundus imaginalis*," the "man of light," and the "purple angel" (*Suhrawardi*)[3] as well as Gilbert Durand's theory[4] of the *imaginaire* and the *anthropological trajectory*. But we will leave this as a marginal commet for now.

The Experience of Dasein as the Appearance of Language and an Explosion

By introducing *Dasein*, Heidegger does not so much follow the logical philosophical discourse (where ontology requires logical justifications, which cannot be introduced, giving birth to a vicious circle and endless nihilism), but rather—language. The latter, despite all the chords of disontologization, operates with a concept like *Dasein*, "*This-Being*" as if nothing happened. "*This-Being*." "*Being—this*." Focusing our attention on the meaning of these words does not take us to philosophy, but leads us to language. The words "this" and "*Being*" attempt to express something—something incredibly important—but, at the same time, something fleeting, vague, and uncertain. Here, Heidegger proposes that we make a leap, trust words rather than concepts, sounds and guessed meanings rather than the

---

3 Henry Corbin, L'*Imagination créatrice dans le soufisme d'Ibn' Arabi*, 2-e éd. (Paris: Flammarion, 1977).
4 Gilbert Durand, *Les Structures anthropologiques de l'imaginaire* (Paris: PUF, 1960).

strict philosophical discourse. Philosophical knowledge and obsessive interest in the ontological set of problems, naturally, have an effect on the choice of the verbal object for the purpose of comprehension, but comprehension itself is missing at the starting point. *Dasein* appears instantly and immediately with all the contents it already comprises. *Dasein* is an axial phenomenon, appearing in a priority fashion; *Dasein* is that which makes appear and that which appears. But, at the same time, this is the call of the language itself.

The experience of *Dasein* belongs to pre-philosophy. It is incredibly naïve and is linked with language both directly and unscientifically. (Perhaps, this is the result of Nietzsche's lessons with his *We Philologists*[5] and Husserl's *Lifeworld*). In essence, Heidegger constructs philosophy from scratch. And the first sound, step, and statement in this philosophy (later, he will conceptualize this as a "new Beginning," *der neue Anfang*") is *Dasein*.

Heidegger is highly critical of and attentive to terms, concepts, and the meaning of words, constantly placing them into the original context and trying to precisely determine their correct historical-philosophical meaning (including nuanced translations and etymology). He proposes to make one single exception and to simply "believe" the meaning of the word *Dasein*: it is *Being* that it records, not "somewhere," but "this," "this here."

Dasein is the first, most important, and, in essence, the only axiom of Heidegger's philosophy. Having grasped it, we will grasp everything else. But herein lies the difficulty: understanding it correctly is impossible without being competent in fundamental-

---

[5] Friedrich Nietzsche, *We Philologists*, tr. J. M. Kennedy (Teddington: The Echo Library, 2007).

ontology and, at the same time, without the direct experience of colliding with *Being* in a factually specific manner of "this."

Dasein is a sudden and explosive discovery of *Being this*. *This* itself is constituted with this explosion as well as that which reveals itself. At the same time, the purity of this experience is guaranteed only by the fact that it takes places under the conditions of total nihilism as a natural and logical conclusion of establishing the entire process of Western European philosophy. In all other situations and contexts, this phenomenon would have been impossible and would have been subject to a completely different and, most likely, rather banal interpretation. In order for *Being* to reveal itself in the explosive and direct way of *this*, it must be preemptively and completely *forgotten*. Otherwise, there will not be an explosion, uniqueness, or *Beingness* in this discovery. Therefore, the emergence of *Dasein* and the philosophy based on it at its core, is philosophy's transition from one stage to another, from the pre-Socratics to Nietzsche. In order for *Dasein* to appear, philosophy must begin, blossom, reach its pinnacle—followed by decline and tragic completion. Only afterward—and, to a large extent, because of it—can *this-Being* reveal itself in the way that it did to Heidegger.

From Essence to Existence

Heidegger himself underscores the fact that the correct approach to *Dasein* and its discovery is possible not through returning to the ontological triangle that we have irreparably lost (this loss was of fundamental significance, according to Heidegger), but through courageously recording the realm of triumphant nihilism. *Dasein* is what records nihilism without corresponding to it. Yet it does not evade its own responsibility for its emergence; furthermore, it wants to travel along the path of this responsibility all the way.

Pushing off *Dasein*, Heidegger proposes to fundamentally change the philosophical settings. Throughout its entire history, Western European philosophical thinking originated from defining thought about *essence, οὐσία (ousia)*. Essence was understood either as God or an idea, subject, object, monad, etc.

Heidegger believes that the essentialist approach expresses that very error that brought the entire philosophical process from the "first Beginning" (pre-Socratics) to the end of philosophy (Nietzsche). Starting from essence as the "common "attribute (*κοινόν, [koinon]*) inherent to *Seiende (ens)* as *Seiendheit (essentia)*, philosophy was doomed to endlessly repeat the same metaphysical route, sooner or later leading thought toward alienation, pragmatism, positivism, and, therefore, nihilism. The attempt to construct an ontology on the basis of *essence* leads to disontologization.

Instead of this, he suggests to begin philosophizing from *Dasein* perceived as *existence* rather than essence, as something undoubtedly present, but in the ontic, not ongological sense.

"The essence (*Wesen*) of *Dasein*," repeats Heidegger in *Sein und Zeit*, "is found in existence." This might cause confusion: encouraging us to think starting from existence rather than essence, Heidegger himself defines *Dasein* (existence) through essence (*Wesen*). But here we must account for the original German context. *Das Wesen* for Heidegger is not a translation of "*οὐσία*" (*ousia*) or the Latin "*existentia*." Moving along the line of language, not philosophical terminology, Heidegger adds a fundamental-ontological meaning to the word "*Wesen*" (the passive participle of the verb *sein*). *Wesen* is complicity with *Seyn* as *Being*, which must only be grasped in its proper capacity, pushing off from grasping the entire philosophical process from the first Beginning until the End as an incorrect ontological course. Whence Heidegger's linguistic novelties such as the usage of a verbal noun *Wesen* as a verb—*ich wese, du wesest, er (sie, es) west, wir wesen, ihr weset, sie wesen*—these forms do not exist in the German language. This is another language—Heidegger's metalanguage of fundamental-ontology.

Therefore, the expression the "essence of *Dasein* is found in existence" must be translated into the correct metalanguage: "*Dasein's Wesen* in existence." This means *Dasein is* not through correspondence with essence as something external or different than itself, but rather by itself. Therefore, *Wesen* is not an essence (*οὐσία*), but an expression (discovery, leading out from unconcealment) of *Dasein's self-Being*. Heidegger does not translate the word "*existentia*" and its derivatives ("*existential*," "*existentiell*") into the German language (even though he attempts to translate everything into German: he even transforms the word "subject" into the German "*Geworfenheit*", "thrownness," which corresponds to the Latin etymology: "*sub*" ["under," "below"] and "*jacere*" ["to throw"]). Even less useful for translating "*existentia*" is the Russian word "*sushchestvovanie*" (*существование*), since it corresponds to the German *Wesen* much closer than it does to the Latin. The verb "*sushchestvovat*'" (*существовать*) transmits what Heidegger wanted to say by inventing the verb "*wesen*," which does not exist in the German language. That said, there is no direct analogy to the Latin "*existentia*" in the Greek language either, and, in rare cases, Heidegger uses the word "*οὗτος*" ("*outos*," "that one," "this one") in an attempt to find an analogy to existence, likely, supported by the etymology of the German *Dasein*.

Therefore the axiomatic phrase in Heidegger's philosophy, "*Dasein's Wesen* in existence," is, in a certain sense, a triple pleonasm, whereas its Germano-Latin etymology is called upon to turn the fundamental axioms of all philosophy upside down, where everything was examined not through itself but through another (φύσις [*physis*], ἰδέα [*idea*], οὐσία [*ousia*], θεός [*theos*], ἐγώ [*ego*], κοινόν [*koinon*], essentia, objectum, subjectum, res, realitas, etc.). With his pleonasmic formula, Heidegger lays the foundation of the new Beginning in philosophy, in which, from now on, he proposes to examine everything from the standpoint of *Dasein* as a factual and ontic authority, which is not preceeded by anything logically, chronologically, or ontologically. Therefore, a significant portion of *Sein und Zeit* is dedicated to apophatic definitions of *Dasein*.

Dasein is neither an essence nor substance: "I," subject, object, world, psyche, life, *Being*, Nothingness, *non-Being*, the greatest kind of *beings*, idea, God, man, any kind of *beings* along with others, *beings-as-a-whole*, the universal, the unified. *Dasein* is linked with *Wesen* and with existence, but this equals the fact that *Dasein* is *Dasein*, and its form of existing is the possibility of *Being*. However, the "*ex*" in "*existentia*" is already part of "*da*" in *Dasein*, and "*Wesen*" is part of "*Sein*" (*Being*) of *Dasein*. In order to explain this, Heidegger repeats the following refrain, "*Dasein* exists factually," "*Dasein existiert faktisch*." "Factually" means "ontically," in the direct, unconditional, specific, totally perceptible presense.

Three Ontological Layers

The introduction of *Dasein* and the beginning of thought, according to Heidegger, lead us to a new formulation of the ontological set of problems. Thus arise three ontological layers.

The question about *Being* may be phrased as follows:

- ontically

- ontologically

- fundamental-ontologically

"Ontically" means a direct empirical correlation to *Dasein*. In a certain sense, we can equate the ontic with the phenomelogical, if only we approach phenomenology not from Husserl's standpoint but from Heidegger's own point of view, that is, as ἀλήθεια (*aletheia*), unconcealment of *Being* in the fact of *Dasein's* presence. In this sense, we may say that *Dasein* is a phenomenon, that it is a given and given unconditionally, in advance and without any justifications as to who, whence, when, what for, and what. Here, the given excludes both the giver and the receiver. Only the act of presenting a gift—giving, presence —remains, hanging over the bottomless abyss of Nothingness.

The ontic is the unconditional presence in the unconditional given of *Dasein*. The ontic precedes any kind of work on the part of consciousness, thought process, and even perception. The ontic comprises neither certainty nor truth (as a correlation), neither subjectness nor objectness. *Being* in the ontic acts in a certain almost "barbaric" sense, as a fact of a resilient, non-differentiated life that includes death and movement, tranquility and presence, disappearance and finitude.

The ontic is *Being before* it has been thought of and focused on, *Being before* nature, *before* φύσις, *before* idea, *before* object, *before* subject, *before* category, *before* concept, *before* philosophy, *before* man, *before* "I" and its predicates.

The "ongological" means comprehending *Being* in the philosophical context. Ontology includes all the shades of philosophically comprehending *Being*, as φύσις (*physis*), and as idea, and as reality, and as the universal, and as subject, and as object, and as an object-based world, and as matter, and as consciousness, and as experience, and as the rational mind, and as the absolute, and as finitude, and as singularity, and as unity. But herein lies the main problem: for Heidegger, the entire ontology—all versions of philosophical comprehension, description, and definition of *Being* in Western European philosophy from the *first Beginning* until the *End*—lead in a knowingly false direction. In pre-Socratic philosophy, ontology is as close as possible to ontics, but even they let in a nuanced error. Later on, this error grows until it reaches gigantic proportions in the philosophy of pragmatism, positivism, understanding *Being* as a moral, value, ideal, worldview, and, finally, product. Plato's teaching about ideas, Aristotle's logic and metaphysics, Creationist theology, essentialism, idealism, realism, and nominalism in Medieval debates, conceptual thought, monadology, the Absolute idea, Hegel's *Science of Logic*, Nietzschean will to power—all of these are variations of incorrect thought about the kind of philosophy that was a majestic and grandiose monument to the same error. The latter comprised ignoring *Dasein* as the basic authority in philosophizing. But at the same time, this work of *ontology as a misconception* prepared the soil (*Grund*) for the bottomless (*Abgrund*) guess about *Dasein*.

"Ontologically," according to Heidegger, means "philosophically," "incorrectly," "nihilistically," "Platonically," "in an alienated way," distracted from the ontic, losing the pulse of *Being* that comprises the basis of the ontic. In the teaching about *Dasein*, between the *ontic* and the *ontological*, there are the following proportions. The ontic is given before the experience of thought, directly. We do not know by whom and to whom it is given. Only one thing is clear: it is given ("it exists factually"). *Dasein* is ontic, it is *the ontic*. Ontology is constructed over *Dasein*; it is the ontic comprehended through philosophy. In the optics of *Dasein*, this ontology is taken as something general, but not as something common for *beings* (which it wants to be), but rather as something common for the erroneous interpretation of *beings*, which it is from the standpoint of transitioning to the new Beginning of philosophy. The first step in the latter process is *Dasein*. Ontology is what flows out of *Dasein*, overcomes it, surpasses it in various ways, rises above it, but, at the same time, forgets it, ignores it, and replaces it with an abstract schema. Ontology is systematized nihilism.

The origins of nihilism comprise the equation of *Being* with *beings* and attributing the greatest normative status to a certain kind of *beings*.

Now, what is fundamental-ontology? It is the transition to the new Beginning. It is the construction of the kind of ontology that, in contrast to regular ontology, would be created in close and constant contact with *Dasein*, without being torn away from it, verifying every following step with the element of the ontic, expressing the ontic, allowing it to speak for itself about itself in the way that is the most suitable for it itself, without imposing any alienating framework, categories, or representations. In order to underscore this particular meaning of the fundamental-ontological, Heidegger, at times, uses the expression *ontic-ontological*.

Fundamental-ontolgy is different from the ontic in the sense that this is a thought process, comprehsion of *Being*, that it traces back to the directness of *Dasein* toward its indirectness. But fundamental-ontology is different from ontology in that the ascension from *Dasein* remains organically linked to *Dasein* itself. Fundamental-ontology does not make mistakes of all the philosophical ontologies and does not propose any additional authorities (ideas, essences, the Creator, subject, object, etc.) *outside* of *Dasein, above* it, *around* it, *underneath* it, and even *inside* it. Fundamental-ontology is the thought process that dwells in *Dasein's Being*, in its element, without giving birth to dualities and relationships, singularities and correspondences— nothing of what could be placed across from one another.

Fundamental-ontology is the yet-to-be-created philosophy of the "future ones" (*Künftige*), which will manifest themselves (in the way that *Being* truth-"*aletheia*" manifests itself, as watermarks appear on a sheet of paper).

Fundamental-ontology always remembers the distinctions between *Being* and *beings* and, therefore, perceives *Dasein* as *beings*, on the one hand, but, at the same time, as the possibility of *Being* (*Seyn*), which makes *Dasein* not only *beings* but also something else.

Dasein as Being-in-Between

It is of outmost importance to emphasize from the onset that *Dasein* is neither "external," nor "internal," since these philosophical and spatial dimensions emerge with it, in it, and through it, not prior to it. Furthermore, their structures depend on *Dasein's* regime, on the way it develops its "*da*" and its "*Sein*," and where the accent is placed. *Dasein* by itself is spatial, and this *spatiality* comprises one of its qualities, which does not allow it to be placed in what it already is—into one of its aspects.

326

At the same time, *Dasein* is neither "preceeding" (a beginning), nor "following" (a result of something that was present before it). *Dasein* is not a function of time, since time does not have autonomous *Being*, in which *Dasein* could settle. The relationship between *Dasein* and time is even more complex as compared to space, which is described in the second part of *Sein und Zeit*.

But the existential and factual character of *Dasein* makes it a rather specific presence and, consequently, it must possess a certain kind of localization. For *Dasein*, the concept of "in between" (*zwischen*) can serve as this empirical localization. Earlier, we spoke about the possible symmetry between demonstrative pronouns and the personal counterpart, underscoring the connection between "*da*" with that which is *between* "I" and "he" (in particular, "you," "*du*"). If we search for *Dasein* within the framework of the regular ontological coordinates (which would correspond to the ontic, empirical approach this time around), then we must place it *in between*— between the interior and exterior, between the past and present. Thus, *Dasein* is spatially limited (it dwells on the boundary, *in between*) and temporarily instantaneous (it belongs to the moment *between* the past and present). *Dasein's* "*da*" manifests in this *between*. Therefore, at a certain angle, we could call *Dasein* "Being-in-between" (*Inzwischen-Sein*).

Dasein's Existentials

Carrying out the transition into the new Beginning requires the development of a new metalanguage for fundamental-ontology. Interpretations, meanings, and contexts, linked to the old ontology, permeate traditional philosophical terms at their very foundation and are, therefore, unsuitable. This led Heidegger to the gradual replenishing of the fundamental-ontological dictionary in which all lexical positions were either new or old—but rethought in the fundamental-ontological vein. Thus, instead of "categories," Heidegger proposed to describe *Dasein* with the help of its predicates, dividing and specifying it. Heidegger refers to *Dasein's* predicates as "*existentials.*"

At the same time, Heidegger introduces a strict distinction in *Sein und Zeit* between the adjectives "existential" and "*existentiell.*" The former refers to *Dasein's* thought process while developing fundamental-ontology. The latter is a description of *Dasein's* ontic aspects in its direct expression, without the movement of thought toward the new Beginning. Therefore, *Dasein's* "existential" is not simply a description but its philosophical fundamental-ontological establishment. "*Existentiell,*" on the other hand, is a factual description (although Heidegger uses this term only as an adjective).

Heidegger presents a brief list of *Dasein's* existentials. The list itself is the process of creating a new philosophy.

In-Der-Welt-Sein (Being-in-the-World)

Heidegger refers to one of the most crucial existentials for *Dasein* as "*in-der-Welt-Sein*" ("*Being-in-the-world*").[6] *Dasein* is "*in-der-Welt-Sein.*" "*This-Being*" is "*Being-in-the-world,*" Heidegger asserts.

Here, it is important to understand why this is called an "existential" and what comprises the "existentiality" of this kind of predicate. The point is that "*Being-in-the-world*" taken as an existential (i.e., within the optics of fundamental-ontology) does not render any kind of judgement in regard to *what* is

6 Martin Heidegger, *Sein und Zeit, op. cit.,* 175.

located in the world, *what* the world is, whether it *is* at all, and whether it has any kind of autonomous *Being*. "*Being-in-the-world*" does not respond to the question "where": it precedes the emergence of a question like this, making it "possible." "*Being-in-the-world*" is an existential (and not a category) as well because the "world" is constituted here not through distinction, space, and place (topography) but through *Being*. "*Being-in-the-world*" is, first and foremost, *Being*, specifically—the kind that carries with it "in" and "world," not "in" and "world" as two separate figures. It is a kind of setting in which "in" is inseparable from the "world," whereas the "world" is inseparable from "in," and both of these—from *Being*. Torn away from the "world," "in" is inconceivable as simply "in." Similarly, the "world" is inconceivable as something separate. The "world" from *Dasein's* existential is always "*in-what-Being*," rather than an essence.

The importance of this existential will be clear to us if we consider the fact that Heidegger talks about the role of "*φύσις*" as a concept in the establishment of pre-Socratic philosophy. Its introduction gradually led to the referential theory of truth. Consequently, the *new Beginning* of philosophy must move in a different direction from the onset. "*Being-in-the-world*" as an existential is fundamental because it prevents the introduction into philosophy of the "world" as nature, object, or reality, as a certain kind of *beings* strictly separate from *Dasein*. "*Being-in-the-world*" is a vaccination against the appearance of the world as an essence. Therefore, this is only the predicate (existential) of *Dasein* and, consequently, it pertains to *Being* directly, without the divisions of the old philosophy into *who* is in the world (*ψυχή*, subject) and the world itself as something different. *Dasein* is always *Being-in-the-world*. When there is *Dasein*, there is *Being-in-the-world*. And the opposite is true: *Being*-in-the-world calls

329

for the presence of *Dasein*, since without *Dasein* as such, to which the existential applies, it is unthinkable (in terms of fundamental-ontology).

In a certain way, this is quite reminiscent of the phenomenological method—with one fundamental difference: for Heidegger, the question of *Being* bears great and paramount significance, direct intuition of *Being* and language (the *Being* of language, the language of *Being*).

In order to better understand *Dasein* from the existential point of view, we must successively reject two axioms absorbed within classical ontology: being convinced of the "I's" existence and that of the "world." At the same time, in the metaphysics of Modernity, these axioms attained hysterical significance with the threat of extinguishing consciousness. This was not always the case, but became the norm following the recorded "death of God." For those in traditional societies, the ontological argument comprised faith in God. "I" and the "world" were the ontological consequences and, in some cases, could have been acknowledged as illusions (Maya in Hinduism) when faced with the Absolute. Therefore, rejecting the "I" and the "world" was a rather acceptable cultural phenomenon that did not violate anything under normal circumstances.

But during Modernity, ontology rejected the "God hypothesis," asking man to substantiate his *Being* either through the subject (*cogito*) or the outside world (empiricism, materialism). It is this kind of Modern man that the perceptiveness of Heidegger's philosophy addresses. It is the man of Modernity that he addresses. It is for him that *Dasein* and the understanding of "*Being-in-the-world*" as an existential carry the most piercing, revolutionary message. The man of Modernity only has his "I" and the "world."

Heidegger begins by suggesting that we part with these proofless illusions, but not in favor of a certain other kind of transcendent reality (God, the Absolute, and so on), but, rather, favoring *Dasein*, factually existent, present in the here and now. Heidegger does not call us back into ongology. He fully acknowledges the legitimacy and predictability of nihilism in Western European philosophy. He invites us forward, further ahead, beyond the ultimate limit of the night and Nothingness, where we will discover not something new as that which *has not been* but something unique, which *is*, was, and will be. This is *Dasein* and its existentials.

Dasein is, and it is in the world, but the world is the consequence of *Dasein*. Sucking in and amazing with its *Being*, *Dasein* is a presence that refuses to be called the "I," refuses to be called the "world," and refuses to correspond to anything else. As *Being-in-the-world*, *Dasein* is a spatially moving *Being*, which organizes itself and everything around itself. First comes "*in-der-Welt-Sein*," "*Dasein*," and only then—the world, and only in the case that it has the chance to justify its autonomy. The latter is not at all simple under the circumstances of Heidegger's acute vigilance in terms of preventing repeating the ontological mistakes of philosophy's first Beginning. From now on, the world becomes an existential hypothesis. We know that there is *Being-in-the-world*, but we do not know (we can only guess and speculate) about the world's *Being*.

Being-in and Being-with

Developing this crucial existential, Heidegger also formulates it somewhat differently, introducing two other parallel existentials *Insein* and *Mitsein*.[7]

---

7 *Ibid.*, 52, 130–134.

"Insein" means *"Being-in."* We have already mentioned that fundamental-ontology always tries to avoid essentializing the world. The *"Insein"* existential, *"Being-in,"* underscores the role of *Dasein* in developing the world as that *in* which *Dasein* dwells. Even prior to the world, it dwells in something. Once again, the given *in*—Heidegger traces the German *"in"* to the Gothic *"innan," "*to live," from which the contemporary German *"wohnen"* is derived—is revealed only through *Being.* This *Being* lives, it resides, it inhabits, it "dwells in."

We must analogously interpret *"Mitsein," "Being-with."* This existential tells us nothing as to *who* dwells with *whom.* But it underscores the fact that *Dasein* is never alone, i.e., singular, i.e., separate, basing its identity on self-identity. Fichte's formula of "I" as equal to "I," on which he based his post-Kantian ontology, is completely inapplicable here. *Dasein* does not yet contain the one who could or must remove his solitude, there are no singularities of dialogue, nor is there a dialogue itself. Here, commonality preceeds its components, commonality—"with" (*"mit"*)—is, whereas those that comprise and establish it *are not.* In this case, "with," *"mit,* " transforms, as in the case with "with," into a derivative of *Being. Being* tells us that it can only be "with"—without "with" there is no *Being.* When *Being* discovers itself, it does so as *"Being-with,"* establishing non-solitude as an inalienable feature of *Dasein. Dasein* is not alone.

Care (Die Sorge)

Heidegger also describes other existentials of *Dasein.* Another notable example is *Die Sorge,* care.[8] *Dasein* is concerned thereby expressing *Being. Being per se* represents *care.* This is an extremely important designation. *Dasein* is not something

---

8 *Ibid.,* 117.

alienated, cold, concerned only with itself, and indifferent. *Dasein* is concern. Theoretically, this existential is derived from the three preceeding ones, "*Being-in-the-world*," "*Being-in*," and "*Being-with*," but it also deciphers them. *Dasein* radiates *care*, and is *care* itself—*care* in its purest form, without the one at whom it is directed. Existing is partial, interested, and involved with the course of existing.

The world's "being at hand" is formed through care in its direction. This trajectory of "*Being-in-the-world*" constitutes something "present," "available" (*das Vorhandene*) as something that is at hand (*das Zuhandene*). *Being-in-the-world* becomes *Being-in-the-home*, in which presence is conceptualized as being surrounded with care, constituted by care.

There is always *care*, *care* is the quintessence of *Dasein*. However, when *care* pushes *Dasein* to step over an unseen barrier (thereby establishing it), to reconsider something, to touch, and eat, then care as an existential can transform being "at hand" into objectivization. Thus, this existential of *Dasein* demonstrates the way in which the oblivion of *Being* commenced in Western European philosophy. At a certain moment, concern that is natural for *Dasein* transformed the world, in which *Being* (*Being-in-the-world*) manifested, into something *excessively*" at hand." Here we can observe the initial movement toward the emergence of φύσις. We begin to understand that fundamental-ontology does not simply constitute the *new Beginning* in philosophy, but also demonstrates the trajectories along which *Dasein* became alienated from itself in the *first Beginning*. Placing the new philosophy into itself and explaining in detail how the old metaphysics arose, the errors in relation to *Dasein's* existentials that served as its basis, and the way in which it formed on its own foundations, Heidegger's analysis of *Dasein* asserts its identity as fundamental-ontology.

333

A little later, we will see that *Dasein* itself can have two basic modes—authentic and inauthentic. And each of the existentials can also act as an expression of either authentic or inauthentic *Dasein*. In the case of the *care* existential, this is obvious, and we can imagine how *Dasein's* existentials in the inauthentic regime constitute the historical-philosophical process from the first Beginning to Nietzsche.

Herein lies the entire significance of Heidegger. Not only does he demonstrate that what finished has finished, but also explains *what* exactly finished, when *it* began, and why this occurred. In addition, Heidegger constructs a bridge toward the new Beginning.

Thrownness (Geworfenheit)

Another highly important existential of *Dasein* is *thrownness* (*Geworfenheit*). *Dasein* was *thrown*. Herein lies its fundamental basis, more specifically, the lack thereof.

Dasein was thrown. It was thrown by someone, into somewhere, in some direction, from somewhere, but there is no someone or somewhere *outside* of and *before Dasein* itself. It was thrown in every sense, including psychological. *Dasein* was thrown since there is no authority that it could have addressed with a complaint, request, behest, or demand. Herein lies the significance of transitioning from the thought process that pushes off essence to the kind of thought that pushes off existence. *Dasein* was thrown because it is on its own, in complete absence of any presence outside itself. We could say that it dwells in a *throw*, it flies, since *thrownness* does not find a *bottom* (*Grund*), but occurs under the conditions of an *abyss* (*Abgrund*).

334

Even though the concept of *Geworfenheit* has become accepted by now, and is actively used in philosophy and psychology, it is not difficult to determine Heidegger's own etymological intentions. Much like "*Unverborgenheit*" (literally, "unconcealment") has the meaning equivalent to the "truth" for him (as a literal transmission of Greek etymology in the word ἀλήθεια), the word "*Geworfenheit*" is none other than the German copy of the Latin "*subjectum*"— from "*sub*" ("under") and "*jacere*" ("to throw"). It is *subjectum* that is the thrown one. In the Russian language, there is something similar in the word "*подлежащее*" ("*podlezhashchee*," grammatical subject)—a copy of another Latin word "*substantivus*", literally "lying," more specifically, "standing under."

The subject is also *thrown in*, but this is a particular case of *thrownness*. Thrownness as *Geworfenheit's* existential is an original and fundamental concept. It is characteristic of both the old philosophy (where it is called ψυχή [*psyche*], δαίμον [*daimon*], "subject," "I," etc.) and the new, where it appears in pure form.

Another existential is connected to *Dasein's* thrownness: "*sketch*" (*Entwurf*). The Russian language, much like German, contains the stem "throw" in the word "sketch" (*набросок* [*nabrosok*]). Having been *thrown*, staying in flight, *Dasein* itself undertakes a *throw*. This throw is a "throw-onto" as an answer to *thrownness*. Here, too, there are parallels with the Latin philosophical term "*proectum*," "project," which etymologically means "thrown forward"—practically the same thing as the German "*Entwurf*" or the Russian "*nabrosok*." In Latin, "*subjectum, quia subiectum est, se proicit*," "being thrown, the subject creates a project."

335

But the "subject" and "object" are not simply Latin words; they are also philosophical notions that belong to the conceptual topography of the old philosophy and, consequently, relate to the metalanguage of metaphysics. Heidegger's "throwness" (as well as the "sketch," *Entwurf*) in the place of the subject serve the following purpose:

- demontaging the metaphysical meanings of philosophical terms and their return to the element of language (from terms to words);

- developing a metalanguage of the new philosophy which is based on Germanic roots.

Let us note that these operations must be conceptualized in the context of the Russian language, and then Heidegger's philosophy will become clear in Russian, too. Also, using Slavic etymology will help in understanding the movement of Heidegger's own thoughts. At the same time, they can serve as the basis of establishing a philosophical metalanguage on the basis of returning to the original etymologies, i.e., language *per se*, which will open up the possibility of constructing Russian philosophy (which never was) relying on the origical Slavic-Russian meanings (with free usage of comparative etymologies of other Indo-European languages).

Befindlichkeit (Findability) and Fear

Dasein's next existential is *findability, Befindlichkeit.*[9]

Dasein's specific throwness manifests in that it acutely perceives it itself as *Befindlichkeit*, as "findability." *Dasein is found.*

---

9 *Ibid.*, 180–200.

The ambiguity in terms of the transitive and intransitive uses of the Russian verb *"находиться"* ("*nakhoditsia*," literally "to be found," meaning "to be located"—*"befinden"* and *"sich befinden"* in German) is quite useful here. By using the transitive verb incorrectly, i.e., without specifying "where" one is located, we transmit the very core of this existential. To be found—not somewhere, but simply to be found. The Russian grammar tries to seek a way out by using the following interpretation: *Dasein* is "found" ("*nakhoditsia*") which means that it was found by someone. And this second meaning, an accurate one this time, can also be accepted from the grammatical standpoint with the following correction: no one finds *Dasein* since, outside of *Dasein*, there is nothing and no one. However, at the same time, it does not find itself (for now), since *Dasein's* "self" (*Selbst*) comprises another topic of its analytical description. Thus, *Dasein* does not "find itself," but *is* rather *found*. [10]

Anxiety in regard to *Dasein being found* is expressed in the mode of this "findability," which is fear (*Furcht*).[11] As a result of the latter, it is quite accurate to say that *Dasein fears*. It *fears* both *thrownness* (*a throw*), *Being-in*, and *orientation toward the "world"* as a place of dwelling. Therefore, *fright* comprises one of *Dasein's* most important existentials, in which general "findability" expresses itself. *Dasein* is frightened and can express its fright in different ways. But it is pierced by fear from the onset, in a fundamental ontic way, even prior to these expressions.

Verstehen (Understanding)

Heidegger thinks that *Verstehen*[12] ("understanding," "comprehension") is also an existential of *Dasein*. "To

---

[10] This formula can be accepted as a fundamental statement from a new philosophy in the Russian language.

[11] *Ibid.*, 140.

[12] *Ibid.*, 134.

understand" ("*понимать*" [*ponimat'*]") in its Russian etymology means to "take something"; "to understand" originates in "*-ять*," "*-нять*" ("*-iat'*," "*-niat'*") which means to "take," to "lift" something. Thus, the Russian language conceptualizes understanding as appropriation, capture, turning into private property (domestication, acquisition, use, taking into care). Even if we could use the Russian word for "understanding" in this case, then it could only be used to describe the existential of the inauthentic *Dasein*. Only *beings* turned into "things-at-hand" can be "understood" by "taking", making a step over the barrier where the sacred relationship with *Being* ends, and from where—with all the domesticity—it is better not to take, and if taking occurs, then to give back immediately. "*Being-in-the-world*," constituting "things-at-hand," actually prepares through *care* these "things-at-hand" for taking. But *Dasein's* authentic existential clearly opposes this. This means that *Verstehen* must be conceptualized differently from conventional "understanding." The German stem of this word contains the meaning "rearrange," "relocate"; the English "to understand" means "to place (stand) under." The French "*comprendre*" (from the Latin "*comprehendere*"), much like the Russian, in contrast to the Germanic languages, is dominated by the stem "*prendre*," i.e., "to take," "to appropriate." We encounter something akin to this meaning in the German word "*das Vernehmung*," "*vernehmen*," ("perception," "to perceive"). By using this word, Heidegger himself occasionally transmits such an important Greek term as "*νοῦς*," "*νοεῖν*" ("*nous*," "*noein*")—"intellect," "rational mind," "thought process," "to think."

For *Dasein*, it is customary to "rearrange," change places. It is possible that this expresses its *care*, its empathy, its complicity in *Being-in-the-world*. By "rearranging," *Dasein* comprehends what it rearranges; identifies the meaning of what is being rearranged; places what is far away closer to itself and what is too close—further away, thereby constructing an intellectual order. In terms of meaning, this is "understanding," although both the Russian and French equivalents are too tied to etymology.

There is a certain linguistic problem here. If we begin examining all these nuances, we will then lose the possibility of translating Heidegger and will be forced to discuss him in the German language only. But if, on the contrary, we try to simplify the situation by rejecting these etymological excursions, then we risk ending up with total nonsense instead of a well-constructed and completely clear Germanic philosophy.

I envision the following solution. When it comes to the most important, key points in Heidegger's philosophy, especially those dealing with his creation of a *metalanguage* for this philosophy, i.e., *constructing a bridge toward the new Beginning*, we must stay as close to the German original as possible. This risks making the text more complex and excessively bulky, but also provides intellectual and philosophical clarity and certainty. At the same time, when it comes to general presentation, we can step away from this rule and use certain words without the etymological and terminological specifics, that is, approximately. Heidegger himself often strays from his metalanguage, sporadically turning from the commonly used connotation of the word or term to specialized meanings unique to his philosophy, then again, without warnings or explanations, he returns to the common usage.

Here is another example. When it comes to *Sein und Zeit* or his other works from the first period, Heidegger uses the word "*Sein*" in all cases where he discusses *Being*. In the 1930s, he begins to carefully differentiate between "*Sein*" (as "*Being* in ontology") and "*Seyn*" (as "*Being* in fundamental-ontology"). These are not translatable into Russian or any other language, but remain significant and foundational for Heidegger's metalanguage.

Therefore, coming back to *Verstehen* and explaining why we cannot generally translate it as "comprehension," we can say, despite stretching it, that *understanding* (as interpretation, decoding, even though none of these is an exact etymological equivalent of *Verstehen*) is an existential of *Dasein*, that *Dasein* is "understanding *Being*," or, more specifically, "understanding," but not "appropriating," *Being* (in order to expel the meaning of "taking" embedded in "comprehension").

Speech (Rede)

"Findability" (*Befindlichkeit*) and "understanding" (*Verstehen*) of *Dasein* express themselves in *speech*.[13] Heidegger emphasizes that in the very definition of man, ancient Greeks often embedded the *ability to speak*, ζῷον λόγον ἔχον (*zoon logon echon*) as the main attribute. The latter, according to Heidegger, should be translated as a "speaking animal," rather than the Latin formula of a "rational animal" ("*animalis rationalis*"). (*Speaking* does not always reveal the presence of a rational mind, but always the presence of *Dasein*.)

Heidegger writes, "Man expresses himself as *beings* through speech."[14] It is important to note here that it is *beings* (ontically) that man expresses himself as, not man. *Dasein* itself lets itself be known through speech. Therefore, speech and the language that it reveals find their source in *Being*. At the same time, it is important to note that it is language, not its grammar and logic, that expresses the deep-rooted fundamental-ontological layer of *Dasein*. Herien lies the most significant trajectory of

13 *Ibid.*, 148.
14 *Ibid.*, 165.

Heidegger's entire philosophy. *Dasein's* ontics as a language must be "understood" (*verstehen*) differently than by using the logical apparatus based on the old philosophy and, consequently, ontology. Heidegger's entire opus is based on this principle: while moving toward the *new Beginning*, he addresses language as *Dasein's* existential directly. On its basis, he creates a metalanguage of fundamental-ontology radically differing from the language of Western European philosophy—from the *first Beginning* (Anaximander, Paramenides, Heraclitus) until its *End* (Nietzsche).

Language is Dasein's Sein

Heidegger emphasizes that *speech as an existential* organically includes *listening* and *silence*. Silence, according to Heidegger, is not simply the lack of speech or its rejection, but a source of speech, speech in its pure *Being*. Speech as a saying conceals silence, eclipsing its all-encompassing and all-containing, life-giving darkness with its presence.

Heidegger pays special attention to the process of hearing and listening. He brings up the image of a sentinel at his station at night surrounded by absolute darkness. The sentinel is tuning into the surrounding silence of *beings* in an attempt to catch the tinest signs of the sound's barely detectable emergence amidst its absence. This kind of silence and this kind of listening take *Dasein* back to the very origins of speech, to that point in the ocean of language where the rivers of speech find their source.

Speech and silence can resemble *beings* and *Being*. *Being* both *is* and *is not beings*. The case of silence is similar: it calls both for the presence of speech and its removal for the sake of an all-encompassing, solemn truth. From the standpoint of *Dasein's* authentic existence, hearing speech and, to an even greater extent, tuning into life-giving silence, is even more significant than speech itself or natural sounds articulated by man.

Stimmung

"Stimmung," "Stimme" is another existential of Dasein. This is a very interesting word. It simultaneously means "voice" and "melody," "setting" and "mood." Being tuned in is also Dasein's existential since it cannot be "on its own." In other words, it cannot be out of tune: it will not play by itself and make sound. Dasein is necessarily in one of the moods. It either laughs or cries, feels sad, calmly observes, feels wrathful, basks. Without these, it is unthinkable: we cannot imagine Dasein lacking its Stimmung existential.

In the old philosophy, mood was considered a secondary quality unworthy of a philosopher. It is impossible to imagine that a stoic, a follower of Seneca, Zeno of Elea, or Marcus Aurelius—who despised affects—saying all of a sudden, "We were sad today, but yesterday was enjoyable." Thinkers must be indifferent, insensitive, alienated. They must think about the eternal and unchanging principles, observe ἀρχή ("arche," the original source) in the state of ἀταραξία ("ataraxia," indifference).

Heidegger suspects that this is a thesis of the false ontology. Alienation from mood, equating Stimme with affect, indicates the already complete divison of Dasein into a soul (consciousness, νοῦς [nous]) and nature (φύσις [physis]), i.e., the alienation and loss of correlation to Being, substituting the question about Being with the question about beings and the general.

Dasein is *attuned*, and *Dasein's* moods leave an impact on the modes of philosophizing in the fundamental-ontological vein. If affects were, in the old philosophy, considered the lowest domain of the thought process, then in the *new Beginning*, moods are inseparably connected to the thought process.

This is linked to Heidegger's own attitude toward art (poetry, in particular). Captivated by *mood*, *Stimme*, poets and artists are capable of reaching the furthest horizons in this direction, the most unreachable heights, which, in terms of their significance, are comparable to the greatest philosophical insights. Heidegger considered philosophers and artists the two types of people that reach an equally great height, but by using different mountain peaks and following diverging paths. They originate from the same *Dasein*, but move along different trajectories. This is why Heidegger addressed the poetry of Hölderlin, Novalis, Rilke, and Georg Heym, as well as the paintings of Vincent van Gogh, for the purpose of interpreting many of his philosophical ideas. *Stimme* is, without a doubt, a poetic existential.

IV. INAUTHENTIC REGIME OF DASEIN'S EXISTENCE

Authenticity and Inauthenticity of Dasein

Having described *Dasein* and its existentials, Heidegger introduces a highly significant distinction into *Dasein* itself. He mentions the presence of two opposite modes of *Being* for *Dasein*: "*eigene*" and "*uneigene*." These are normally translated as "*authentic*" and "*inauthentic*." In German, "*eigene*" means "one's own," in other words, "that which belongs only to oneself." "*Uneigene*" is "not one's own," "inauthentic," "alienated." The Greek word "*αὐθεντικός*" (*authenticos*) is based on the root "*αὐτός*," i.e., "oneself," "one's own," which closely corresponds to the German "*eigene*."

The introduction of this fundamental distinction leads us to describing these two types of *Dasein's* existence and, consequently, to dividing all existentials into two modes: each existential can be viewed in its authentic (*eigene*) and inauthentic (*uneigene*) version.

Heidegger demonstrates that the "natural" (in the very least, most frequently encountered) state of *Dasein* is *inauthentic*. *Dasein* exists in the inauthentic, not one's own. It can exist (and must do so) authentically, but most often (almost always) this is not the case. The inauthenticity of *Dasein's* existence is one of the fundamental attributes of *Dasein*, specifically. This is a certain addition to *Dasein* from the side (there is no such side): it is its inseparable and fundamental attribute. *Dasein's* inauthenticity has its own deep-rooted foundations.

345

In addition, all forms of inauthentic existence are rooted in *Dasein's* authentic structure. It is important to note that *Dasein* appears (does not conceal itself any longer, reveals itself) in the authentic mode, whereas it conceals itself (hides, disappears) in the inauthentic mode. But both unconcealment and concealment comprise the essence of its existence.

The All-Piercing Everyday

What comprises the core of *Dasein's* inauthentic existence? Heidegger calls this *"durchdringliche Alltäglichkeit"*[1], which means "all-piercing" or *"penetrating everyday (everydayness)."* It seems that the term "everyday" is a lightweight. But the latter does not presuppose what occurs daily, because very different things occur "every day" that cannot serve as a predicate for such a fundamental notion like *Dasein*. The inauthentic register of existence itself gives birth to the "everyday," establishes, and constitutes it, transforms everything into it, which may not be the "everyday" by itself, and makes this everyday "piercingly penetrable." "Everydayness" and "extraordinarity" are predetermined by *Dasein's* setting. In the inauthentic mode, everything, even the most extraordinary event, turns into routine, becomes banale, is included in the common. In addition, the power of *Dasein* is so great that it is capable of ensnarling *everything* in the "everyday," keeping actions, thoughts, events, gestures, occurrences, and feelings in this state. No one and nothing are capable of slipping away from this register when it is turned on; the piercing rays of inauthenticity control everything.

---

[1] Martin Heidegger, *Sein und Zeit, op. cit.*, 160.

Decay (Verfallen)

Since *Dasein* exists, its existentials are not something additional to it, but rather express certain aspects of it itself. Consequently, *Dasein's* existentials in the inauthentic mode function as expressions of this inauthenticity. They do not fall under the "all-piercing everyday," but rather each constitutes the latter in its own way. Operating in the inauthentic regime, *Dasein's* existentials create the everyday.

Thus, "thrownness" (*Geworfenheit*) transforms into "breakdown," "decay" (*Verfallen*) inside inauthentic *Dasein*.[2] This kind of existence expresses, in its own way, furnishes, moderates, and emits the fundamental element of the "throw." *Dasein* falls, breaks apart, collapses, thereby creating the "everyday" as distraction, dispersion, decomposition, dilapidation, confusion, and multiplicity.

This affects other existentials as well. For instance, "*Being-in-the-world*" in *Dasein's* inauthentic existence becomes "falling-into-the-world." The "world" itself emerges as a result, torn away from "*Being-in-the-world*," alienated from this kind of *Being*, preemptively fallen. Every world is a fallen world, and this fallenness, the world's fall into sin, is a form of *Dasein's* existence as that of fall and decay. The world falls away from *Being-in-the-world* becoming the world; by becoming the world, it becomes the world of decay, falls apart into multiplicity, immediately begins to turn into dust, dissipates in the entropic process. Yet this is not an attribute of the world, or even the attribute of the world that has fallen away from "*Being-in-the-world*," but rather the attribute of *Dasein's* inauthentic existence. The world transforms into the everyday world through *Dasein's* inauthentic regime.

---

2 *Ibid.*, 127.

But it is not just the world that falls. *Dasein* itself *falls* and *falls into* the everyday. This *fall* into the everyday becomes *Dasein's* fate, its history. The history of *Dasein* in its inauthentic regime is the history of its *fall* (as an inauthentic expression of *thrownness*). This is precisely why the history of Western European philosophy inexorably moves in the direction of nihilism: it embodies the fall of *Dasein*.

The fall is the fall into inauthenticity (*Uneigentlichkeit*).

Chatter (Gerede)

Inauthentic *Dasein* possesses other attributes such as *chatter* (*Gerede*), *curiosity* (*Neugierigkeit*), and *ambiguity* (*Zweideutigkeit*).[3]

Chatter is a variant of speech (this is obvious in German: *Gerede*—*Rede*), which narrates about *Dasein* as it appears in its inauthentic regime. Here, chatter expresses itself exactly like speech and, exactly like speech, it is one of *Dasein's* existentials. The difference is that chatter is speech pierced with the everyday, creating this everyday, submerging the one who speaks and the one who listens into it, as well as the one who is silent (in this case, the one who keeps quiet). When it comes to chatter, it is impossible to tell clearly who is speaking, what about, to whom, and for what purpose. It represents background murmur, white noise, abstracted from the speaker himself and from the one whom he addresses. *Dasein* reveals itself in this (even if in its inauthentic regime); it is the one for whom it is customary to narrate, through speech, about the *Being* present in it, addressing everyone and no one at the same time. Chatter transfers this existential of *Dasein* into a message about "this" (*da*) rather than *Being* (*Sein*). "This" appears in chatter (*Gerede*)—"this,

---

3 *Ibid.*, 175, 167, 170.

this, this." Chatter attracts one's attention to *factuality* (which is also one of *Dasein's* existentials), but detracts from *Being*. This is why factuality becomes insignificant, negligible.

Endless muttering about all that is insignificant weaves the structure of the everyday, fills it with endless discourse as a kind of totalitarian radio, which can never be turned off, since it broadcasts in our consciousness. Any attempts to focus on any statemen's meaning result in failure, since *Gerede* transitions to the next subject of conversation at the very moment when the rational mind tries to comprehend the previous statement.

Inauthentic *Dasein* cannot handle silence as an aspect of authentic speech, nor can it handle full-fledged speech narrating about *Being*, asking about it, encouraging to listen to its voice. *The voice of Being* is always quiet but, so that there are no chances left to hear it, *Gerede* rings louder and louder. It seems to express everything so as not to say anything—only to fill inquisitive silence with a stream of ordinary statements.

Chatter is an inalienable attribute of many, even the most non-talkative and sullen people (anti-social loners are even more prone to chatter on the inside). People talk constantly on the inside. Something always goes on inside their heads with spinning fragments of words, thoughts, concepts, and phrases. It is this that is the existential chatter of the inauthentic *Dasein*. It has no beginning or end. When man first emerges into the world, he hears squeaking, ringing, rattling medical instruments, whispering nurses, doctors' self-assured deep voices, screaming women giving birth, newborn crying (including oneself); later on appear the continuously muttering father, mother, brothers, sisters, grandparents, cats, television, later yet—television announcers, teachers, bosses, employees, insurance agents,

349

cashiers, administrators, and, again, at the end—nurses and doctors. Man passes accompanied by the same cantankerous and senseless rumbling of the daily phrases strung onto one another and lacking the narrative about *Being*.

In *chatter*, *Dasein* is thrown, and in *chatter* it is liquidated. When man dies, chatter continues since it is the fundamental attribute of the inauthentic *Dasein*.

Curiosity (Neugierigkeit)

Understanding (*Verstehen*) transforms into curiosity and a neurotic desire to get acquainted with more and more new types, concepts, states, things, places, and events without submerging into their *Being*. It is *curiosity* that is an attempt to appropriate, take upon oneself, privatize the world torn away from its *Being*. And, based upon its satisfaction level, curiosity only grows, since it takes the world without its *Being*. Inauthentic *Dasein* does not obtain anything, but only loses, dispersing its most important attribute while falling (it is *curiosity* that is the fall of *understanding*—*Verstehen*), *Being* embedded in "*this-Being*" (*Dasein*).

In the German language, *Neugierigkeit* literally means "hunger for novelty." The Russian "*любо*" (*liubo-* from "*любовь*" [*liubov'*], "love") and "*-пытство* ("*-pytstvo*" from "*пытать*" [*pytat'*], here, to "find out," "learn," "unravel") does not contain the same negative connotation. *Hunger for novelty* expresses *Dasein's* inauthentic vanity much more acutely. It pushes *Dasein* toward constant sliding from one thing to another, as we get used to the last thing, we move on to the next. But "getting used to something" does not mean "to be understood" ("*verstanden*"). Inauthentic *Dasein* "understands" in the sense that it "lifts" a certain something that it could discard in the next moment, since the intention of inauthenticity is not to explore the *Being* in what was "lifted," but the gesture of "false" appropriation itself. At the same time, the aforementioned Russian word for "curiosity" etymologically means neither an attempt to appropriate nor the transition into novelty: it can be a quality of asking for one and the same, it can be triggered by the same thing if it is worth it for *Dasein* to ask about its *Being*.

Elements reproduced by *Dasein* in its inauthentic *Being* become a constant, continuous, *prodigal contemplation* which gravitates toward nothing. Hunger for novelty is a form of the greatest kind of ignorance: running from one thing to another and grabbing everything in sight, only to drop it a second later, inauthentic *Dasein* makes everything *old*, meaningless, uninteresting, and does not inspire any kind of advancement. Thus *Neugierigkeit* becomes an escape from meaning, thought, content —in other words, *Being*.

Heidegger asserts that curiosity (*Neugierigkeit*) expresses man's aspiration to *see*. Seeing means failing to understand. The fact of seeing does not communicate anything to *Dasein* or make it advance in terms of grasping *Being*. Seeing is the least ontic of all perception forms. The everyday replaces thoughtful understanding (*Verstehen*) with appearances (δόξα [doxa], "renown") and submerges inauthentic *Dasein* into a continuous chain of appearances, sightseeing.

The thought process demands *limits* to seeing, a focused contemplation on one and the same so that this contemplation could open up *Being* of the contemplated thing — or *Dasein* itself. Whence come traditional meditative practices, concentrating one's attention on the same objects. The less man sees, the more chances he has for recognition and comprehension. But this is the case with the authentic *Dasein*. In its inauthentic counterpart, everything is the opposite. Its purpose is to collect appearances that replace meaning. The more total is its ability to observe, the more meaningless are the observed images.

We can compare two exemplars of inauthentic *Dasein*, *chatter* and *curiosity*. When it comes to *chatter* (*Gerede*), the same thing is repeated over and over again, as a rule. This intrusive nonsense does not even stop at night when man closes his eyes and looks at nothing. *Curiosity* constantly pushes him toward *novelty*— what he "had not seen" earlier. Thus, the eternal return of the same kind of nonsense in the form of *Gerede* is complemented with a "refreshing" stream of new nonsense in the form of *Neugierigkeit*. Not yet ready for public consumption when *Sein und Zeit* was being written, the television handles this ideally. The television combines the flow of half-comprehended, inconsistent information with the flow of images. In this way, the television is one of the greatest embodiments of the *piercing everyday* and, consequently, a privileged form of *Dasein's* inauthentic existence.

Ambiguity (Zweideutigkeit)

The fact that *Dasein* is always found *in between* (*zwischen*) generates constant ambiguity in the inauthentic regime along with uncertainty, vagueness, and always confused ontic trajectories of *Dasein's* development in the direction of spatial or temporal horizons. In contrast to authentic *Dasein*, which grasps *Being* in *Being-in-between*, liberating it from false identities with *beings-outside-of* (φύσις, *physis*) and *beings-inside-of* (ἰδέα [idea], ψυχή [*psyche*]), inauthentic *Dasein* falls into a pattern of thrashing between the exterior and the interior and, spinning in a cycle of uncertainties growing like a snowball, ends up being unable to focus and prove ontologically the basis for either one.

We can examine ambiguity as a layer of *chatter* over the *hunger for novelty*. Meaningless repetition of one and the same in chatter generates simulated consistency in inauthentic *Dasein*. The latter establishes a fictitious row of meanings as a certain kind of muttering consistency of pseudo-meanings. *Curiosity*, on the other hand, introduces the pseudo-dynamic of flashing images. Since both are the opposite of meaning, both processes function in a de-synchronized state, achieving ambiguity through layering two kinds of nonsenses over each other (auditory and visual).

Fear as an Escape

As part of inauthentic existence, *fear*, typical of *Dasein* as such, pushes it toward *flight*. This *flight* (or an escape) is not characterized by *whither* it could run but *whence* and *from what*. Inauthentic *Dasein* interprets *fear* as a fear faced with *Being* and turns it into a panicked *flight from Being*.

An escape from *Being*, that is, from what is inside *Dasein* corresponding to *Sein*, can be carried out in two directions: *without* and *within*. An escape *without* means constituting the world as a world torn away from *Being-in-the-world*. This world, as something autonomous, becomes the result of *Dasein's* inauthentic existence escaping from itself, whereas the direction of this *escape without* creates the world as whitherto one flees from *Being*. At the same time, the same world that has fallen out of *Being-in-the-world* can be described as a result of inauthentic thrownness. When thrownness becomes a fall and decay, it, first and foremost, does not constitute the one that

353

falls, but where one falls, falling apart afterward. Where one falls is the same where one escapes.

A different form of fear can be caused by that very world that is constituted by *tearing away from Being*. In this case, fleeing from *Being* becomes fleeing from the world. Inauthentic *Dasein* constitutes the internal dimension of the subject, which becomes autonomous in response to the fear inspired from the outside. In this case, this can also be presented as *thrownness*, only not into the world but in the opposite direction, as alienation from the world, a *turn away* from *beings* and *from the Being of beings*. In all of these cases with *Dasein's* inauthentic existence, this fear accompanying *Being*, fear of *Being*, and fear as *Being* become fear faced with *Being*.

The Figure of Das Man

Describing the existence of inauthentic *Dasein*, Heidegger introduces the figure of *das Man*.[4] This is a neologism for the German language. In German, "man" is "*der Mann*," a masculine noun with "nn" at the end. At the same time, German contains such forms as "*man spricht*," "*man sieht*," "*man denkt*," meaning "one speaks," "one sees," "one thinks."[5] The French language contains a direct analogy to "*das Man*" — "*on*," "*l'on*" (which is formed from the French "*homme*," "*l'homme*," "man" in the same way as the German "*Man*" is from "*der Mann*," "man," and "*Mensch*" in contemporary German). In English, this expression can be translated in the way that "they say" is used without specifying who "they" are.

---

[4] *Ibid.*, 173.
[5] There is no direct analogy to this in the Russian or English languages, and the corresponding forms either use a third-person verb without a personal pronoun ("they say," "they think"), a reflexive verb in the third-person singular ("it is considered," "it is sung"), or a third-person plural verb with the pronoun "everyone" ("everyone thinks," "everyone believes"). "*Das Man*" has often been translated as "the They," which conveys the relation to "conventional wisdom."

Heidegger introduces *"das Man"* as an expression of the inauthentic *Dasein* that has fallen into the everyday. *Das Man* is the "I" of the inauthentic *Dasein*, its personified expression. *Das Man* is the answer to the question "Who?" in relation to the inauthentic *Dasein*.

Das Man expresses the inauthentically taken existential of "Being-with" (*Mitsein*). Since *Dasein* reveals both *Being-with* and *Being-together*, in the inauthentic regime this means the transfer of subjectivity onto an uncertain, vague, and unrecorded authority found *in between* (*zwischen*), like *Dasein* itself. In this particular case, *das Man* is not an "I" of a certain person, or a "he," "you," and "everyone put together." Rather, *das Man* is no one, since he is the target of projecting the refusal to accept any responsibility for statements, opinions, actions, conclusions, and projects—an escape from them, a flight—rather than responsible statements, conclusions, actions, results, and projects. The density of movement away from responsibility generates the existence of *das Man*, which becomes the reference point for everything and everyone. What man does not think through himself or someone else for him—someone specific nearby or even far away from him—ends up in the category of "they think," "they think that," "it is believed." As a rule, no one specifically (neither individually, nor collectively) does not think as "they think" (as *das Man thinks*). Nonetheless, it is this absence of a specific position personified in anyone that grants the (inarticulate) "thoughts" of *das Man*" the greatest authority, indisputable "truth," unconditionality, and obviousness.

Das Man is constituted together with the everyday as its faceless personification, as its core, which contains nothing specific, definitive, clear, and transparent. *Das Man* is concentrated *ambiguity* (*Zweideutigkeit*). His "declarations" are never unequivocal and orderly, but this makes them all the more mandatory, oppressive, and self-imposing. The more *das Man* establishes himself in justifying his actions and judgements, the more absurd and unfounded he becomes.

In *das Man*, writes Heidegger, "each one is the other, and no one is himself." [6]

Das Man is the main *acteur* and, at the same time, creator of the everyday. *This is Dasein's "who" during a fall, in decay (Verfallen). Das Man* falls without noticing, thinking instead that he "has a good seat."

Das Man is the one that generates inauthentic ontology; it is he who speaks of the subject and object. A chain of inauthentic existentials, a system of ontological judgements, concepts of a subject, object, and, it is frightening to admit, "God" emerges, and is constructed in him. "God" as an ontological construct of the inauthentic *Dasein* is established through his inability to truly address the *other*, much like the authentic state of oneself.

According to Heidegger, the man who says "I" is a ridiculous madman, since correct philosophical comprehension of the first-person pronoun makes its practical usage impossible in principle. When man says, "I," he is being encouraged by *das Man* to do so; "I" turns into citing an indefinite, trustworthy and, at the same time, unprovable authority. By pronouncing "I," man dissipates through *das Man* throughout the "falling world," filled with *das Man's* mirrors, a multitude of caricatures of integrity, personhood, reason, and determination.

An analogous situation emerges with the terms *"objective," "real," "reality."* Assuming that the external is a *given*, man, once

---

[6] *Ibid.*, 126.

again, operates in the dimension of *das Man*. The latter, instead of relating to *beings* through *questioning about his own Being*, crosses out its essence and even its existence, annihilating them, replacing them with *Nothingness*. Reality, objectivity, and, especially, materiality are deeply nihilistic concepts. The very possibility of their existence is rooted in the *all-piercing everyday* and in foolish wisdom of *das Man*. Modern American English has an established expression, "conventional wisdom," which means, literally, the "kind of wisdom agreed upon by everyone that it is, indeed, wisdom," representing the "public place." The latter, specifically, is the formula of *das Man's* existence, a form of his wisdom-making agreed upon by everyone (even though no one specific was asked about it), but which can neither point nor prove its origins and its intellectual genesis, the roots of which could contain errors, mistakes, absurdity, or an obvious stretch.

Das Man also has its own "god." This "god" is calm, lazy, and does not participate in the lives of people. Lazy, lounging god (*deus otiosis* of religious origins) is also a creation of *das Man*.

Das Man always thinks practically and, therefore, creates a daily ontology, in which everything profound and problematic is subject to doubt, while he gladly and confidently accepts the emptiest of chimeras as reliable evidence. Let us propose a schematic diagram of *das Man's* ontological triangle (see below).

Of course, *das Man* could do without a "god," since he has a sufficiently firm belief in the reliability of the erroneous and unprovable ("I" and "reality") along with doubt in everything else (often much more justified and self-evident) in order to exist.

357

Nonetheless, "just in case," he reserves this greatest ontological authority where he could place the following instead of "god": an "idea," "values," "ideals," "worldviews," the "state," "society," and so on.

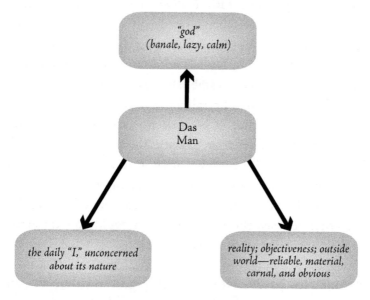

schematic diagram featuring ontological poles of inauthentic Dasein

The image of inauthentic *Being*, the image of our ordinary everyday woven from us ourselves, in the eyes of Heidegger becomes a process of fundamental ontological decay—turbulent, active, frightening, constant, and continuing every second. The world, which normally and calmly opens up in *das Man's* everyday (and everyone else), in reality is something frightening in this optics—a catastrophe, crisis, fall, and decay. Falling for the charms of *das Man* and his "conventional wisdom" is more frightening than a serial killer's paws. In the latter case, one could recall authentic *Being*. Evading the killer, however, one cannot remember *Being*, even though the former had already caught him and dismembered him, as he slept quiety while cozily snoring. And if consciousness touched this mood even briefly, man would awaken, because there is nothing more monstrous, violent, and pathological than what occurs in the *piercing everyday*. *Das Man* dismembers *Being*, forces it to rot and decompose, turns the living into the dead, and life-saving questioning into the suffocating and preemptively wrong answer.

Das Man as Dasein's Existential

In order to understand Heidegger's thought process, we must avoid any hint of dualism. *Dasein's* inauthentic existence, the transformation of its existentials—"thrownness" into "fall" and "decay," "understanding" into "curiosity," "*Being-in-the-world*" into the illusion of objectivity, "*Being-in-between*" into "ambiguity," etc.; the centrality of *das Man*; the all-piercing everyday—all of these are not something external, foreign, or other than *Dasein* itself. This is *Dasein*, its own choice, *decision* (*Entscheidung*). The terms "good"/"bad" are inapplicable here, along with "true"/"false," "kind"/"evil," and so on. In all cases and in both regimes—authentic and inauthentic—we are dealing with the one and the same: *Dasein*, which, regardless of the way it exists, always and only expresses *Dasein's* existence.

Thus, in order to avoid any hint of dualism in describing *das Man* and his attributes, Heidegger emphasizes the following: "*Das Man* is an existential and, as an original phenomenon, belongs to the positive structure of *Dasein*."[7] This is an incredibly important clarification. Existing inauthentically, *Dasein* nonetheless remains the main and only distributor of *Being*, meaning, content, structure, and orientation of processes, even if this distribution is expressed in nihilism, false ontology,

---

7 *Ibid.*, 128; here, translated from the Russian.

alienation, nonsense, inarticularity, confusion, and decay. It is *Dasein* exclusively that bears the responsibility for both the inauthenticity and authenticity of existence. It is *Dasein* that is at the core and is the existence of everything, predetermining *what* is, *how* it is, and *for how long what is* will be.

Heidegger calls upon *Dasein's* own inauthenticity to think *positively*.

V. AUTHENTIC DASEIN

Authentic Dasein and Being

What is *authenticity?*

Heidegger defines it as the *antithesis of the inauthenticity* described through various forms of existence that we discussed earlier.

The most important aspect of *authentic (eigene) Dasein* is the fact that it is *focused on the possibility to be*, on the kind of *Sein (Being)* that is *(ist) this-one-here (da)*. The presence of *Sein* is embedded in *Dasein*, but *Dasein* itself, in its existence, may treat this *Sein* in two ways. It could get distracted from it, shrug it off, turn away, focus on something else (for instance, the pure "*da*," i.e., "this"). In the case of this decision, it enters into the inauthentic regime and begins existing through unleashing the "piercing everyday," with all its characteristic existential versions—*das Man*, "curiosity," "panicked flight," "chatter," "ambiguity," and so on.

Authentic *Dasein* exists in the fact that it *is*, that *Being prevails in it*, that *it exists as Being*. Authenticity is found where we move away from inauthenticity, from the endless chatter and novelty as well as the "conventional wisdom" of *das Man*; when we stop running away from *Being* into the world or into ourselves, dwelling in the world, when we begin to focus specifically on *Being*, and, through this focus, carefully and attentively reach "*where*" this *Being* is; when we respond to the call of thrownness with an intense recognition of *findability*, but do not allow *findability* to calm us, *cultivating thrownness and its inquisitiveness*. But in all of these authentic existentials, the most important aspect is the *concentration on Being* in all its modalities and combinations. We must address it with the question about it itself. Then *Dasein* will develop according to its fundamental-ontological regime.

Being Which Is "This" and Which Is

What can "this-here-*Being*" say about itself dwelling in its own authentic mode? It could say two of the last frightening and beautiful words, *"this here-Being"*; *"this-here—Being"*; *"this here, Being is."* Instead of the *"I,"* instead of the *"world,"* instead of *"god,"* we must say the original and correct word, *"is." "Is"* is in the beginning, only then comes "what," "who," "how," "where," "when," "why," "for what purpose." But more often than not, this *"is"* falls out, is erased, and sometimes disappears.

At one point, the Russian language contained the connecting verb *"быть"* (*byt'*, to be) which was an unconditional participant of any affirmative sentences in all of its forms. *Being* was the required element of grammar. In contemporary Russian, we say, "I—a child," "she—a subject of criminal liability," "man—disabled person," "we—excellent fellows." Then what happened to *"is"*? We speak about the "I," about "her," "man," "child," "a subject of criminal liability," "a disabled person," but nowhere do we state that they *are*, that they *pertain to Being*, and that *Being speaks through them*. One could end up with the impression that all parties in question do not exist, that they are symbols, that *Being* left them, or that they escaped from it themselves, slipped away, backed away, and collapsed into "No thing." Earlier, this was impossible in the Old Church Slavonic; the verb "to be" was conjugated and necessarily present in such forms.[1]

---

[1] *азъ есмь, azm esm'*, I am;

Thus, the phrase, "I—a child" would have sounded as "*азъ чадо есмъ*" ("*az chado esm*"). But a child's *Being*, his "am (is)," is incompatable with the "I": the latter is something that pertains to adolescence.

If this saying were given back to *Being*, the latter would forbid us to pronounce it. "She is a subject of criminal liability" means that she is not worth a dime with her *Being* lowered to the level of criminal law. Thus, she did not simply commit a crime, but her *Being* revolves around the ontology of criminal law, and her place is in prison. "This man is a disabled person" means that his disability is the equivalent of his *Being*. By acknowledging this, we lower his masculinity to disability, which is a contradiction. Thus, a man without an arm or an eye will always remain something other than a disabled person. He will try to remain a man, while repressing his disability, pushing it further away from the pure illumination of *Being's* light. He might even be cured. Traditional societies either ignored warriors' wounds or considered them an embellishment. Looking the wrong way at a veteran wounded by an enemy's spear would cost its source dearly—both eyes or even a broken neck. In the past, the armless, legless, and scarred were men; their peers and they themselves *honored* their *Being* and masculinity. The case with the excellent fellows: if we are "excellent fellows," then we bear responsibility. *If we brag through Being, then we will answer to Being.* This motif often occurs in Russian epic tales, in which bragging leads to dark miracles: death in the epic tale of Fedor

---

ты еси, ty esi, you are;

(*он, она, оно, on/a/o,* s/he, it—previously, not personal but demonstrative pronouns—*есть, est',* are;

мы есмы, my esmy, we are;

вы есте, vy este, you are;

(*они) сутъ (oni) sut',* they are.

Buslaev, resurrection of the Tatar army in the epic tale of Ilia Muromets and Batyga, etc.

Dasein's authenticity is its turn toward *Sein*, its desire and will to *be*, and determination to discover oneself as *Being*. In this case, *Dasein* is etymologically focused on itself as *Being*, which is not somewhere over there, inside or out, but *"this (here),"* *"in between."* Thrownness and findability apply to *Being*. "Being-with" becomes *" "Being-with-Being."* *Being-in-the-world* becomes *Being-in-Being*. Speech narrates about *Being*. Fear turns into terror (*Angst*), which does not disseminate or force to flee, but rather turns all of its power toward *Being*, which contains both threat and salvation, the terrifying and terrified, baring its finality and accepting it.

Spaciality as an Existential of Dasein

The space within which *Dasein* exists authentically is sacred, living, fundamental-ontological. This space is born out of "*this-Being.*" Spaciousness (*Räumlichkeit*) reveals itself as one of *Dasein's* existentials.[2]

Space is the development of *Dasein's* "thisness" (*da*). But the point where it begins is not arbitrary and abstract, but rather that which points to *Being* (*Sein*) as its own presence (*Dasein*). In this case, *Being* is conceived not as independent of "this" ("this here"), "there," or "somewhere over there," but specifically *this here*. The kind of terror that this concentration of *Being* in *Dasein's* factuality inspires in it, transforms into the affirmation of *Dasein's* selfness (*Selbst*) in its authentic existence.

---

2 Martin Heidegger, *Sein und Zeit, op. cit.,* 129.

The "Who" of Authentic Dasein

Heidegger speaks about the "who" that appears in authentic *Dasein*. Answering the question of "who?"[3], authentic *Dasein* responds with the "self," "it itself" formula (*Selbst* in German). The *Selbst* of authentic *Dasein* comprises its equivalence with *Being*, *Sein*. *Dasein* may be. It may be itself, in which case it *is*, or it may be *not itself*, in which case *das Man* and other inauthentic existentials operate in the place of *Selbst*.

We could approach the authentic selfness of *Dasein* through negating *das Man*, through a determined and conscious *turn away from the piercing everyday*, but this turn will be actualized only in the case of *Dasein* undertaking it by itself, through relying on *Being*, which is present in it and speaks through it.

Being-toward-Death (Sein-zum-Tode)

One of the most significant aspects of *Dasein* in its authentic existence is *Being-toward-death*.[4] The everyday does not like the subject of death. *Das Man* always lives, always tempting and violating us with the thought that he might be immortal, and we, too, as a result. As soon as *Dasein* pays attention to death, as soon as death reveals itself "here and now," as soon as death without any intermediate realities is launched into *Dasein*, there emerges the greatest possibility for *Dasein* to transition into its authentic regime. In this regime, *fear* transforms into *terror*, which originates in *Dasein's* lighting-fast realization of its finality. "Being-toward-death," writes Heidegger, "is existential [сущностный] terror, *Angst*." *Dasein* is finite, mortal, and is present facing death. When it turns toward it, focusing on it, it reveals itself in intense, absolute, ultimate terror.

---

3 *Ibid.*, 110.
4 *Ibid.*, 114.

Terror is the opposite of fear. Fear provokes filling the external world with things, and the internal world—with empty thoughts and concerns. Piling up a multitude of things and ideas is an expression of *Dasein's* fear faced with its own mortality and finality. This trick works inside inauthentic *Dasein*, which is barricaded by the dissipated multitude from the simplicity and severity of the death's moment. But this safety of the multitude is the flipside of the fear coin. It does not remove it, but exacerbates it, making it flat, small, and pathetic. Its alternative is the peaceful triumph of *terror* (*Angst*) faced with clearly contemplated death. Colliding with death through *terror* is the necessary result of *Dasein's* primacy and its ontic status. Having nothing before or after itself, much like inside or out, *Dasein* can only carry out a dialogue with *Nothingness*. *Being* embedded in *Dasein* is too indivisible for the authentic state to postulate something outside itself; authentic *Dasein* is collected and consolidated—it is yet to be dispersed throughout the multitude of *beings* which emerges specifically through its transition into the inauthentic regime. Thus, *Dasein* by itself, inside its own *Selbst*, can maintain a dialogue only with death and the *element of pure Nothingness*. It is the direct collision with this element that is the state of terror. Terror is the most important form of *Dasein's* authentic existence. In terror, *Dasein* is *Dasein*, that is, *Dasein* to the greatest extent, since it is fully concentrated on its own *Being* which, as *Being* in the fullest sense (not an individual or a common case of *Being*), can only assume *non-Being* outside itself, i.e., death.

Being always exists *toward death* and is *faced toward death*. In the place where death's presence is at its greatest, deep-rooted and perfect terror reigns. This terror is a true sign of *Being's* presence, since death inspires terror only because it *is* and because it *may not be*. That which *is not* does not experience any kind of terror; *non-beings* feel wonderful inside death. It triggers terror specifically in *beings* which recognizes that they *are* with lightning speed.

Das Man attempts to conceal *Dasein* in various ways and avoid colliding with terror and *Being* when faced with death. He is engaged in non-stop chatter; he expresses interest and curiosity, moves around, fills the world with objects, and the soul—with concerns for a single purpose only—in order to take refuge from this terror. But it is only possible to hide from it by refusing to focus on *Being* as a finality, i.e., through the cost of imitating *non-Being*. Inside the inauthentic regime, *Dasein pretends* in such a way that it would not be noticed either from the standpoint of death or that of *Being*. It is as if this inauthentic *Dasein is* and *is not* at the same time. Thus, it attempts to slip away from absolute terror by imitating immortality.

Conscience (Gewissen)

Heidegger describes the process of calling onto *Dasein's* authentic *Being* by introducing conscience into the game. "Conscience," he writes, "summons *Dasein's* seflness (*Selbst*) out of being lost in *das Man*."[5]

The German word "*Gewissen*" means both "conscience" and "consciousness" at the same time. The Russian language contains a similar etymology: "*совесть*" (*sovest'*, conscience) is formed from "with" and "news" ("*co-*" and "*весть*"—"*so-*" and "*vest'*"), whereas the German "*Gewissen*"—from the general suffix "*ge-*" and the stem "*wissen*" ("to know"). Consciousness springs up from the depths of *Dasein* and calls onto it to focus its attention on *Being*. "*Dasein* is the one who calls and the one who is called," writes Heidegger.[6]

5 *Ibid.*, 231–267.
6 *Ibid.*, 274.

A "clear conscience" is illusionary. Normally, the conscience reveals itself when it reproaches us. *Gewissen* is the constant feeling of guilt, which *Dasein* experiences. In Heidegger's view, *Dasein* is fundamentally *guilty* in principle. But only in its inauthentic state does it try to explain itself or somehow escape from condemntation and cover up its guilt. But *Dasein*, listening to the voice of its consciousness, reveals itself in *guilt* since it is through *guilt*, as a fundamental reproach, that its true *Being* manifests itself. Revealed in guilt, *Dasein* returns to what it is. Recognizing guilt, pure guilt, guilt as such, reminds *Dasein* that it is operating in an inauthentic regime.

Dasein is guilty of the piercing everyday, guilty of *das Man*, guilty of curiosity and chatter, guilty of fear, postulating reality and the "I," decay and decomposition, i.e., all versions of inauthentic existence. *Dasein's* guilt is always proven and sabsolute. In order to feel the extent of its endless and absolute guilt, *Dasein* should not commit anything reprehensible. In that case, *Dasein* will have no opportunity to evade understanding the greatest level of its guilt in the face of *Being*. Every specific fault must be rectified. The only kind of guilt that cannot be redeemed is the delay in transitioning from inauthentic existence to the authentic counterpart. This delay, this "*noch nicht*," contains the drama of *Dasein's* historic presence as "*Sein*" placed into "*da*."

Dasein's fault is that this "*da*" is not the way it should be, and even in that *Dasein* itself cannot change anything here solely with its own will. *Dasein* is guilty in an absolute way, always, and preemptively. The way from "*da*" toward "*Sein*" does not lie in this guilt's redemption, but rather in its profound realization.

370

"*Noch nicht*" is neither an accident nor an error, it is the constituting side of "*this-Being*," which cannot be canceled or overcome, but can be recognized and accepted as guilt. In this gesture of recognition and acceptance, guilt becomes the *passage toward the horizon of another authentic Beginning.*

Positive Analysis of Dasein in Both Regimes

Authentic *Dasein* is *Dasein per se*, and its existentials in the authentic regime express their ontic essence as the attributes of this *Dasein*. But it is none other than the same *Dasein* and its existentials that activate inauthentic existence. Herein lies the principal motif of *Sein und Zeit*, in which Heidegger attempts to underscore his main idea in a thousand different ways: inside both the authentic and inauthentic *Dasein*, we are dealing with the same authority, the same "*this-Being*." The most important point is not to denounce inauthenticity and break through toward authenticity (although this is also important), but to comprehend the *way in which* inauthentic *Dasein* is responsible for the process of developing the entire Western European philosophy from its Greek pre-Socratic heights and until the bottomless collapse into Modernity's nihilism. And under the majestic and meaningless architecture of this philosophy and its consequences (culture, politics, sociology, ideology, economics, etc.), we must recognize—always and everywhere—its main character, hidden under a giant heap of theories, concepts, ideas, systems, doctrines, and religious dogmas.

Positive analysis of *Dasein* in relation to the inauthentic regime comprises the fact that philosophy must be fundamentally demystified and reduced to its true and principal point from which it draws its origins, and which is the main character in the *history of Being*. Uncovering

Dasein in a place where it veils itself particularly well, we conquer the opportunity for understanding its structure. And even if we are dealing with the inauthentic regime, this inauthenticity belongs to *Dasein*, specifically, which could also be authentic. Without untangling the ball of alienating and concealing inauthenticities, we would have remained amidst our illusions regarding *Dasein* and its central role in constituting the world, thoughts, man, consciousness, space, and time. But, understanding that everywhere, even when it is not obvious, we are dealing with *Dasein* and only *Dasein*, we could decipher its message, addressed to itself in the most unusual way—through flipping its own existentials, through self-concealment under the guise of *das Man*, through flight from oneself and renouncing one's own *Being*. If we focus our attention on *Dasein*, specifically, then its *self-concealment* will be identified as its indirect *self-unconcealment*. The latter will allow us to prepare the foundations for its direct and complete self-unconcealment in an explosion of *Being*. This explosion must occur during the transition into a *new Beginning* of philosophy and achieving *Ereignis*.

Dasein and Seyn

In *Sein und Zeit*, Heidegger does not yet arrive at the distinction between *Sein* with an "i" and *Seyn* with a "y," which he makes in the 1930s during the cycle of discussing the problem of *Ereignis*. But he lays the foundations for the basic fundamental-ontological orientation of his philosophy specifically in this early period. In order to briefly highlight the problem of *Being* in relation to *Dasein*, we can project Heidegger in the middle and late periods onto the set of problems in his early work. In this case, we get the following picture.

At the basis of Heidegger's thought lies the distinction between *Being (Seyn)* and *beings (Seiende)*. This distinction is incredibly subtle since *beings (Seiende) are*. This means that they, as *beings (Seiende)*, express *Being (Sein)*, which cannot be defined in any other way than through *beings (Seiende)*, and that they *are*. This is how the ancient Greeks treated this subject. Following this path further, they transitioned from understanding *Being* as an *attribute of Beings* to generalizing this ontic observation and constructing a philosophy in which *Being* was conceptualized not simply as a fact that *beings (Seiende) are*, but as a *common attribute (κοινόν [koinon])* that is inherent to all *beings (Seiende)* as *beings (als Seiende)*. It was this generalization that was taken for *Being* and indistinguishably equated with *beingness* ("*οὐσία*" [ousia] in Greek, "*Seiendheit*" in German). According to Heidegger, the entire upcoming philosophical ontology and all Western European metaphysics are based on this. The latter, no matter how it formulated the question of *Being* and regardless of the ontological arguments that it accepted or rejected, forever remained within the bounds of comprehending *Being* through *beings*.

At the same time, it is here that we should expect a certain trick, according to Heidegger. Understanding *Being* through *beings (Seiende)* is the source of a colossal and progressing misconception, an illness lasting two and a half thousand years, the name of which is "Western European philosophy." Born amidst the pre-Socratics who conceived of *Being* through *beings* (Heraclitus, Anaximander, Parmenides), this ontology comes to completion in Nietzsche's philosophy. The latter definitively demonstrated the kind of nihilism that is present in Modern philosophy. Later, Heidegger will define *Being as a common attribute of beings* through *Sein*, and it is to this initial operation that he will reduce the catastrophic history of Western European philosophy as a progressive oblivion of *Being*.

Heidegger insists that the *Being* that is common for all *beings*, *Sein*, is not *Being per se*, but only one of its aspects. This aspect, taken exclusively, closes the possibility of understanding *Being* in the full sense of *Seyn*. The fact of the matter is that apart from discovering oneself as the *Being of beings (Sein des Seiende)*, *Being (Seyn)* is also *Nothingness (Nichts)* and *non-beings (μή ὄν, mi on)*, because it includes everything and excludes nothing. It is this that explains the ultimate nihilism of Western philosophy, and the fact that *Nothingness* entered the stage at the end of its history. At the same time, the microscopic chasm between *Seyn* and *Sein* at the beginning was unnoticeable, and it seemed that it could be overlooked.

Seyn is Sein, but it also is das Nichts (Nothingness). The second part of the previous phrase, "but it also is *das Nichts* (Nothingness)," let itself be known through the implicit and destructive work on the part of man's *logos*, alienating *beings* from their *Being* further and further and replacing it with *re-pre-sentations* (ideas, concepts, hierarchies of creation, subject and object, *a priori* statements, etc.) more and more. Thus, inaccurately understood *Seyn*, reduced to *Sein*, attempted to remind man about the real proportions through the nihilism of the Western European thought process, initially hidden and only evident at the end of Modernity.

Since this cycle has finished, Heidegger suggest a transition to a *new Beginning*, which includes conceiving of *Seyn* directly—*not through beings (Seiende), but differently*. How so?

Dasein serves this purpose as a fundamental basis of a new philosophy, as a starting position of constructing fundamental-ontology.

On the one hand, *Dasein* is *beings* (*Seiende*). But it is not regular *beings among beings,* since it is the *kind of beings* that is the *Being of beings.* For this reason, the word "*Dasein*" contains "*Sein*" rather than "*Seiende.*" *Dasein* is not *Da-Seiende.* Directly addressing the word is not a philological game, but a breakthrough to fundamental-ontology. And the first and most important element of this language is *Dasein.* As one of *beings, Dasein* fundamentally differs from the other *beings* since it precedes them. It is impossible to evaluate the presence or absence of *beings* outside of *Dasein,* since it is *Dasein* that calls *beings*—*beings,* whereas *beings* themselves, perhaps, do not recognize that they are *beings.* This is why man is an animal with a *logos,* a "talking animal." By calling *beings*—*beings, Dasein* introduces *Being* (*Sein*) into the game.

At one point[7], Heidegger writes that *Being (Sein) battles with beings (Seiende). Dasein is the kind of beings that is on the side of Being in this battle.*

In relation to *beings* (*Seiende*), *Being as Seyn* acts as *Nothingness,* since nothing corresponds to it. Through its "*da*" ("this") shines the light on *Being* (*Seyn*), its coming to fruition. Thus, *Dasein* undermines *beings* as that which perceives its own *Being* as an expression of *Being* as a common attribute for all *beings.* In this way, *Dasein* "nihilates" (annihilates) it. But, at the same time, *Dasein* recovers *beings* in *Being* (*Seyn*) through its authentic existence, drawing it toward participating in the

---

[7] Martin Heidegger, *Beiträge zur Philosophie (vom Ereignis)* (Frankfurt am Main: Vittorio Klostermann, 1989), 249.

event, coming to fruition (*Ereignis*). Thus, Heidegger writes[8], "At first, we must undertake differentiation (between *Seyn* and *Seinde*) and determine it, and *then* we must overcome it." Both of these operations are carried out through *Dasein*, by *Dasein*, and inside *Dasein*; furthermore, it is they that are the form of *Dasein's* authentic existence.

Thus, the notion of "*Dasein*" introduced in *Sein und Zeit* becomes the key concept for Heidegger's entire philosophy, and is located at the basis of fundamental-ontology and its new metalanguage.

---

[8] *Ibid.,* 277.

VI. ZEIT-TIME AND ITS HORIZONS

Introducing the Expression "Zeit-Time"

In order to approximately understand Heidegger's philosophical approach to the subject of time, let us begin with the fact that the semantics and etymology of the German word *"Zeit"* fundamentally differs from the semantics and etymology of the Russian word for "time." In fact, it differs so fundamentally, that we must pose the question as to whether it is correct to literally translate *"Sein und Zeit"* into Russian, let alone copying those formations that are related to the root *"Zeit"* and similar-sounding words in Heidegger's philosophy (for instance, *"zeitigen"*). The question is not as problematic with the term *Being*. After all, both Slavic and Germanic roots related to *Being* trace back to common Indo-European origins in one way or another, with two forms—*"bhū-"*(with the initial meaning "to grow") and *"es-"* (meaning "to be," "to be in availability," "be present"), which fused in conjugating the same verb with forms based on different stems (this is the case both in the German and Russian languages).

But the case of the word *"Zeit"* and the Latin *"tempus"* (which is the source of the French *"le temps,"* English "time," etc.) is much more complex. After all, *"Zeit"* originates from the Indo-European stem *"dá (i),"* which means to "chop," "separate from one another," "tear apart." The Latin base has the same meaning. Yet the Russian word *"время"* (vremia) is formed from the stem *"вертеть"* (vertet', to spin), and its meaning is linked to "continuity," "repetition," "linking one to another" (e.g., Russian "верёвка," *verevka*, rope). The German "*Zeit*" and Latin "*tempus*," on the contrary, "separate," "cut into moments," whereas the Russian "time" "connects," "ties together," "spins," and, in a certain sense, "repeats." The German "*zeitigen*" literally means to "predetermine a start," "set in motion" (evidentaly, as a one-off action), "cause the appearance of fruit," so that it could be collected. Derivatives from the Russian word for "time," by definition, cannot have similar meanings: "*повременить*" (*povremenit'*, to wait a while), in contrast, means to save the fruit on the tree for as long as possible and not to hurry with the blossoming and ripening of the fruit, etc.

This creates serious difficulties in terms of understanding Heidegger in Russian. For him, one of the most important tasks was to trace the concepts in the old philosophy back to their original meaning, and, on this basis, pushing off them as *Dasein's* direct speech about *Sein*, to create a new metalanguage. *Zeit* plays a central role in this language, but using the Russian word for "time" instead of the German "*Zeit*" will always prevent understanding Heidegger. For this reason, the correct thing to do is to maintain the German word "*Zeit*" in the Russian text. Heidegger's most important book would be called *Bytie i Zeit* in Russian. The sound of "*Zeit*" itself resembles clanging a well-sharpened knife. Russian "*vremia*," in contrast, is akin to the soothing sound of a lullaby. But, as in the case with "understanding," we should still follow a different path and offer the following wild-looking expression, "*Zeit-time*," i.e., the kind of time that is at the end of all time, the kind of time that does not loop, but is, instead, cut: time-moment, time-lightning. Therefore, we translate *Sein und Zeit* as *Being and Zeit-time*. [1]

---

[1] The editor has kept the expression "*Zeit-time*," even though the English word, "time," is closer to the German original, as per the author's discussion of the Latin "*tempus*" above. (*Ed.*)

Finality of Zeit-Time

The most important aspect in Heidegger's understanding of *Zeit-time* is that it is neither an attribute of an object (according to empiricists and materialists) nor of a subject (according to Kant). *Dasein* does not exist in *Zeit-time*. *Zeit-time* is not the subject's mode either. *Zeit-time* is not found outside of *Dasein*, it is inside *Dasein*. But *Dasein* has no dimensions or space, since *spatiality* (*Räumlichkeit*) is one of its existentials. Thus, *Zeit-time* should be understood as *Being*. *Dasein*, in a certain sense, is *Da-Zeit*. Since *Dasein* is finite—this is one of its principal attributes—so is *Zeit-time*.

Heidegger contests the infinity of *Zeit-time*. *Zeit-time* cannot be infinite, since, by definition, *Zeit* is separation, cutting up, dismemberment. Dismemberment is a chasm, not a bond. *Being* cannot be placed into *Zeit-time*, since it predates the break and instead coincides with it as a fundamental finality. Therefore, *Zeit-time* does not, *a priori*, precede *Dasein*, but coincides with *Dasein*, if the latter exists authentically. Once *Dasein* comes to an end, there is no more subject, object, or *Zeit-time*. Yet *Dasein* ends when it becomes *Being-toward-death* (*Sein-zum-Tode*), staring into death's eyes. This occurs through *Ereignis*. *Zeit-time* begins to work through *Ereignis* and *Dasein's* recognition of its finality.

It is important to note that in contrast to space, which is *Dasein's* existential, *Zeit-time* is not an existential. In a certain sense, it is more profound and fundamental than an existential, and also more problematic. *Being* as *Seyn* operates within *Zeit-time*. Thus, in contrast to the permanently present existentials in *Dasein*, *Zeit-time* is unique and occurs only once.

381

Three Ecstasies of Zeit-Time

Heidegger interprets the manifestation of *Seyn* through *Zeit-time* as three forms of frenzy, ἔξτασιζ (*ekstasiz*) in Greek. *Zeit-time steps out of itself* in three ecstasies.

The first ecstacy of *Zeit-time* is linked with *what was*, the second—with the *present*, whereas the third—with *what will be*. The most important ecstacy among all three is linked to *what will be*.[2]

The significance of *Dasein* is to throw the will so as to be and so as to *be able to be (Seinkönnen)*. This is a constant concentrated project of *Dasein's* existence in the direction of its authenticity. The ultimate horizon of this throw is a *leap (Sprung)*. *This is a leap of Dasein into Sein.*

Zeit-time understood in a fundamental-ontological way is the kind of *Zeit-time* the frenzy of which is contained in *what will be*. To the extent that *Dasein* is *Being*, this *Being of frenzy in what will be* reveals itself. *Zeit-time* becomes that which unfolds from a point in *what will be*, which constitutes the other horizons.

Zeit-time corresponds to *Dasein's* question as to how *Being (Seyn)* exists. In the ecstasy of *what will be*, *Being (Seyn) will be (wird wesen)*, that is, will be specifically as *Being (Seyn)*, rather than *beings* and ontological constructs based on it. Thus, *Zeit-time* develops and carries events in it not by itself; it is *Dasein* that develops it in its decision in favor of authentic

---

2 The author differentiates between the past, present, and future and those tenses based on the verb "to be"; the translation follows this distinction closely. In the Russian language, there is an overlap; e.g., "*budushchee*" means both the "future" and, literally, "that which will be." (*Ed.*)

existence. This means that *what will be* is a horizon of the *new Beginning*, the moment of *Ereignis*, in which *Being* begins *to be* in full.

This moment of *Ereignis* cannot be in any other horizons of *Zeit-time* (present or *what was*). If this were not the case, then neither the present nor the past would be either. But since they *are* and *were*, they are connected to the moment of *what will be* in one way or another. *Dasein* is what connects these three ecstasies in existence. *Dasein*, despite not yet existing authentically (otherwise, the future, *that which will be*, would have become the present or past), exists inauthentically, but exists nonetheless. Therefore, it participates in *Being*, *is*, even if in a roundabout way through keeping quiet and inauthentic.

Heidegger separates *what was* from *what passed*, the present—from *what is* now, and *what will be*—from the upcoming. Each ecstatic horizon of *Zeit-time* contains a link to *Dasein's Being* and the concealment of this link, which is expressed in the presence of *Dasein*. This connection as unconcealment, ἀλήθεια (*aletheia*), the truth of *Being* (*Seyn*) constitutes an ontological core of the horizons: it is *what was*, *what is*, and *what will be*. What truly *is* and *was* is *what will be* (in the future—*what will be*—*Sein=Seyn*). But that which *was* and *is* ecstatically anticipates this, and, to the extent that this anticipation is real, it *was* and *is*.

All three horizons also have an inauthentic modality. Among all that which passed, which belongs to the past, *was as that which was*, there only is what is the most important, most mysterious, and least obvious. The rest *was* simply *that which is passed*, and as such, it belongs only to what is passed and, to a certain extent, it *was not*, even though it *was* in the past after all.

The case with the present is similar: what occurs in the present is the continuation of the "walk" ("has passed," "occurred," "is coming," "will be going on later"). This "walk" of the horizons has a difficult relationship with the *Being* thereof. Something from the past *was*, and something else passed, i.e., something *that once was*, and something else—only *what passed*.

The same is the case in the present and the upcoming that could become *what will be* or simply the upcoming. This comprises the very core of *Dasein*.

Dasein, according to Heidegger, must make a fundamental choice between the upcoming and *what will be*, that is, a direct choice about authentic existence and questioning *Being (Seyn)*. Then, the *upcoming* will become *what will be*. If it makes the choice in favor of inauthentic existence, then the upcoming will only remain thus, which means that it *will not be*.

The *past, that which is arriving*, and the *upcoming* comprise three inauthentic ecstasies of *Zeit-time* in three horizons. In this chain, the past is completely incomprehensible for what is occurring, and the latter, in turn—for what is upcoming. Instead of the history of *Being (Seinsgeschichte)*, the aggregate of these three horizons of inauthentic existence comprises a nonsensical cast of futility.

And on the contrary, a group of three authentic ecstasies of *Zeit-time* produces that line of *Being (Seyn)* which makes all three horizons contemporaneous to each other. What was in *that which was* cannot disappear anywhere, since *Zeit-time* does not precede *Dasein*. *What is*, having links to *Being (Seyn)*, cannot not be, since it already *was*. Thus, *what was* still *is* now. Heidegger describes this as instantaneity and almost simultaneity, synchronism of authentic thought. Each philosophical era had its own heights and, even though they are separated by centuries, they are separated by moments and conceive of themselves as contemporaries. After all, truly serious thought (thought about *Being*) of one thinker is picked up by another thinker as the most relevant in terms of measuring depth. For profound thought, only the deep is contemporary, regardless of to which horizon it belongs. The most current and deep is the kind of future—*what will be*—that is the fulfillment of *Zeit-time's* ecstacy in the form of the instantaneous, unique, and finite *Ereignis*.

What *was, is*. Both are preparations for what *will be*. But what *will be*, to the extent that it *will be*, already *is*, and it transforms the past into what once *was*, and the transitional—into what *is*.

CONCLUSION: HEIDEGGER AND THE STATE OF PHILOSOPHY

Martin Heidegger's philosophy is a moment in the thought process we cannot avoid. More precisely, we could do so, but it would negatively affect us. Looking for the approach to comprehending *beings*, deciphering philosophical heritage, grasping the temporal and spatial features of where we find ourselves, we could say for certain: *Heidegger is a reference point from which we could measure thought trajectories in various directions*. It is possible to assume that we would stumble upon this point even without Heidegger, but even in that case, we would discover the same structural lines, notice the same subtle flashes of the "desolate times," the same ominous shadows of European nihilism, the same indecipherable whisper of the weary and worn-out *Dasein*. Heidegger is an eternally new idea in us ourselves, in it itself. Without colliding with this wealth, our thought process is invalid.

But Heidegger neither gives us any answers, nor points the way. His philosophy is something opposite of a system, teaching, or theory. Instead, it is the life-giving flesh of thoughts that excludes any closed and irreversible trajectories, any fixation, or any construction.

At first glance, it may seem that Heidegger deliberately complicates his thought, and those who get confused at times are surprised that, in certain works, he writes in an incredibly

387

clear way. However, the opposite is the case: the more unclear and vague—his words, the clearer and brighter—his thoughts. His words are a quiet and genuine flame that remains elusive for the devious strategies of an ice-cold, rational mind. Heidegger himself wrote that the Greeks called Heraclitus "the Dark," since their own intellectual light turned into a wretched shadow as compared to his genius. He burned and sculpted. Immersed into darkness. This is why he was "ὁ Σκοτεινός" (o Skoteinos), "the Dark."

We must appreciate Heidegger—incomprehensible, imprecise, avoiding strict definitions, dodging systematizations, contradictory, and unclear. He used to say that in its squeamish quest to liberate itself from the irrational, Western European philosophical thought forgot to focus its attention on the most important aspect—on the *sacrament of its own emergence*, its own appearance out of the dusk of the pre-philosophical, pre-rational era. And it is there, in the twilight, where it is unclear whether we are already dealing with thought or *"not yet," "not quite,"* that we pass the *currents of philosophical fate*, the fate of the West, and those of men connected to it. Heidegger immersed into this twilight with pleasure, awe, and terror, as if fulfilling his destiny.

Zealously researching the Beginning of thought, he discovered for himself and for us the ability to live and think in the element of this Beginning. It is there that the trajectory of mankind's history originated at one point. It is there that a period should have been placed, a single period, in a terrifying steam of absolute freedom. If this period placed by the first philosophers coincided with the unseen center of emptiness, the pole of Nothingness, then the streams of *Geviert*, the "Fourfold," would have removed the fatality of complex and false paths in Western European metaphysics leading to the cliff of nihilism. But this period was placed *somewhere nearby*. It was very *close* to the pole of Nothingness, but a tiny bit away, by a micron. This miniscule distance, present nonetheless, made the Beginning into the *first Beginning*, predetermining everything else— from Parmenides through Plato and Aristotle to Augustine, Descartes, Hegel, and Nietzsche.

Only *one* straight line connects any two points. And in our case— only in *one* direction. This is the direction *away from Seyn— Being*. Having done so, Heidegger substantiated the case for the abyss of European nihilism through obtaining an unshakable foundation in it itself—*"fundamentum inconcossum."* And it so turned out that it was in Heidegger himself, as in the *"prince of philosophers"* (*princeps philosophorum*), that philosophy *came to fruition*. The light ray reached the point from which, from now on, it was called to *reflect* as if it were smooth mirror-like flesh.

What Heidegger had done with the history of philosophy gave us *philosophy* as what "has happened" and "has finished." But, at the same time, if we carefully observed the development of its grand creation, we obtained *that which is most important*. With the price of the original error in establishing the point of the first Beginning, tragically paid for by more than two millennia of dramatic Western history, we know *reliably and for certain*, rather than arbitrarily guessing, where *it was necessary* to place this period in order to avoid what had happened. Heidegger himself clearly saw: with its path into the abyss, immersing into the element of pure nihilism, with its ambiguous, disastrous anthem to *Gestell* and technical development, the West was the *first* to reach the lowest boundary of *Being's* abandonment. With its sacrifice, it demonstrated not only where not to go, but also *how to commence the second Beginning*, free from the inexorable abyss.

Through the *retreat* from the possibility of an authentic *Geviert*, from venerating *Seyn-Being* as a creative nihiliation and nihilating creation, Western metaphysics outlined the blueprint of the way in which *it should have been done* and *should be done* so as to avoid deviating from it. When? *Always. Now.* The second Beginning, although dependent on *Dasein's* existential choice in favor of authenticity, at the same time, *depends on nothing.* It has already been roughly outlined.

As a result of the calm, passionately indifferent acceptance, *"not yet"* has lost the fatality of its hypnosis in Heidegger's philosophy. We are no longer fighting in its snares, feeling nervous, but we accept it as it truly is, trying to find the sign of *another Beginning* with solemn gratitude in the last smoldering ruins of Western culture.

Grateful peoples from those cultures that are different from the West will be able to appreciate the greatness and significance of the West's last thinker, the last European, the one who uttered the most beautiful, most profound, the brightest, and the most poignant *funeral speech* about Western metaphysics, Western history, and the history of Western civilization.

Another Beginning is a matter of the future, of those who will be upcoming, as Nietzsche dreamt. But the Sun does not rise in the West. And from now on, we have grasped the meaning of the sunset, necessary for moving toward the horizon *from another direction. Heidegger's another Beginning cannot address the people of the West. Therefore, it addresses us.*

POSTSCRIPT

I envision this book as exactly *half* of what I would like to say about Martin Heidegger and another Beginning. Having found the point of this other Beginning, we will try to move ahead in the direction of the *possibility of Russian philosophy*. It is quite obvious that the Russian thought lay fallow, ripening with bloody juices of premonitions, muttering in its sleep, attempting to say a certain something, but fatally locating no words, images, or signs. Perhaps, the Russian thought has been waiting. It has been waiting for the right time, not wanting to *participate* in the end of Western European philosophy, being neither in solidarity, nor vitally involved in the development of Western European metaphysics.

Many Russians minds have asked the following question, "*What are we waiting for?*"

And we are, indeed, still waiting for something all the time...I will risk suggesting that we have been waiting *specifically for that*. We have been waiting for the moment when the West comes to an end in order to *enter philosophy* with our Russian power amassed over the centuries, but. . . only truly and into genuine philosophy—the kind that will be worthy of our silent, mysterious Russian dream hidden deep inside. And this could only be the *philosophy of another Beginning*.

This is the title of this book's second volume dedicated to the greatest Western thinker: *Martin Heidegger: the Possibility of Russian Philosophy*.

GLOSSARY

Abyss (Abgrund)—an aspect of *Seyn-Being* expressed through *"nihilation"* (*Nichten*); the *openness* of man and *Dasein*; *beings'* lack of reliable foundations (contrary to the topography of Platonic metaphysics); the risk inherent in freedom; traces of *Seyn-Being* in *beings* facing *Dasein*, first and foremost.

Ambiguity (see Zweideutigkeit)—an *existential of inauthentic Dasein*, the uncertaintly of everyday thought tracing back to the extremely simplified referential theory of *truth*; the limit of vulgarized Platonism.

Americanism—the ultimate expression of the metaphysics of the subject in the form of individualism, the triumph of technology, consumerism, calculation; the final expression of Western European metaphysics in the form of pure *Gestell* and *Machenschaft* of capitalist markets; the final form of mankind's degeneration; aggressive Liberalism; the choice in favor of the infinite *End* instead of *another Beginning* (*Anfang*); the same thing as "planetary idiocy."

Authentic (eigene)—one's own, genuine, that which corresponds to the *fundamental-ontological essence* (*Wesen*) as a direct *relationship* (*Bezug*) with *Seyn-Being*.

Be, to be (see Sein, εἶναι)—the main concept in Heidegger's philosophy; in the ontic sense, it means to *be one of beings*, to *be like beings*; in the ontological and theological sense, it means to *be the essence of beings*, the *greatest kind of beings*; in the fundamental-ontological sense, it means to exist (*wesen*), to "be in accordance with essencing," i.e., to *be a participant in Seyn-Being*.

Beginning—transitioning the *thought process* from simple (ontic) to the philosophical, posing the *question about Being* in its purest form, up until receiving a definitive answer, that is, through to establishing a full-fledged *ontology*; see the *first Beginning, another Beginning.*

Beginning, another (andere Anfang)—Heidegger's philosophy, which invites us to *fundamental-ontology*, preparing for *Ereignis*, burying Western European *metaphysics*, and a radical leap into *Geviert.*

Beginning, first (erste Anfang)—the transition from *thinking to philosophy* carried out in ancient Greece by the pre-Socratics and completed under Plato.

Being (Seyn, Seyn-Being, Sein, Sein-Being)—the general name of what makes *beings* (that, which is)—*beings; thought* trajectory that transforms *thought into philosophy*; the horizon of the deepest and most accurate understanding of *beings*; Heidegger interprets this in two ways: old (Platonic and post-Platonic) *metaphysics* and *fundamental-ontology*. In the first case, he conceives of *Being* as the *essence of beings*, the *greatest kind of beings*, idea, ego, subject, object, will, power, appearance, as well as *techne, Gestell*, writing it with an "i" ("*Sein*"); in the second case, Heidegger interprets this as *non-beings*, as that which makes *beings—beings*, but that does not become *beings* in the process, writing it with a "y" ("*Seyn*"). Not all of Heidegger's texts closely adhere to this rule. Thus, in order to understand him correctly, we must always specify what he means when using "*Sein*" without any additional information—*Seyn* or *Sein*.

Being-in (Insein)—a neutral *existential* of *Dasein* that can be interpreted both as *inauthentic* (scattering throughout *beings*) and *authentic* (participation in the Fourfold, *Geviert*) modes.

Being-in-the-world (In-der-Welt-sein)—the most important and fundamental *existential* of *Dasein* that characterizes its main attribute; see *World*.

Being, this-Being (Dasein)—the center of the *thought* process that renders judgement about *beings* and, in certain cases, about the *Being of beings*; has a unique relationship with *Seyn-Being*; unconditional presence which makes the *ontic*—the *ontic*, and the *world (Welt)*—the *world (Welt)*; the location of *Seyn-Being's* dwelling in *beings*; the *abyss (Abgrund)* is its foundation *(Grund)*; the moment of *illumination (Lichtung)* of *beings* by *Seyn-Being* (as if by lightning); a certain something that is defined through *existentials*; that which is localized inside *Geviert's* "world region" *(Weltgegend)* in the direction of *man*; that which *exists factually*; one of the most important words in Heidegger's *philosophy*.

Being-toward-death (Sein-zum-Tode)—an *existential of authentic Dasein*; a fundamental attribute of man, the only kind of *beings* capable of facing death; man is a "mortal" *(Sterbliche)* by definition; only man can die, while all the other *beings* perish.

Being-with (Mitsein)—a neutral *existential* of *Dasein* that signifies that *Dasein* neighbors *beings* (as a *multitude*, πάντα) or *Being*.

Being's abandonment (Seinsverlassenheit)—*Seyn-Being's* refusal to remind us about itself under the circumstances of incorrectly posing the question about it and receiving an even more incorrect answer; ignoring Western European *philosophy* and history on the part of *Seyn-Being*; the *fundamental-ontological essence (Wesen)* of Western European *philosophy* and history; the meaning and internal contents of *European nihilism*.

397

Being's guardian—man in *another Beginning*, inside *Geviert* unleashed by *Ereignis*.

Being's oblivion (Seinsvergessenheit)—refusal to place the *question about Being* at the center of the philosophical process; gradual exacerbation of Platonic theory of *ideas* until the emergence of contemporary pragmatism, technocracy, Marxism (*Machenschaft*), and "Americanism" (*planetary idiocy*).

Beings (Seiende)—that which is present around the thing; that which is perceived through the *ontic throught process* as that which *is*.

Beings-as-a-whole (Seiende-im-Ganzen)—the answer (especially in Plato and Aristotle) to the ontological question about *what* differentiates *beings* from *Being* in the spirit of early *metaphysics*; the same thing as *Sein-Being*.

Beings, highest, supreme, "beingful" (ὄντως ὄν)—the basic element in Platonic *philosophy* and subsequent *metaphysical* topography of Western European *philosophy*; the same thing as the *idea, beings* (*Seiendheit*), *Sein-Being*; God in Western Christian theology.

(In) Between (see Zwischen)—*Seyn-Being's* location inside *Geviert* (between men and gods, Sky and Earth); *Dasein's* location between the internal and external, between the past and future, between the ontic and ontological.

Care (Sorge)—one of the most important *existentials* for *Dasein*; in its *authentic* regime, it signifies *Dasein* facing *Being*, whereas in its *inauthentic* regime, it turns toward *beings*.

Chatter, gossip (Gerede)—an *existential of inauthentic Dasein*; a steady stream of consciousness of a conventional man; reciting (aloud or silently) words and phrases the meaning of which one does not fully grasp or does not grasp at all; analogous to the *speech (Rede)* existential of *authentic Dasein*.

Conscience (Gewissen)—*Dasein's existential*, which signifies the correspondence between *Dasein* in the depth of its *findability* (*Befindlichkeit*) with itself, with its own *Selbst* (as *Seinkönnen*).

Curiosity (Neugierigkeit)—an *existential of inauthentic Dasein*; *inability* to focus one's thought process on things in order to grasp their meaning, their connection to other things and structures of thought; the expression of everyday idiocy; the aspiration to obtain "new" information without the accurate comprehension of the "old."

Decay (Verfallen)—*Dasein's inauthentic existential, Dasein's* fall into *beings, Dasein's* alienation from itself (*Selbst*).

Desert, desertification (Wüste, Verwüstung)—widening the area of *Nothingness (Nichts)*, the result of replacing natural *beings* with artificial, objectified, technical *beings*; exacerbation of the *abandonment of Being (Seinsverlassenheit)*; the same thing as "desolate times" (*durftige Zeit*).

Decision (Entscheidung)—the ontological and philosophical choice of fate as an answer to the question about *beings' Being*; in a narrow sense, a turning-point decision by contemporary mankind about recognizing or not recognizing *European* nihilism, *Gestell*, and τέχνη as the completed, ultimate fate (*Geschick*) of Western Europe and, consequently, its transition (or not) into *another Beginning*.

399

Destruction, phenomenological destruction (Destruktion, phänomenologische Destruktion)—taking a statement back to its context within the space of *metaphysical* topography; the same thing as that which was later called "deconstruction" in structuralism (Lacan, Derrida).

Difference, ontological difference (Differenz, ontologische Differenz)—the basis of *philosophy*, the ability to differentiate between *Being* and *beings* and provide an answer to the question, "What is *Being* like?"

Earth (Erde)—world region (*Weltgegend*) in *Geviert*; the beginning of concealment, objectness, giveness, presence; *beings* that lean toward attempting to become the *World*; cover for the *abyss*; is in the state of *war* with the *Sky* (*World*).

Ecstacy—leaving the boundaries, forms of *existence* and *essenting* in *Zeit-time*.

End—the establishment of Platonic ontology, Aristotelian logic, physics, and *metaphysics* within the framework of the *first Beginning*; Nietzsche's discovery of *European nihilism*—within the framework of the entire Western European *philosophy*—as the main attribute of Modernity and of the *will to power* as the main driving force behind Western European *philosophy* and history.

Essence, fundamental-ontological (Wesen)—everything that has direct relationship with *Seyn-Being*.

Essence (Seiendheit, οὐσία)—the answer to the theological question as to what differentiates *beings* from *Being* in the spirit of early *metaphysics*; *idea* in Plato; the basis of the two-dimensional philosophical topography and the referential theory of *truth*; the same thing as *Sein-Being*.

Event (Ereignis)—*Seyn-Being in another Beginning*; that which comes to fruition like *Seyn-Being in fundamental-ontology*; a key word in Heidegger's philosophy.

Existence—affirmation made as part of a (non-philosophical) *thought* process about the *fact* of an *ontic* presence of a certain kind of *beings*.

Existence, the way in which Seyn-Being is (Wesung)—*presence* in accordance with *Wesen*, that is, with *Seyn-Being*.

Existential—one of the meaningful aspects of *Dasein's phenomenological existing*.

Fate, destiny (Geschick, Geschichte)—the message of *Seyn-Being* embedded into the basis of Western European philosophical process.

Findability (Befindlichkeit)—neutral *existential of Dasein*, the fact of *Dasein's* discovery of itself.

Fourfold (Geviert)—a figure of a *fundamental-ontological* understanding of *beings* through *Seyn-Being*; comprises two intersecting axes of the *World-Sky* (*Himmel, Welt*) with the *Earth* (*Erde*) and *gods* (divinities, *Göttern*) with men (*Menschen*); *each of the axes* (*gods-men, Sky-World*) represents a line of *war* (battle, *Streit*); *Seyn-Being, Ereignis*, and the thing (*Ding*) are located at the intersection.

Fundamental-ontology—a *philosophical thought process* focused on *Seyn-Being*; conceives of *Seyn-Being* directly, not from the standpoint of *beings* but through *itself*; rejects the double topography of the old *metaphysics* and constructs *philosophy* without tearing it away from the *ontic* (non-philosophical) thought process and its obvious aspects; the same thing as *onto-ontology*.

God—the *highest of beings* in Western European theology and Scholasticism, Creator of the world, religious figure put in the place of the *idea of good* (truth, good, and beauty) by Plato; the root cause, *causa sui* as part of Modernity's deism.

God, gods, divine (Göttlichkeit, Gott, Göttern)—one of the *"world regions"* (*Weltgegenden*); one of the four components of the Fourfold (*Geviert*); we cannot say that gods are (*sind*), or that they are not (*sind nicht*); "gods need *Seyn-Being*"; gods are light and prone to fleeing; gods are at war with men (see also the *"Last God"*).

God, last (letzte Gott)—the figure of the *god* in the *Fourfold* (*Geviert*) developing in *another Beginning* at the moment of *Ereignis*; eschatological figure crowning *Seyn-Being* with its arrival; the last horizon in *fundamental-ontology*; see the *Divine, gods, God*.

Idea—visual appearance of Plato's philosophy, which is at the basis of creating *metaphysical* topography and classic *ontology*; Plato's teaching about ideas predetermined the fate of Western European *philosophy* and, consequently, the course of Western European history; the idea is *beings*, but the *greatest kind of beings, supreme beings* (ὄντως ὄν), the *essence of beings* (οὐσία, *Seiendheit*), beings-as-a-whole (*Seiende-im-Ganzen*); later, in this topography, without changing its two-tier (referential) structure, the place of Plato's *idea* is taken by form, energy, God, subject, ratio, object, will to power, values, world view, *τέχνη* at various stages; the *idea per se* is the pure embodiment of *Gestell*; the teaching about ideas fixes the principle of *Being* as *Sein-Being* until the end of Western European *metaphysics*; Plato's teaching about *ideas* as the correlation between things and ideas (Plato's *Republic*) is at the foundation of Western European theory of knowledge (gnoseology).

Idiocy, planetary—projecting the *metaphysics of the subject* onto an individual in contemporary Anglo-Saxon (American), technical, Liberal, capitalist culture that has reached global proportions; transfer of the entire set of problems into the sphere of satisfying the private interests of a single individual; the ultimate form of *"Being's abandonment"* (*Seinsverlassenheit*), *nihilism*, and degeneration; maximization of the *will to power* in the realm of the utilitarian and non-heroic everyday approach; the same thing as *Americanism*.

Inauthentic (uneigene)—not one's own, counterfeit, turned away from one's essence, from oneself (*Selbst*), a distorted relationship with *Being* or forgetting of the latter.

Language (speech, Rede)—*Seyn-Being's* statement about itself through *Dasein's authentic existence*; is entrusted to a people (*Volk*), whence *thinkers and philosophers* draw it.

Leap (Sprung)—addressing *Seyn-Being* through bypassing *beings*; the same thing as the *transition* (*Übergang*).

Lightning (κεραυνός)—the name of *Being* in Heraclitus, alongside "war" (*πόλεμος*), "fire" (*πῦρ*), etc.

Man—a kind of *beings* that differs from other *beings* with his unique relationship with *Seyn-Being*; that, through which

Seyn-Being expresses itself; the approximate location of *Dasein*; *beings* that have no *essence*, the *Wesen* of which leads into the abyss; in old *metaphysics*, man is one of the names for the *subject*, an "animal in procession of a rational mind" (ζῷον λόγον ἔχον, *animalis rationalis*); the "*guardian of Being*" in the *philosophy of another Beginning*.

Metaphysics—philosophical topography, based on a system of doubling *beings* through postulating a "higher" plane (ideas, thought process, God, values, representations, subject, object, and so on will); the fate of Western European mankind; initially, clearly prepared in the philosophy of Plato and Aristotle; *overcoming metaphysics* is a necessary step to prepare the *transition* (*Übergang*) toward *another Beginning and fundamental-ontology*.

Metaphysics, overcoming of—a necessary act in terms of recognizing the fatal inadequacy of *posing the question about Being* and its answer in Western European *metaphysics* (Plato, Aristotle, Scholasticism, Modernity); discovering the "*abandonment of Being* (*Seinsverlassenheit*) and accurately deciphering its meaning; understanding *techne* (τέχνη) and *Gestell* as *fate* (*Geschick*, *Schicksal*); the operation of "*phenomenological destruction*" (*Destruktion*), i.e., placing any *philosophical* statement into the original *metaphysical* topography.

Nihilate, nihilation (nichten, Nichten)—an attribute of *Seyn-Being* in relation to *beings*; *Seyn-Being's war* against *beings*.

Nihilism, European—the final phase of the "*oblivion of Being*" (*Seinsvergessenheit*), "*abandonment of Being*" (*Seinsverlassenheit*), the *End* of Western European *philosophy*, the crash of *metaphysical* topography, the discovery of τέχνη, *Machenschaft*,

Gestell, and the "will to power" as the main trajectory of this philosophy; Nietzsche's discovery of the real state of Western European history.

Nothingness (Nichts)—1) in *Seyn-Being*, the side that does not correspond to the power that generates *beings*, killing source; the same thing as "*nihilation*"; 2) *Seyn-Being* as *non-beings*, as that which *differs from beings*; 3) simply *non-beings* without specifying whether it belongs to *Seyn-Being* or not; 4) the *fundamental-ontological essence* (*Wesen*) of Western European philosophy and history as *Gestell*; 5) in certain cases, this is the *abyss*.

Object (objectum)—what is in front of the *subject* in the *metaphysics* of Modernity.

Object (Gegenstand)—in the culture of Modernity, this is an *object* that was manufactured or used in the process of production.

Ontics, ontic—a form of *thought* that remains within the limits of *beings* and does not raise the *question about beings' Being*; a non-philosophical *thought process*.

Onto-ontology—the same thing as *fundamental-ontology*. *Illumination* (*Lichtung*): *philosophical* address to *Seyn-Being* and its result for *Dasein* and *beings*.

Ontology, ontological—1) *thought process* that raises the *question about beings' Being* and gives a certain answer to it; 2) incorrectly formulated *question about beings' Being in the first Beginning* and *metaphysical and philosophical* topography constructed on its basis; in this sense, it is the opposite of *fundamental-ontology*.

Openness (Offene)—unconcealment; see *Illumination*.

(A) People (narod, Volk)—those entrusted with *language* as *Seyn-Being's* statement about itself.

Question in philosophy, basic (Grundfrage)—what is the *truth of Seyn-Being?* How does *Seyn-Being exist (west)?* Addressing *Seyn-Being* not as *beings* and not from the standpoint of *beings*; a *leap into the abyss.*

Question in philosophy, key (leading) (Leitfrage)—what is the *essence of beings?* What are *beings-as-a-whole?*

Question in philosophy, transitional (Übergangsfrage)—why is there something (*beings*) instead of *Nothingness* (Leibniz)?; an intermediate *question* between the *"leading question"* of the old *metaphysics* ("What is the *essence of beings?* "What are *beings-as-a-whole?"*) and the *basic question of fundamental-ontology* ("*What is the truth of Seyn-Being?*)

Philosophy—the kind of *thought process* that poses the question about the *Being of beings* and develops it inside the kind of topography that is explained with the answer to this question.

Sacred, holy (Heilige)—the name of *Seyn-Being* in poetry (Hölderlin).

Setting, voice (Stimme, Stimmung, πάθος)—*Dasein's existential* defining its positioning in relation to *beings* and *Being*.

Seynsgeschichte, seynsgeschichtliche—fate linked to *Seyn-Being, Seyn's* message through the structure and history of Western European *philosophy* about itself with the help of self-removal and self-concealment during the course of developing the *first Beginning* (up until the triumph of *nihilism* and *Machenschaft*) and self-discovery in *another Beginning* (*Ereignis*); one of the most important terms in Heidegger's philosophy.

Sky (Himmel)—a *world region* (*Weltgegend*), one of the four components of the Fourfold (*Geviert*), along with the *Earth, gods, and men*; embodies the principle of light, celestiality, openness, appearance, unconcealment; in some cases, Heidegger equated the Sky with the *World* (inside *Geviert*).

Spaciality (Räumlichkeit)—*Dasein's existential.*

Subject—in the *metaphysics* of Modernity, it is the carrier of the rational source and an authority that makes the most important *ontological* judgement (Descartes's *cogito*) about the *Being of beings.*

Surprise—the kind of setting (*Stimmen*, πάθος) that leads one toward philosophizing inside the *first Beginning* (according to Plato and Aristotle).

Terror (Angst)—*Dasein's existential* generated from its groundlessness, *thrownness,* and *findability* at a distance from all *beings*; the experience of coming into contact with *Seyn-Being* as a "*nihilating*" power; the *leap into the abyss*; the emergence of *Sein,* which opens up and Is illuminated in *da* (*this, here*); the main setting (*Stimmen*, πάθος) of thought in *another Beginning* in contrast with the *first Beginning,* in which that setting was *surprise.*

Theology—Christian religious philosophy of Western Europe established on the basis of Platonic and Aristotelian *metaphysics; God-Creator* personifies the *greatest, surpreme kind of beings.*

Thing—initially, *beings* in their relation to *Seyn-Being,* something sacred, holy (*Heilige*); is positioned at the center of *Geviert*; in Western European *metaphysics,* the thing gradually becomes an *object* (*objectum, Gegenstand*), something technical, manufactured, or used in production (a resource).

This—the side of *this-Being* (*Dasein*) in which *Being* (not as *beings,* but rather as *Being*) may reveal itself and appear in the way that it exists (*west*), directly rather than indirectly through *beings*; the moment of *fundamental-ontology* focus.

Thought process—1) ontic thought: evaluating *beings* individually and collectively, comparing individual parts of *beings* with each other; man's attributes; 2) philosophical thought: posing the *question about Being* and its relationship with *beings*; philosopher's attribute.

Thrownness—one of *Dasein's* crucial *existentials* related to the absence of *Dasein's* obvious cause *inside beings*; *Dasein's* set of problems, its foreignness in relation to *beings,* its "homelessness"; a hint about the etymology of the word *"subject"* (literally: "thrown under.")

Times, desolate—the period of *desertification* (*Verwüstung*), *oblivion of Being* (*Seinsvergessenheit*), triumph of *European nihilism.*

Transition (Übergang)—the transition from the *End of philosophy* toward *another Beginning*; the same thing as the *leap* (*Sprung*).

Truth (see Unverborgnheit, ἀλήθεια)—unconcealment, which can mean: 1) *Seyn-Being's* unconcealment (*fundamental-ontology*), 2) unconcealment of *beings* (the *philosophy of the first Beginning*), 3) the correlation between one kind of *beings* (*thing*) to another (*supreme* beings—*idea, place in the hierarchy of creation, concept, etc.*), which is the source for the referential theory of truth.

War, battle—the name of *Being* in Heraclitus; the "father of all and king of all," the relationship between the polar "*world regions*" (*Weltgegend*) inside *Geviert*.

Who (Wer)—the question in regard to who is the "I" for *Dasein*; may be *authentic* (*Selbst, Seinkönnen*) and *inauthentic* (*das Man*).

Will to power (Wille zur Macht)—deep-rooted contents of Platonic *ontology* and the old *metaphysics*, finally revealing themselves in today's world, noted and outlined by Friedrich Nietzsche; domination, "premediated imposition" (*Vorsetzende Durchsetzung*), nihilism, the same thing as *Gestell, τέχνη, Machenschaft*.

World (Welt, κόσμος)—order, openness; *beings* permeated by *light rays, logos, lightning, and fire* in Heraclitus; *beings-as-a-whole* as a "world region" (*Weltgegend*) of *Geviert*; the same thing as the *Sky*; that in which and how *Dasein* is found (see *Being-in-the-world*).

World region (Weltgegend)—one of the four components in the Fourfold (*Geviert*): *Sky* (*World*), *Earth, gods, and men*, unthinkable without the others.

German Terminology Used by Heidegger in a Particular Way

Abschied—farewell.

Als—as.

Abendland —the West; literally "evening land."

Abgrund—abyss.

Abkehr—departure from.

Alltäglichkeit, dürchdringliche Alltäglichkeit—everyday(ness), all-piercing everyday.

Anfang, anfängliche—beginning, initial.

Angst—fear, terror.

Anwesen—presence, presencing.

Aufgehen—rise up, come up, sprout, the act of $\varphi v\sigma\varepsilon\iota v$, whence $\varphi\grave{v}\sigma\iota\zeta$.

Aufstellung—setting, installation.

Befinden, sich befinden—to be located, found.

Befindlichkeit—findability.

Besinnung—comprehension, contemplation.

Bezug—relation, relationship.

Da—this, (t)here.

Dasein—this-Being; in a regular sense: existence, *Being*.

Destruktion (phänomenologische Destruktion)—destruction, phenomenological destruction.

Differenz (ontologische Differenz)—difference, ontological difference.

Ding—thing.

Durftige Zeit—desolate time.

Dort—there.

Du—you (singular).

Eigene—one's own, authentic.

Entscheidung—decision.

Entwurf—draft, project, sketch.

Er—he.

Ereignis, Er-Eignis—event; Heidegger artificially brings its meaning closer to *eigene* (authentic).

Erinnerung, Er-Innerung—memory, reminder; Heidegger artificially brings its meaning closer to *"inner."*

Ermächtigung—legitimization, authorization.

Erstaunen—wonder, amazement.

Entsetzen—terror.

Existential—an existential (noun), pertains to the fundamental-ontological analysis of *Dasein*.

Existentiel—existential (adj.), pertains to the ontic description of *Dasein*.

Ewige—eternal.

Furcht—fear.

Gefüge—structure.

Gegenstand—object.

Gerede—chatter, gossip.

Geschichte—history; for Heidegger, this is the *fate* of Western European philosophy embedded into its ontological structure and linked to this structure and topography.

Geschick—fate, message.

Gestell—that which was positioned, affixed (like a shelf); joint; one of the most important words in Heidegger's philosophy which signifies the relationship to *beings* from the standpoint of *metaphysically* comprehended *Being* and, consequently, man operating within the topography of this *ontology*.

Gewicht—weight.

Gewissen—conscience, one of *Dasein's* existentials.

Geworfenheit—thrownness, one of *Dasein's* existentials.

Gleiche, ewige Wiederkehr des Gleichens—one and the same; Nietzsche's Eternal Return.

Grund—foundation, basis.

Heilige—sacred, holy.

Herstellung—production.

Hier—here.

Holzwege—paths in the woods, for Heidegger, something between a path and thick brush of the woods.

Ich—I.

Insein—*Being-in*, one of *Dasein's* existentials.

Inzwischen-Sein—Being-in-between.

Kommen, das Kommendste—to come, arrive, that which arrived (in regard to the *Last God*).

Können, sein können—to be able to, the main attribute of authentic *Dasein*.

Künftige—the future ones, those who pertain to *another Beginning*.

Lichtung—illumination, clearing.

Machen—to do, make.

Machenschaft—mechanicity, a relationship of technical production toward *beings* and *Being*; the main attribute of Marxism and capitalism; the fundamental-ontological essence (*Wesen*) of *Machenschaft* is *Gestell*; close to τέχνη.

Macht—power, from *machen*.

Man, das Man—the "who" of inauthentic *Dasein*.

Mitsein—*Being-with*, one of *Dasein's* existentials.

Neugierigkeit—curiosity, one of *Dasein's* existentials.

Nichten—nihilation.

Nichts—nothing, Nothingness.

Offene—open.

Räumlichkeit—spatiality, one of *Dasein's* existentials.

Rede—speech.

Schützen, Schutz, Schutzlosigkeit—protect, secure.

Seiende—*beings*.

Seiende-im-Ganzen—*beings-as-a-whole*.

Seiende ist—*beings are*.

Seiendheit—essence.

Sein (in Sein-Being)—*Being* in ontology.

Seinsvergessenheit—oblivion of *Being*.

Seinsverlassenheit—abandonment of *Being*.

Selbst—oneself, the *who* of authentic *Dasein*.

Seyn (in Seyn-Being)—*Being* in *fundamental-ontology*.

Seyn west—*Being exists*.

Sorge—care, one of *Dasein's* existentials.

Sprung—leap.

Sterbliche—mortal.

Stimmen—voice, mood, setting, one of *Dasein's* existentials.

Streit—war, battle.

Tod, Sein-zum-Tode—death, *Being-toward-death*, one of *Dasein's* authentic existentials.

Übergang—transition, passage.

Übergangsfrage—transitional question.

Uneigene, Uneigentlichkeit—inauthentic, inauthenticity.

Unheil—disaster, evil.

Unverborgnheit—unconcealment, truth (*aletheia*).

Verbergen—hide, conceal, cover.

Verfallen—decay, ruin, one of *Dasein's* inauthentic existentials.

Vernehemen—perceive, examine.

Verstehen—understanding, one of *Dasein's* existentials.

Verstellen—disguise, conceal, obstruct.

Verweigerung—refusal, denial.

Verwüstung—desertification.

Volk —a people, *narod* (Rus.).

Vorhandene—available, present.

Vorstellung—re-presentation; thought-process specifics within the famework of Western European *metaphysics*; traces back to Plato's theory of ideas.

Vorsetzende Durchsetzung—predetermined imposition.

Wächterschaft —guardianship.

Wage—balance.

Wagnis—venture, risk, danger.

Wahrheit —truth.

Weg—way.

Weltgegend—world region (inside *Geviert*).

Weisung—direction, instruction.

Wendung—turn.

Wesen—fundamental-ontological essence.

Wesen als Verb (ich wese, du wesest, er, sie, es west, wir wesen, ihr weset, sie wesen)—to exist.

Wesentliche—that which is according with existence.

Wesung—presence in accordance with Wesen.

Wille zur Macht—Will to Power.

Wink—nod, wink.

Wohnen—to live.

Zeit (Zeit-time)—time in the Germanic understanding as that which separates (unlike the linking idea of time in Slavic "*vremia*").

Zufall—accident, literally "that which falls."

Zuhandene—that which is at hand.

Zukunft—future, that which is coming.

Zweideutigkeit—ambiguity, *Dasein's* existential.

Greek Terminology

αἰὼν παῖς ἐστι παίζων, περρεύων: παιδός ἡ βασιληίη—
"Time is a child playing, throwing dice. The ruling power is a child's." (See Heraclitus.)

ἀλήθεια (aletheia)—truth.

αὐθεντικός (authentikos)—own, genuine, authentic.

γὲνεσις (genesis)—origin.

δαίμον (daimon)—god, minor deity.

δεινόν (deinon)—terror, something inspiring fear.

δίκη (dikē)—justice.

δόξα (doxa)—visibility, appearance.

εγώ (ego)—I.

εἶδος (eidos)—type.

εἶναι (einai)—to be.

ἕν (hen)—one, unified. (See Heractlitus.)

ἐνὲργεια (energeia)—action, energy.

ἔον, ἔοντα (eon, eonta)—*beings* (archaically active present participle from εἶναι).

ἐκστάσις (ekstasis)—ecstasy, leaving oneself.

ἔσχατον (eschaton)—end.

εὔκυκλος σφαῖρος (eukyklos sphairos)—well-rounded sphere. (See Parmenides.)

ἦθος ἀνθρώπῳ δαίμων (ethos anthropo daimon)—"*ethos* is a *daimon* for man." (See Heraclitus.)

ζωή (zoi)— life.

ζῷον λόγον ἔχον (zoon logon echon)—animal processing the rational principle (speech, thought).

θαυμάζειν (thaumazein)—to wonder.

θεός (theos)—god.

ἰδὲα (idea)— idea.

ἴδιος (idios)—one's own, individual.

κεραυνός (keraunos)—lightning.

κοινόν (koinon)— that which is shared, common.

λέγειν (legein)—to speak, think; initially, to reap.

λόγος (logos)—word, thought, speech; initially, harvest.

μάχομαι (machomai)—to fight, battle.

μὲθοδος (methodos)—method, direction sign.

μηχανική (mechanike)—mechanics, machine.

νοεῖν (noein)—to think, understand.

νοῦς (nous)—thought process, mind.

ὄν (on)—*beings*. (See Heractlitus.)

ὄντως ὄν (ontos on)—the greatest (supreme) kind of *beings*.

Οὐκ ἐμοῦ ἀλλὰ τοῦ λόγου ἀκούσαντας ὁμολογεῖν σοφὸν ἐστίν ἕν πάντα εἶναι. (Ouk emou alla tou logou akousantas homologein sophon estin hen panta einai.)—"If you do not listen to me, but to the logos, it would be wise, abiding by it, to say: everything is one." (See Heraclitus.)

οὐράνιον (ouranion)—of the sky, heavenly, celestial.

οὐρανάς (ouranos)—sky, heavens.

οὐσία (ousia)—essence, substance.

οὗτος (autos)—oneself.

πάθος (pathos)—state, impression, pathos.

πάντα (panta)—all *beings*, all things.

ποιεῖν (poiein)—to create, make.

ποίησις (poiesis)—creation.

πόλεμος (polemos)—war, battle.

πῦρ (pyr)—fire.

τέμνειν **(temnein)**—divide, cut.

τέχνη **(techne)**—technique, craft, skill.

ὕλη **(yli)**—matter, substance; initially, wood.

φαίνεσται **(phainesthai)**—to appear.

φθορὰ **(phthora)**—decay, destruction, death.

φυσειν **(physein)**—produce, generate, sprout.

φύσις **(physis)**—nature.

ψυχή **(psyche)**—soul.

Latin Terminology

animalis rationalis—rational animal, i.e., man.

causa sui—self-caused cause, cause generated within itself.

cogito ergo sum—"I think, therefore I am." (See Descartes.)

creare—to create.

ens—*beings*.

ens creatum—created *beings*.

esse—to be.

essentia—essence.

existentia—existence.

fundamentum inconcussum—unshakable foundation.

homo economicus—self-interested, economic man.

jacere—to throw, cast, hurl.

mundus imaginalis—imaginary world.

negatio—negation, rejection.

objectum—object, literally "that which was cast in front."

ordo—order.

positium—positive, set, established.

ratio—rational mind.

res—thing.

res cogitans—thinking thing, mind. (See Descartes.)

res creata—created thing.

res extensa—corporeal substance. (See Descartes.)

subjectum—subject, literally "that which was cast down."

substantia—substance, literally "that which stands under."

templum—temple.

tempus—time, as that which is "split," closer to the German "*Zeit*" than the Russian "*vremia*."

transcendens—transcendent, on the other side of the boundary.

vis primitive active—original active force. (See Leibniz.)

SELECTED BIBLIOGRAPHY

Anders, Günther. *Über Heidegger*. München: C. H. Beck, 2001.

Babich, Babette. *From Phenomenology to Thought, Errancy, and Desire*. Dordrecht: Kluwer Academic Publishers, 1995.

Bech, Joseph. *De Husserl a Heidegger: la transformación del pensamiento fenomenológico*. Barcelona: Universitat de Barcelona, 2001.

Biemel, Walter. *Martin Heidegger mit Selbstzeugnissen und Bilddokumenten dargestellt*. Reinbek: Rowohlt, 1973.

_____. *Martin Heidegger und Karl Jaspers: Briefwechsel 1920–1963*. Frankfurt am Main: V. Klostermann, 1992.

Blattner, William. *Heidegger's Being & Time A Reader's Guide*. London: Continuum Books, 2006.

Blitz, Mark. *Heidegger's Being and Time and the Possibility of Political Philosophy*. Ithaca: Cornell University Press, 1981.

Brito, Emilio. *Heidegger et l'hymne du sacré*. Leuven: University Press., 1999.

Brogan, Walter. *Heidegger and Aristotle: The Twofoldness of Being*. Albany: State University of New York Press, 2005.

Caputo, J.D. *Demythologizing Heidegger*. Bloomington: Indiana University Press, 1993.

Clark, Timothy. *Derrida, Heidegger, Blanchot*. Cambridge: Cambridge University Press, 1992.

_____. *Martin Heidegger*. London: Routledge, 2002.

Collins, Jeff. *Heidegger and the Nazis*. New York: Totem Books, 2000.

Cooper, David. *Heidegger*. London: Claridge Press, 1996.

Cordón, J.M.N. *Heidegger o el final de la filosofía*. Madrid: Fernández Ciudad, 1993.

Coriando, Paola-Ludovica. *Herkunft aber bleibt stets Zukunft. Martin Heidegger und die Gottesfrage*. Frankfurt am Main: V. Klostermann, 1998.

Crowe, Benjamin. *Heidegger's Phenomenology of Religion*. Bloomington: Indiana University Press, 2008.

_____. *Heidegger's Religious Origins Destruction and Authenticty*. Bloomington: Indiana University Press, 2005.

Dastur, Françoise. *Heidegger y la cuestión del tiempo*. Buenos Aires: Ediciones del Signo, 2006.

Davis B.W. *Heidegger and the Will On the Way to Gelassenheit*. Evanston: Northwestern University Press, 2007.

Denker, Alfred. *Heidegger-Jahrbuch*. Freiburg; München: Verlag Karl Albert, 2004.

_____. *Historical Dictionary of Heidegger's Philosophy*. Lanham: Scarecrow Press, 2000.

Dreyfus, Hubert. *Being-in-the-World: A Commentary on Heidegger's Being and Time*. Cambridge: MIT Press, 1991.

_____. *Companion To Heidegger*. Oxford: Blackwell, 2005.

_____. *Heidegger: A Critical Reader*. Oxford: Blackwell, 1992.

Edwards, Paul. *Heidegger's Confusions*. London: Prometheus, 2004.

Emad, Parvis. *On the Way to Heidegger's Contributions to Philosophy*. Madison: University of Wisconsin Press, 2007.

Farrell, David. *Intimations of Mortality: Time, Truth, and Finitude in Heidegger's Thinking of Being*. University Park: Pennsylvania State University Press, 1986.

Faye, Emmanuel. *Heidegger. Die Einführung des Nationalsozialismus in die Philosophie*. Berlin: Matthes und Seitz, 2009.

Fell, Joseph. "Heidegger's Notion of Two Beginnings" *The Review of Metaphysics* 25 (2) (1971): 213 - 237.

Figal, Günter. *Dimensionen des Hermeneutischen. Heidegger und Gadamer*. Frankfurt am Main: V. Klostermann, 2005.

_____. *Heidegger Lesebuch*. Frankfurt am Main: V. Klostermann, 2006.

_____. *Heidegger und Husserl. Neue Perspektive*. Frankfurt am Main: V. Klostermann, 2009.

_____. *Martin Heidegger. Phanomenologie der Freiheit*. Frankfurt am Main: Athenäum, 1988.

_____. *Martin Heidegger zur Einführung*. Hamburg: Junius, 2007.

Fink, Eugen. *Alles und Nichts*. Den Haag: Nijhoff, 1959.

_____. *Erziehungswissenschaft und Lebenslehre*. Freiburg: Rombach, 1970.

_____. *Grundfragen der antiken Philosophie*. Würzburg: Königshausen & Neumann, 1985.

_____. *Grundfragen der systematischen Pädagogik*. Freiburg: Rombach, 1978.

_____. *Grundphänomene des menschlichen Daseins*. Freiburg: Alber, 1979.

_____. *Hegel*. Frankfurt am Main: V. Klostermann, 2006.

_____. *Heraklit. Seminar mit Martin Heidegger*. Frankfurt am Main: V. Klostermann, 1970.

_____. *Metaphysik und Tod*. Stuttgart: W. Kohlhammer, 1969.

_____. *Nachdenkliches zur ontologischen Frühgeschichte von Raum–Zeit–Bewegung*. Den Haag: Nijhoff, 1957.

_____. *Nietzsches Philosophie*. Stuttgart: Kohlhammer, 1960.

_____. *Sein und Mensch. Vom Wesen der ontologischen Erfahrung*. München: Alber, 1977.

_____. *Spiel als Weltsymbol*. Stuttgart: Kohlhammer, 1960.

_____. *Vom Wesen des Enthusiasmus*. Freiburg: Hans V. Chamier, 1947.

_____. *Welt und Endlichkeit*. Würzburg: Königshausen & Neumann, 1990.

Fried, Gregory. *Heidegger's Polemos*. New Haven: Yale University Press, 2000.

_____. *Companion to Heidegger's Introduction to Metaphysics*. New Haven: Yale University, 2001.

Frings, Manfred. *Heidegger and The Quest For Truth*. Chicago: Quadrangle Books, 1968.

Fynsk, Christopher. *Heidegger: Thought and Historicity*. Ithaca: Cornell University Press, 1993.

Gadamer, Hans-Georg. *Der Anfang der Philosophie*. Stuttgart: Philipp Reclam, 1996.

_____. *Heideggers Wege*. Tubingen: J. C. B. Mohr, 1983.

_____. *Heidegger. Freiburger Universitätsvorträge zu seinem Gedenken*. Freiburg; München: Alber, 1977.

_____. *Wahrheit und Methode. Grundzüge einer philosophischen Hermeneutik*. Tübingen: Mohr, 1960.

Gander, Hans-Helmuth. *Europa und die Philosophie*. Frankfurt am Main: V. Klostermann, 1993.

_____. *Von Heidegger her. Wirkungen in Philosophie–Kunst–Medizin*. Frankfurt am Main: V. Klostermann, 1991.

_____. *"Verwechselt mich vor Allem nicht!" Heidegger und Nietzsche*. Frankfurt am Main: V. Klostermann, 1994.

Gasché, Rodolphe, ed. "Heidegger: Art and Politics." *Diacritics* 19:3-4. Baltimore (1989).

Geier, Manfred. *Martin Heidegger*. Reinbek: Rowohlt, 2005.

Gelven, Michael. A *Commentary on Heidegger's Being and Time*. DeKalb: Northern Illinois University Press, 1989.

Glazebrook, Trish. *Heidegger's Philosophy of Science*. New York: Fordham University Press, 2000.

Greisch, Jean. "The Eschatology of Being and the God of Time in Heidegger." *International Journal of Philosophical Studies* 4:1. (1996): 17-42.

Gross, Daniel. *Heidegger and Rhetoric*. Albany: State University of New York, 2005.

Großmann, Andreas *et al. Rudolf Bultmann und Martin Heidegger: Briefwechsel 1925 bis 1975*. Frankfurt am Main: V. Klostermann, 2009.

Guerra, Jorge Acevedo. *Heidegger y la época técnica*. Santiago: Ed. Universitaria, 1999.

Guignon, Charles. The *Cambridge Companion to Heidegger*. Cambridge: Cambridge University Press, 1993.

Haar, Michel. *Heidegger et l'essence de l'homme*. Grenoble: Millon, 1990.

_____. *Le Chant de La Terre: Heidegger et Les Assises de L'histoire de L'Etre*. Paris: Herne, 1985.

_____. *La fracture de l'histoire. Douze essais sur Heidegger*. Grenoble: Millon, 1994.

_____. *The Irony of Heidegger*. London: Continuum, 2007.

Han, B.-C. *Martin Heidegger*. München: Fink, 1999.

Heidegger, Martin. *Aristoteles Metaphysik IX 1–3. Von Wesen und Wirklichkeit der Kraft (Sommersemester 1931), Gesamtausgabe (GA) 33*, edited by H. Hüni (Frankfurt am Main: V. Klostermann, 1981).

_____. *Aus der Erfahrung des Denkens (1910–1976)*, GA 13, ed. H. Heidegger (*Ibid.*, 1983).

_____. *Beiträge zur Philosophie (Vom Ereignis) (1936–1938)*, GA 65, ed. F.-W. von Herrmann (*Ibid.*, 1989).

_____. *Besinnung (1938/39)*, GA 66, ed. F.-W. von Herrmann (*Ibid.*, 1997).

_____. *Bremer und Freiburger Vorträge*, GA 79, ed. P. Jaeger (*Ibid.*, 1994).

_____. *Der Begriff der Zeit (1924)*, GA 64, ed. Hrsg. F.-W. von Herrmann (*Ibid.*, 2004).

_____. *Der deutsche Idealismus (Fichte, Schelling, Hegel) und die philosophische Problemlage der Gegenwart (Sommersemester 1929); Im Anhang: Nachschrift "Einführung in das akademische Studium" (Sommersemester 1929)*, GA 28, ed. C. Strube (*Ibid.*, 1997).

_____. *Der Satz vom Grund (1955–1956)*, GA 10, ed. P. Jaeger (*Ibid.*, 1997).

_____. *Die Frage nach dem Ding. Zu Kants Lehre von den transzendentalen Grundsätzen (Wintersemester 1935/36)*, GA 41, ed. P. Jaeger (*Ibid.*, 1984).

_____. *Die Geschichte des Seyns*, GA 69, ed. P. Trawny (*Ibid.*, 1998).

_____. *Die Grundbegriffe der Metaphysik. Welt–Endlichkeit–Einsamkeit (Wintersemester 1929/30)*, GA 29/30, ed. F.-W. von Herrmann (*Ibid.*, 1983).

_____. *Die Grundprobleme der Phänomenologie (Sommersemester 1927)*, GA 24, ed. F.-W. von Herrmann (*Ibid.*, 1975).

_____. *Die Metaphysik des deutschen Idealismus. Zur erneuten Auslegung von Schelling: Philosophische Untersuchungen über das Wesen der menschlichen Freiheit und die damit zusammenhängenden Gegenstände (1809)*, GA 49, ed. G. Seubold (*Ibid.*, 1991).

_____. *Einführung in die Metaphysik (Sommersemester 1935)*, GA 40, ed. P. Jaeger (*Ibid.*, 1983).

_____. *Einführung in die phänomenologische Forschung (Wintersemester 1923/24)*, GA 17, ed. F.-W. von Herrmann (*Ibid.*, 1994).

_____. *Einleitung in die Philosophie (Wintersemester 1928/29)*, GA 27, ed. O. Saame et I. Saame-Speidel (*Ibid.*, 1996).

_____. *Erläuterungen zu Hölderlins Dichtung (1936–1968)*, GA 4, ed. F.W. von Herrmann (*Ibid.*, 1981).

_____. *Feldweg-Gespräche (1944/45)*, GA 77, ed. I. Ingrid Schüssler (*Ibid.*, 1995).

_____. *Frühe Schriften (1912–1916)*, GA 1, ed. F.-W. von Herrmann (*Ibid.*, 1978).

_____. *Gedachtes*, GA 81, ed. Paola-Ludovika Coriando (*Ibid.*, 2007).

_____. *Geschichte der Philosophie von Thomas von Aquin bis Kant (Wintersemester 1926/27)*, GA 23, ed. H. Vetter (*Ibid.*, 2006).

_____. *Grundbegriffe (Sommersemester 1941)*, GA 51, ed. P. Jaeger (*Ibid.*, 1981).

_____. *Grundbegriffe der antiken Philosophie (Sommersemester 1926)*, GA 22, ed. F.-K. Blust (*Ibid.*, 1993).

_____. *Grundbegriffe der aristotelischen Philosophie (Sommersemester 1924)*, GA 18, ed. M. Michalski (*Ibid.*, 2002).

_____. *Grundfragen der Philosophie. Ausgewählte "Probleme" der "Logik" (Wintersemester 1937/38)*, GA 54, ed. F.-W. von Herrmann (*Ibid.*, 1984).

_____. *Grundprobleme der Phänomenologie (Wintersemester 1919/20), GA 58*, ed. H.-H. Gander (*Ibid.*, 1992).

_____. *Hegel* / Hrsg. I. Schüssler. Fr./M., 1993 (GA 68).

_____. *Hegels Phänomenologie des Geistes (Wintersemester 1930/31), GA 32*, ed. I. Görland (*Ibid.*, 1980).

_____. *Heraklit. 1. Der Anfang des abendländischen Denkens (Sommersemester 1943); 2. Logik. Heraklits Lehre vom Logos (Sommersemester 1944), GA 55*, ed. M.S. Frings (*Ibid.*, 1979).

_____. *Holzwege (1935–1946), GA 5*, ed. F.-W. von Herrmann (*Ibid.*, 1977).

_____. *Hölderlins Hymne "Andenken" (Wintersemester 1941/42), GA 52*, ed. C. Ochwaldt (*Ibid.*, 1982).

_____. *Hölderlins Hymne "Der Ister" (Sommersemester 1942), GA 53*, ed. W. Biemel (*Ibid.*, 1984).

_____. *Hölderlins Hymnen "Germanien" und "Der Rhein" (Wintersemester 1934/35), GA 39*, ed. S. Ziegler (*Ibid.*, 1980).

_____. *Identität und Differenz (1955–1957), GA 11*, ed. F.-W. von Herrmann (*Ibid.*, 2006).

_____. *Kant und das Problem der Metaphysik (1929), GA 3*, ed. Hrsg. F.-W. von Herrmann (*Ibid.*, 1991).

_____. *Logik als die Frage nach dem Wesen der Sprache (Sommersemester 1934), GA 38*, ed. G. Seubold (*Ibid.*, 1998).

_____. *Logik. Die Frage nach der Wahrheit (Wintersemester 1925/26), GA 21*, ed. W. Biemel (*Ibid.*, 1976).

_____. *Metaphysik und Nihilismus, GA 67*, ed. H.-J. Friedrich (*Ibid.*, 1999).

_____. *Metaphysische Anfangsgründe der Logik im Ausgang von Leibniz (Sommersemester 1928), GA 26*, ed. K. Held (*Ibid.*, 1978).

_____. *Nietzsche 1 (1936–1939)*, GA 6.1, ed. B. Schillbach (*Ibid.*, 1996).

_____. *Nietzsche 2 (1939–1946)*, GA 6.2, ed. B. Schillbach (*Ibid.*, 1997).

_____. *Nietzsche metaphysische Grundstellung im abendländischen Denken: Die ewige Wiederkehr des Gleichen (Sommersemester 1937)*, GA 44, ed. M. Heinz (*Ibid.*, 1986).

_____. *Nietzsche: Der europäische Nihilismus, (1940)*, GA 48, ed. P. Jaeger (*Ibid.*, 1986).

_____. *Nietzsche: Der Wille zur Macht als Kunst (Wintersemester 1936/37)*, GA 43, ed. B. Heimbüchel (*Ibid.*, 1985).

_____. *Nietzsches Lehre vom Willen zur Macht als Erkenntnis (Sommersemester 1939)*, GA 47, ed. E. Hanser (*Ibid.*, 1989).

_____. *Nietzsches Metaphysik (für das Wintersemester 1941/42 angekündigt, aber nicht vorgetragen) / Einleitung in die Philosophie—Denken und Dichten (Wintersemester 1944/45)*, GA 50, ed. P. Jaeger (*Ibid.*, 1990).

_____. *Ontologie. Hermeneutik der Faktizität (Sommersemester 1923)*, GA 63, ed. K. Bröcker-Oltmanns (*Ibid.*, 1988).

_____. *Parmenides (Wintersemester 1942/43)*, GA 54, ed. M.S. Frings (*Ibid.*, 1982).

_____. *Phänomenologie der Anschauung und des Ausdrucks. Theorie der philosophischen Begriffsbildung (Sommersemester 1920)*, GA 59, ed. C. Strube (*Ibid.*, 1993).

_____. *Phänomenologie des religiösen Lebens. 1. Einleitung in die Phänomenologie der Religion (Wintersemester 1920/21); 2. Augustinus und der Neuplatonismus (Sommersemester 1921); 3. Die philosophischen Grundlagen der mittelalterlichen Mystik*, GA 60, ed. C. Strube, M. Jung, T. Regehly (*Ibid.*, 1995).

_____. *Phänomenologische Interpretation ausgewählter Abhandlungen des Aristoteles zu Ontologie und Logik (Sommersemester 1922)*, GA 62, ed. G. Neumann (*Ibid.*, 2005).

_____. *Phänomenologische Interpretation von Kants Kritik der reinen Vernunft (Wintersemester 1927/28)*, GA 25, ed. I. Görland (*Ibid.*, 1977).

_____. *Phänomenologische Interpretationen zu Aristoteles. Einführung in die phänomenologische Forschung (Wintersemester 1921/22)*, GA 61, ed. W. Bröcker et K. Bröcker-Oltmanns (*Ibid.*, 1985).

_____. *Platon: Sophistes (Wintersemester 1924/25)*, GA 19, ed. I. Schüssler (*Ibid.*, 1992).

_____. *Prolegomena zur Geschichte des Zeitbegriffs (Sommersemester 1925)*, GA 20, ed. P. Jaeger (*Ibid.*, 1979).

_____. *Reden und andere Zeugnisse eines Lebensweges (1910–1976)*, GA 16, ed. H. Heidegger (*Ibid.*, 2000).

_____. *Sein und Wahrheit. 1. Die Grundfrage der Philosophie (Sommersemester 1933); 2. Vom Wesen der Wahrheit (Wintersemester 1933/34)*, GA 36, 37, ed. H. Tietjen (*Ibid.*, 2001).

_____. *Sein und Zeit (1927)*, GA 2, ed. F.-W. von Herrmann (*Ibid.*, 1977).

_____. *Seminar: Vom Wesen der Sprache. Die Metaphysik der Sprache und die Wesung des Wortes. Zu Herders Abhandlung "Über den Ursprung der Sprache,"* GA 85, ed. I. Schüssler (*Ibid.*, 1999).

_____. *Seminare (1951–1973)*, GA 15, ed. C. Ochwadt (*Ibid.*, 1986).

_____. *Seminare: Nietzsche: Seminare 1937 und 1944*, GA 87, ed. P. von Ruckteschell (*Ibid.*, 2004).

_____. *Schelling: Vom Wesen der menschlichen Freiheit (1809) (Sommersemester 1936)*, GA 42, ed. I. Schüssler (*Ibid.*, 1988).

_____. *Unterwegs zur Sprache (1950–1959)*, GA 12, ed. F.-W. von Herrmann (*Ibid.*, 1985).

_____. *Vom Wesen der menschlichen Freiheit. Einleitung in die Philosophie (Sommersemester 1930)*, GA 31, ed. H. Tietjen (*Ibid.*, 1982).

_____. *Vom Wesen der Wahrheit. Zu Platons Höhlengleichnis und Theätet (Wintersemester 1931/32)*, GA 34, ed. H. Mörchen (*Ibid.*, 1988).

_____. *Vorträge und Aufsätze (1936–1953)*, GA 7, ed. F.-W. von Herrmann (*Ibid.*, 2000).

_____. *Was heißt Denken? (1951–1952)*, GA 8, ed. P.-L. Coriando (*Ibid.*, 2002).

_____. *Wegmarken (1919–1961)*, GA 9, ed. F.-W. von Herrmann (*Ibid.*, 1976).

_____. *Zu Ernst Jünger "Der Arbeiter,"* GA 90, ed. P. Trawny (*Ibid.*, 2004).

_____. *Zu Hölderlin / Griechenlandreisen*, GA 75, ed. C. Ochwadt (*Ibid.*, 2000).

_____. *Zur Bestimmung der Philosophie. 1. Die Idee der Philosophie und das Weltanschauungsproblem (Kriegsnotsemester 1919); 2. Phänomenologie und transzendentale Wertphilosophie (Sommersemester 1919); 3. Anhang: Über das Wesen der Universität und des akademischen Studiums (Sommersemester 1919)*, GA 56, 57, ed. B. Heimbüchel (*Ibid.*, 1987).

_____. *Zur Sache des Denkens (1962–1964)*, GA 14, ed. von F.-W. von Herrmann (*Ibid.*, 2007).

_____. *Über den Anfang (1941)*, GA 70, ed. F.-W. von Herrmann (*Ibid.*, 2005).

Heim, Michael. *The Metaphysics of Virtual Reality*. Oxford: Oxford University Press, 1993.

Held, K.. "Heidegger und das Prinzip der Phänomenologie." In *Heidegger und die praktische Philosophie*, edited by A. Gethmann-Siefert, O. Poggeler, 111-39. Frankfurt am Main: Suhrkramp, 1989.

Hodge, J. *Heidegger and Ethics*. London: Routledge, 1995.

Holland, Nancy and Patricia Huntington. *Feminist Interpretations of Martin Heidegger*. University Park: Penn State University Press, 2001.

Inwood, Michael. *Heidegger Dictionary*. Oxford: Blackwell, 1999.

_____. *Heidegger*. Freiburg: Herder, 1999.

Jacobs, David, ed. *The Pre-Socratics After Heidegger*. Albany: State University of New York Press, 1999.

Janicaud, Dominique. *Heidegger en France*. Paris: Albin Michel, 2001.

_____. *L'Ombre de cette pensée: Heidegger et la question politique*. Grenoble: Millon, 1990.

_____. *La Métaphysique à la limite: cinq études sur Heidegger*. Paris: PUF, 1983.

Johnson, Patricia. *On Heidegger*. Belmont: Wadsworth/ Thomson Learning, 2000.

Kaelin, E.F. *Heidegger's Being & Time*. Tallahassee: University Presses of Florida, 1988.

King, Magda. *Guide to Heidegger's Being and Time*. Albany: State University of New York, 2001.

_____. *Heidegger's Philosophy*. New York: Macmillan, 1964.

Kisiel, Theodore. *Heidegger's Way of Thought Critical and Interpretative Signposts*. London: Continuum, 2002.

_____. *The Genesis of Heidegger's Being & Time*. Berkeley, 1993.

Kovacs, George. *The Question of God in Heidegger's Phenomenology*. Evanston: Northwestern University Press, 1990.

Köchler, Hans. *Skepsis und Gesellschaftskritik im Denken Martin Heideggers*. Meisenheim: Anton Hain, 1978.

Lang, Berel. *Heidegger's Silence*. Ithaca: Cornell University Press, 1996.

Large, William. *Heidegger's Being & Time*. Bloomington: Indiana University Press, 2008.

Lehmann, Karl. *Vom Ursprung und Sinn der Seinsfrage im Denken Martin Heideggers*. Freiburg, 1999.

Lemke, Anja. *Konstellation ohne Sterne. Zur poetischen und geschichtlichen Zäsur bei Martin Heidegger und Paul Celan*. München: Fink, 2002.

Ludz, Ursula. *Hannah Arendt und Martin Heidegger: Briefe 1925 bis 1975 und andere Zeugnisse*. Frankfurt am Main: V. Klostermann, 2002.

Löwith, Karl. *Heidegger—Denker in dürftiger Zeit*. Stuttgart: Metzler Verlag, 1984.

Macann, Christopher. *Critical Heidegger*. London: Routledge, 1996.

Macquarrie, John. *Heidegger and Christianity*. New York: Continuum, 1994.

_____. *Martin Heidegger*. Richmond; John Knox, 1968.

Malpas, Jeff. *Heidegger's Topology Being, Place, World*. Cambridge: MIT, 2006.

_____. *Heidegger: Earth and Sky, Gods and Mortals, Freedom and Death*. Hobart: Pyrrho Press, 1999.

Maly, Kenneth. *Heidegger's Possibility Language, Emergence—Saying Be-ing*. Toronto: University of Toronto Press, 2008.

Marx, Werner. *Absolute Reflexion und Sprache*. Frankfurt am Main: V. Klostermann, 1967.

_____. *Das Spiel. Wirklichkeit und Methode*. Freiburg: Schulz, 1967.

_____. *Ethos und Lebenswelt. Mitleidenkönnen als Mass*. Hamburg: Meiner, 1986.

_____. *Heidegger und die Tradition. Eine problemgeschichtliche Einführung in die Grundbestimmungen des Seins*. Stuttgart: Kohlhammer, 1961.

Mattéi, Jean-François. *Heidegger et Hölderlin*. Paris: PUF, 2001.

_____. *Heidegger. L'énigme de l'être*. Paris: PUF, 2004.

_____. *L'Ordre du monde. Platon, Nietzsche, Heidegger*. Paris: PUF, 1989.

McGrath, S.J. *Heidegger: A (Very) Critical Introduction*. Cambridge: Wm. B. Eerdmans Publishing Co, 2008.

Merleau-Ponty, Maurice. *Humanisme et terreur*. Paris: Gallimard, 1947.

_____. *Le visible et l'invisible*. Paris: Gallimard, 1964.

_____. *Les aventures de la dialectique*. Paris: Gallimard, 1955.

_____. *Phénoménologie de la perception*. Paris: Gallimard, 1976.

Moyle, Tristan. *Heidegger's Transcendental Aesthetic An Interpretaton of the Ereignis*. Aldershot: Ashgate Pub Co, 2005.

Mugerauer, Robert. *Heidegger and Homecoming. The Leitmotif in the Later Writings*. Toronto: University of Toronto Press, 2008.

_____. *Heidegger's Language and Thinking*. London: Humanity Books, 1988.

Mulhall, Stephen. *Routledge Philosophy Guidebook To Heidegger and Being and Time.* London: Routledge, 1996.

Murray, Murray, ed. *Heidegger and Modern Philosophy.* New Haven: Yale University Press, 1978.

Myerson, George. *Heidegger, Habermas and the Mobile Phone.* Cambridge: Totem Books, 2001.

Navia, Mauricio. *Hermenéutica: interpretaciones desde Nietzsche, Heidegger, Gadamer y Ricoeur.* Mérida: Universidad Los Andes, 2008.

Nenon, T. "Memphis Heidegger and Praxis." *Southern Journal of Philosophy* 28 (1990).

Nietzsche, Friedrich. *Werke. Kritische Gesamtausgabe.* Berlin; New York: Walter de Gruyter, 1967. Bde. 1–30.

Nolte, Ernst. *Martin Heidegger: Politik und Geschichte im Leben und Denken.* Berlin; Frankfurt: Proyla, 1992.

Okrent, Mark. *Heidegger's Pragmatism Understanding, Being, and the Critique of Metaphysics.* Cornell: Cornell University Press, 1988.

Olson, Alan. *Heidegger and Jaspers.* Philadelphia: Temple University Press, 1994.

Ott, Hugo. *Martin Heidegger. Unterwegs zu seiner Biographie.* Frankfurt am Main, New York: Campus Books, 1988.

Parkes, Graham. *Heidegger and Asian Thought.* Honolulu: University of Hawaii Press, 1987.

Partenie, Catalin and Tom Rockmore. *Heidegger and Plato Toward Dialogue.* Evanston: Northwestern University Press, 2005.

Petkovsek, Robert. *Heidegger—Index (1919–1927).* Ljubljana: Universitas Labacensis Facultas, 1998.

Petzet, H.W. *Auf einen Stern zugehen. Begegnungen und Gespräche mit Martin Heidegger 1929–1976.* Frankfurt am Main: Societäts-Verlag, 1983.

Philipse, Herman. *Heidegger's Philosophy of Being: A Critical Interpretation*. Princeton: Princeton University Press, 1998.

Polt, Richard. *Heidegger: an Introduction*. Ithaca: Cornell University Press, 1999.

_____. *The Emergency of Being: On Heidegger's Contributions to Philosophy*. Ithaca: Cornell University Press, 2006.

Prado, C.G. *A House Divided Comparing Anlytic and Continental Philosophy*. New York: Humanity Books, 2003.

Pöggeler, Otto. *Der Denkweg Martin Heideggers*. Stuttgart: Neske, 1994.

_____. *Heidegger und die hermeneutische Philosophie*. Freiburg: Alber, 1983.

_____. *Philosophie und hermeneutische Theologie. Heidegger, Bultmann und die Folgen*. Paderborn: Fink, 2009.

_____. *Philosophie und Politik bei Heidegger*. Freiburg, München: Alber, 1972.

Raffoul, François. *Heidegger and Practical Philosophy*. Albany: State University of New York Press, 2002.

_____. "Heidegger and the Origins of Responsibility." In *Heidegger and Practical Philosophy*, edited by Raffoul, François and David Pettigrew. Albany: State University of New York Press, 2002.

_____. *Heidegger and the Subject*. Amherst: Humanity Books, 1999.

Rapaport, Herman. *Heidegger & Derrida, Reflections on Time and Language*. Lincoln: University of Nebraska Press, 1989.

Reijen, Willem van. *Martin Heidegger*. München, 2009.

Rentsch, Thomas. *Martin Heidegger—Das Sein und der Tod. Eine kritische Einführung*. München, Zürich: Piper, 1989.

Richardson, William. *Existential Epistemology: A Heideggerian Critique of the Cartesian Project*. Oxford: Clarendon, 1986.

_____. *Heidegger. Through Phenomenology to Thought*. Bronx: Fordham University Press, 1993.

Richter, E. *Die Frage nach der Wahrheit*. Frankfurt am Main: V. Klostermann, 1997.

Risser, James. *Heidegger toward the Turn Essays on the Work of the 1930s*. Albany: State University of New York Press, 1999.

Robinson, J.M. *The Later Heidegger and Theology*. New York: Harper & Row, 1963.

Rockmore, Tom. *On Heidegger's Nazism and Philosophy*. Berkeley: University of California Press, 1992.

_____. *The Heidegger Case On Philosophy and Politics*. Philadelphia: Temple University Press, 1992.

Rosenberg, Alan. *Heidegger and Foucault Critical Encounters*. Minneapolis: U of Minnesota Press, 2003.

Roth, Michael. *The Poetics of Resistance: Heidegger's Line*. Evanston: Northwestern University Press, 1996.

Rée, J. *Heidegger*. New York: Routledge, 1999.

Safranski, Rüdiger. *Ein Meister aus Deutschland*. Frankfurt: Fischer, 1999.

Sallis, John. *Deconstruction and Philosophy*. Chicago: University of Chicago Press, 1987.

_____. *Delimitations Phenomenology and the End of Metaphysics*. Bloomington: Indiana University Press, 1995.

_____. *Echoes: After Heidegger*. Bloomington: Indiana University Press, 1990.

_____. *Reading Heidegger: Commemorations*. Bloomington: Indiana University Press, 1993.

Sartre, Jean-Paul. *L'Etre et le neant. Essai d'ontologie phenomenologique*. Paris: Gallimard, 1943.

_____. *La Transcendance de l'go*. Paris: Vrin, 1966.

Schalow, Frank. *The Incarnality of Being The Earth, Animals, and the Body in Heidegger's Thought*. Albany: State Univ of New York, 2007.

Schmitt, Richard. *Martin Heidegger on Being Human: an Introduction to Sein und Zeit*. New York: Random House, 1969.

Schürmann, Reiner. *Le Principe d'anarchie. Heidegger et la question de l'agir*. Paris: Editions du Seuil, 1982.

Scott, Charles et al. *Companion to Heidegger's Contributions to Philosophy*. Bloomington: Indiana University Press, 2001.

Seidel, George. *Martin Heidegger and the Pre-Socratics*. Lincoln: University of Nebraska Press, 1964.

Seubert, H. *Heideggers Zwiegespräch mit dem deutschen Idealismus*. Köln, Weimar, Wien: Böhlau, 2003.

Shahan, R.W. *Thinking About Being Aspects of Heidegger's Thought*. Norman: University of Oklahoma Press, 1984.

Sharr, Adam. *Heidegger's Hut*. Cambridge: MIT Press, 2006.

Sheehan, Thomas. *Heidegger The Man and the Thinker*. Chicago: Precedent Publishing, 1981.

Simmel, G. *Die Probleme der Geschichtsphilosophie*. Leipzig: Duncker & Humblot, 1892.

Sluga, Hans. *Heidegger's Crisis, Philosophy and Politics in Nazi Germany*. Cambridge: Harvard University Press, 1993.

Souche-Dagues, Denise. *Du Logos chez Heidegger*. Grenoble: Millon, 1999.

Spanos, William. *Heidegger and Criticism*. Minneapolis: University of Minnesota Press, 1993.

_____. *Martin Heidegger and the Question of Literature*. Bloomington: University of Indiana, 1999.

Steiner, George. *Martin Heidegger*. Harmondsworth: Penguin, 1980.

Steinmann, Michael. *Heidegger und die Griechen*. Frankfurt: V. Klostermann, 2007.

Stellardi, Giuseppe. *Heidegger and Derrida on Philosophy and Metaphor: Imperfect Thought*. Amherst: Humanity Books, 2000.

Stenstad, Gail. *Transformations Thinking after Heidegger: University of Wisconsin Press*. Madison, 2006.

Tallis, Raymond. *A Conversation with Martin Heidegger* Basingstoke: Palgrave Macmillan, 2002.

Taminiaux, Jacques. "Heidegger and The Earth." *Diacritics* 19:3-4. Baltimore (1989).

_____. *Lectures de l'ontologie fondamentale. Essais sur Heidegger*. Grenoble: Millon, 1989.

Thiele, Leslie Paul. *Timely Meditations*. Princeton: Princeton University Press, 1995.

Thomson, Iain. *Heidegger on Ontotheology Technology and the Politics of Education*. Cambridge: Cambridge University Press, 2005.

Thomä, D. *Heidegger-Handbuch*. Stuttgart: Metzler, 2003.

Trawny, Peter. *Martin Heidegger. Einführung*. Frankfurt, New York: Campus Verlag, 2003.

_____. *Voll Verdienst, doch dichterisch wohnet/ Der Mensch auf dieser Erde. Heidegger und Hölderlin*. Frankfurt am Main: V. Klostermann, 2000.

Tugendhat, Ernst. *Der Wahrheitsbegriff bei Hussel und Heidegger*. Berlin: Walter de Gruyter & Co, 1970.

Vallega, A.A. *Heidegger and the Issue of Space: Thinking on Exilic Grounds*. University Park: Pennsylvania State University Press, 2008.

Vallega-Neu, D. *Heidegger's Contributions to Philosophy: An Introduction*. Bloomington: Indiana University Press, 2003.

Vogel, Lawrence. *The Fragile We: Ethical Implications of Heidegger's Being and Time*. Evanston: Northwestern University Press, 1994.

Volpi, Franco. *Heidegger e Aristotele*. Padova: Daphne, 1984.

Vycinas, Vincent. *Earth And Gods: an Introduction to the Philosophy Of Martin Heidegger*. New York: Springer, 1969.

Waldenfels, B. "Réponse à l'autre. Éléments d'une phénoménologie responsive." In *Phénoménologie française et phénoménologie allemande*, edited by E. Escoubas, B. Waldenfels, 134-155. Paris: L'Harmattan, 2000.

Ward, J.F. *Heidegger's Political Thinking*. Amherst: University of Massachusetts Press, 1995.

Watts, Michael. *Heidegger. A Beginner's Guide*. London: Hodder & Stoughton, 2001.

Wisser, Richard. *Martin Heidegger im Gespräch*. München: Alber, 1970.

Wittgenstein, Ludwig. *Werkausgabe*. Frankfurt am Main: Suhrkamp, 1984. Bd. 1–8.

Wolin, Richard. *Heidegger's Children*. Princeton: Princeton University Press, 2001.

_____. *The Heidegger Controversy*. Cambridge: MIT, 1993.

_____. *The Politics of Being*. New York: Columbia University Press, 1990.

Wood, David. *Of Derrida, Heidegger, and Spirit*. Evanston: Northwestern University Press, 1993.

_____. *Thinking after Heidegger*. Cambridge: Polity Press, 2002.

Wrathall, M. *How to Read Heidegger*. London: Granta, 2005.

Young, Julian. *Heidegger's Later Philosophy*. Cambridge: Cambridge University Press, 2001.

_____. *Heidegger, Philosophy, Nazism*. Cambridge: Cambridge University Press, 1997.

Zimmermann, Hans Dieter. *Martin und Fritz Heidegger. Philosophie und Fastnacht*. München: C. H. Beck Verlag, 2005.

Zimmerman, Michael. *Eclipse of the Self: The Development of Heidegger's Concept of Authenticity*. Athens: Ohio University Press, 1986.

_____. *Heidegger's Confrontation with Modernity*. Bloomington: Indiana University Press, 1990.

INDEX

M

N

ABOUT THE AUTHOR

ALEXANDER DUGIN (b. 1962) is one of the best-known writers and political commentators in post-Soviet Russia. Born to a well-educated family—his parents held doctorates in medicine and law—he entered the Moscow Aviation Institute in 1979. During the 1980s, he was a principal member of the underground traditionalist movement in the Soviet Union, including dissident author Yuri Mamleev. He later became a translator and journalist, making his earliest foray into politics by joining *Pamiat'*, the first nationalist party to emerge during the twilight years of the USSR.

After the collapse of the USSR opened up new possibilities, Dugin began associating with several of the major figures of the European New Right, such as Alain de Benoist. Between 1994 and 1998, he collaborated with Russian opposition movements, including Eduard Limonov's National Bolsheviks, which sought to synthesize Left and Right doctrines. In 1998-2003, he served as the advisor to Gennadiy Seleznyov, the Chairman of the State Duma.

In 2002, Dugin founded the Eurasia Movement, which he has continued to lead up to the present day. In addition to the many books he has authored on political, philosophical, and spiritual topics, he currently serves on the staff of the Moscow State University and regularly appears on mainstream Russian television. He holds doctorates in political science, sociology, and philosophy. As an advocate of the return of Russia to the global stage and its potential as a counterweight to American hegemony, some commentators have pointed out the influence of Dugin's geopolitical ideas on Vladimir Putin and the modern Kremlin.

Ingram Content Group UK Ltd.
Milton Keynes UK
UKHW022112230323
419066UK00016B/897